岸本斉史

Naruto has passed the 40-volume mark, becoming a long-term series. From here on out, I plan to keep working hard, with my eyes trained on the finish line!

—*Masashi Kishimoto, 2008*

Author/artist Masashi Kishimoto was born in 1974 in rural Okayama Prefecture, Japan. After spending time in art college, he won the Hop Step Award for new manga artists with his manga **Karakuri** (Mechanism). Kishimoto decided to base his next story on traditional Japanese culture. His first version of **Naruto**, drawn in 1997, was a one-shot story about fox spirits; his final version, which debuted in **Weekly Shonen Jump** in 1999, quickly became the most popular ninja manga in Japan.

NARUTO VOL. 42
The SHONEN JUMP Manga Edition

STORY AND ART BY MASASHI KISHIMOTO

Translation/Mari Morimoto
English Adaptation/Deric A. Hughes & Benjamin Raab
Touch-up Art & Lettering/Gia Cam Luc
Design/Gerry Serrano
Editor/Joel Enos

Editor in Chief, Books/Alvin Lu
Editor in Chief, Magazines/Marc Weidenbaum
VP, Publishing Licensing/Rika Inouye
VP, Sales & Product Marketing/Gonzalo Ferreyra
VP, Creative/Linda Espinosa
Publisher/Hyoe Narita

Printed in the U.S.A.

Published by VIZ Media, LLC
P.O. Box 77010
San Francisco, CA 94107

SHONEN JUMP Manga Edition
10 9 8 7 6 5 4 3 2 1
First printing, April 2009

SHONEN JUMP MANGA EDITION

NARUTO

VOL. 42

THE SECRET OF THE MANGEKYO

STORY AND ART BY
MASASHI KISHIMOTO

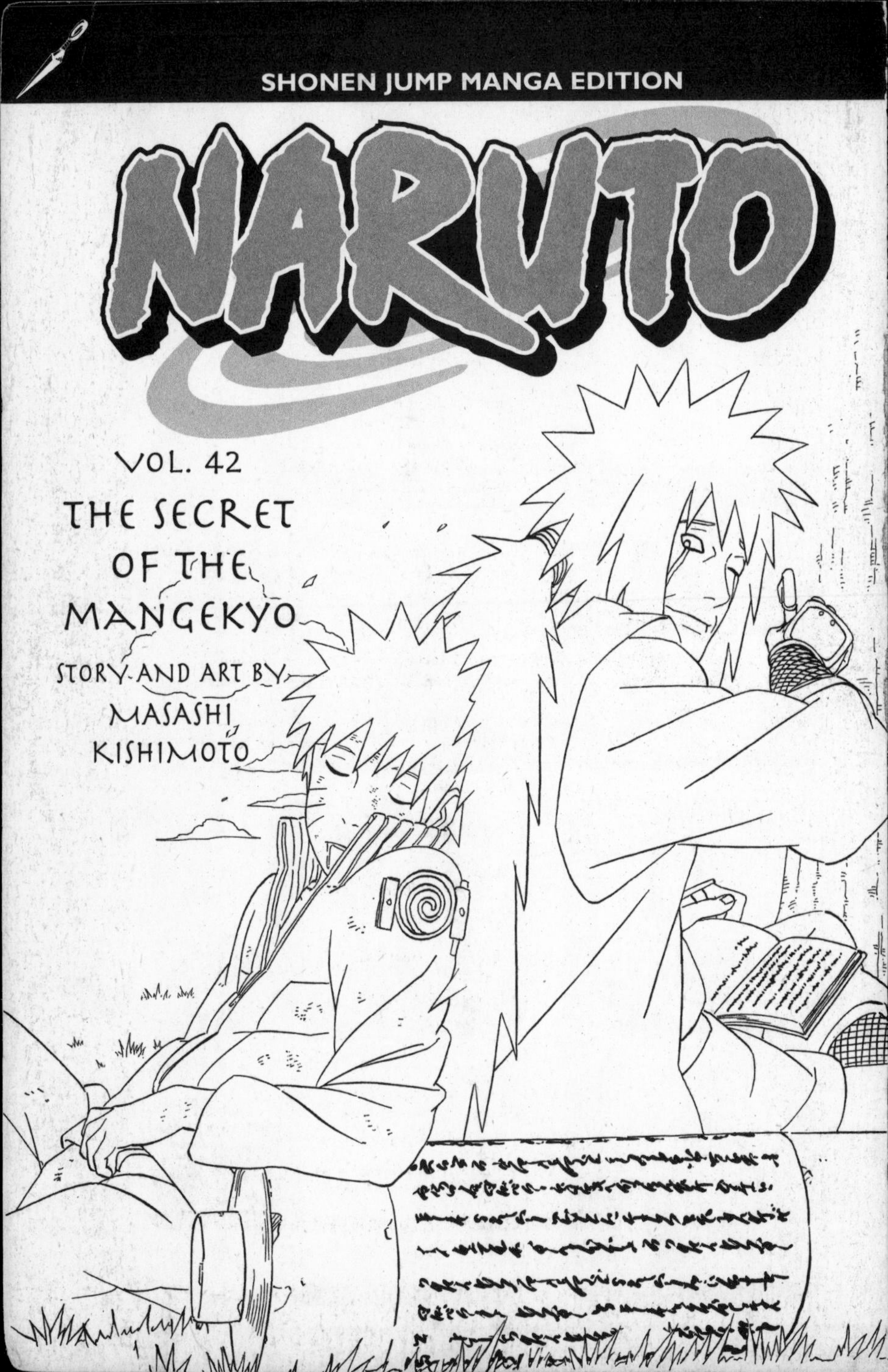

CHARACTERS

Naruto ナルト

Sasuke サスケ

Kakashi カカシ

Sakura サクラ

Sai サイ

Yamato ヤマト

Tsunade 綱手

Jiraiya 自来也

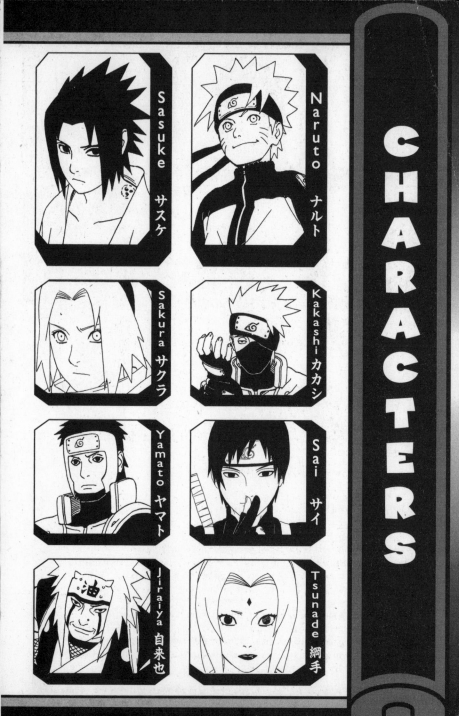

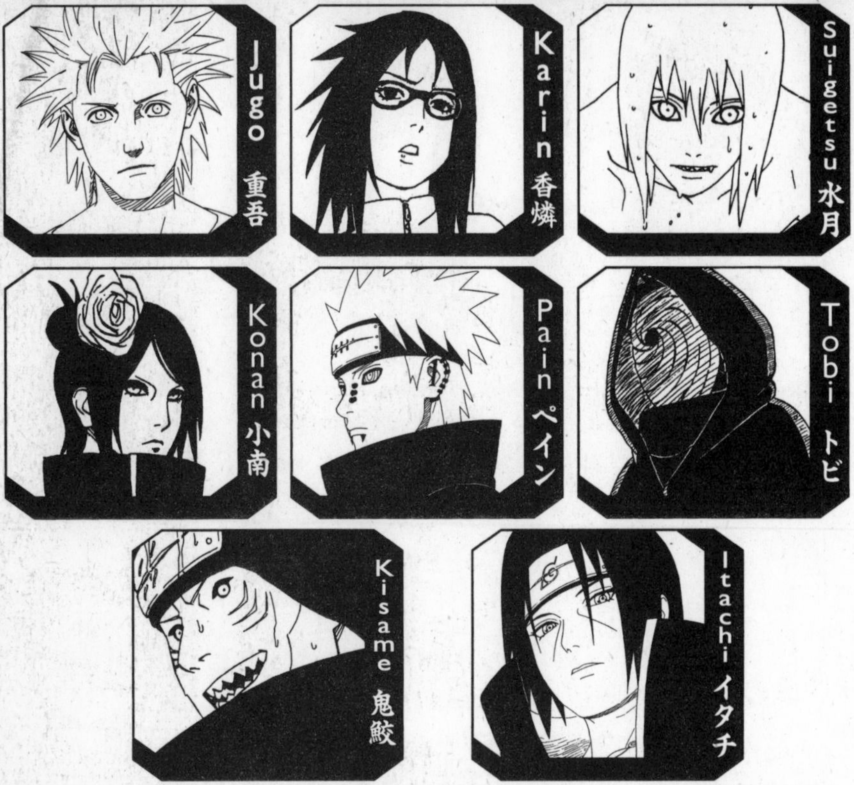
Suigetsu 水月
Karin 香燐
Jugo 重吾
Tobi トビ
Pain ペイン
Konan 小南
Itachi イタチ
Kisame 鬼鮫

THE STORY SO FAR...

Once the bane of the Konohagakure Ninja Academy, Naruto now serves dutifully among the ranks of the Konoha shinobi—an illustrious group of ninja sworn to protect their village from the forces of evil seeking to destroy it from without and within...

Naruto's search for his former classmate and friend, Sasuke—now on a mission of vengeance against his own brother, Itachi—finally bears fruit, and the paths of these two young shinobi are poised to re-converge...

Jiraiya continues his top-secret mission within the Hidden Rain Village and discovers the true identity of the Akatsuki's enigmatic leader, Pain—who turns out to be none other than one of Jiraiya's former disciples!

When Pain reveals his quest to create the ultimate jutsu capable of ending all wars by wreaking havoc and causing rampant destruction, Jiraiya is forced to kill his former student in order to save the world. But as he soon discovers, Pain **never** dies...

NARUTO

VOL. 42
THE SECRET OF THE MANGEKYO

CONTENTS

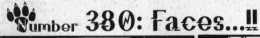

Number 380: Faces...II

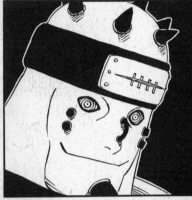

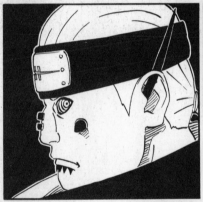

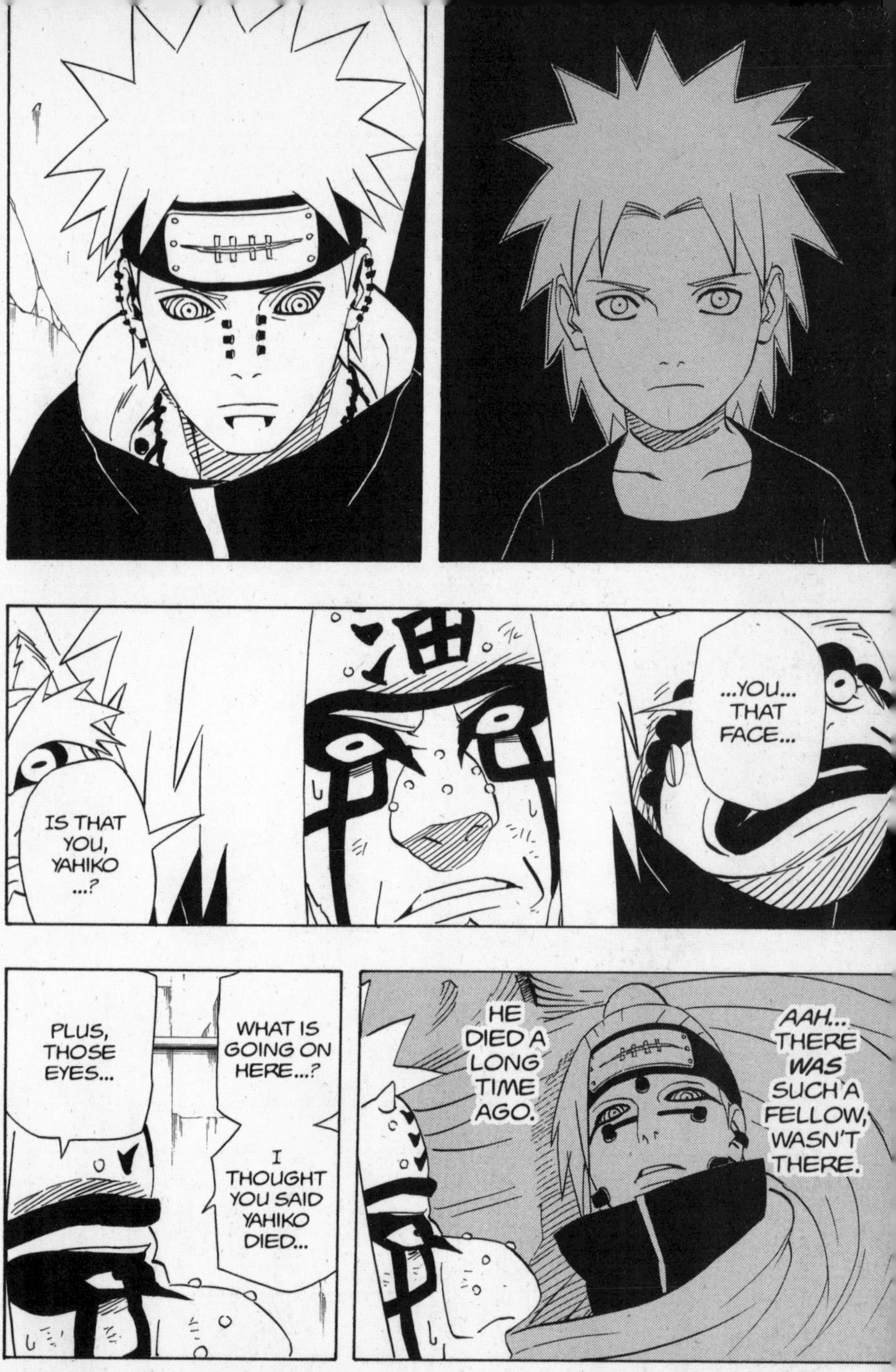
...YOU... THAT FACE...
IS THAT YOU, YAHIKO ...?
AAH... THERE WAS SUCH A FELLOW, WASN'T THERE.
HE DIED A LONG TIME AGO.
WHAT IS GOING ON HERE...?
PLUS, THOSE EYES...
I THOUGHT YOU SAID YAHIKO DIED...

READ THIS WAY

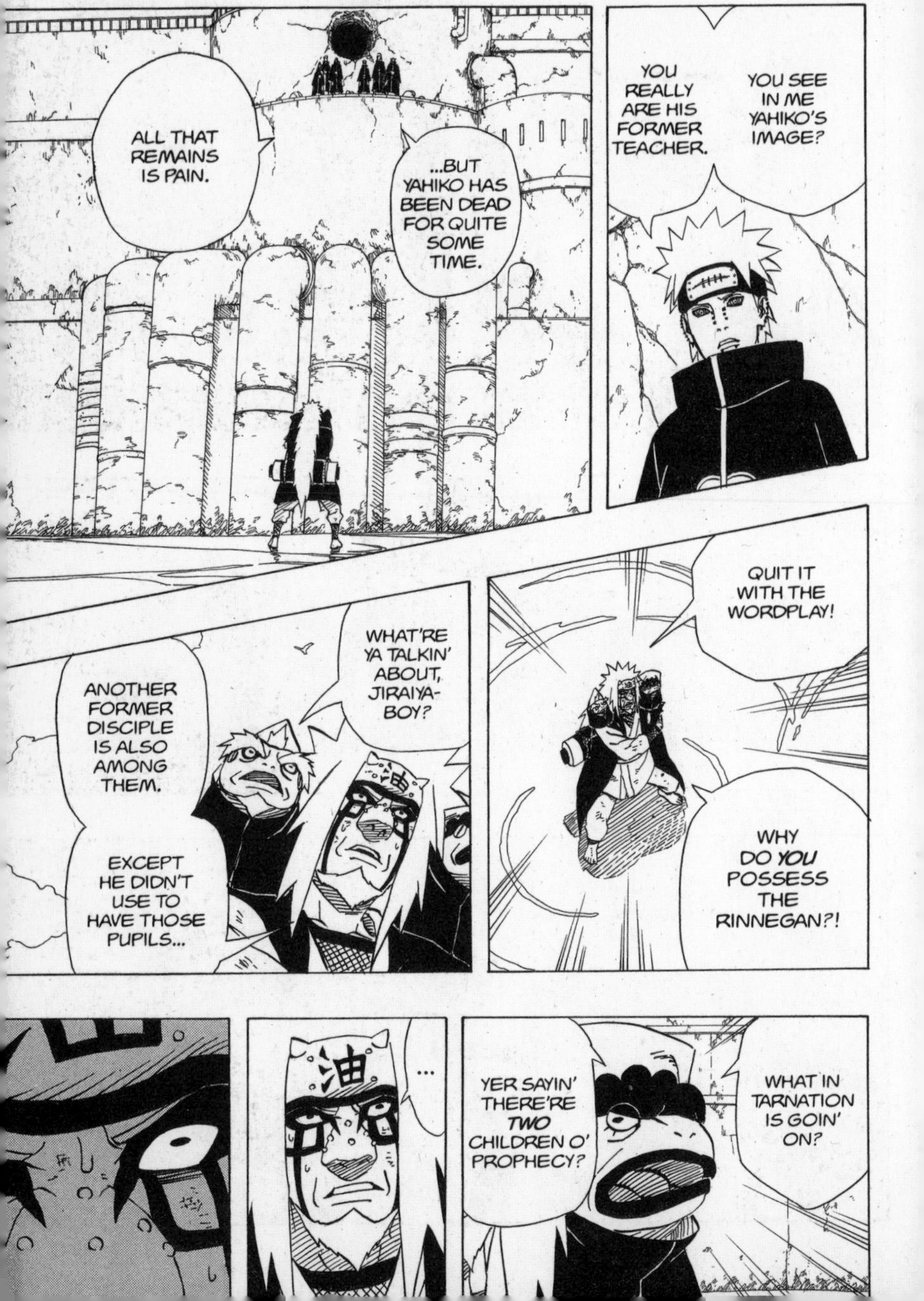
YOU SEE IN ME YAHIKO'S IMAGE?
YOU REALLY ARE HIS FORMER TEACHER.
...BUT YAHIKO HAS BEEN DEAD FOR QUITE SOME TIME.
ALL THAT REMAINS IS PAIN.
QUIT IT WITH THE WORDPLAY!
WHY DO *YOU* POSSESS THE RINNEGAN?!
WHAT'RE YA TALKIN' ABOUT, JIRAIYA-BOY?
ANOTHER FORMER DISCIPLE IS ALSO AMONG THEM.
EXCEPT HE DIDN'T USE TO HAVE THOSE PUPILS...
WHAT IN TARNATION IS GOIN' ON?
YER SAYIN' THERE'RE *TWO* CHILDREN O' PROPHECY?
...

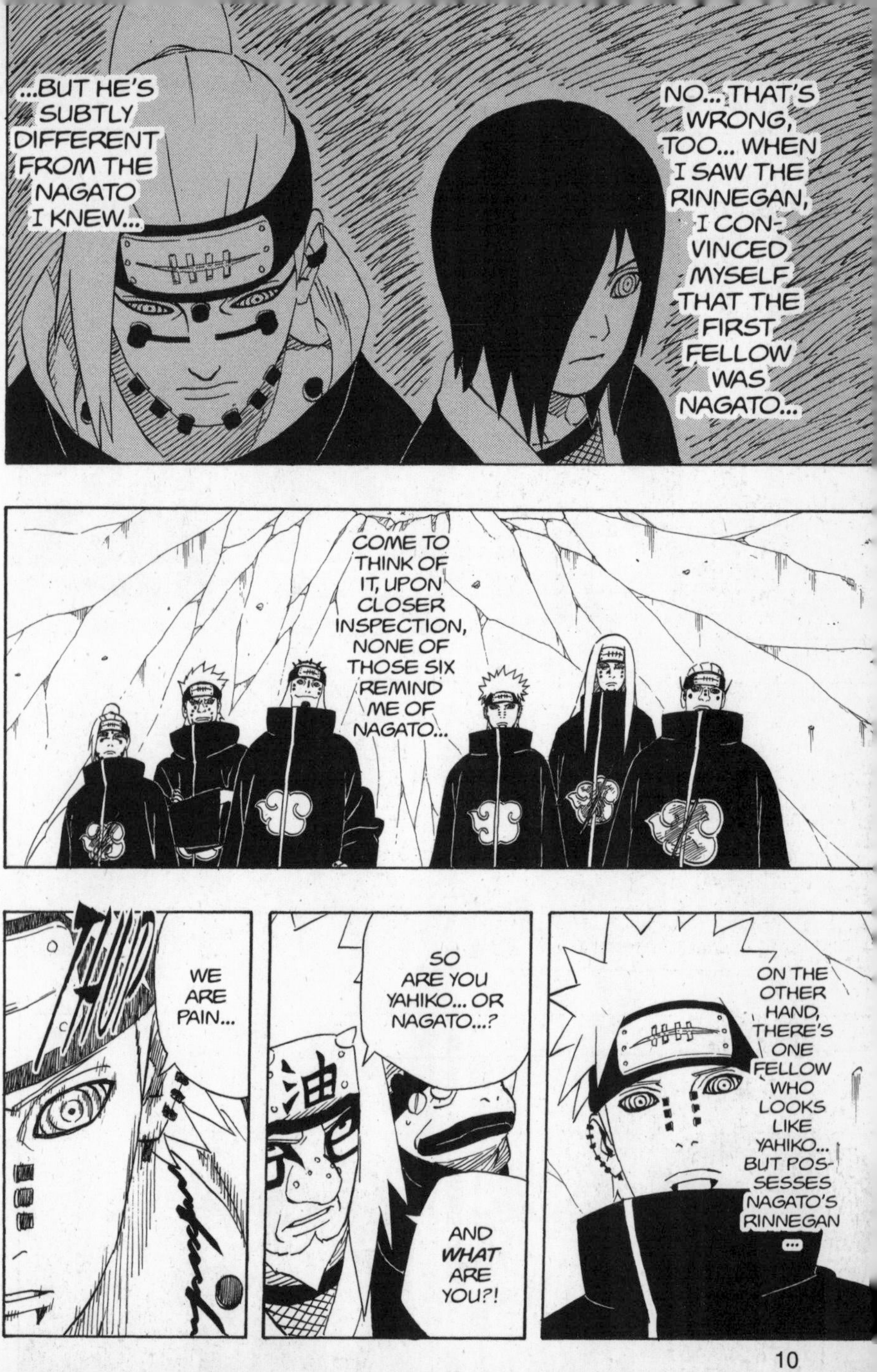
NO... THAT'S WRONG, TOO... WHEN I SAW THE RINNEGAN, I CONVINCED MYSELF THAT THE FIRST FELLOW WAS NAGATO...
...BUT HE'S SUBTLY DIFFERENT FROM THE NAGATO I KNEW...
COME TO THINK OF IT, UPON CLOSER INSPECTION, NONE OF THOSE SIX REMIND ME OF NAGATO...
ON THE OTHER HAND, THERE'S ONE FELLOW WHO LOOKS LIKE YAHIKO... BUT POSSESSES NAGATO'S RINNEGAN ...
SO ARE YOU YAHIKO... OR NAGATO...?
AND WHAT ARE YOU?!
WE ARE PAIN...

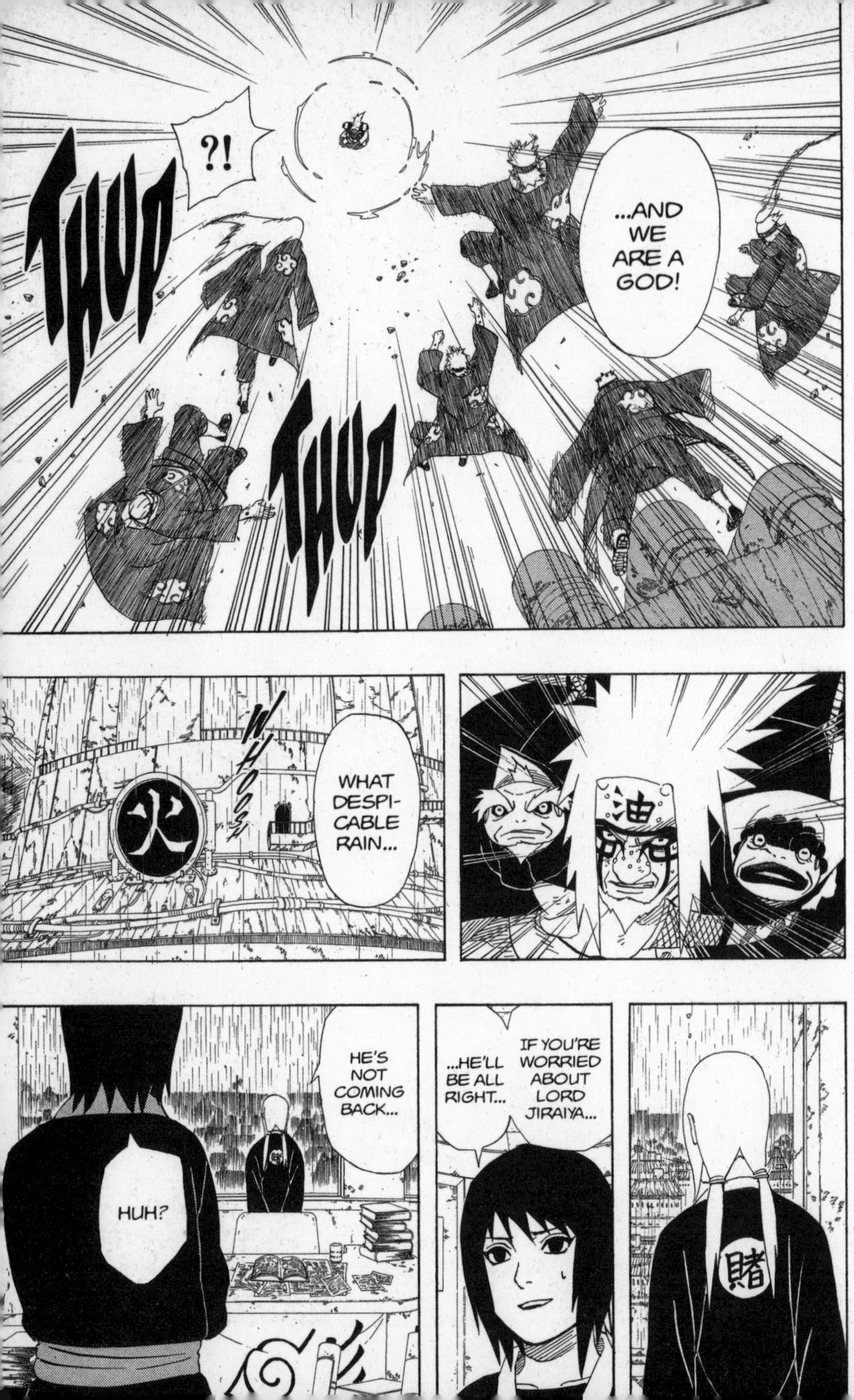
...AND WE ARE A GOD!
?!
THUD
THUD
WHAT DESPICABLE RAIN...
WHOOOSH
IF YOU'RE WORRIED ABOUT LORD JIRAIYA...
...HE'LL BE ALL RIGHT...
HE'S NOT COMING BACK...
HUH?

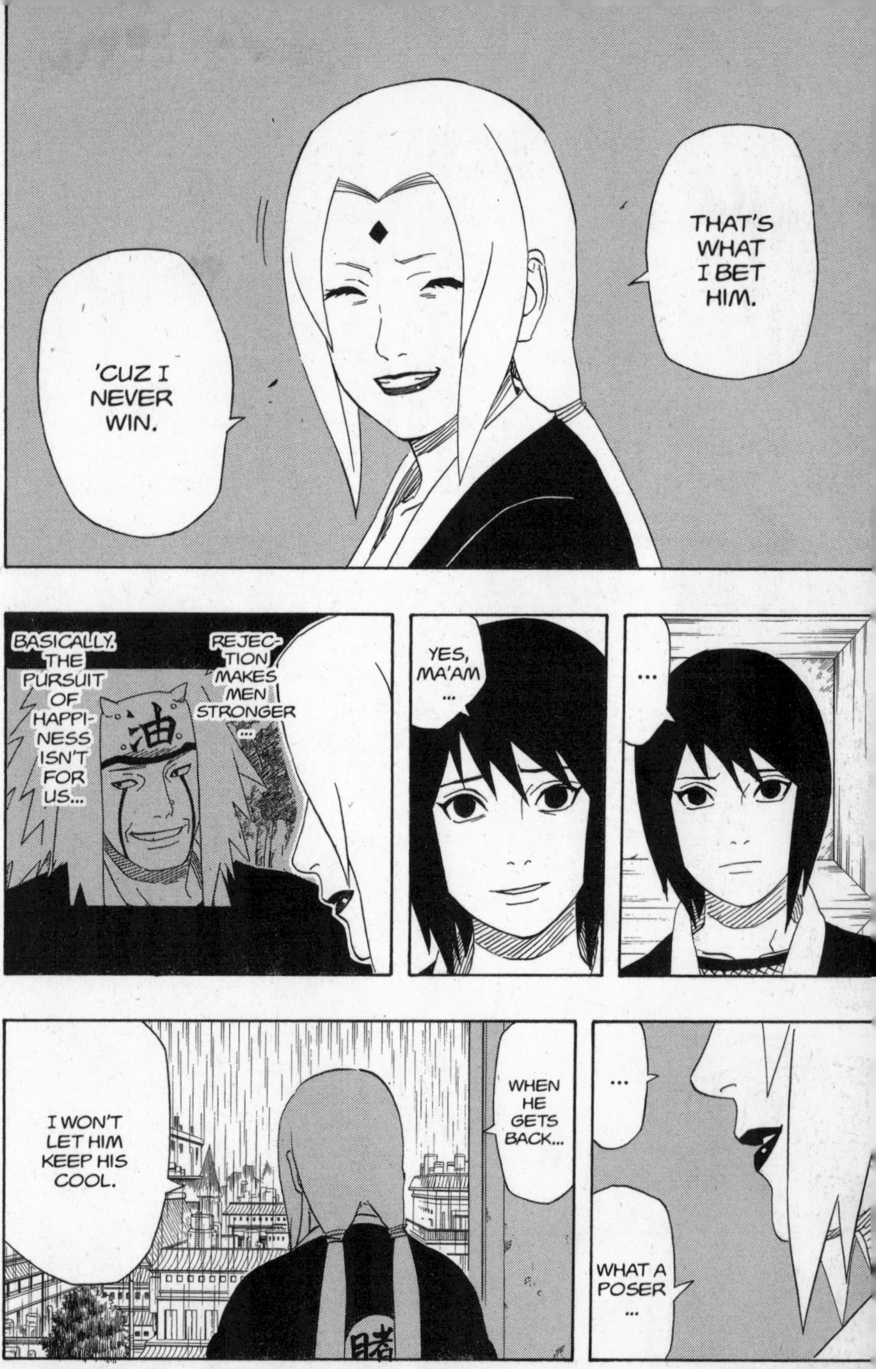
THAT'S WHAT I BET HIM.
'CUZ I NEVER WIN.
...
YES, MA'AM ...
REJECTION MAKES MEN STRONGER ...
BASICALLY, THE PURSUIT OF HAPPINESS ISN'T FOR US...
...
WHAT A POSER ...
WHEN HE GETS BACK...
I WON'T LET HIM KEEP HIS COOL.

READ THIS WAY

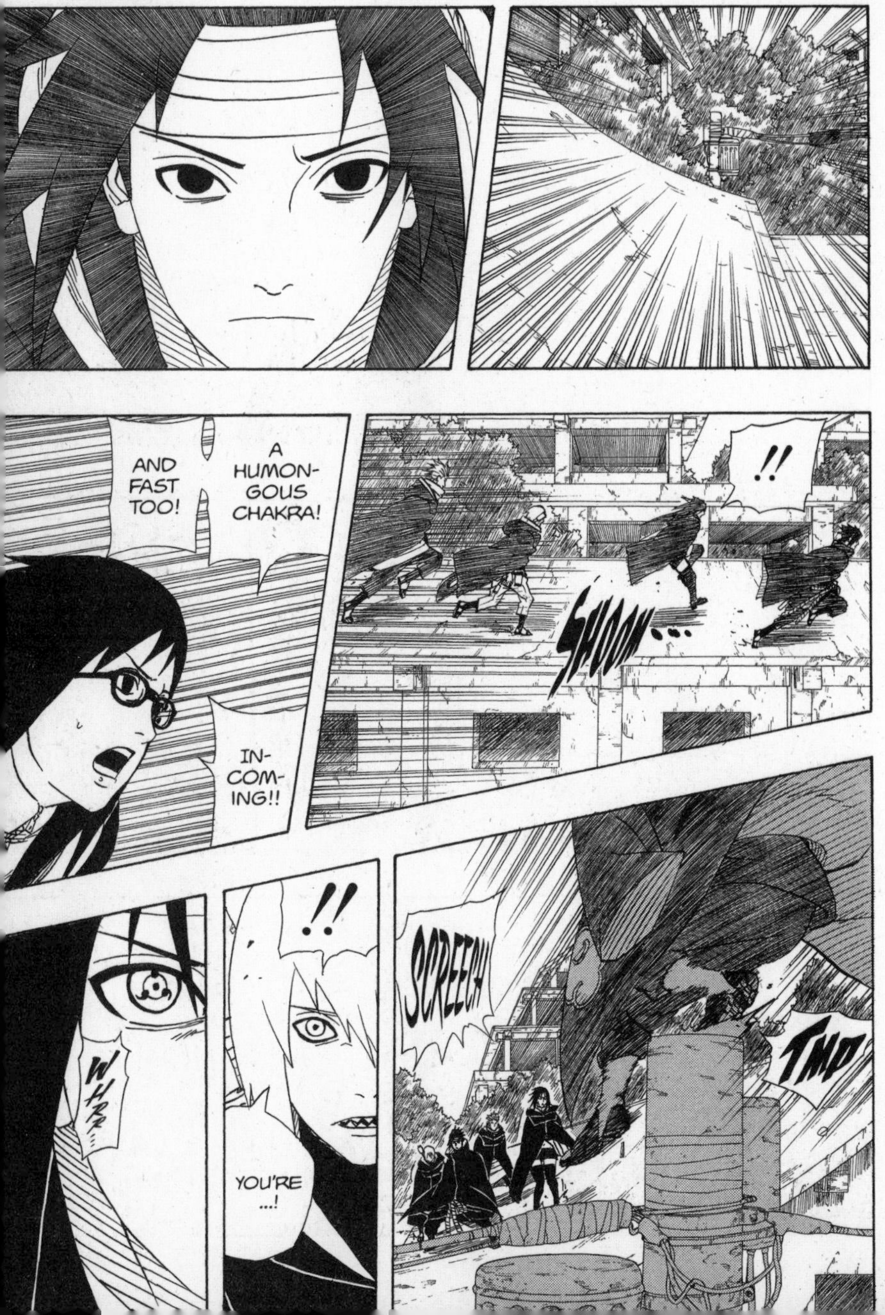
!!
SHOOM...
A HUMON-GOUS CHAKRA!
AND FAST TOO!
IN-COM-ING!!
SCREECH
TMP
!!
YOU'RE ...!
WHRR...

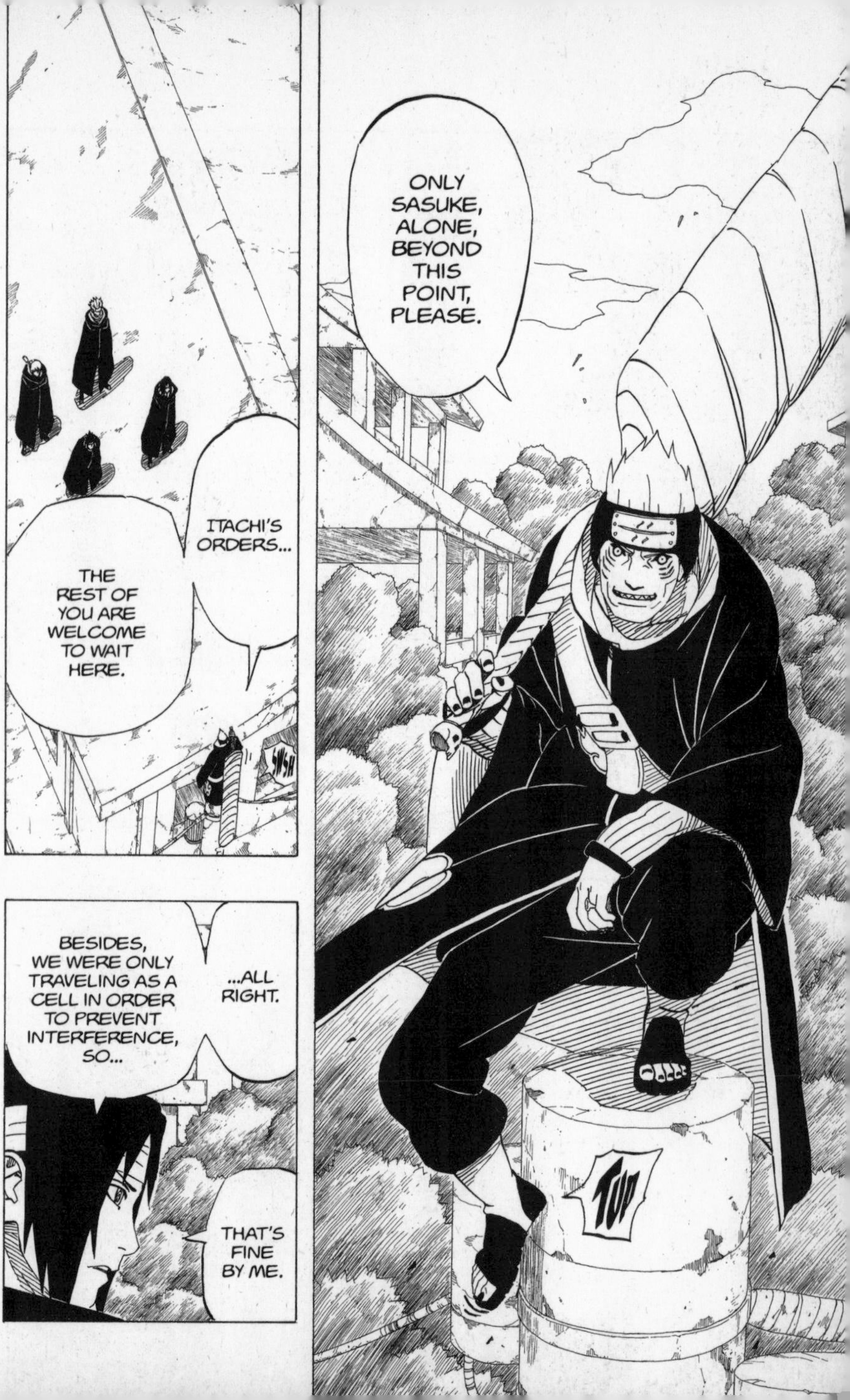
ONLY SASUKE, ALONE, BEYOND THIS POINT, PLEASE.
TUP
ITACHI'S ORDERS...
THE REST OF YOU ARE WELCOME TO WAIT HERE.
SWSH
...ALL RIGHT.
BESIDES, WE WERE ONLY TRAVELING AS A CELL IN ORDER TO PREVENT INTERFERENCE, SO...
THAT'S FINE BY ME.

READ THIS WAY

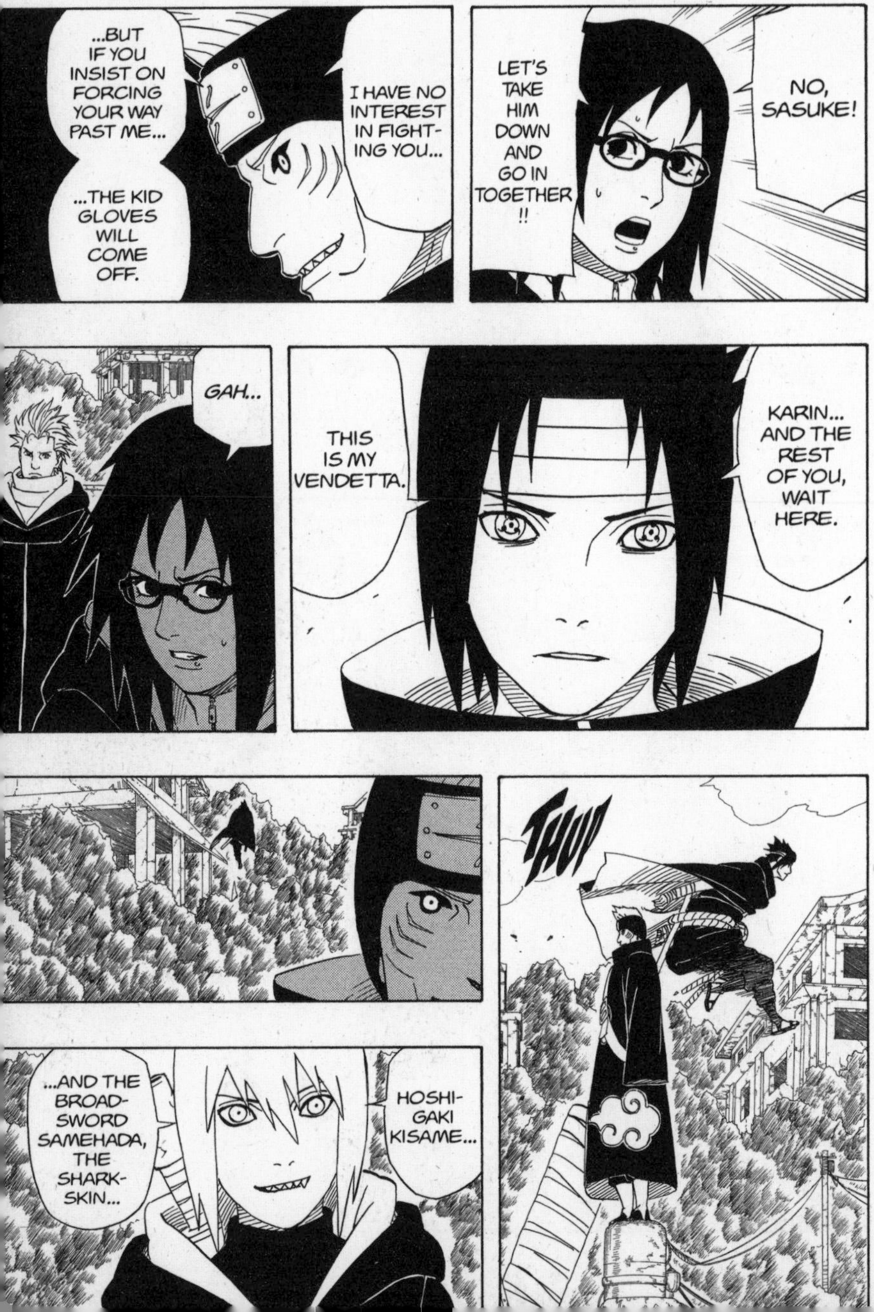
NO, SASUKE!
LET'S TAKE HIM DOWN AND GO IN TOGETHER!!
I HAVE NO INTEREST IN FIGHTING YOU...
...BUT IF YOU INSIST ON FORCING YOUR WAY PAST ME...
...THE KID GLOVES WILL COME OFF.
KARIN... AND THE REST OF YOU, WAIT HERE.
THIS IS MY VENDETTA.
GAH...
THUP
HOSHIGAKI KISAME...
...AND THE BROADSWORD SAMEHADA, THE SHARKSKIN...

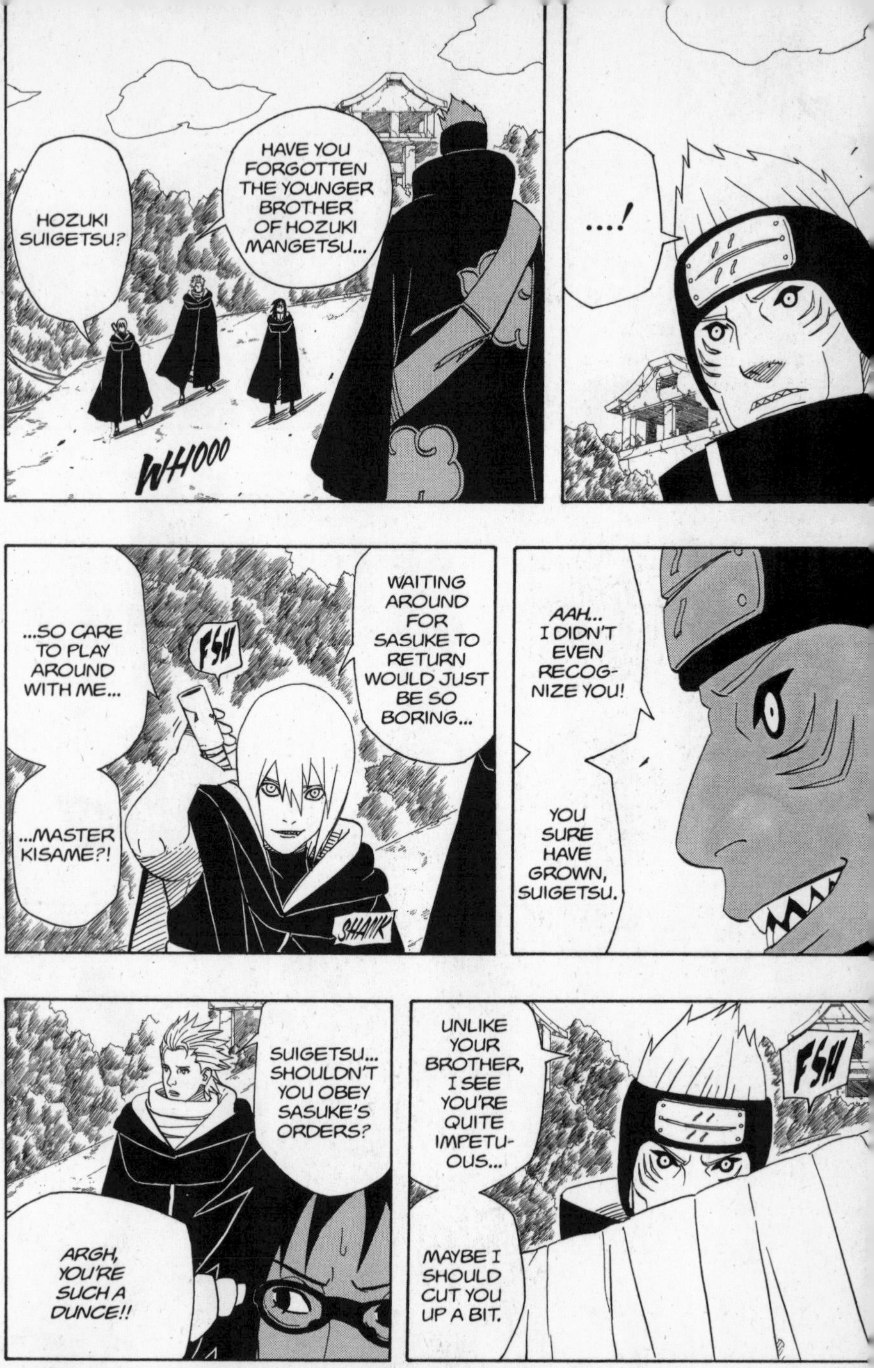
....!
HAVE YOU FORGOTTEN THE YOUNGER BROTHER OF HOZUKI MANGETSU...
HOZUKI SUIGETSU?
WHOOO
AAH... I DIDN'T EVEN RECOGNIZE YOU!
YOU SURE HAVE GROWN, SUIGETSU.
WAITING AROUND FOR SASUKE TO RETURN WOULD JUST BE SO BORING...
FSH
...SO CARE TO PLAY AROUND WITH ME...
...MASTER KISAME?!
SHANK
UNLIKE YOUR BROTHER, I SEE YOU'RE QUITE IMPETUOUS...
FSH
MAYBE I SHOULD CUT YOU UP A BIT.
SUIGETSU... SHOULDN'T YOU OBEY SASUKE'S ORDERS?
ARGH, YOU'RE SUCH A DUNCE!!

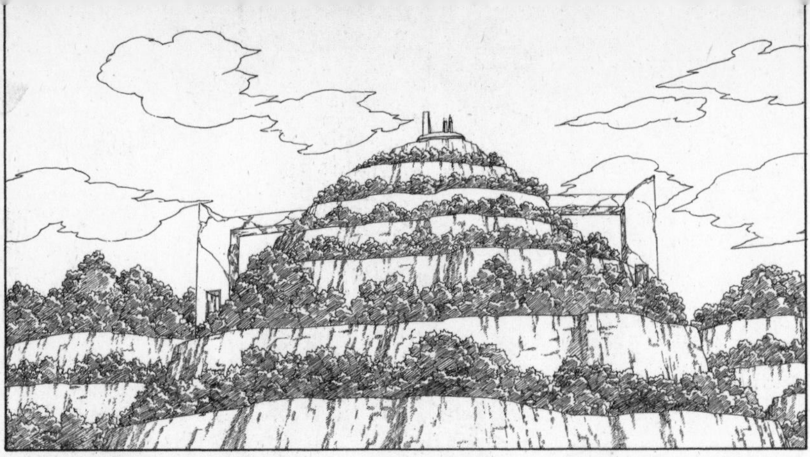

"FOX"

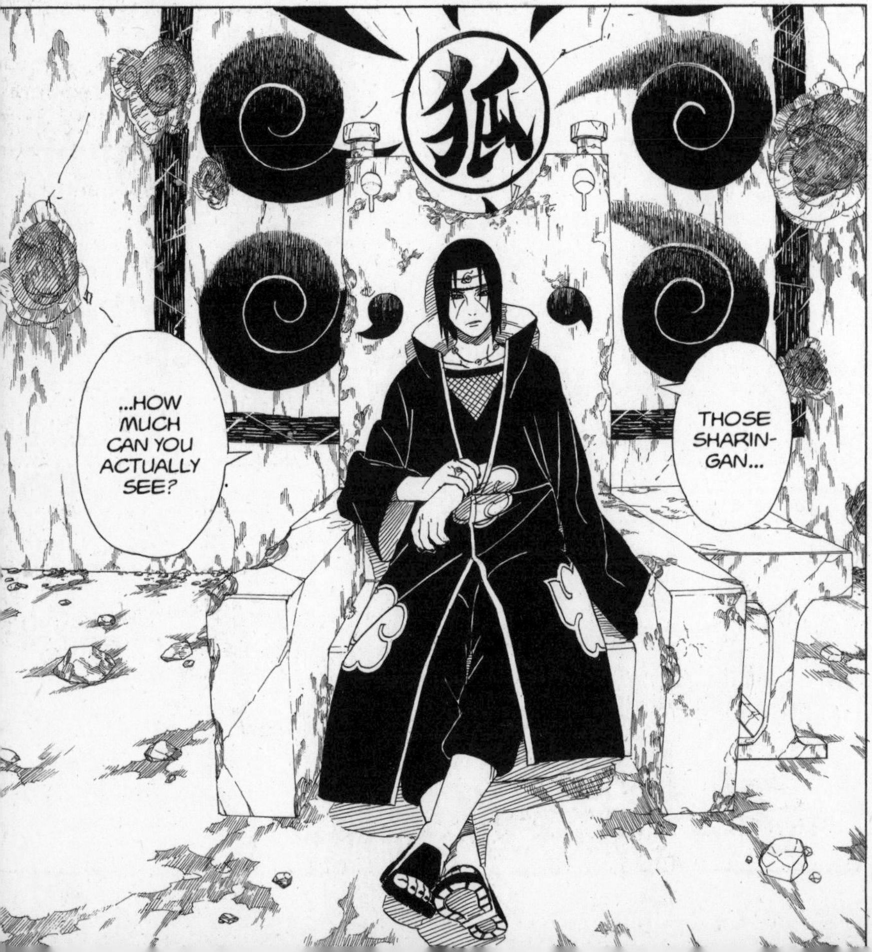
THOSE SHARIN-GAN...
...HOW MUCH CAN YOU ACTUALLY SEE?

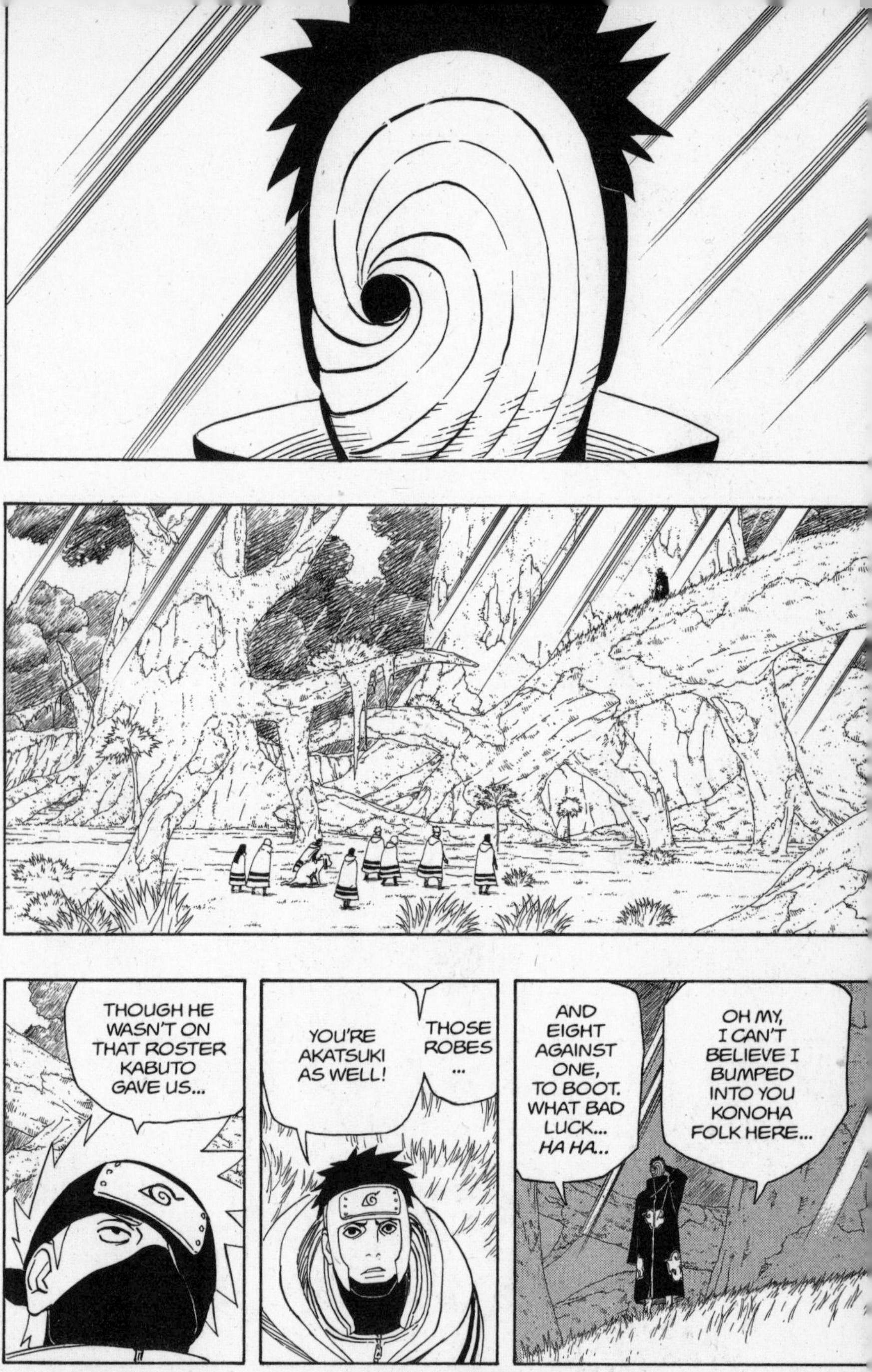
OH MY, I CAN'T BELIEVE I BUMPED INTO YOU KONOHA FOLK HERE...
AND EIGHT AGAINST ONE, TO BOOT. WHAT BAD LUCK... *HA HA...*
THOSE ROBES ...
YOU'RE AKATSUKI AS WELL!
THOUGH HE WASN'T ON THAT ROSTER KABUTO GAVE US...

READ THIS WAY

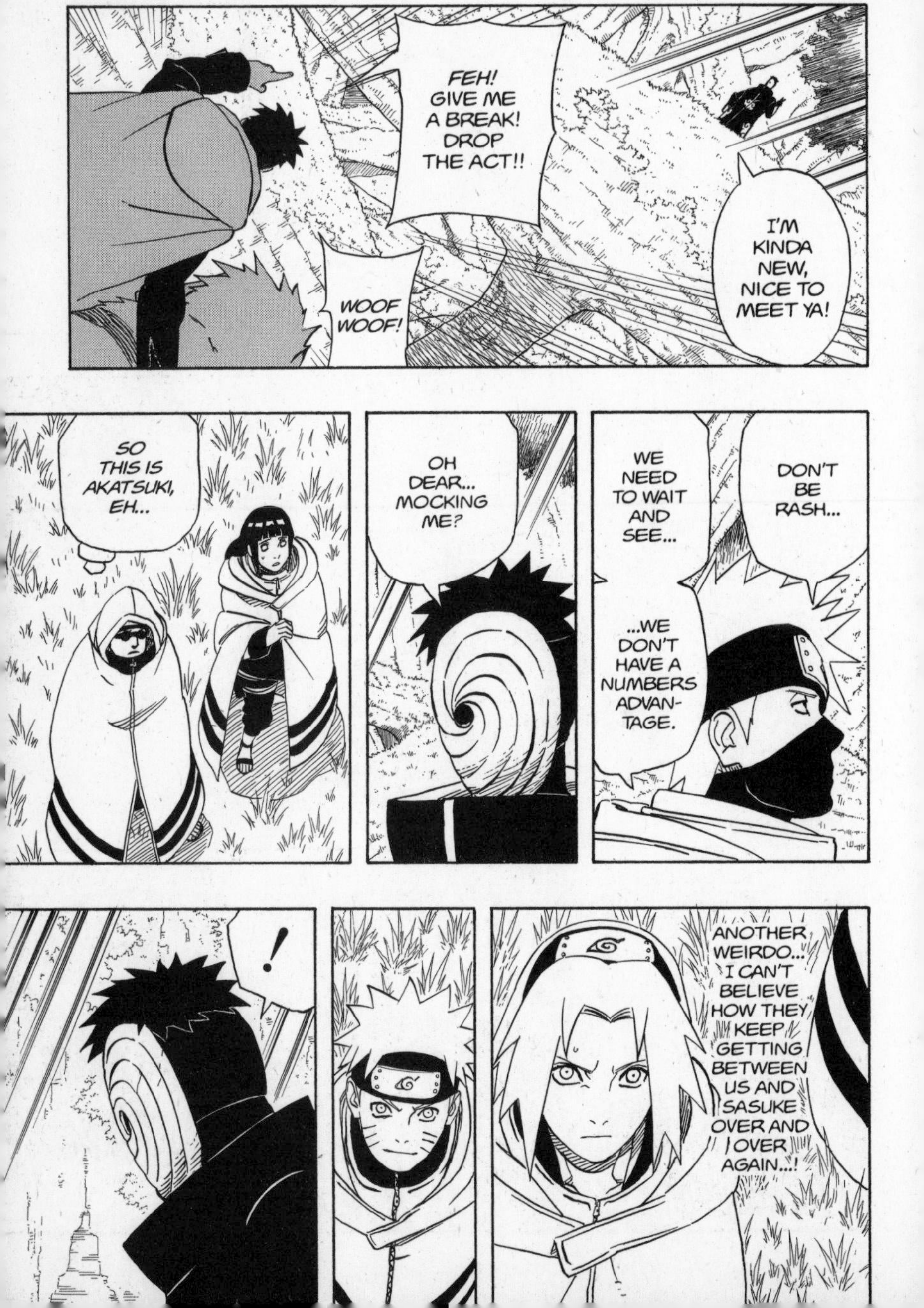
I'M KINDA NEW, NICE TO MEET YA!
FEH! GIVE ME A BREAK! DROP THE ACT!!
WOOF WOOF!
DON'T BE RASH...
WE NEED TO WAIT AND SEE...
...WE DON'T HAVE A NUMBERS ADVANTAGE.
OH DEAR... MOCKING ME?
SO THIS IS AKATSUKI, EH...
ANOTHER WEIRDO... I CAN'T BELIEVE HOW THEY KEEP GETTING BETWEEN US AND SASUKE OVER AND OVER AGAIN...!
!

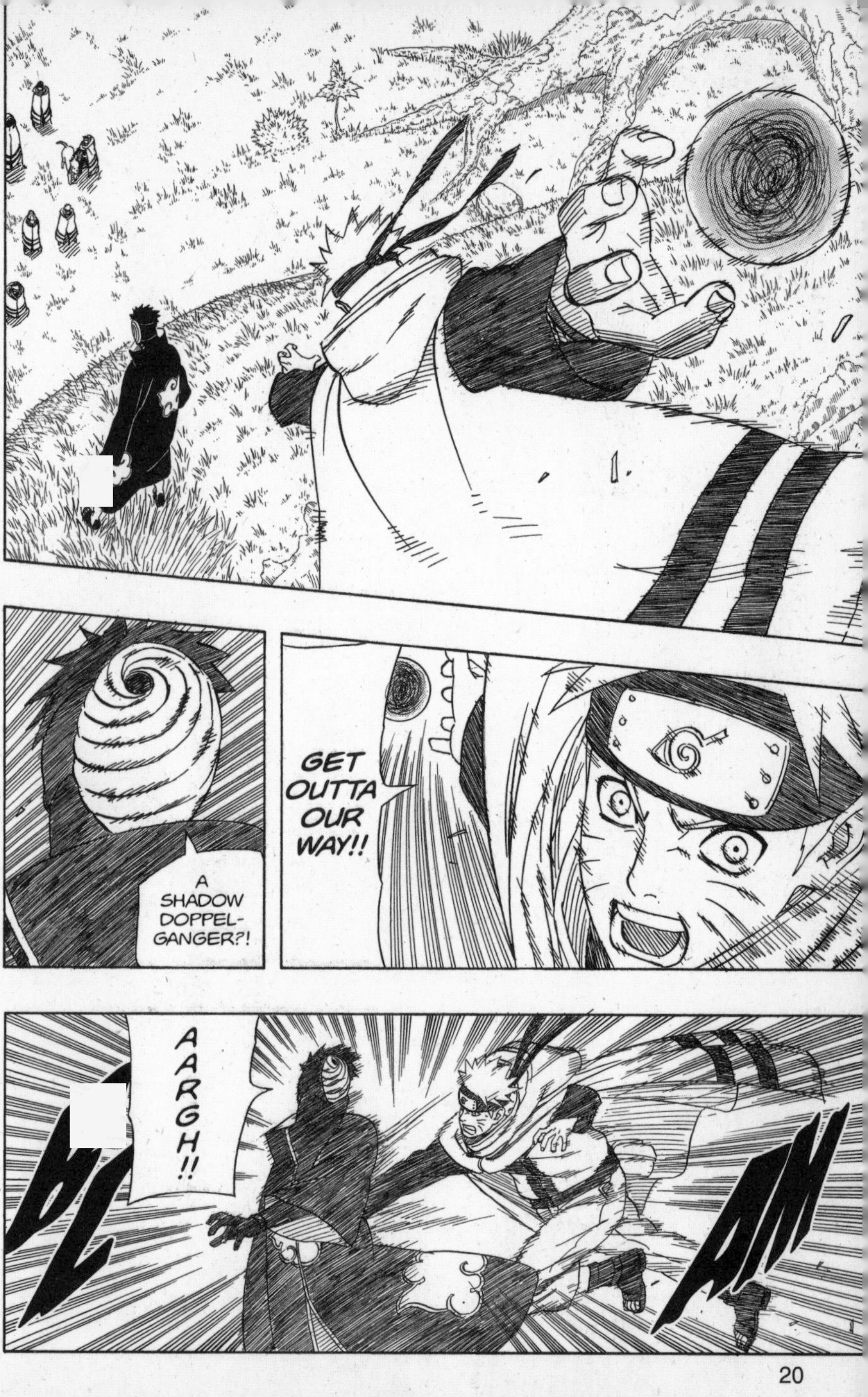
GET OUTTA OUR WAY!!
A SHADOW DOPPEL-GANGER?!
AARGH!!

READ THIS WAY

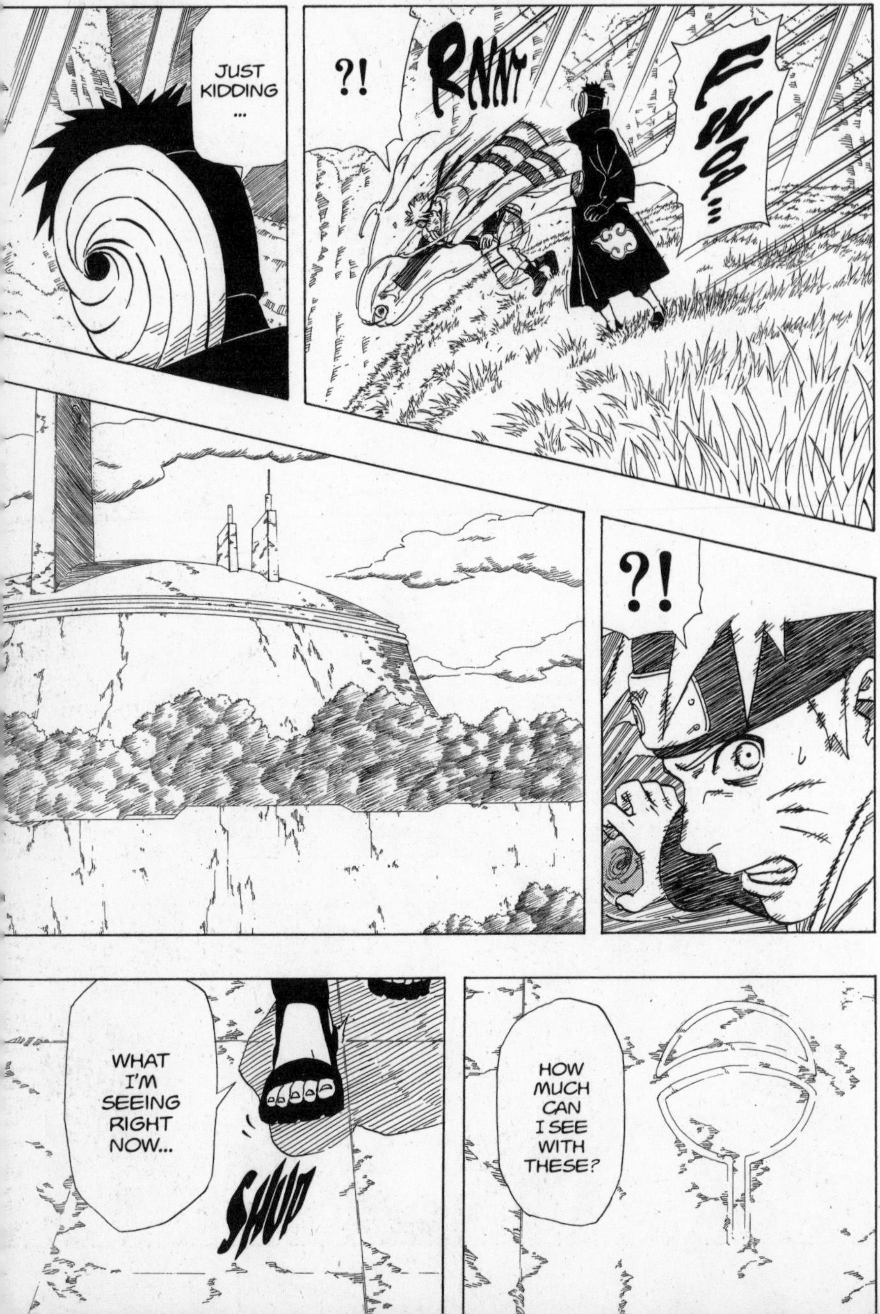
?!
RNNT
FWOO...
JUST KIDDING ...
?!
HOW MUCH CAN I SEE WITH THESE?
WHAT I'M SEEING RIGHT NOW...
SHUP

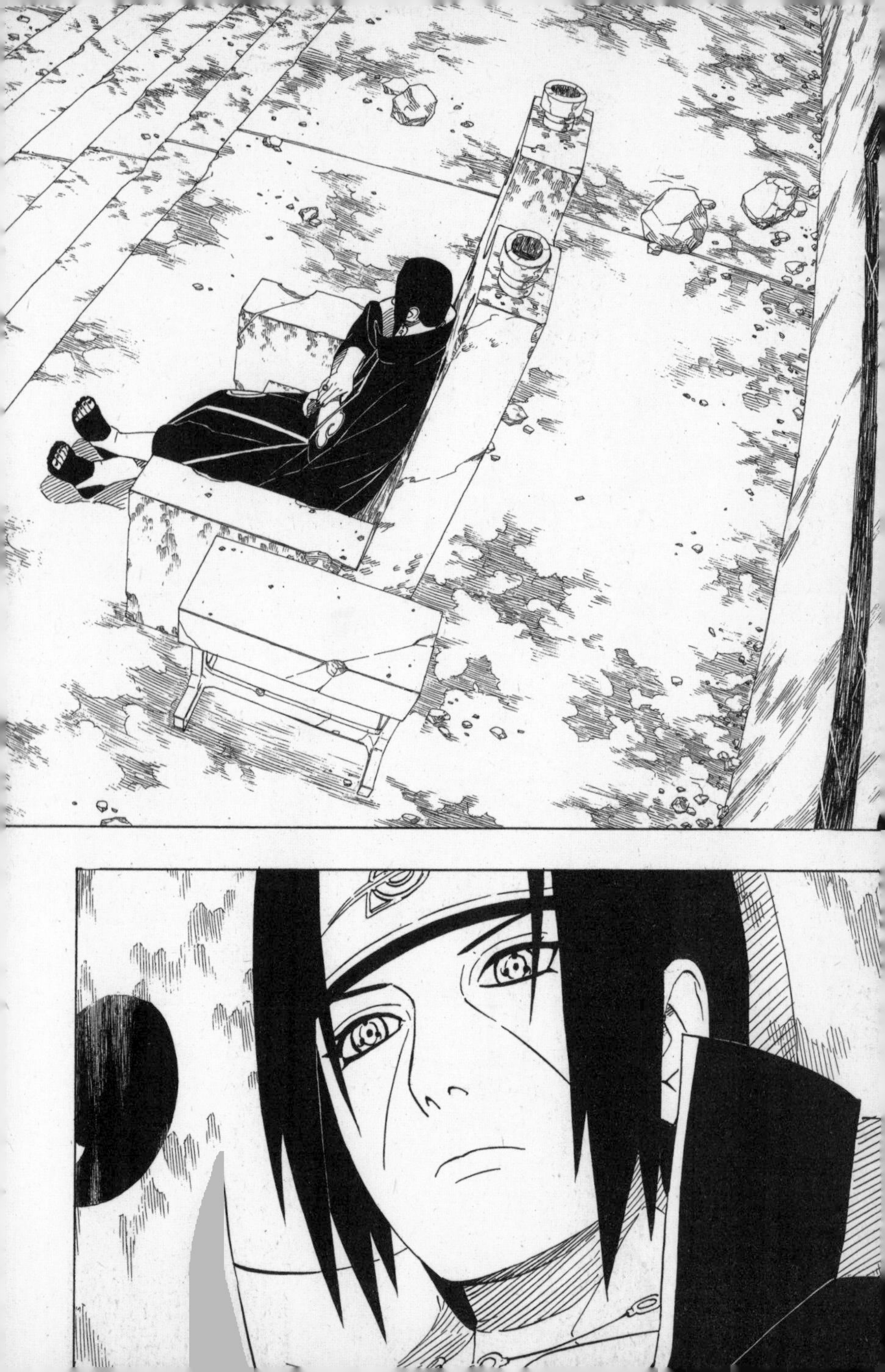

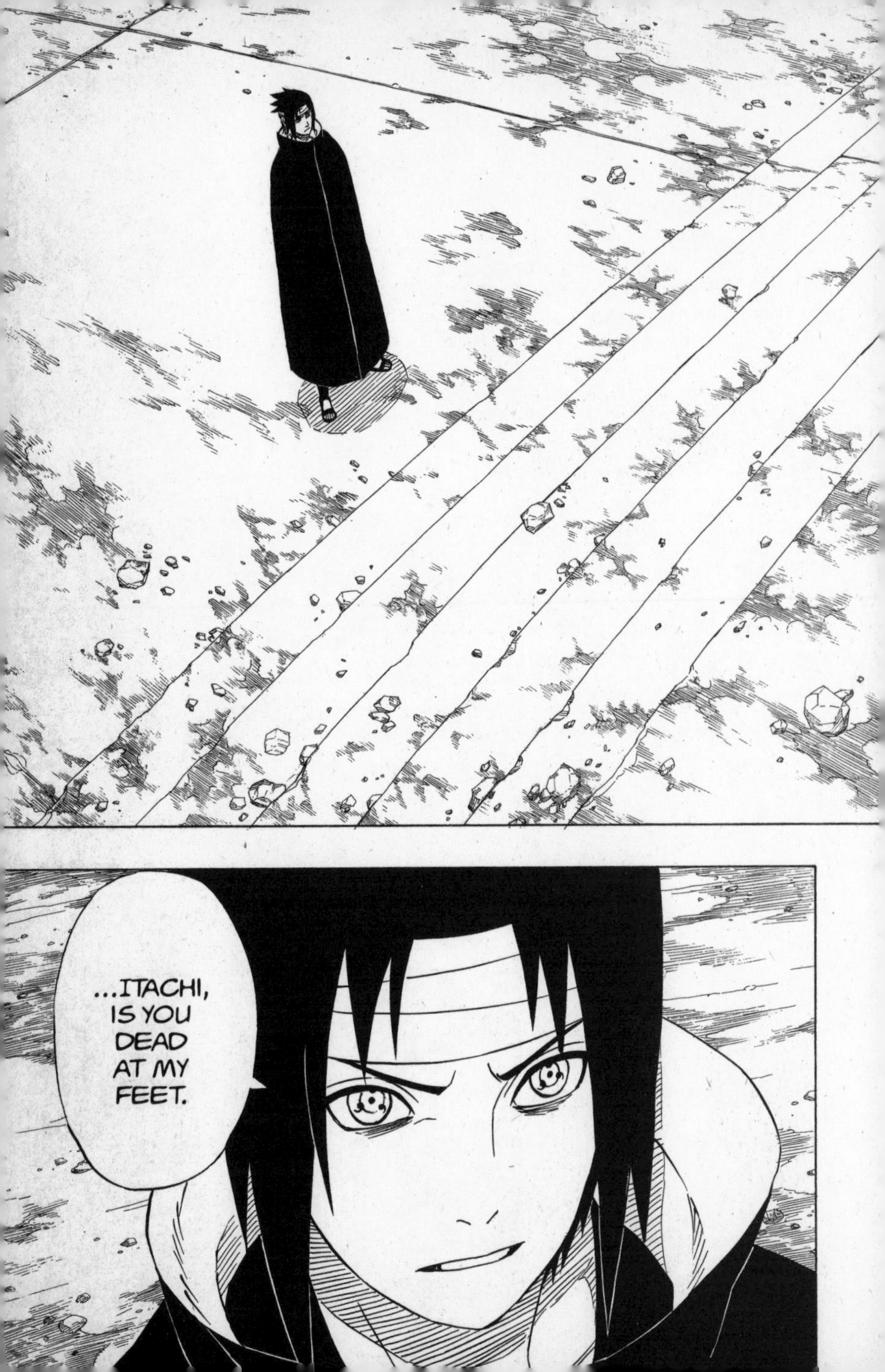
...ITACHI, IS YOU DEAD AT MY FEET.

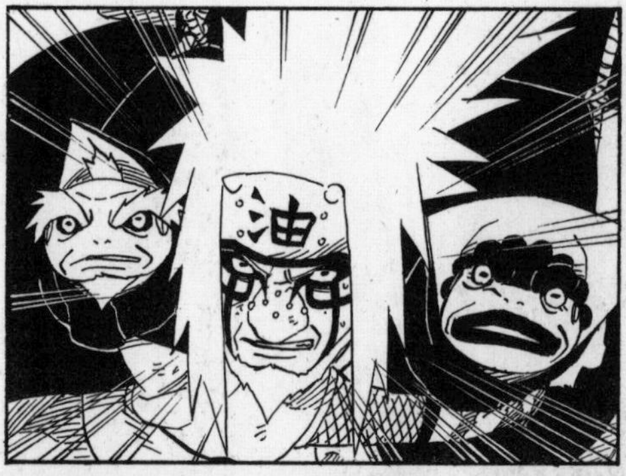
油

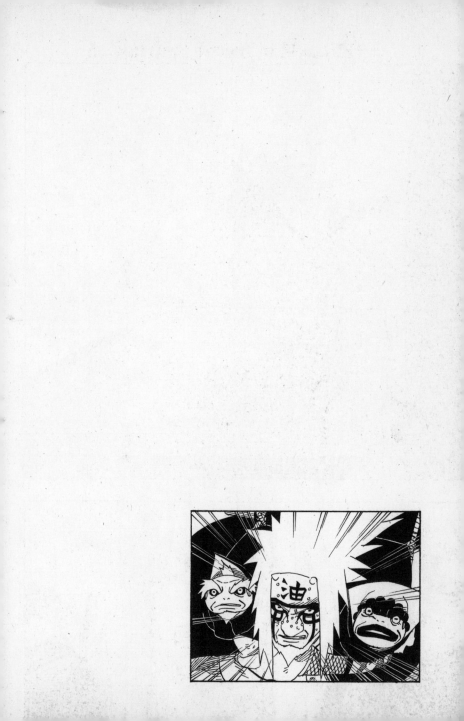

Number 381: True Identities...!!

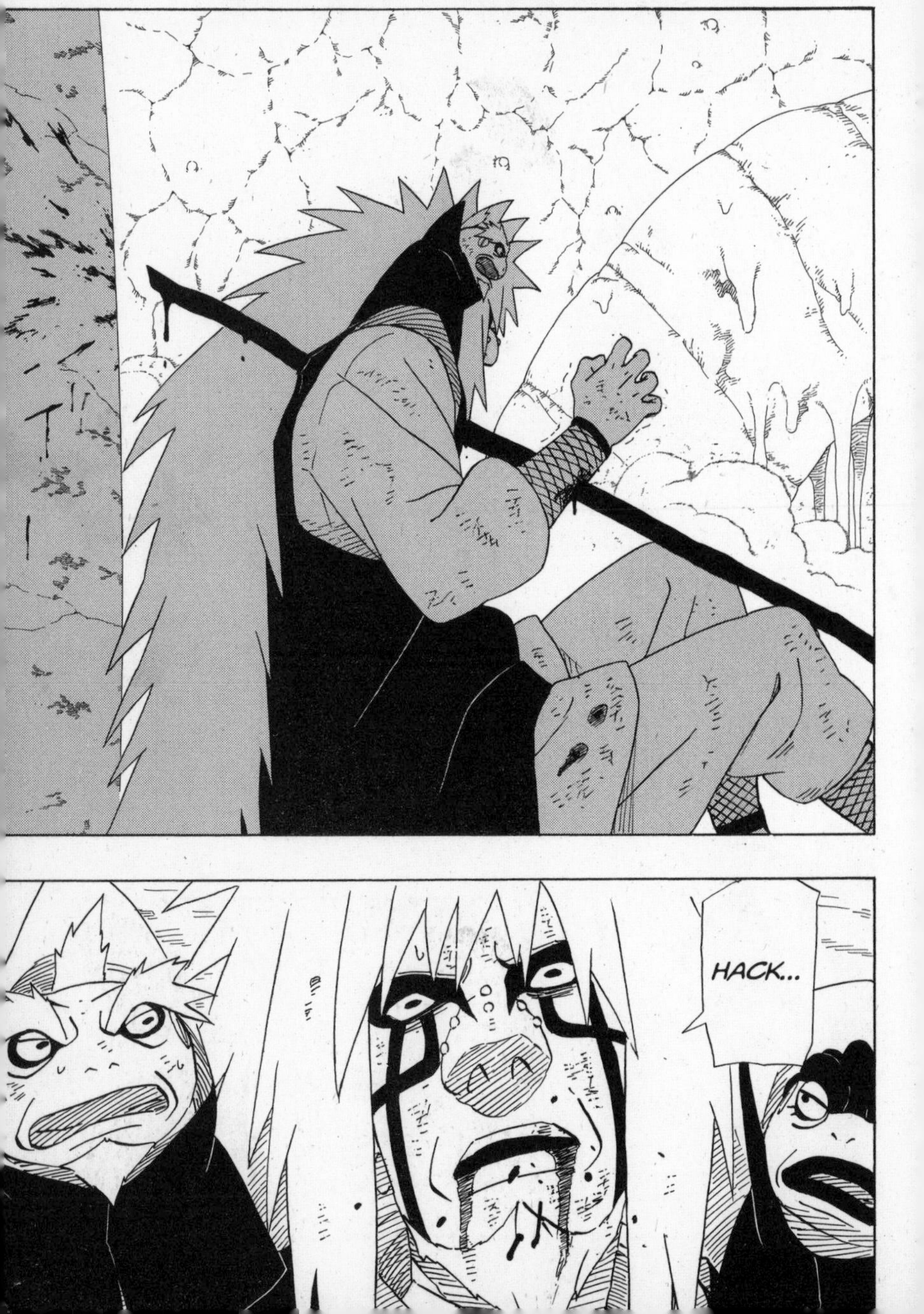
HACK...

Number 381: True Identities...!!

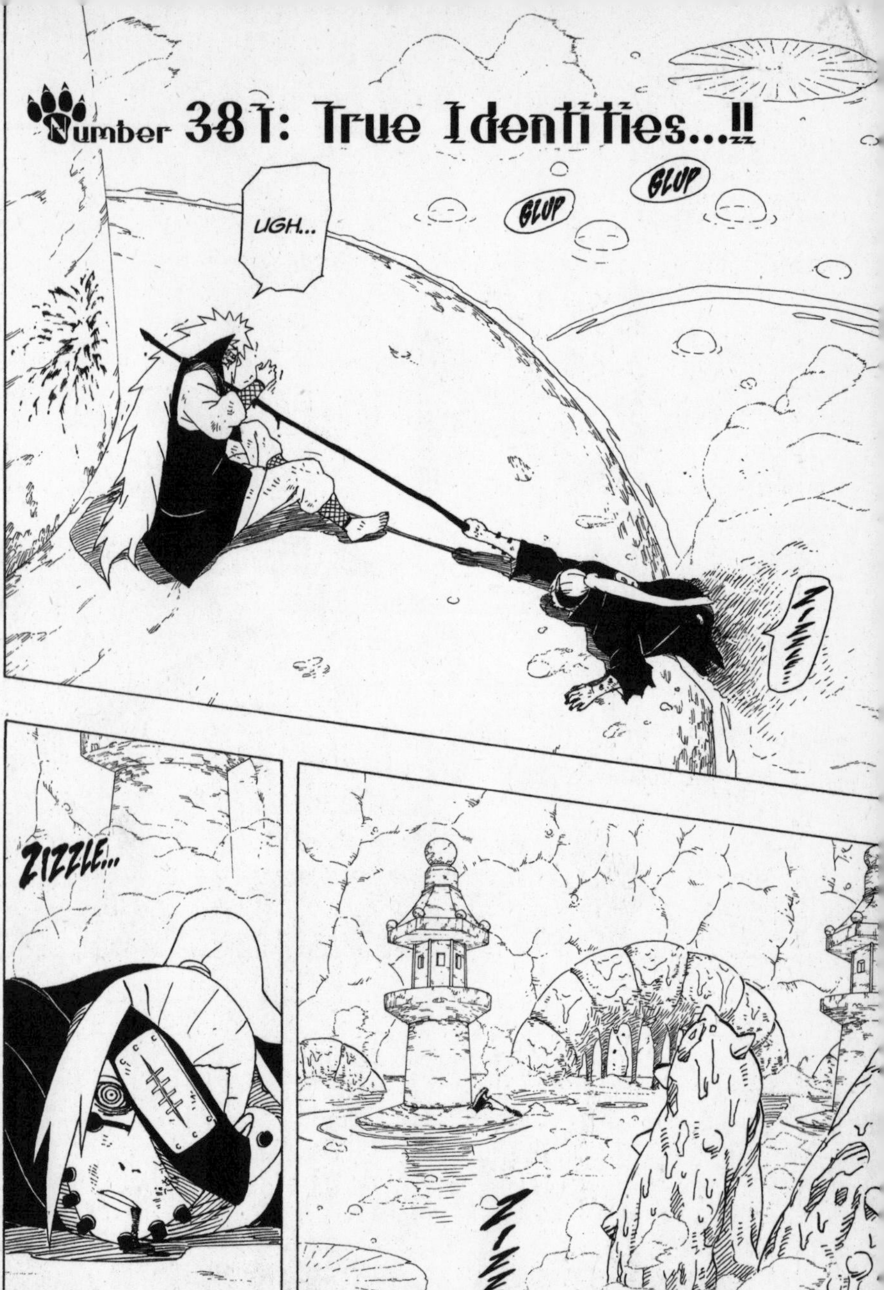
UGH...
GLUP
GLUP
ZIZZLE...

READ THIS WAY

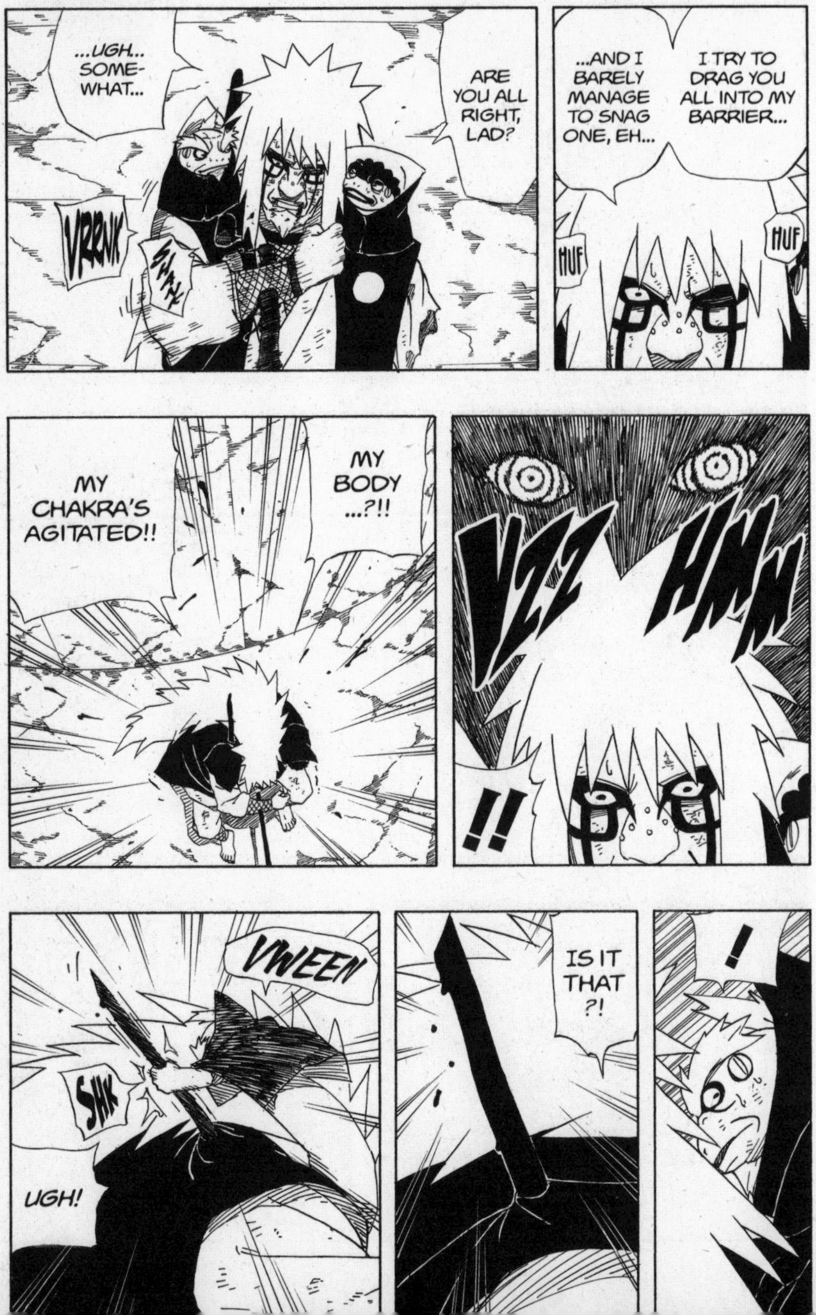
I TRY TO DRAG YOU ALL INTO MY BARRIER...
...AND I BARELY MANAGE TO SNAG ONE, EH...
HUF
HUF
ARE YOU ALL RIGHT, LAD?
...UGH... SOME-WHAT...
VRRNK
SHANK
VZZ
HMMM
!!
MY BODY ...?!!
MY CHAKRA'S AGITATED!!
!
IS IT THAT ?!
VWEEN
SHK
UGH!

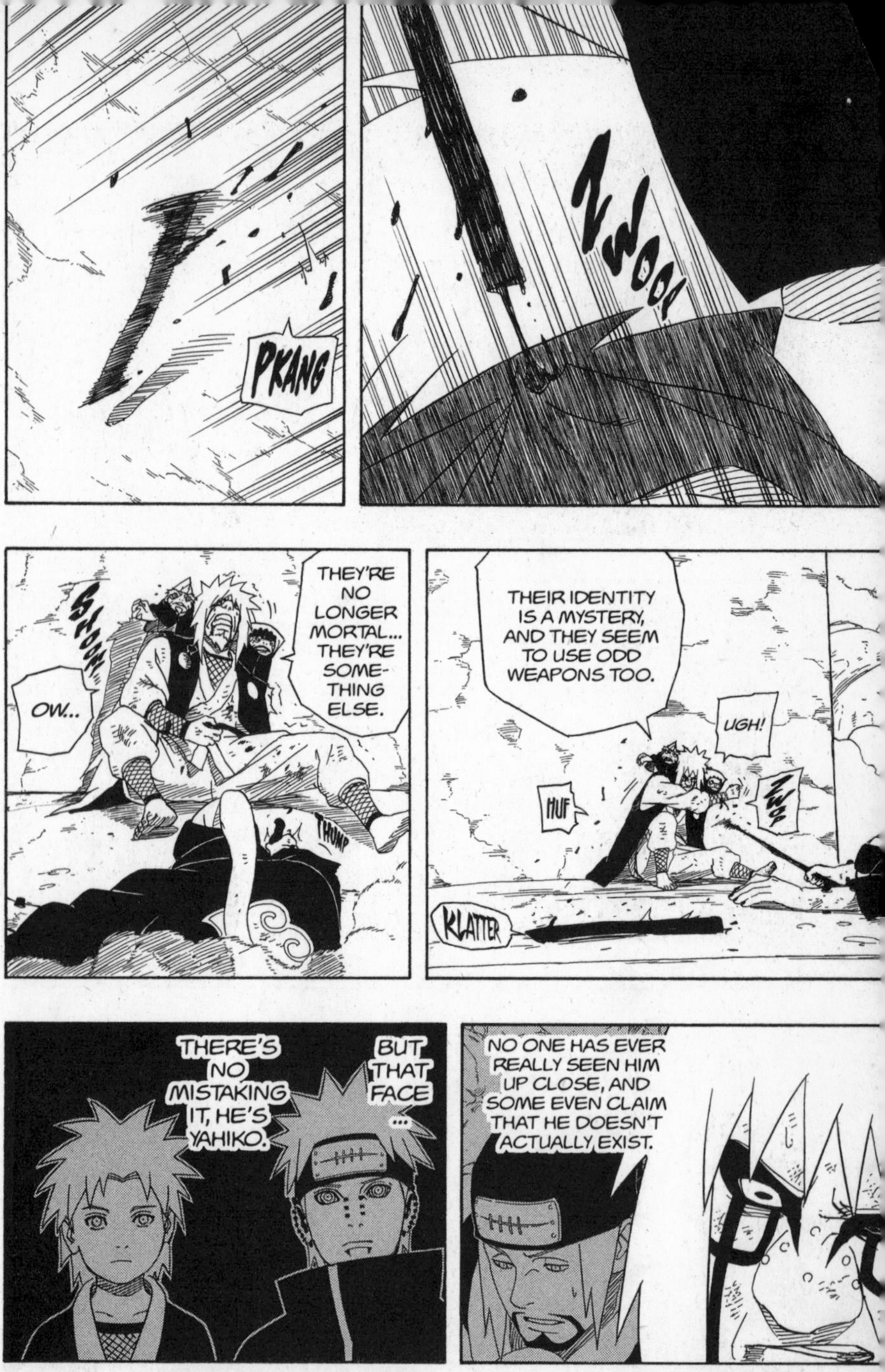
ZWOOP
PKANG
THEIR IDENTITY IS A MYSTERY, AND THEY SEEM TO USE ODD WEAPONS TOO.
UGH!
ZWOP
HUF
KLATTER
THEY'RE NO LONGER MORTAL... THEY'RE SOMETHING ELSE.
SHOOM
OW...
THUMP
NO ONE HAS EVER REALLY SEEN HIM UP CLOSE, AND SOME EVEN CLAIM THAT HE DOESN'T ACTUALLY EXIST.
BUT THAT FACE...
THERE'S NO MISTAKING IT, HE'S YAHIKO.

READ THIS WAY

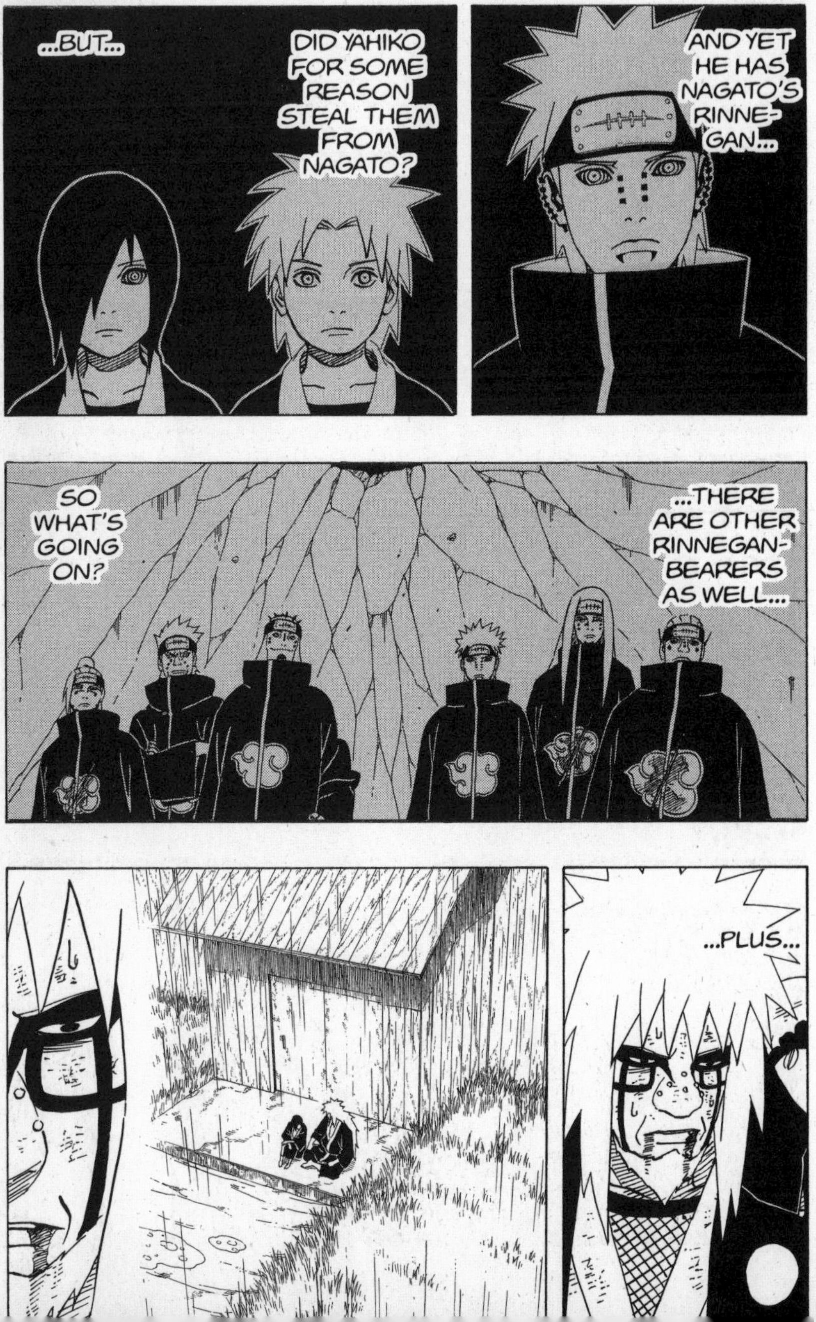
AND YET HE HAS NAGATO'S RINNE-GAN...
DID YAHIKO FOR SOME REASON STEAL THEM FROM NAGATO?
...BUT...
...THERE ARE OTHER RINNEGAN-BEARERS AS WELL...
SO WHAT'S GOING ON?
...PLUS...

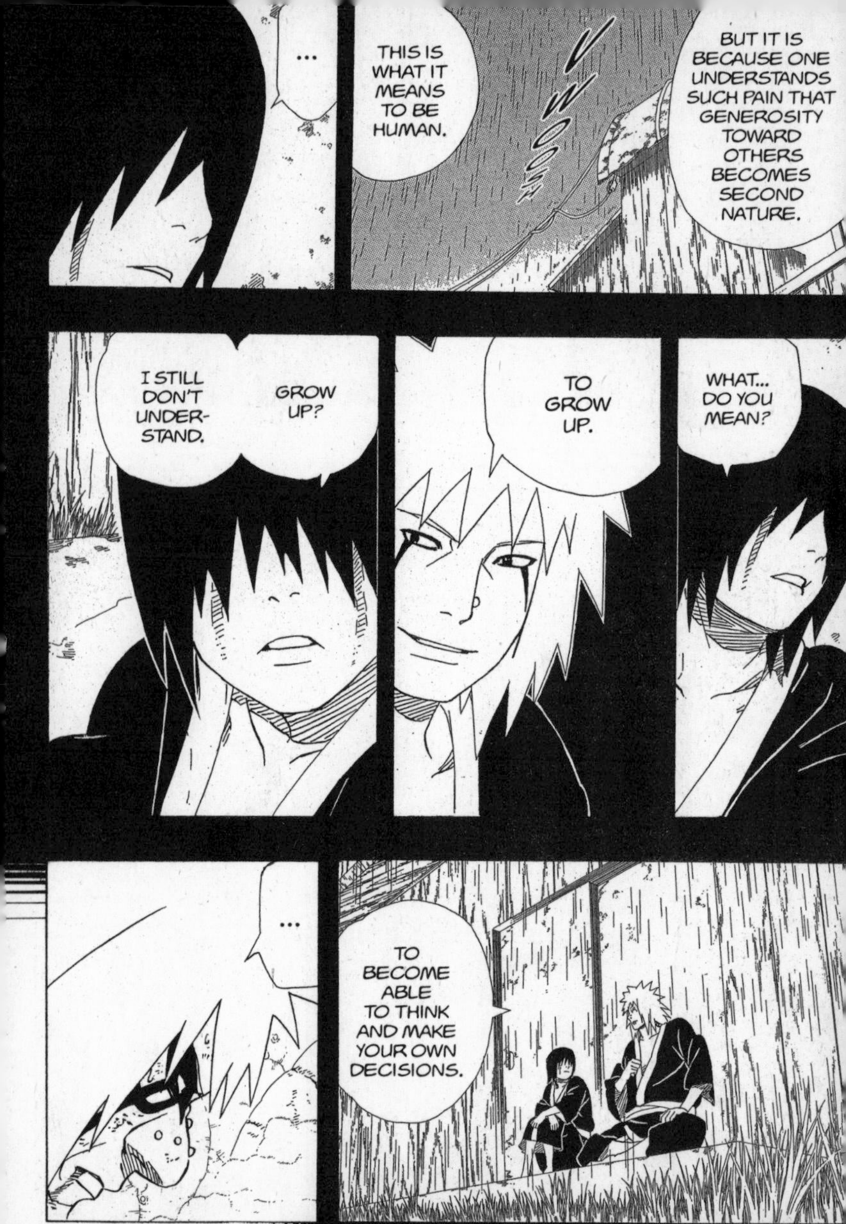
BUT IT IS BECAUSE ONE UNDERSTANDS SUCH PAIN THAT GENEROSITY TOWARD OTHERS BECOMES SECOND NATURE.
THIS IS WHAT IT MEANS TO BE HUMAN.
...
WHAT... DO YOU MEAN?
TO GROW UP.
GROW UP?
I STILL DON'T UNDER-STAND.
TO BECOME ABLE TO THINK AND MAKE YOUR OWN DECISIONS.
...

READ THIS WAY

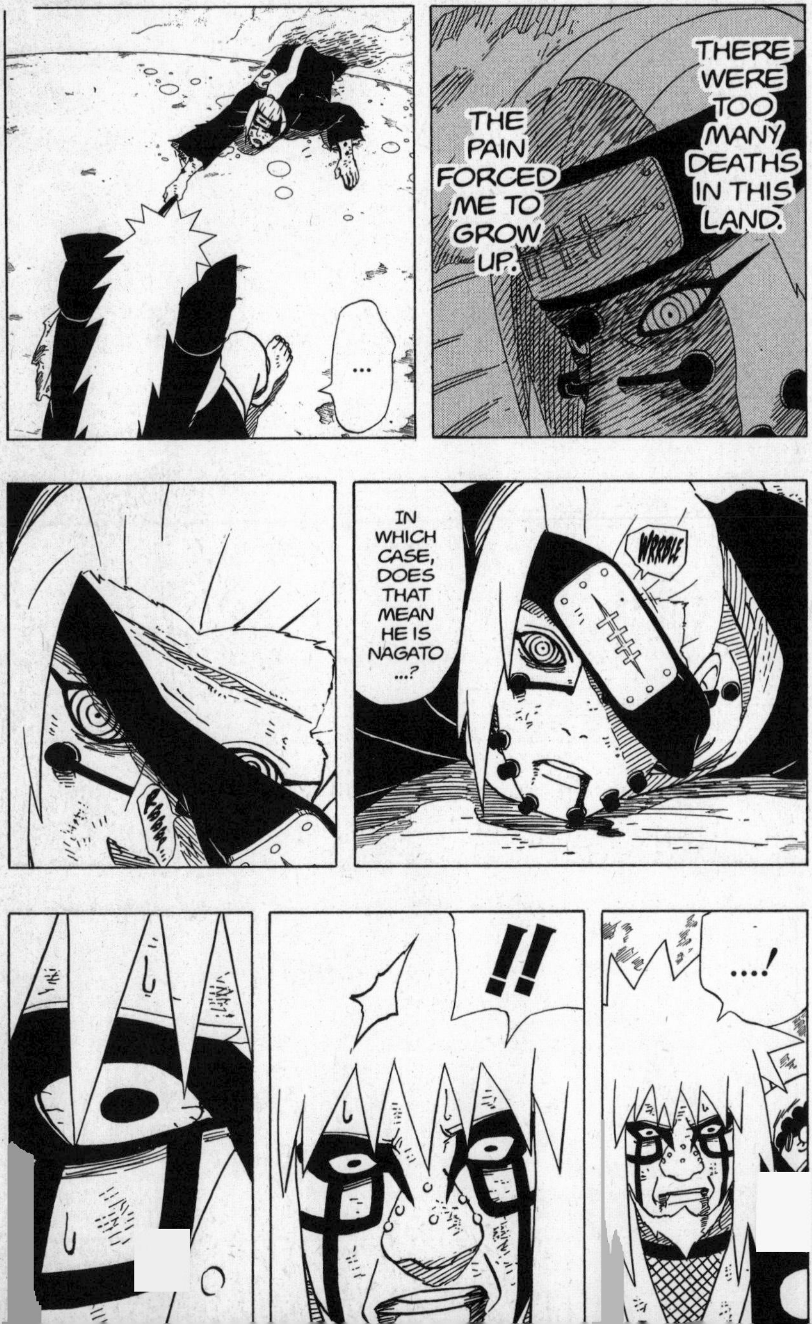
THERE WERE TOO MANY DEATHS IN THIS LAND.
THE PAIN FORCED ME TO GROW UP.
...
WRRBLE
IN WHICH CASE, DOES THAT MEAN HE IS NAGATO ...?
...!
!!

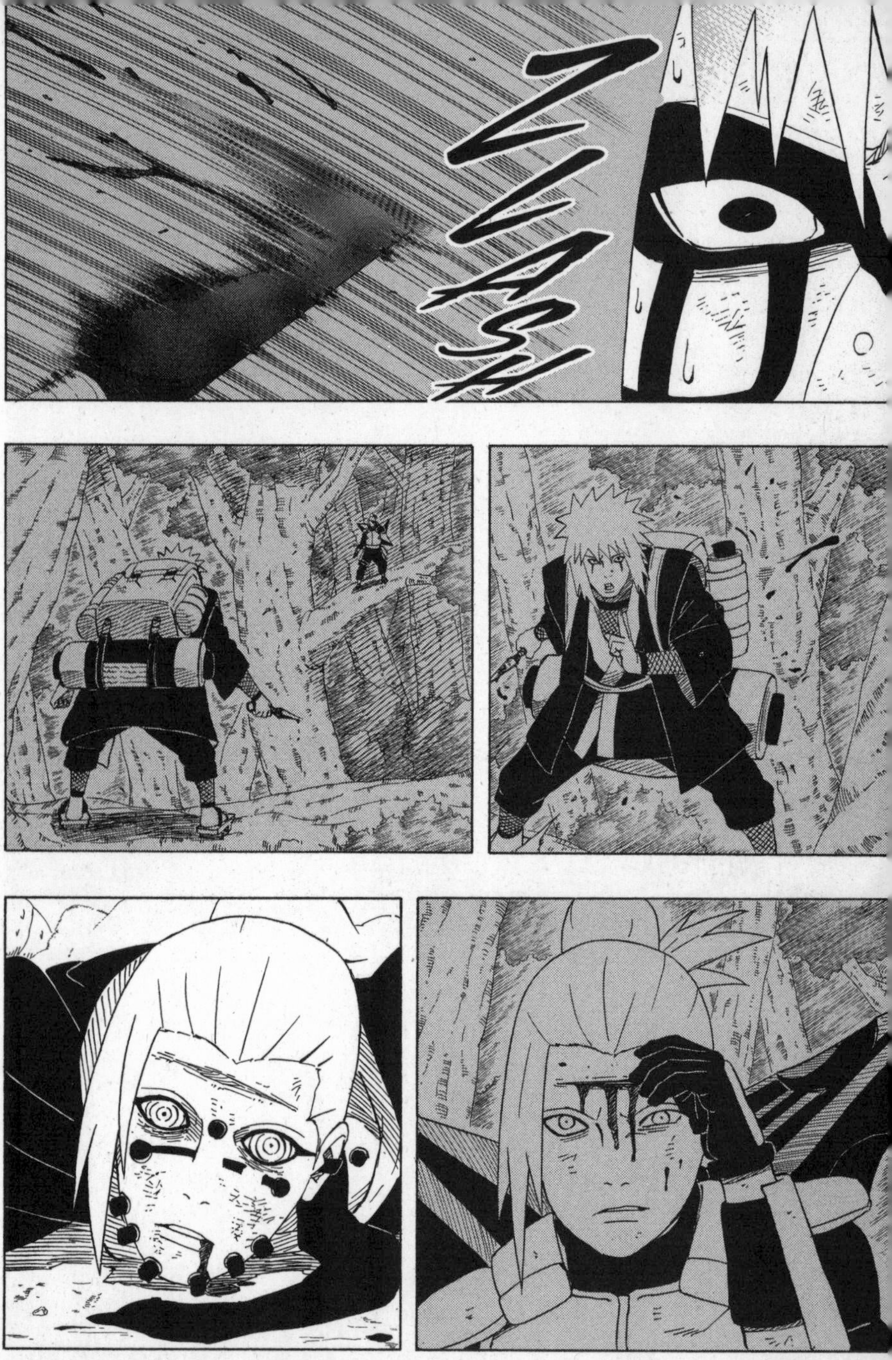
ZWASH

READ THIS WAY

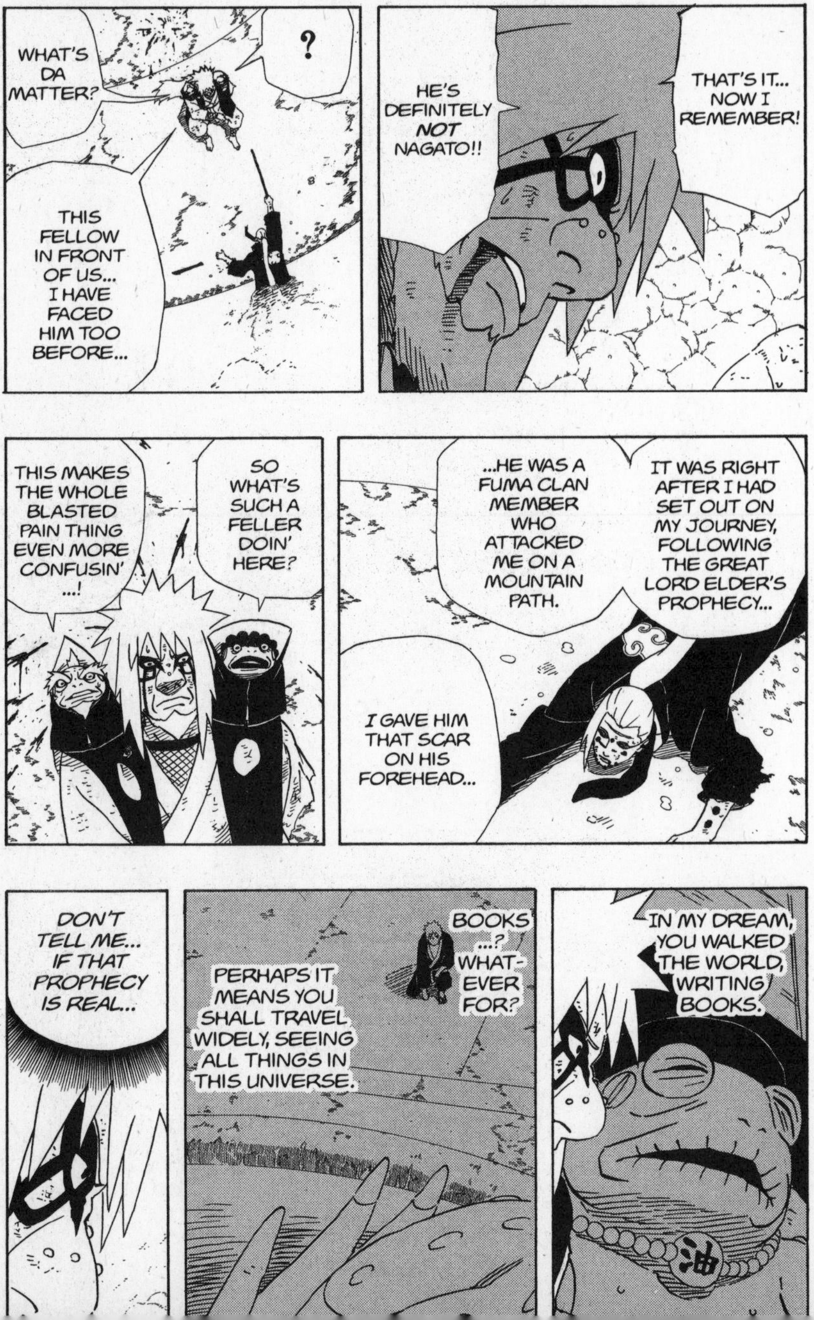

THAT'S IT... NOW I REMEMBER!
HE'S DEFINITELY *NOT* NAGATO!!
?
WHAT'S DA MATTER?
THIS FELLOW IN FRONT OF US... I HAVE FACED HIM TOO BEFORE...
IT WAS RIGHT AFTER I HAD SET OUT ON MY JOURNEY, FOLLOWING THE GREAT LORD ELDER'S PROPHECY...
...HE WAS A FUMA CLAN MEMBER WHO ATTACKED ME ON A MOUNTAIN PATH.
I GAVE HIM THAT SCAR ON HIS FOREHEAD...
SO WHAT'S SUCH A FELLER DOIN' HERE?
THIS MAKES THE WHOLE BLASTED PAIN THING EVEN MORE CONFUSIN'...!
IN MY DREAM, YOU WALKED THE WORLD, WRITING BOOKS.
BOOKS...? WHATEVER FOR?
PERHAPS IT MEANS YOU SHALL TRAVEL WIDELY, SEEING ALL THINGS IN THIS UNIVERSE.
DON'T TELL ME... IF THAT PROPHECY IS REAL...

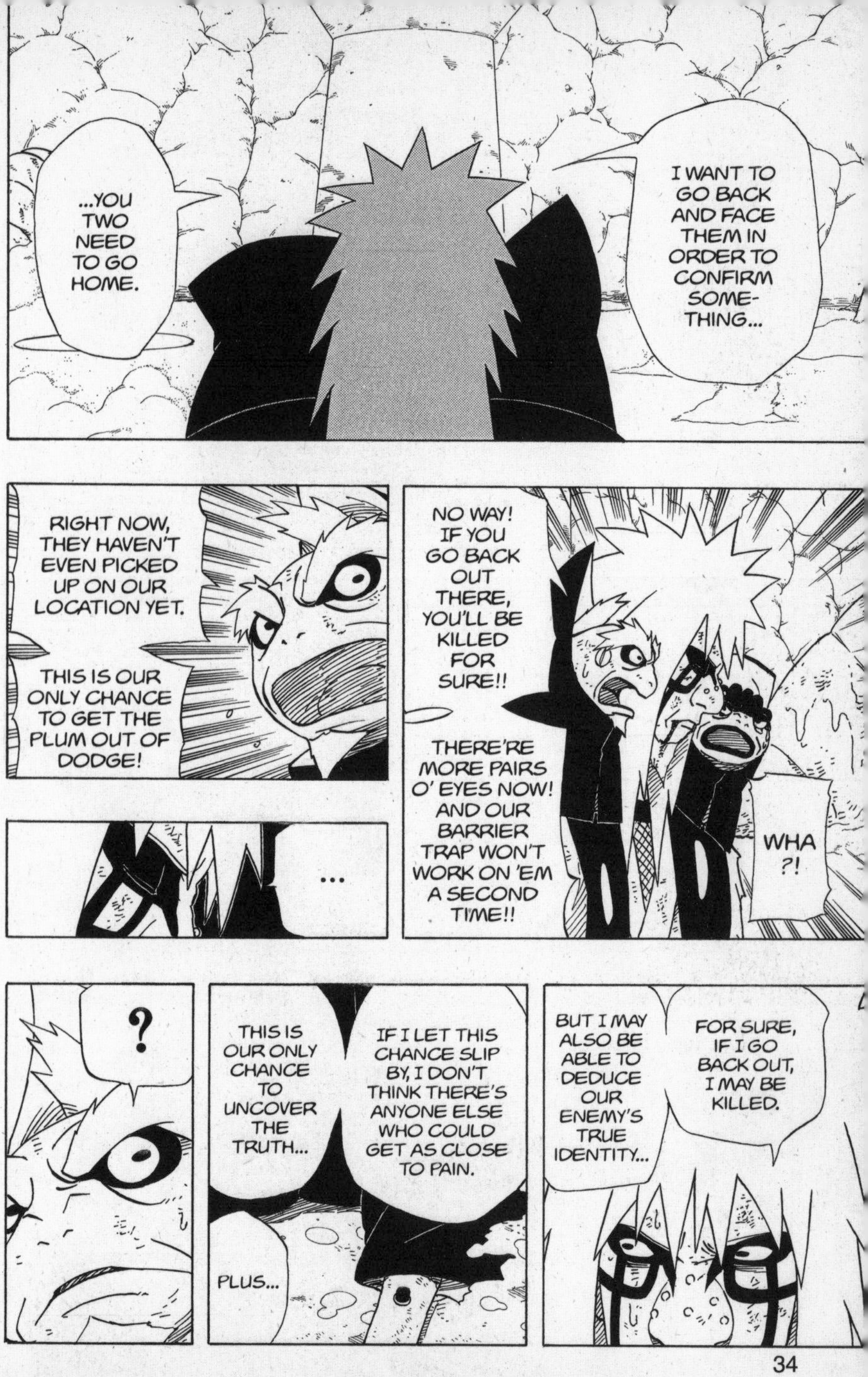
I WANT TO GO BACK AND FACE THEM IN ORDER TO CONFIRM SOME-THING...
...YOU TWO NEED TO GO HOME.
NO WAY! IF YOU GO BACK OUT THERE, YOU'LL BE KILLED FOR SURE!!
THERE'RE MORE PAIRS O' EYES NOW! AND OUR BARRIER TRAP WON'T WORK ON 'EM A SECOND TIME!!
WHA ?!
RIGHT NOW, THEY HAVEN'T EVEN PICKED UP ON OUR LOCATION YET.
THIS IS OUR ONLY CHANCE TO GET THE PLUM OUT OF DODGE!
...
FOR SURE, IF I GO BACK OUT, I MAY BE KILLED.
BUT I MAY ALSO BE ABLE TO DEDUCE OUR ENEMY'S TRUE IDENTITY...
IF I LET THIS CHANCE SLIP BY, I DON'T THINK THERE'S ANYONE ELSE WHO COULD GET AS CLOSE TO PAIN.
THIS IS OUR ONLY CHANCE TO UNCOVER THE TRUTH...
PLUS...
?

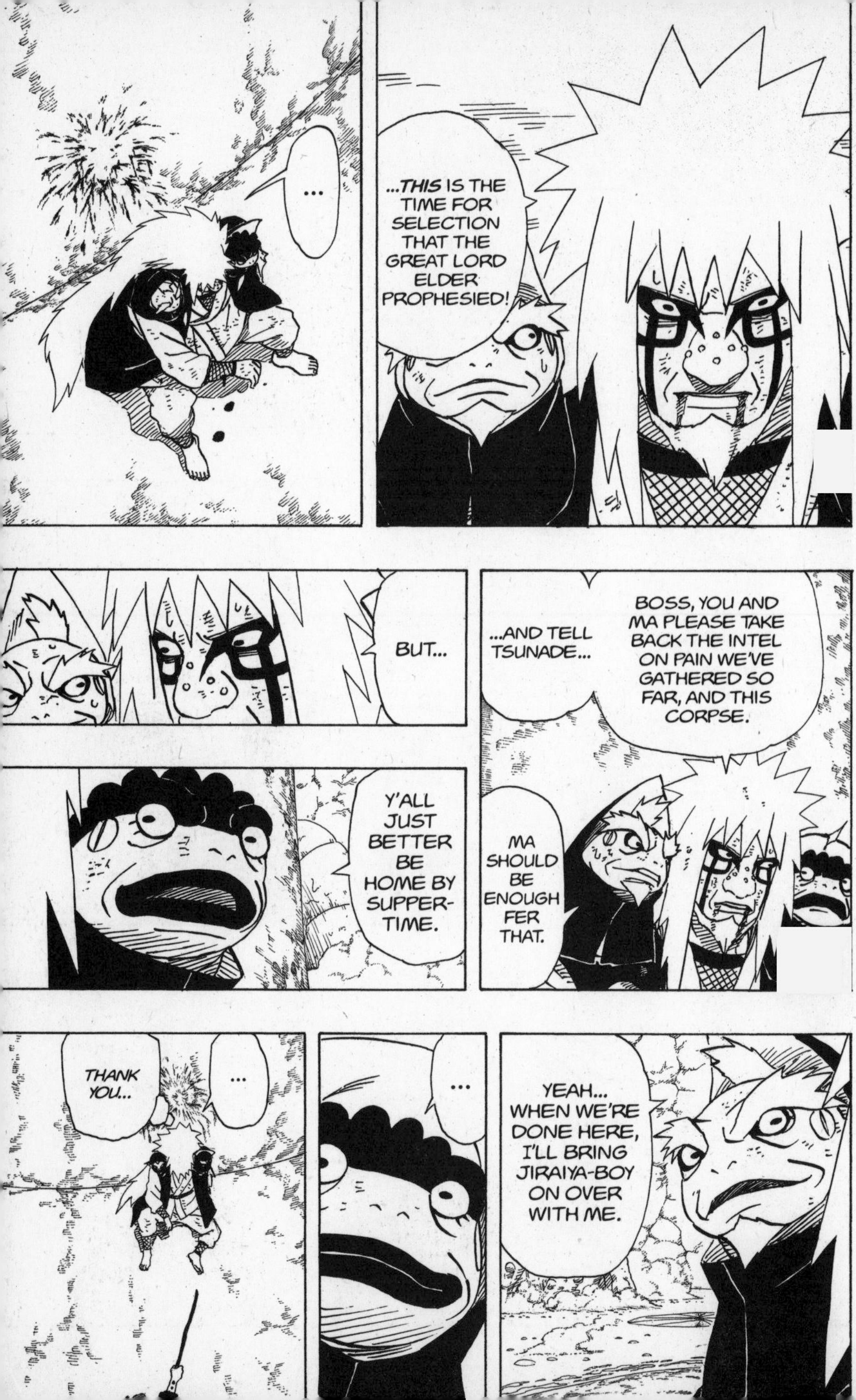
...THIS IS THE TIME FOR SELECTION THAT THE GREAT LORD ELDER PROPHESIED!
...
BOSS, YOU AND MA PLEASE TAKE BACK THE INTEL ON PAIN WE'VE GATHERED SO FAR, AND THIS CORPSE.
...AND TELL TSUNADE...
MA SHOULD BE ENOUGH FER THAT.
BUT...
Y'ALL JUST BETTER BE HOME BY SUPPER-TIME.
YEAH... WHEN WE'RE DONE HERE, I'LL BRING JIRAIYA-BOY ON OVER WITH ME.
...
...
THANK YOU...

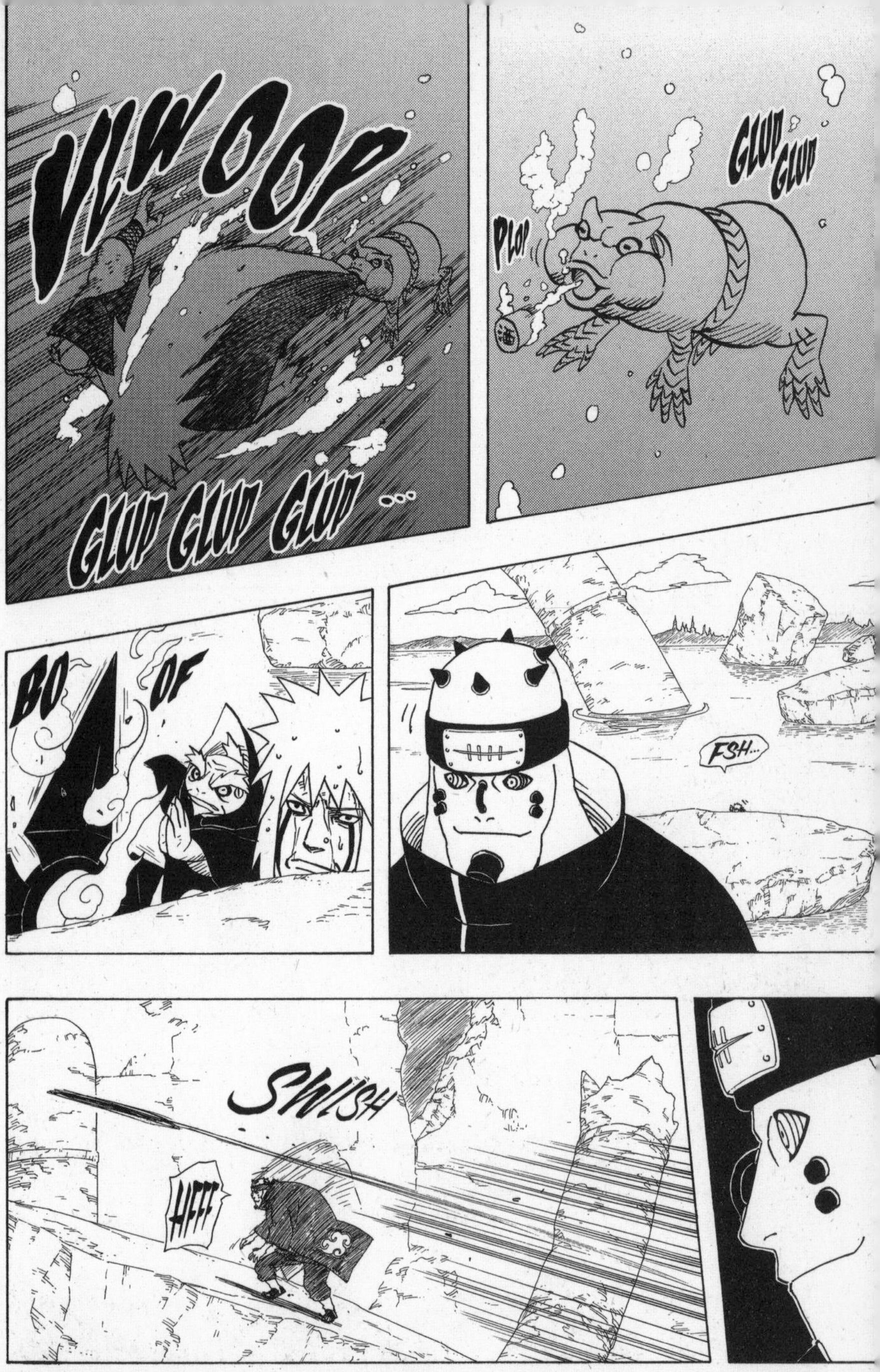
GLUP GLUP
PLOP
VLW OOP
GLUP GLUP GLUP ...
FSH...
BO OF
SWISH
HFFF

READ THIS WAY

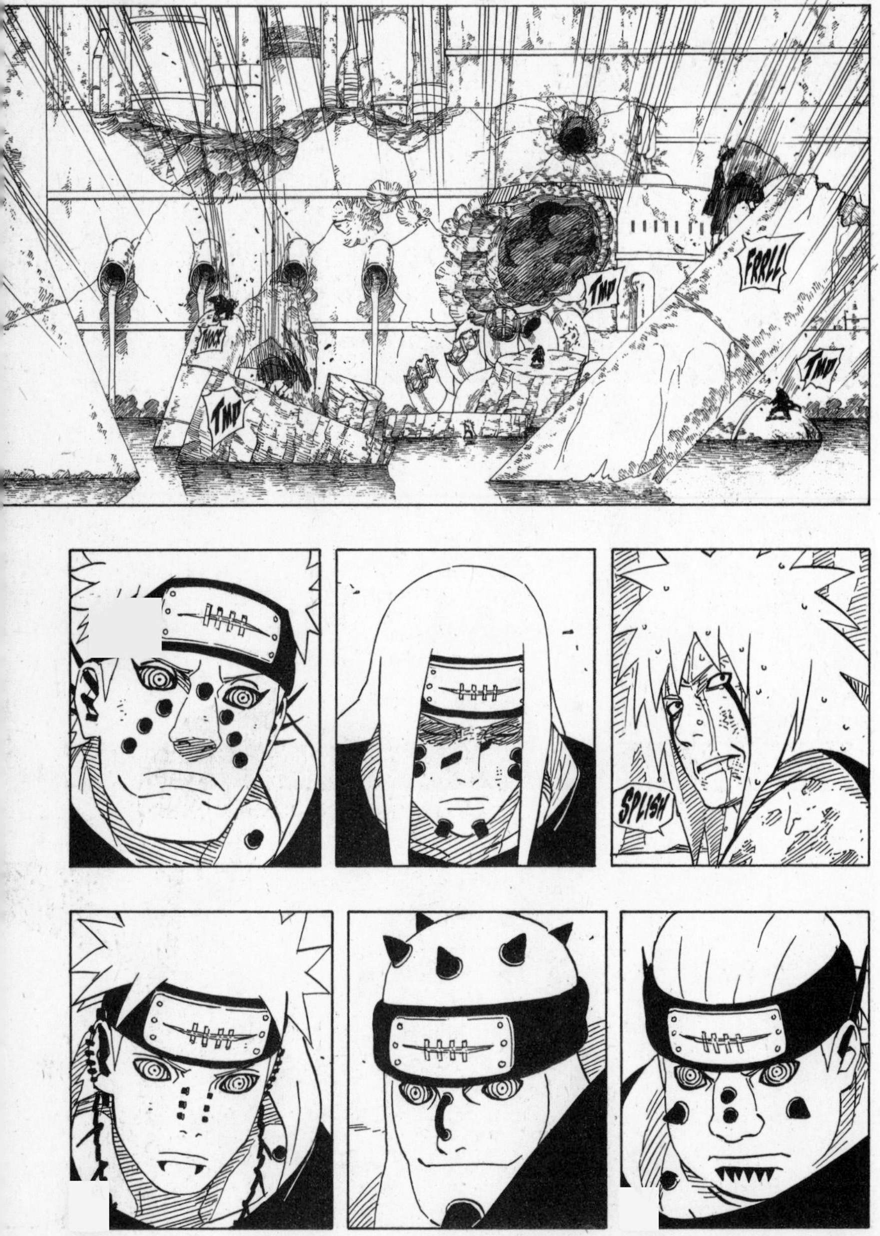
FRRLL
TMP
TMP
THOCK
TMP
SPLISH

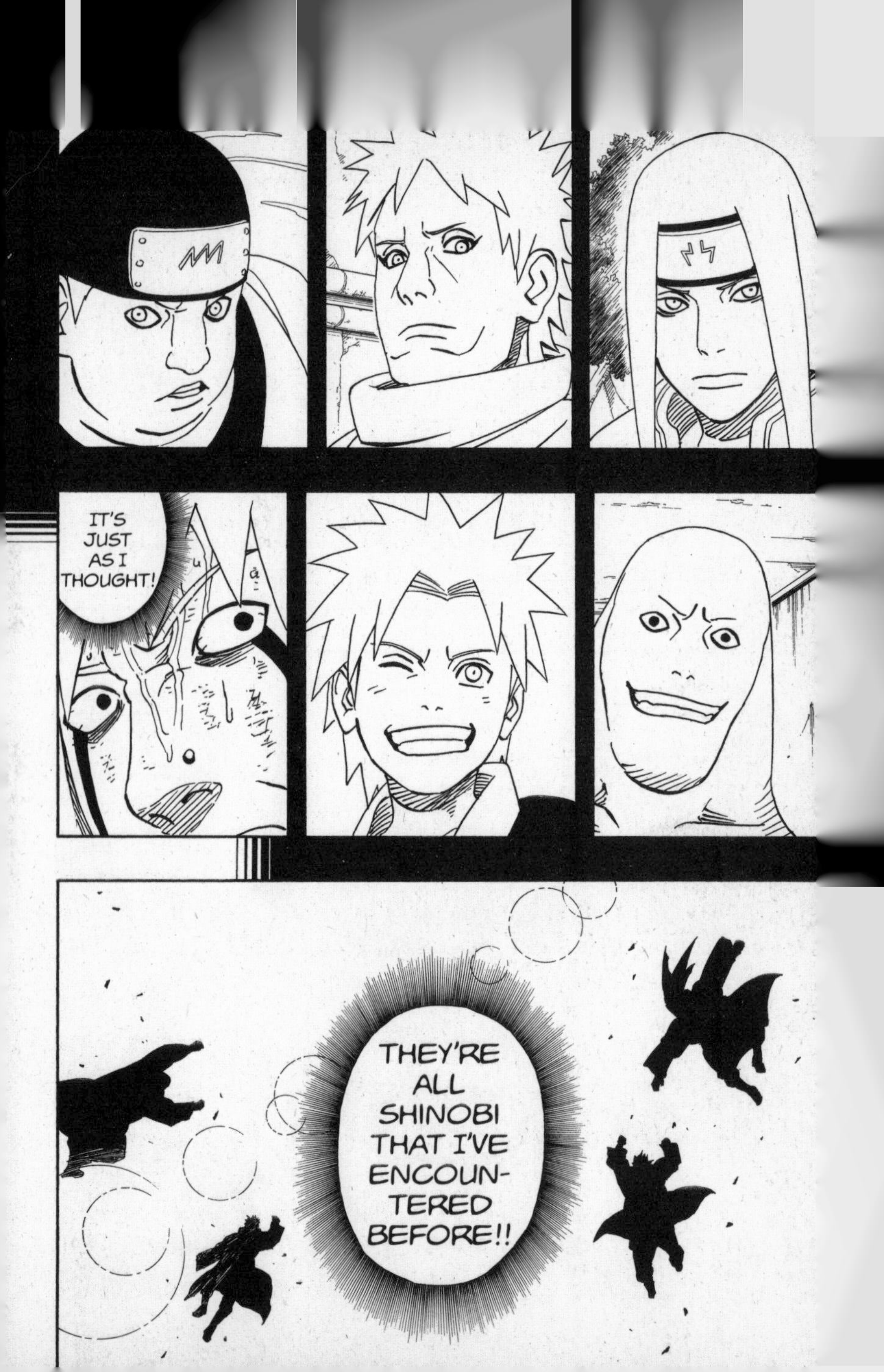
IT'S JUST AS I THOUGHT!
THEY'RE ALL SHINOBI THAT I'VE ENCOUNTERED BEFORE!!

READ THIS WAY

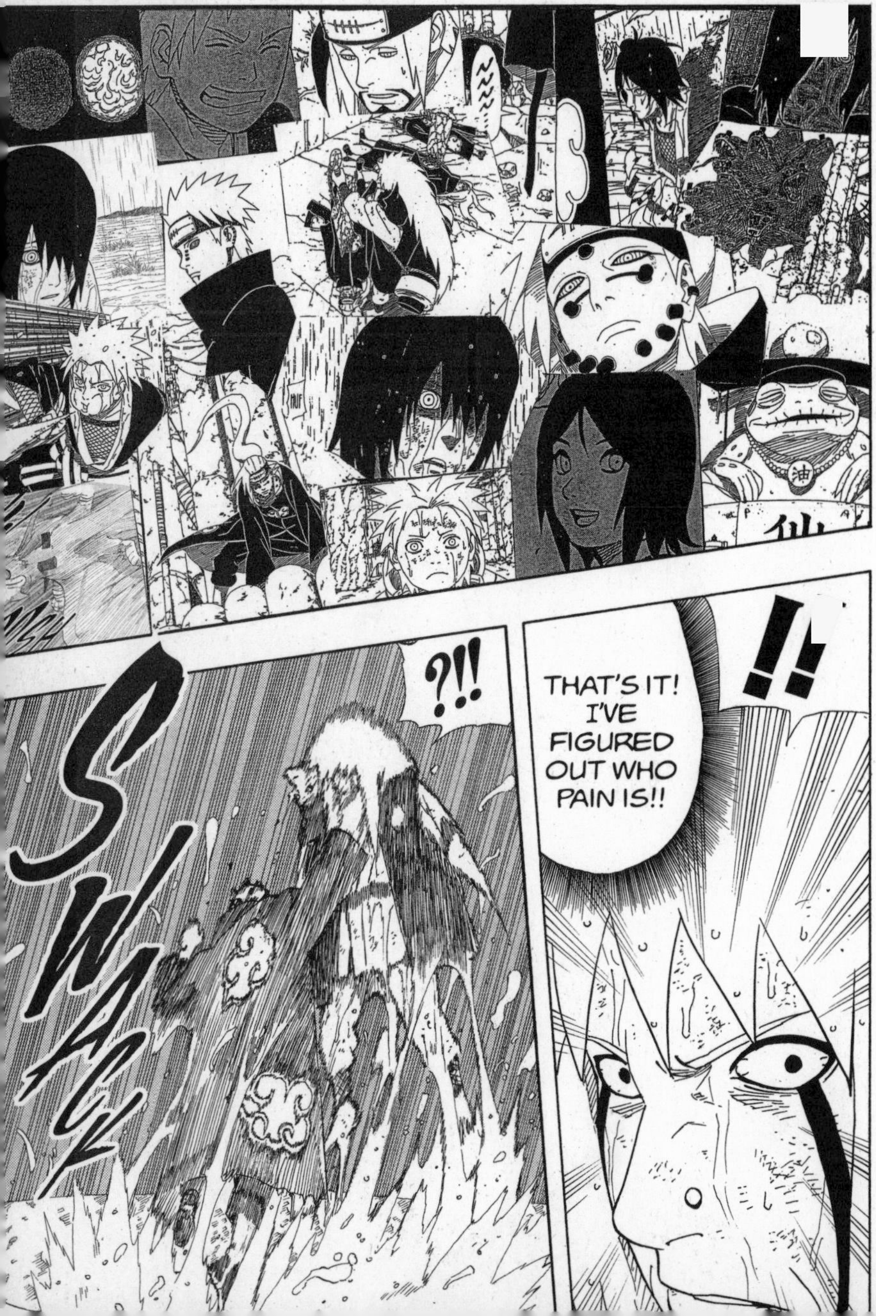
!!
THAT'S IT! I'VE FIGURED OUT WHO PAIN IS!!
?!!

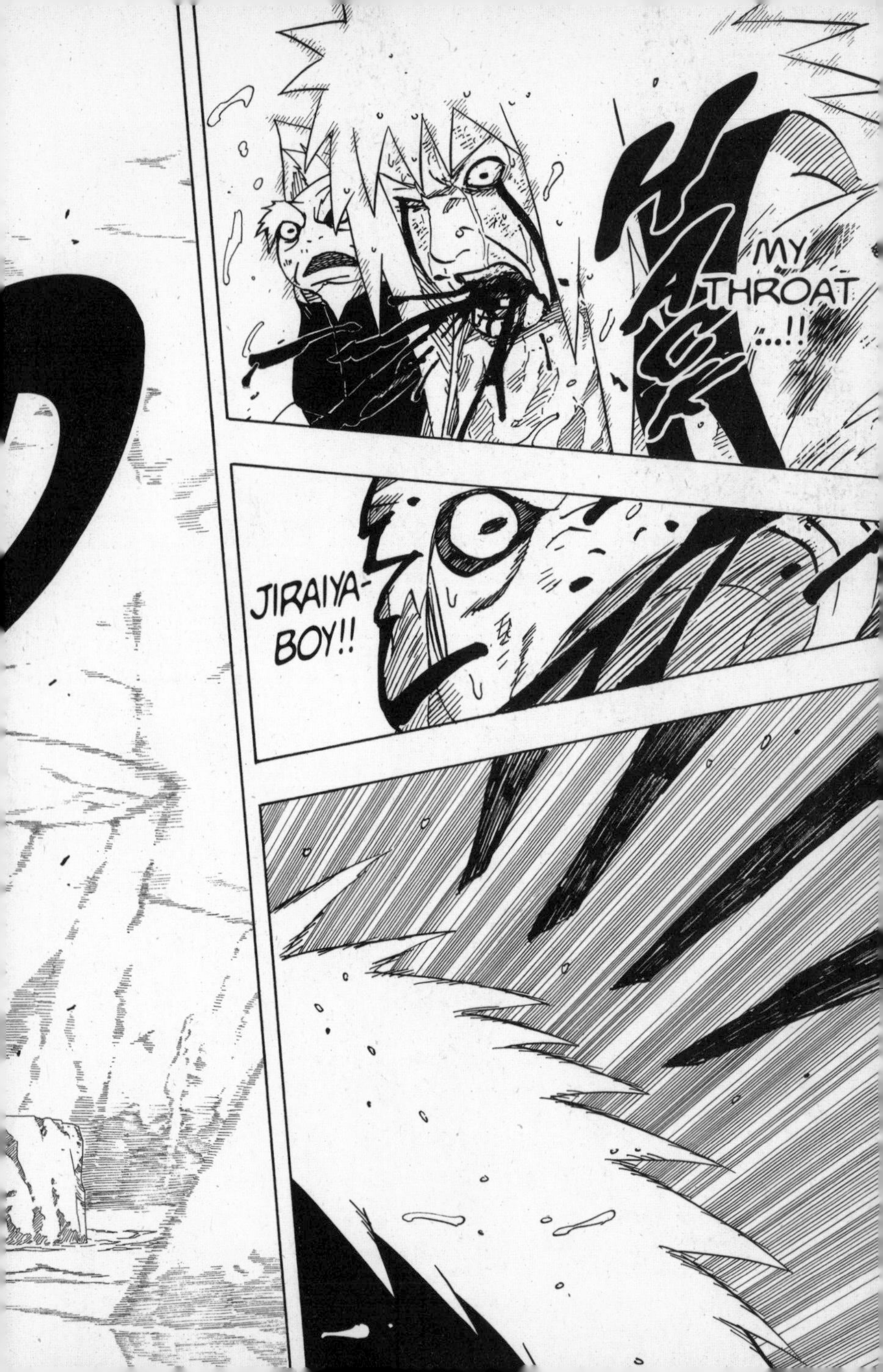
MY THROAT ...!!
JIRAIYA-BOY!!

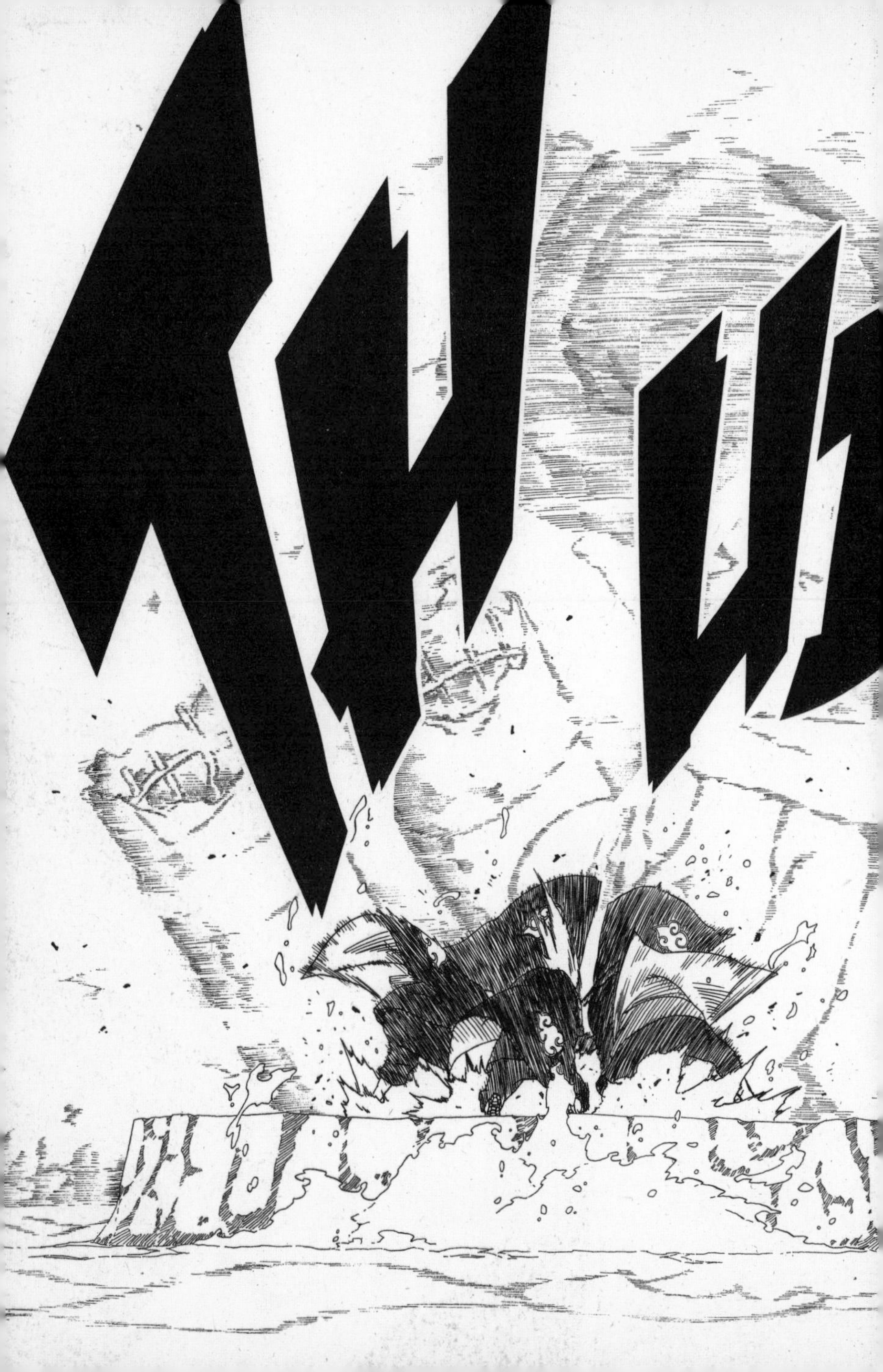

NARUTO

Number 382: The True Choice!!

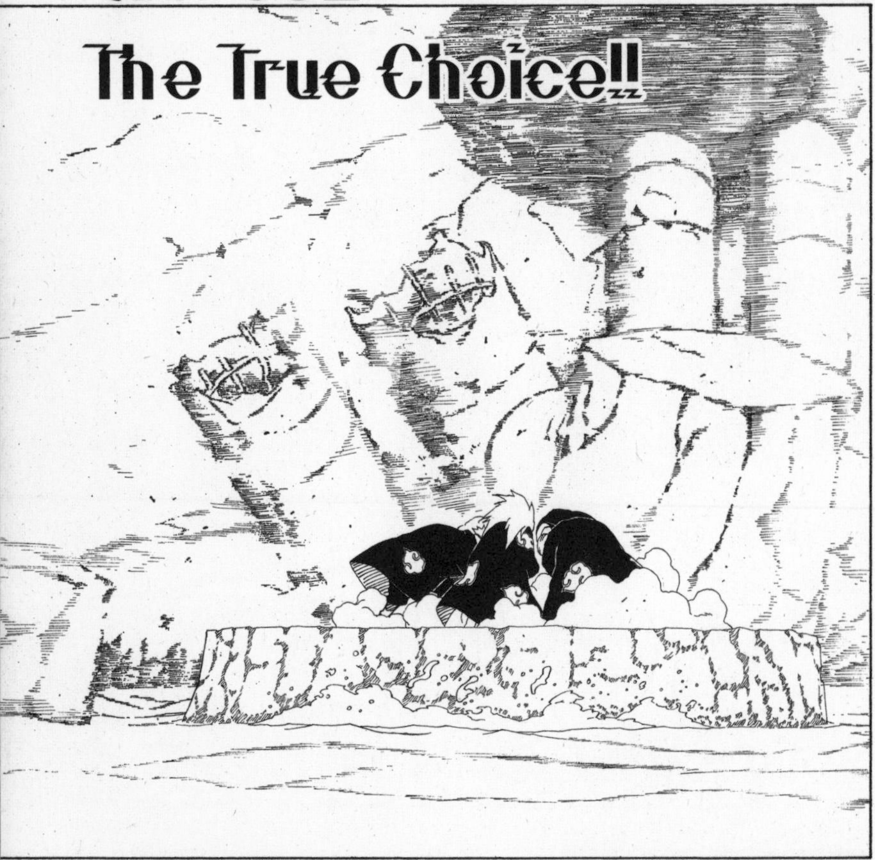

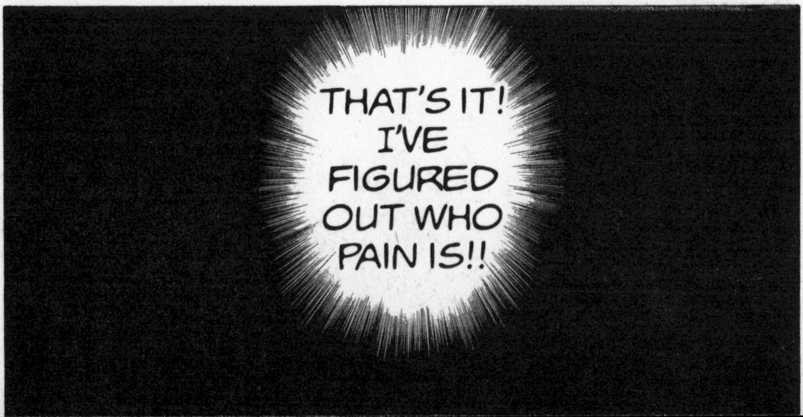
THAT'S IT! I'VE FIGURED OUT WHO PAIN IS!!

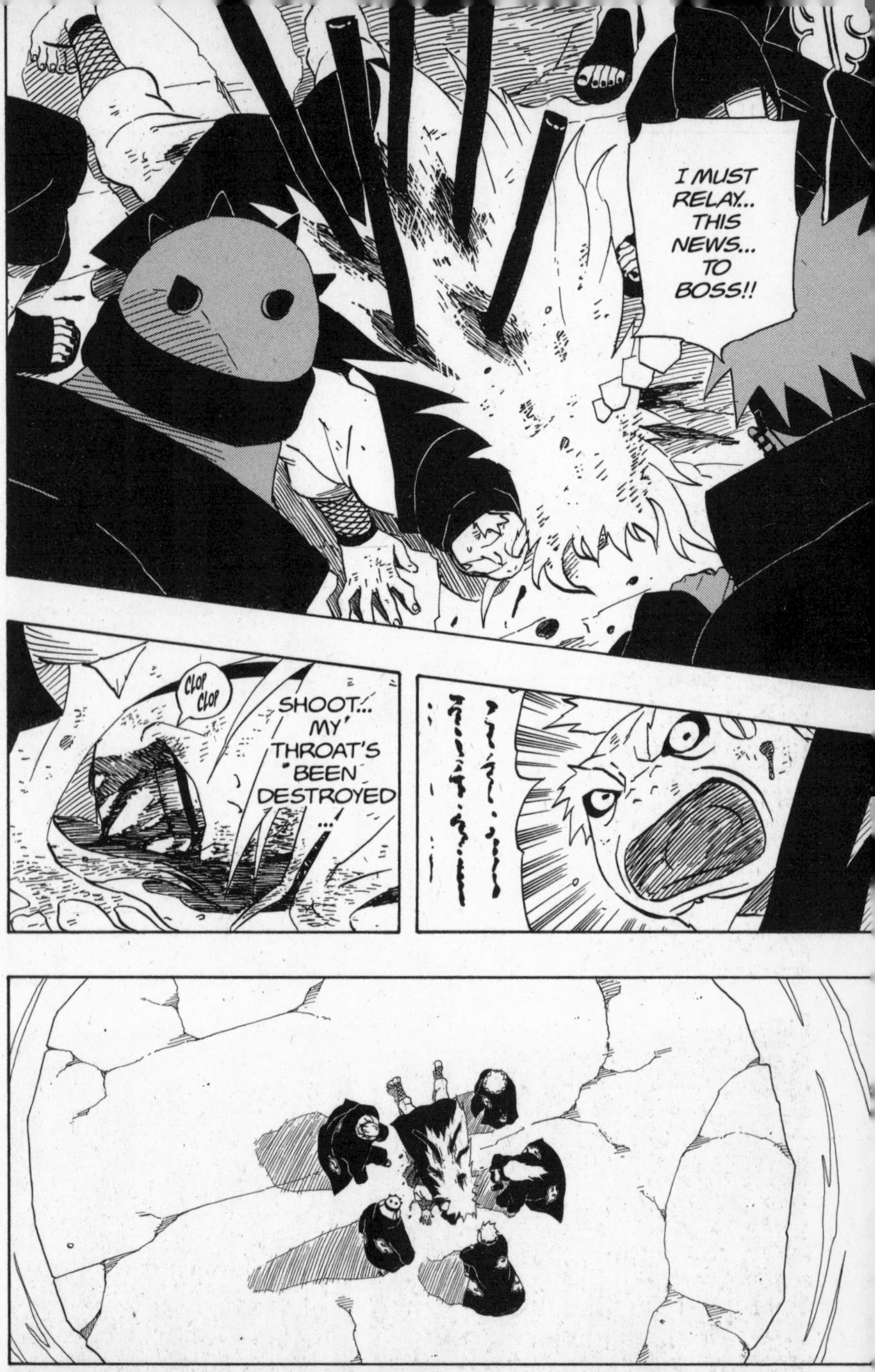
I MUST RELAY... THIS NEWS... TO BOSS!!
CLOP CLOP
SHOOT... MY THROAT'S BEEN DESTROYED...

READ THIS WAY

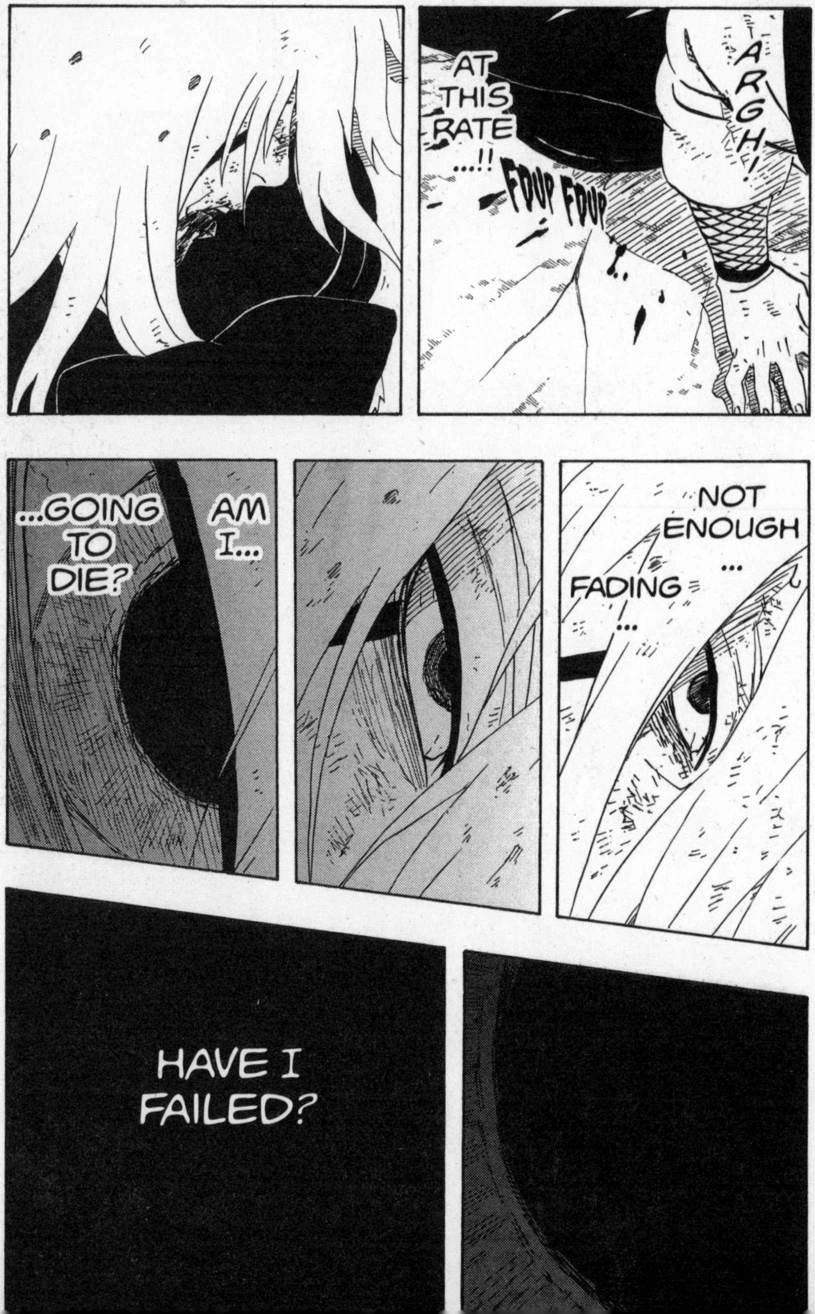
ARGH!
AT THIS RATE ...!!
FDUP FDUP
NOT ENOUGH ...
FADING ...
AM I...
...GOING TO DIE?
HAVE I FAILED?

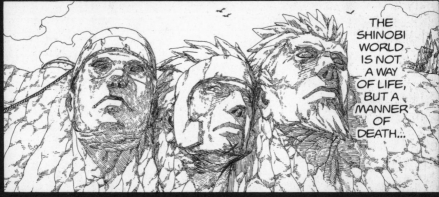

THE SHINOBI WORLD IS NOT A WAY OF LIFE, BUT A MANNER OF DEATH...
A SHINOBI'S LIFE IS NOT MEASURED BY HOW THEY LIVED BUT RATHER WHAT THEY MANAGED TO ACCOMPLISH BEFORE THEIR DEATH.
...AND LOOKING BACK, MY LIFE'S TALE WAS FULL OF FAILURE...

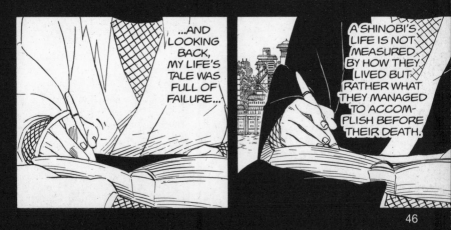

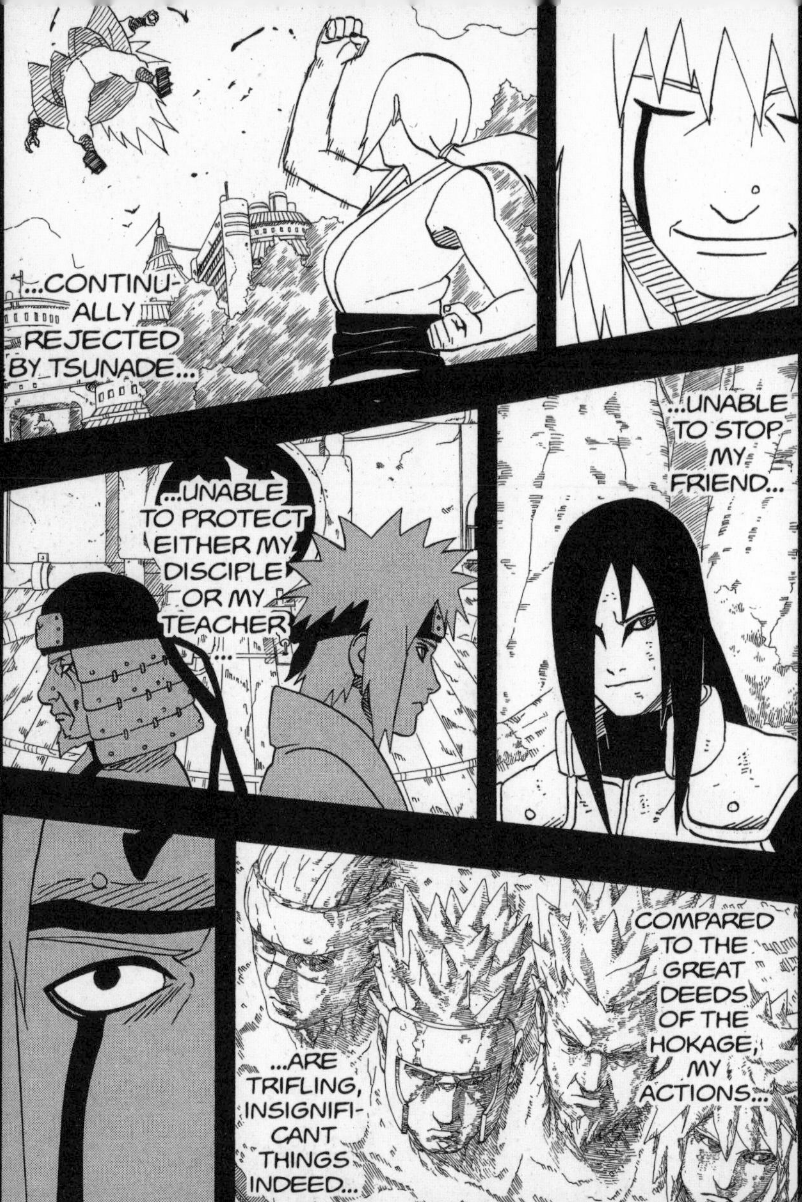
...CONTINUALLY REJECTED BY TSUNADE...
...UNABLE TO STOP MY FRIEND...
...UNABLE TO PROTECT EITHER MY DISCIPLE OR MY TEACHER...
COMPARED TO THE GREAT DEEDS OF THE HOKAGE, MY ACTIONS...
...ARE TRIFLING, INSIGNIFICANT THINGS INDEED...

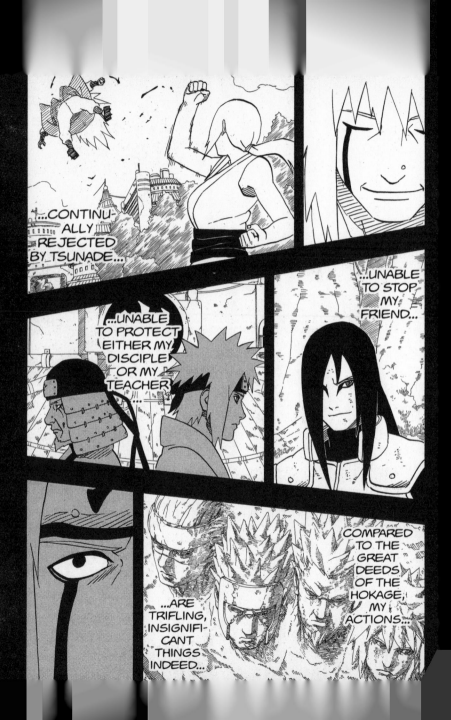

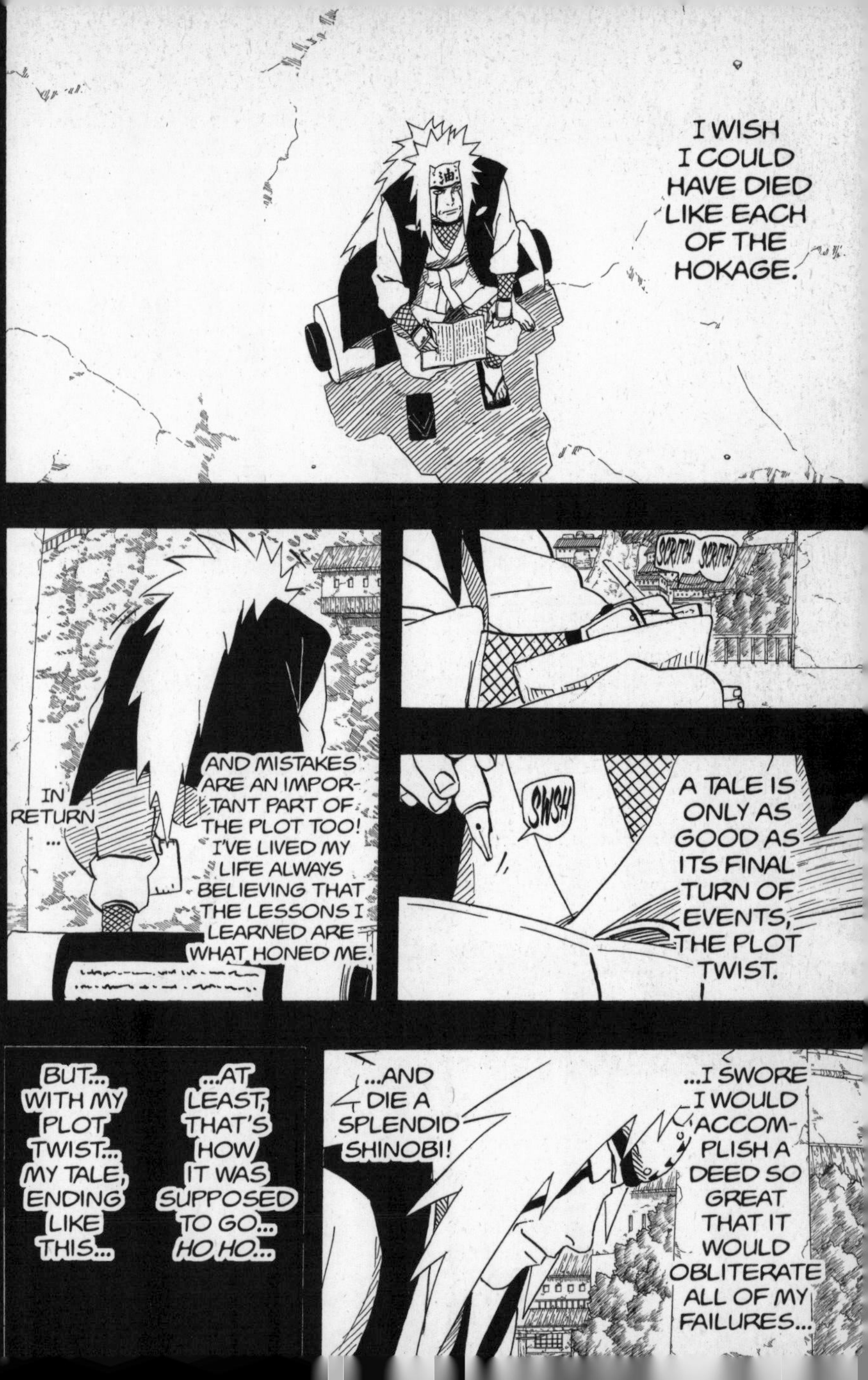
I WISH I COULD HAVE DIED LIKE EACH OF THE HOKAGE.
SCRITCH SCRITCH
SWSH
A TALE IS ONLY AS GOOD AS ITS FINAL TURN OF EVENTS, THE PLOT TWIST.
AND MISTAKES ARE AN IMPORTANT PART OF THE PLOT TOO! I'VE LIVED MY LIFE ALWAYS BELIEVING THAT THE LESSONS I LEARNED ARE WHAT HONED ME.
IN RETURN...
...I SWORE I WOULD ACCOMPLISH A DEED SO GREAT THAT IT WOULD OBLITERATE ALL OF MY FAILURES...
...AND DIE A SPLENDID SHINOBI!
...AT LEAST, THAT'S HOW IT WAS SUPPOSED TO GO... HO HO...
BUT... WITH MY PLOT TWIST... MY TALE, ENDING LIKE THIS...

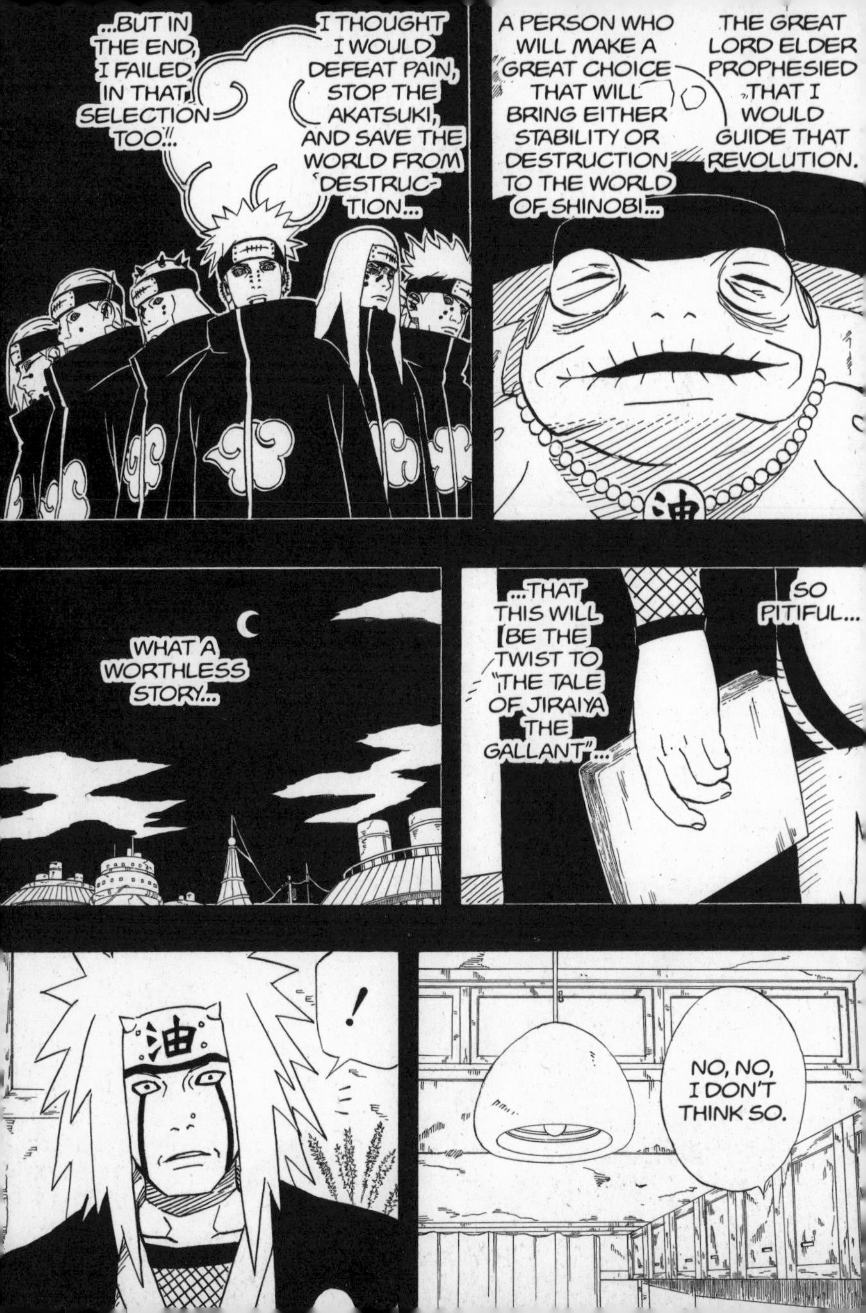
THE GREAT LORD ELDER PROPHESIED THAT I WOULD GUIDE THAT REVOLUTION.
A PERSON WHO WILL MAKE A GREAT CHOICE THAT WILL BRING EITHER STABILITY OR DESTRUCTION TO THE WORLD OF SHINOBI...
I THOUGHT I WOULD DEFEAT PAIN, STOP THE AKATSUKI, AND SAVE THE WORLD FROM DESTRUCTION...
...BUT IN THE END, I FAILED IN THAT SELECTION TOO!!...
SO PITIFUL...
...THAT THIS WILL BE THE TWIST TO "THE TALE OF JIRAIYA THE GALLANT"...
WHAT A WORTHLESS STORY...
NO, NO, I DON'T THINK SO.
!

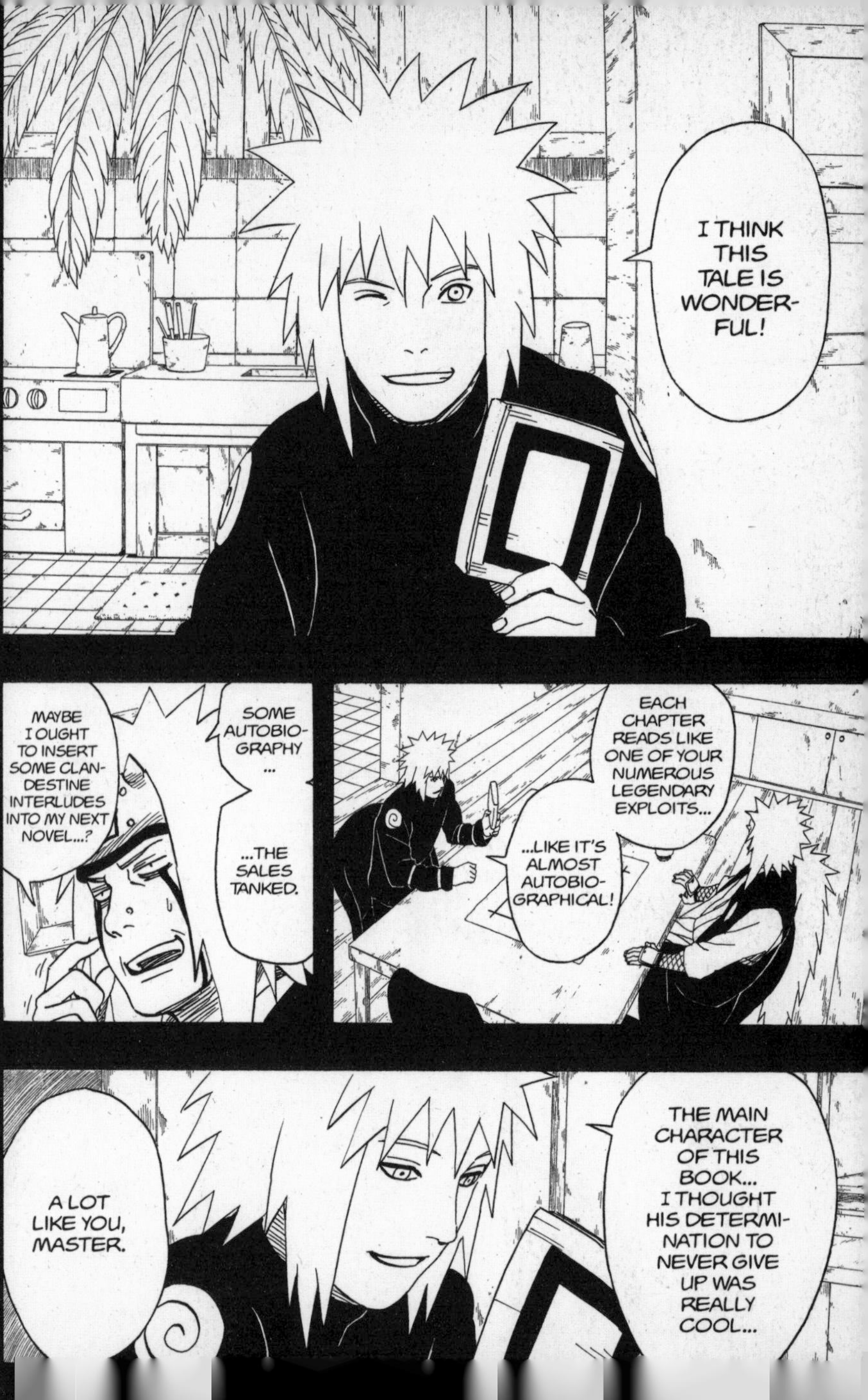
I THINK THIS TALE IS WONDERFUL!
EACH CHAPTER READS LIKE ONE OF YOUR NUMEROUS LEGENDARY EXPLOITS...
...LIKE IT'S ALMOST AUTOBIOGRAPHICAL!
SOME AUTOBIOGRAPHY ... ...THE SALES TANKED.
MAYBE I OUGHT TO INSERT SOME CLANDESTINE INTERLUDES INTO MY NEXT NOVEL...?
THE MAIN CHARACTER OF THIS BOOK... I THOUGHT HIS DETERMINATION TO NEVER GIVE UP WAS REALLY COOL...
A LOT LIKE YOU, MASTER.

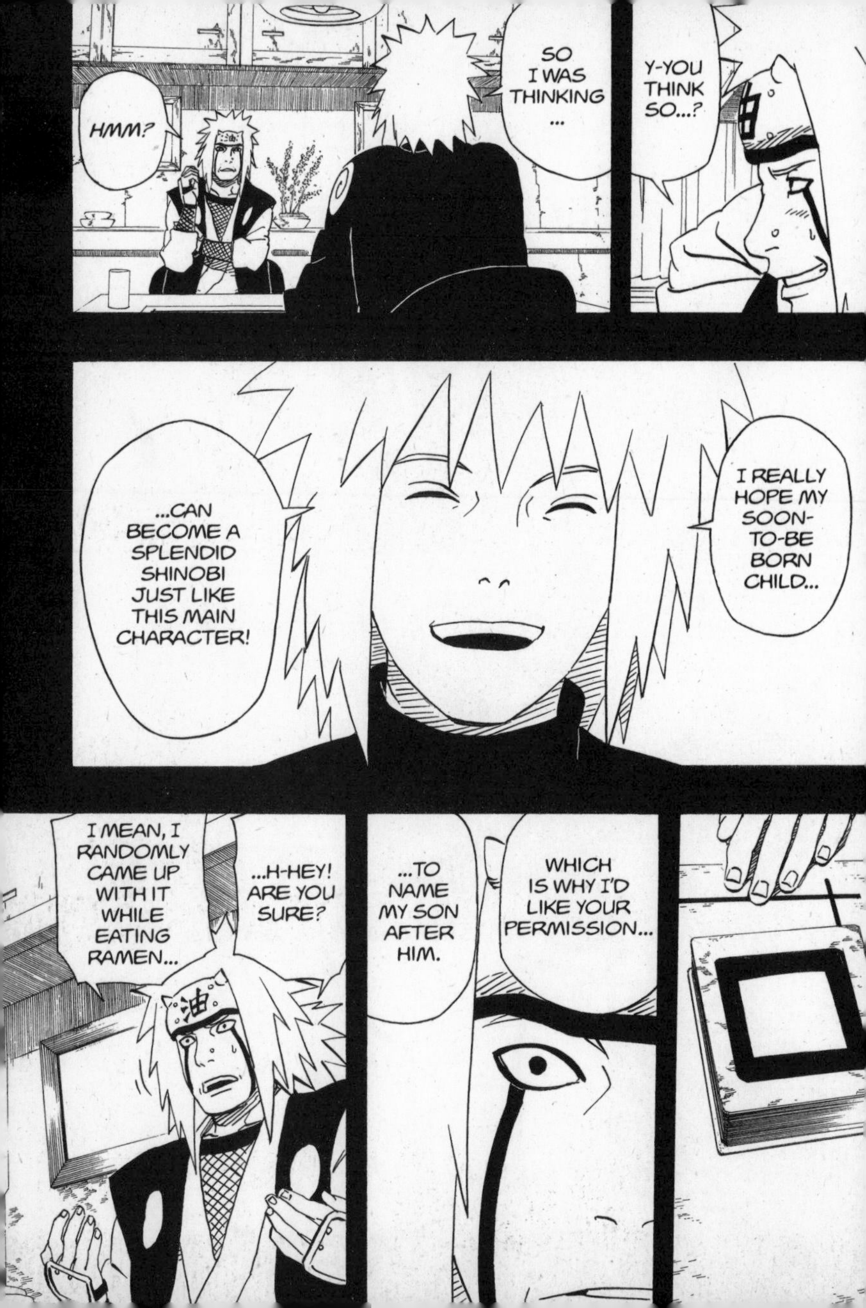
Y-YOU THINK SO...?
SO I WAS THINKING...
HMM?
I REALLY HOPE MY SOON-TO-BE BORN CHILD...
...CAN BECOME A SPLENDID SHINOBI JUST LIKE THIS MAIN CHARACTER!
WHICH IS WHY I'D LIKE YOUR PERMISSION...
...TO NAME MY SON AFTER HIM.
...H-HEY! ARE YOU SURE?
I MEAN, I RANDOMLY CAME UP WITH IT WHILE EATING RAMEN...

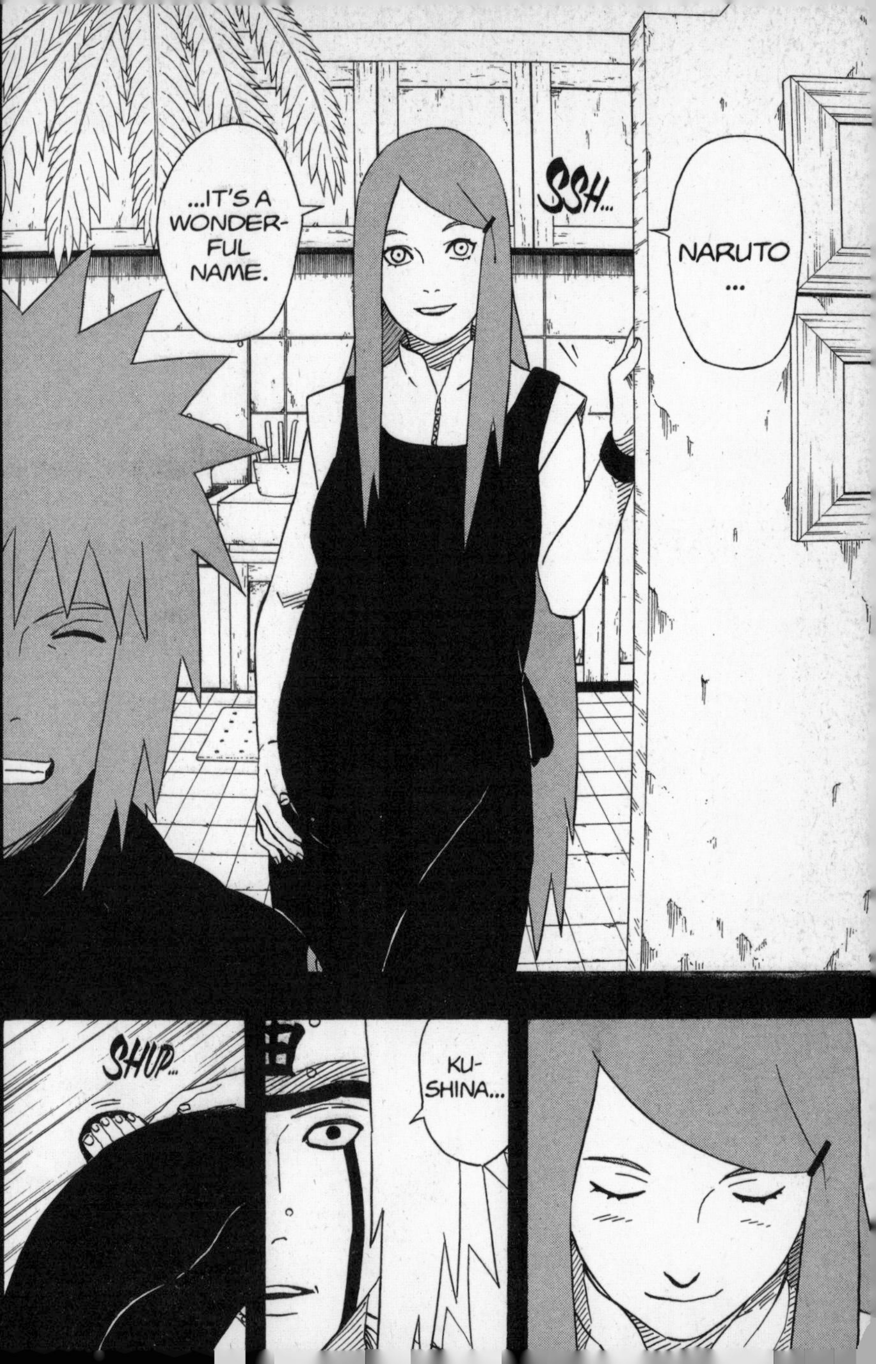
NARUTO ...
SSH...
...IT'S A WONDERFUL NAME.
KU-SHINA...
SHUP...

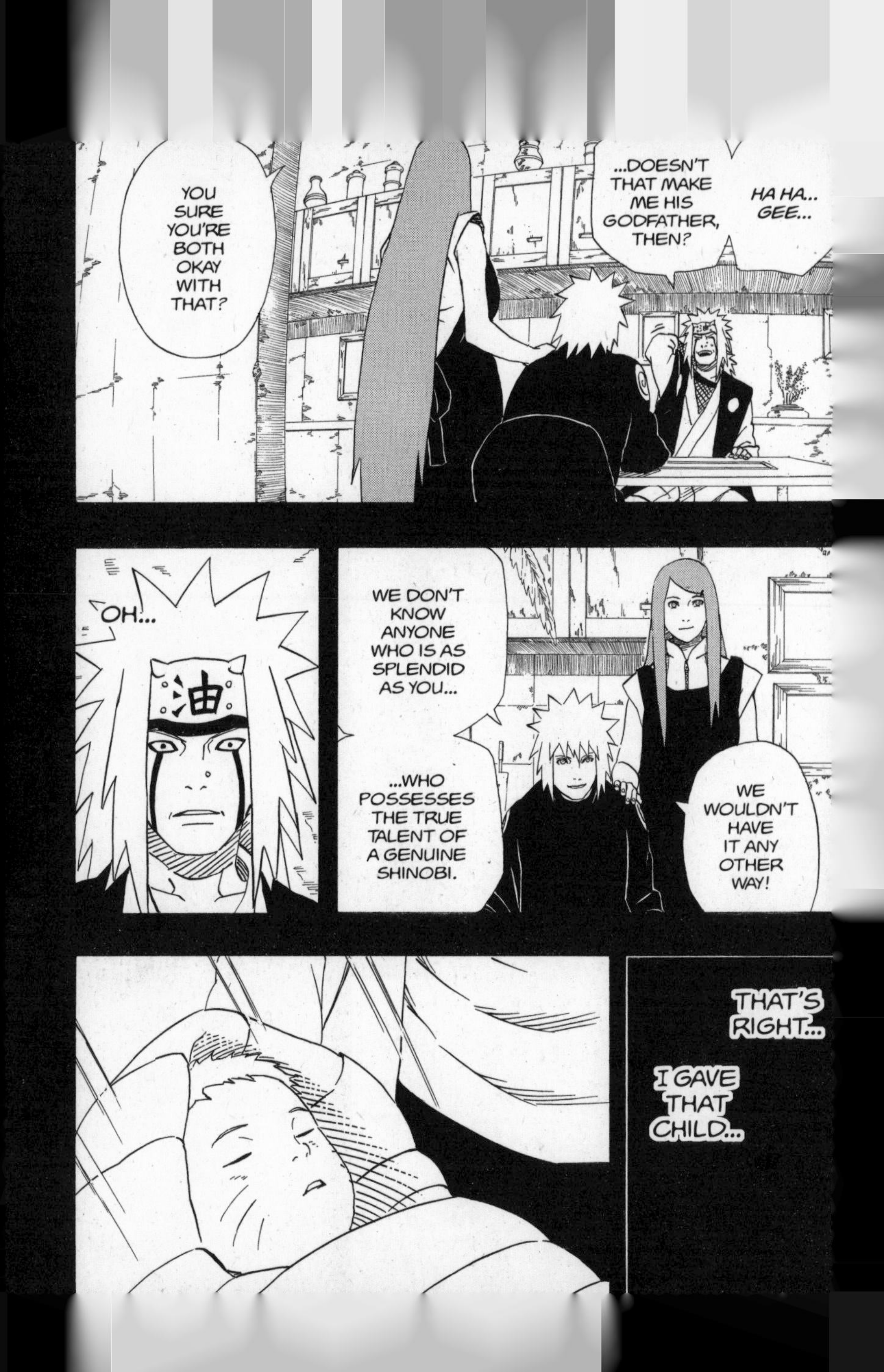
HA HA... GEE...
...DOESN'T THAT MAKE ME HIS GODFATHER, THEN?
YOU SURE YOU'RE BOTH OKAY WITH THAT?
WE DON'T KNOW ANYONE WHO IS AS SPLENDID AS YOU...
...WHO POSSESSES THE TRUE TALENT OF A GENUINE SHINOBI.
WE WOULDN'T HAVE IT ANY OTHER WAY!
OH...
THAT'S RIGHT...
I GAVE THAT CHILD...

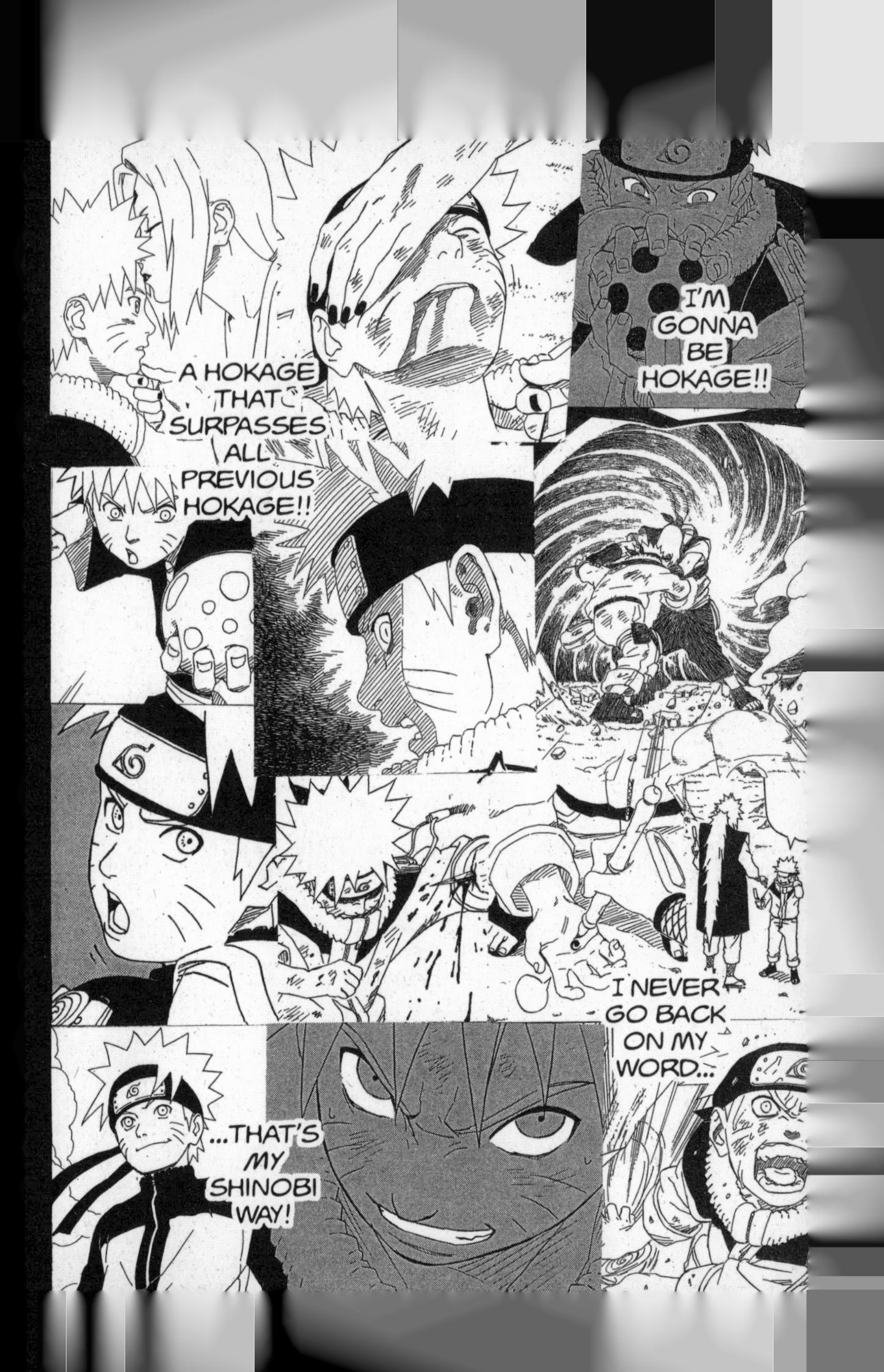
I'M GONNA BE HOKAGE!!
A HOKAGE THAT SURPASSES ALL PREVIOUS HOKAGE!!
I NEVER GO BACK ON MY WORD...
...THAT'S MY SHINOBI WAY!

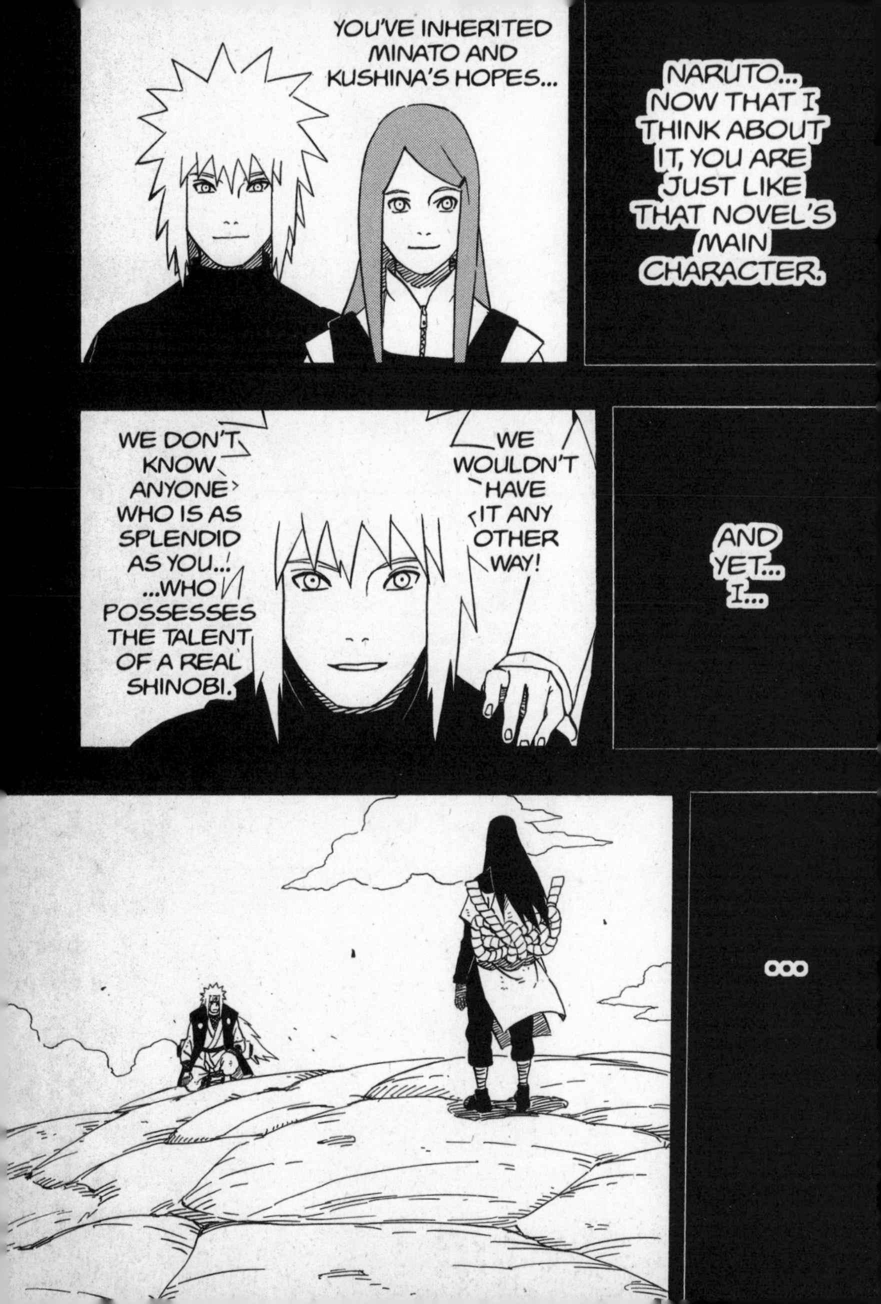
NARUTO... NOW THAT I THINK ABOUT IT, YOU ARE JUST LIKE THAT NOVEL'S MAIN CHARACTER.
YOU'VE INHERITED MINATO AND KUSHINA'S HOPES...
AND YET... I...
WE WOULDN'T HAVE IT ANY OTHER WAY!
WE DON'T KNOW ANYONE WHO IS AS SPLENDID AS YOU...! ...WHO POSSESSES THE TALENT OF A REAL SHINOBI.
...

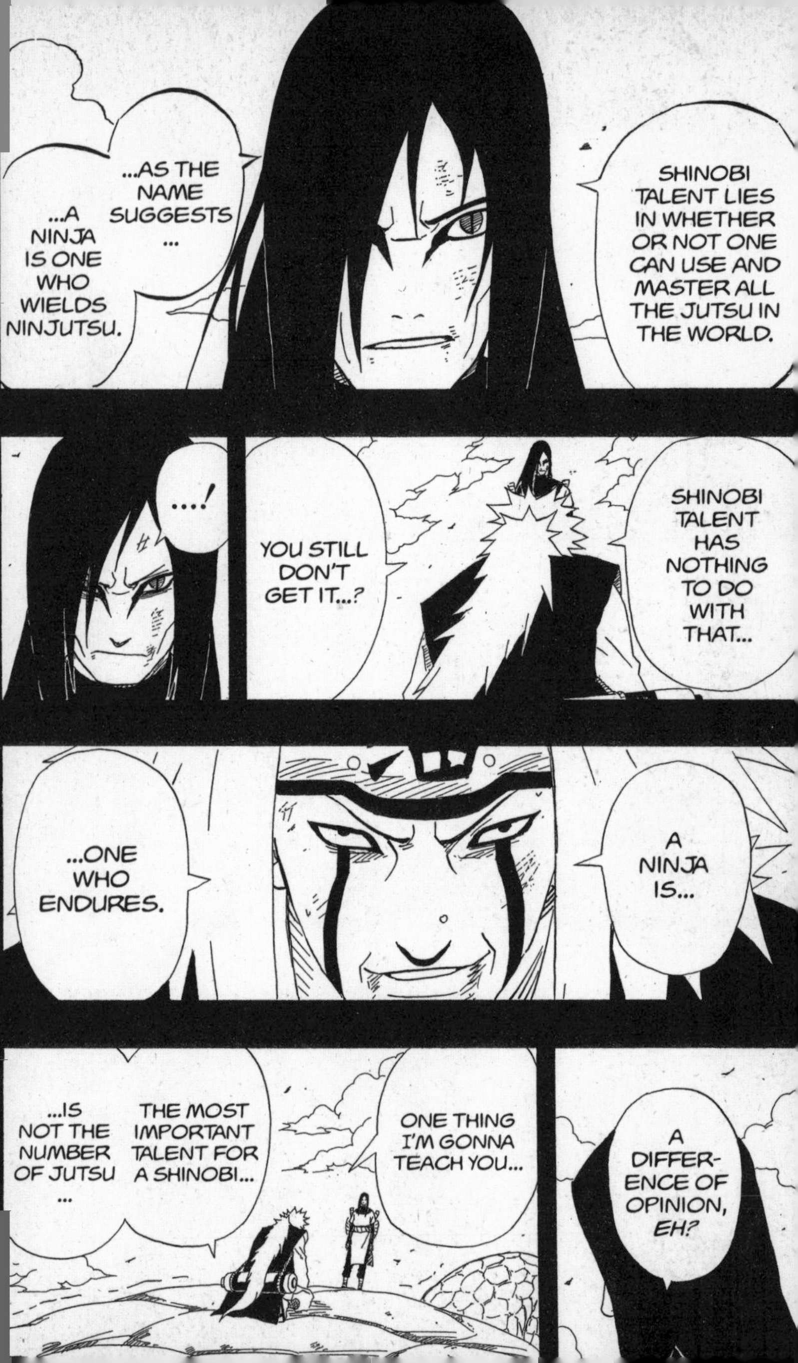
SHINOBI TALENT LIES IN WHETHER OR NOT ONE CAN USE AND MASTER ALL THE JUTSU IN THE WORLD.
...AS THE NAME SUGGESTS ...
...A NINJA IS ONE WHO WIELDS NINJUTSU.
SHINOBI TALENT HAS NOTHING TO DO WITH THAT...
YOU STILL DON'T GET IT...?
...!
A NINJA IS...
...ONE WHO ENDURES.
A DIFFER-ENCE OF OPINION, *EH?*
ONE THING I'M GONNA TEACH YOU...
THE MOST IMPORTANT TALENT FOR A SHINOBI...
...IS NOT THE NUMBER OF JUTSU ...

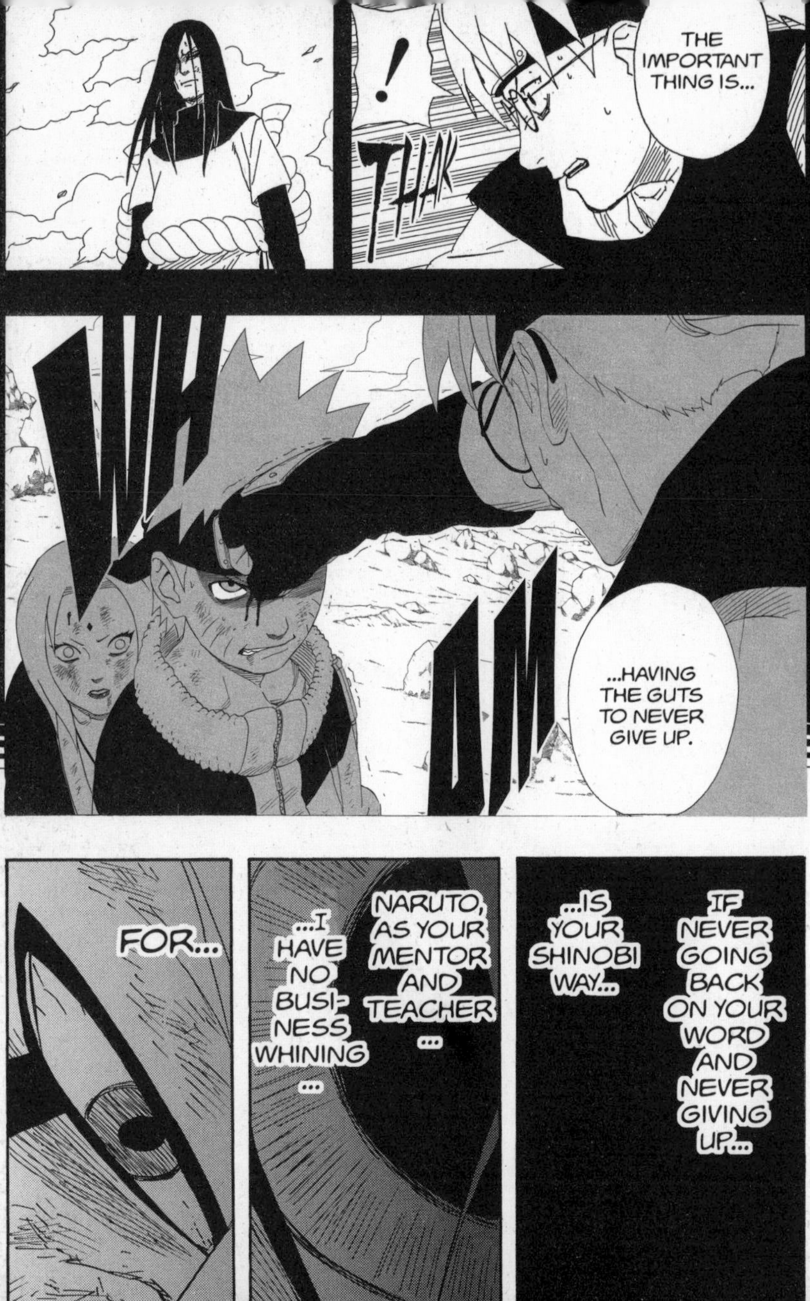
THAK
!
THE IMPORTANT THING IS...
WHAM
...HAVING THE GUTS TO NEVER GIVE UP.
IF NEVER GOING BACK ON YOUR WORD AND NEVER GIVING UP...
...IS YOUR SHINOBI WAY...
NARUTO, AS YOUR MENTOR AND TEACHER...
...I HAVE NO BUSI-NESS WHINING...
FOR...

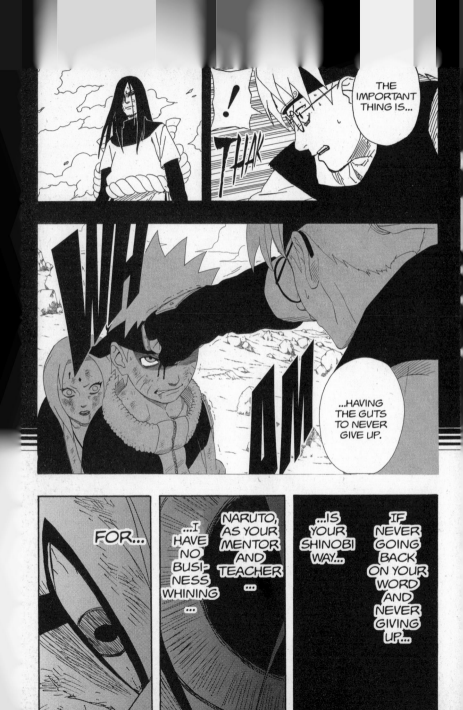

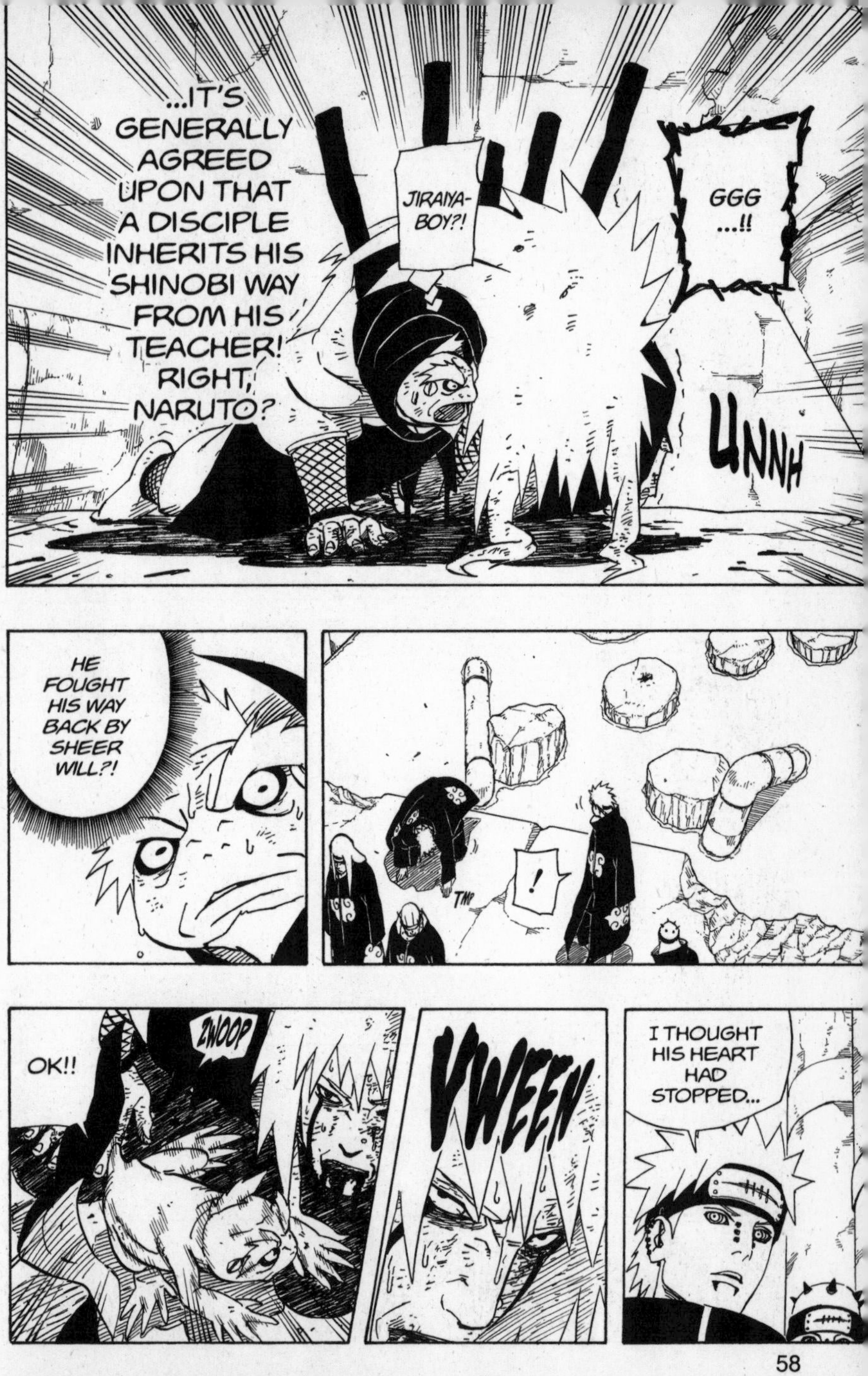
GGG ...!!
UNNH
JIRAIYA-BOY?!
...IT'S GENERALLY AGREED UPON THAT A DISCIPLE INHERITS HIS SHINOBI WAY FROM HIS TEACHER! RIGHT, NARUTO?
!
TMP
HE FOUGHT HIS WAY BACK BY SHEER WILL?!
I THOUGHT HIS HEART HAD STOPPED...
VWEEN
ZWOOP
OK!!

READ THIS WAY

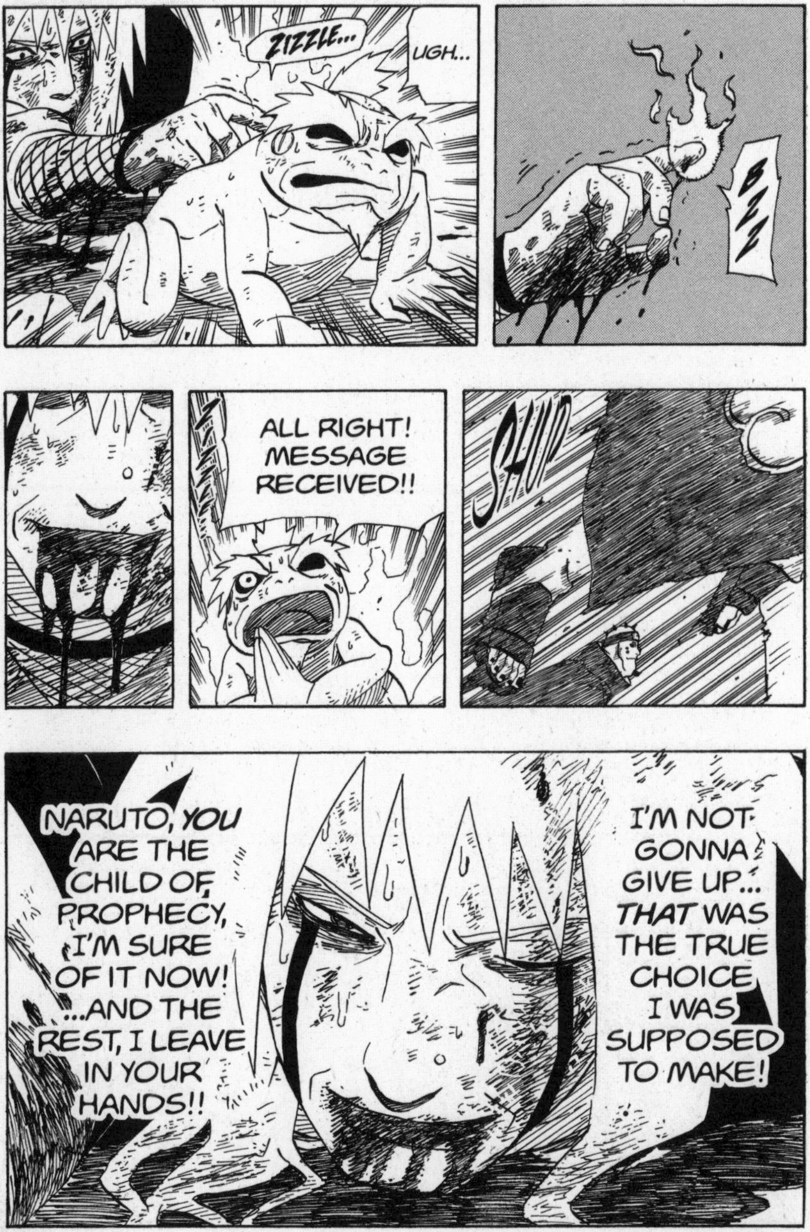
BZZZ
UGH...
ZIZZLE...
SHUP
ALL RIGHT! MESSAGE RECEIVED!!
I'M NOT GONNA GIVE UP... *THAT* WAS THE TRUE CHOICE I WAS SUPPOSED TO MAKE!
NARUTO, *YOU* ARE THE CHILD OF PROPHECY, I'M SURE OF IT NOW! ...AND THE REST, I LEAVE IN YOUR HANDS!!

Number 383: The Final Chapter and...!!

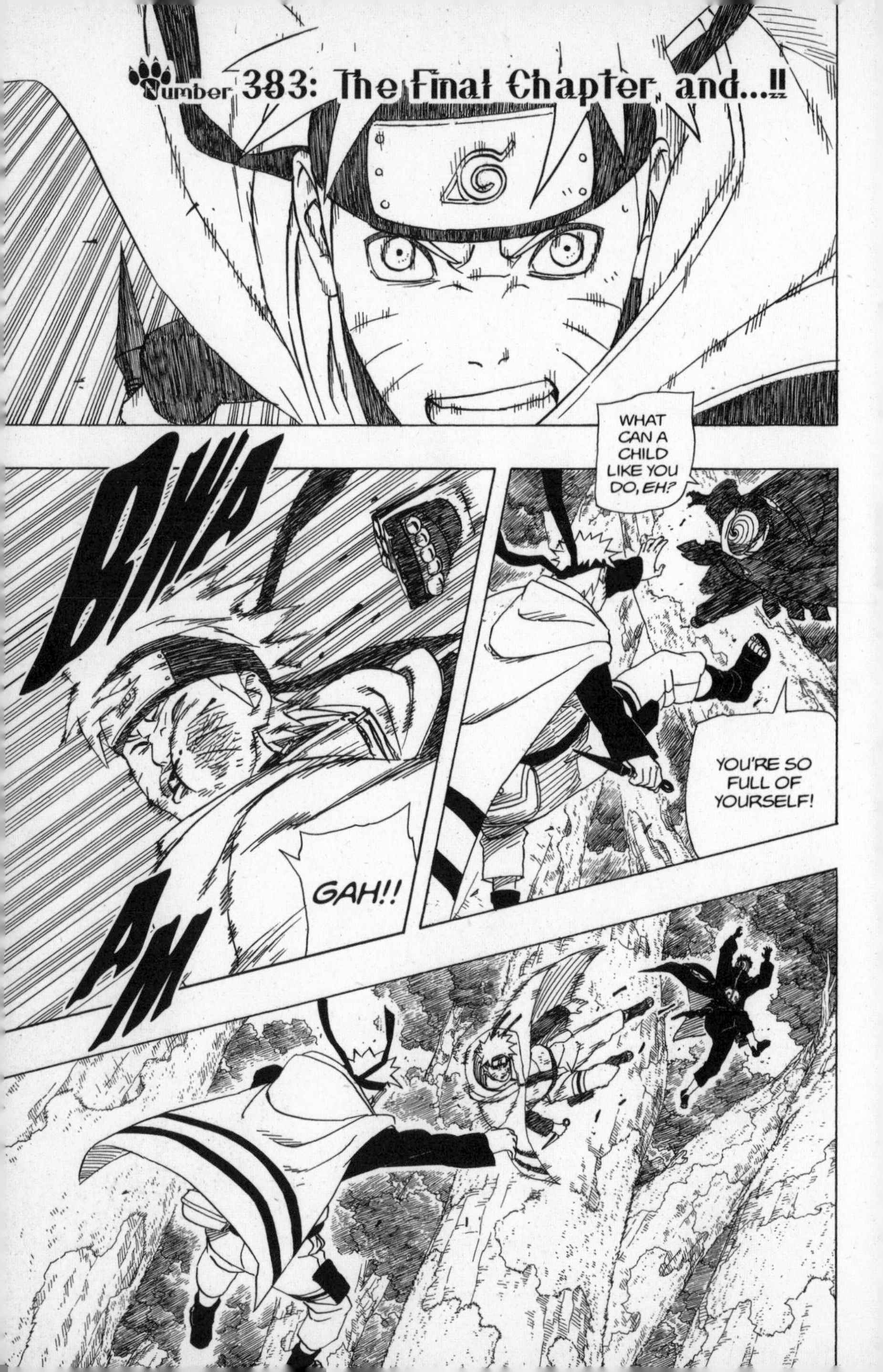
WHAT CAN A CHILD LIKE YOU DO, EH?
YOU'RE SO FULL OF YOURSELF!
BWA
GAH!!
AM

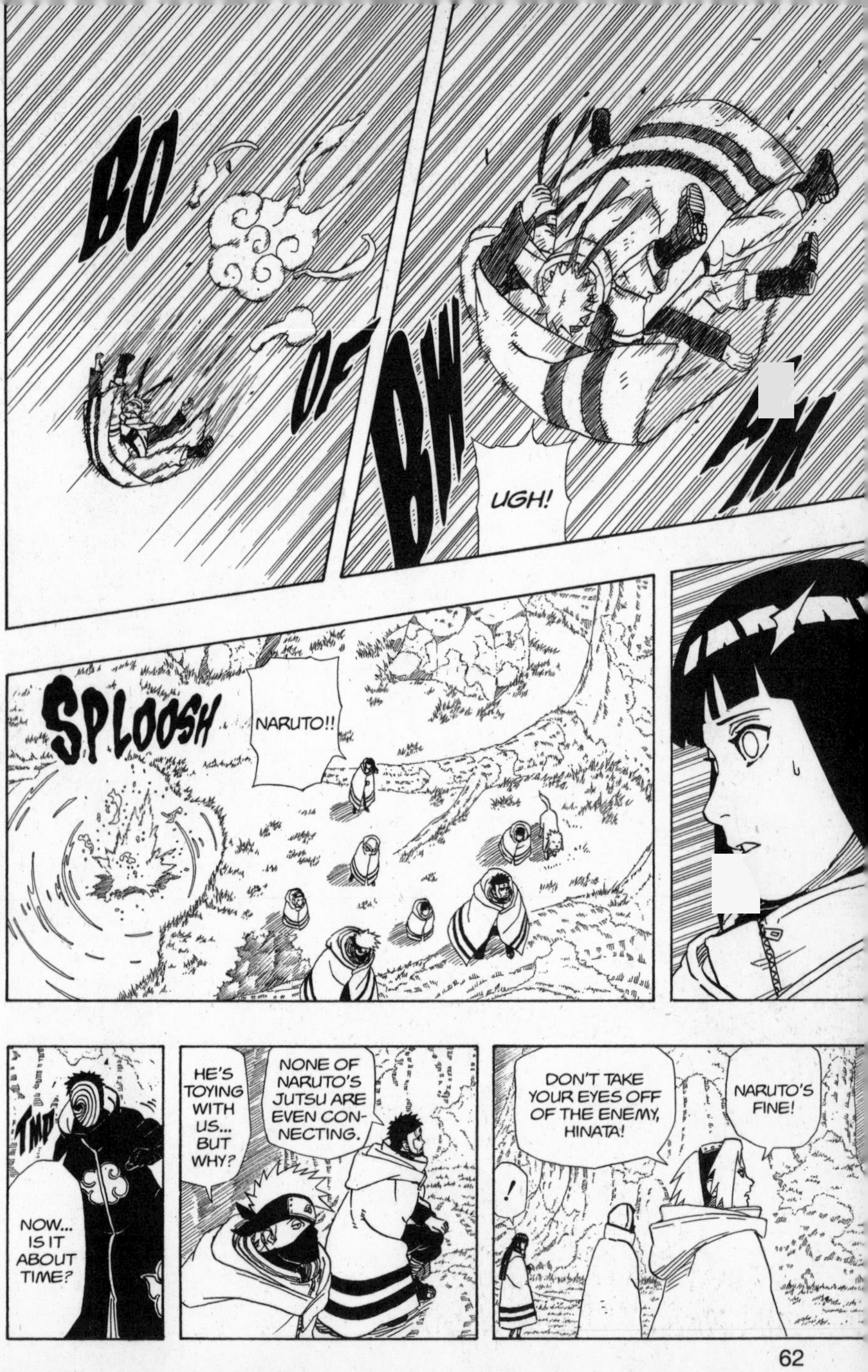
UGH!
BOOF
NARUTO!!
SPLOOSH
NARUTO'S FINE!
DON'T TAKE YOUR EYES OFF OF THE ENEMY, HINATA!
!
NONE OF NARUTO'S JUTSU ARE EVEN CONNECTING.
HE'S TOYING WITH US... BUT WHY?
NOW... IS IT ABOUT TIME?

Number 383: The Final Chapter and...!!

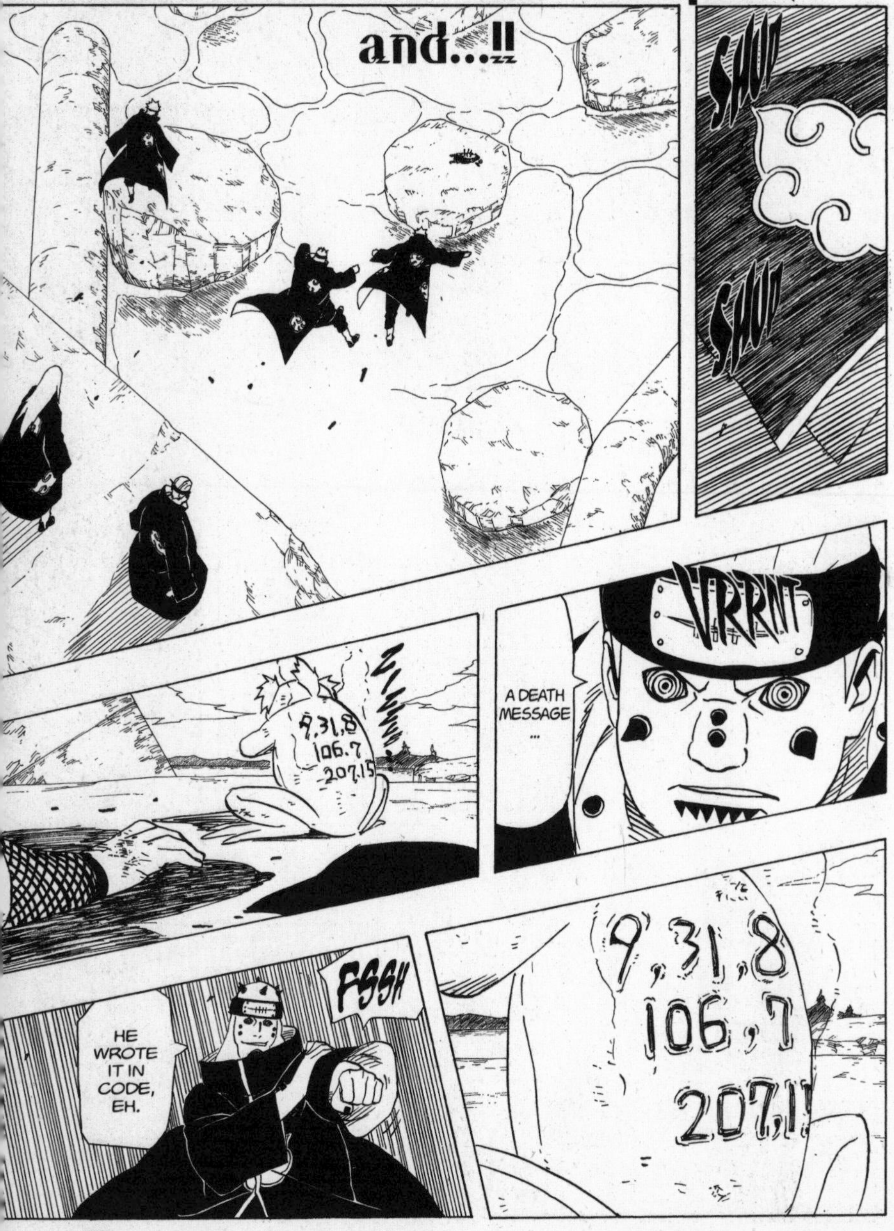
SHUT
SHUT
VRRNT
A DEATH MESSAGE ...
9,31,8
106,7
207,15
FSSH
HE WROTE IT IN CODE, EH.

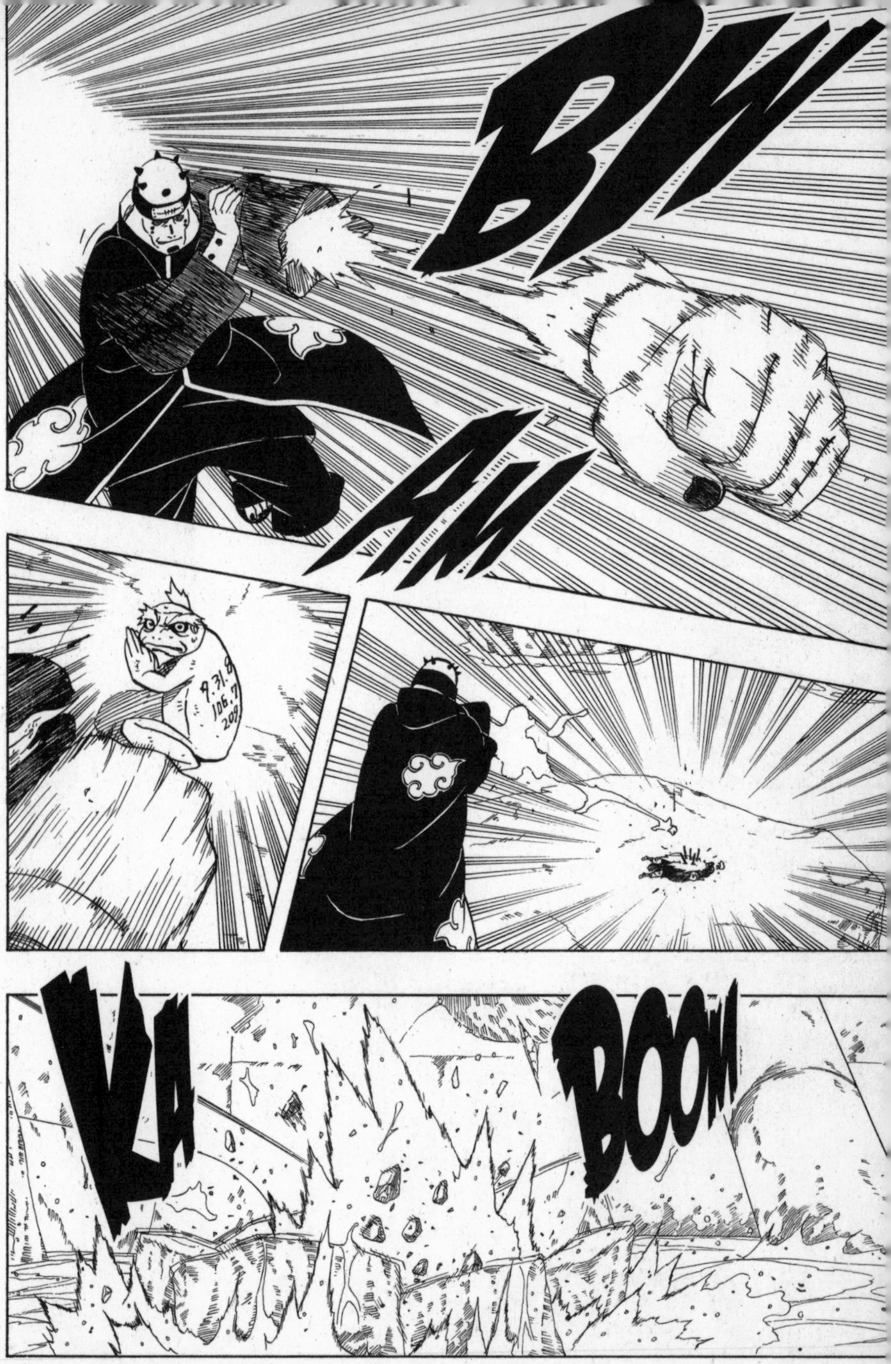
BW
HAM
KA
BOOM

READ THIS WAY

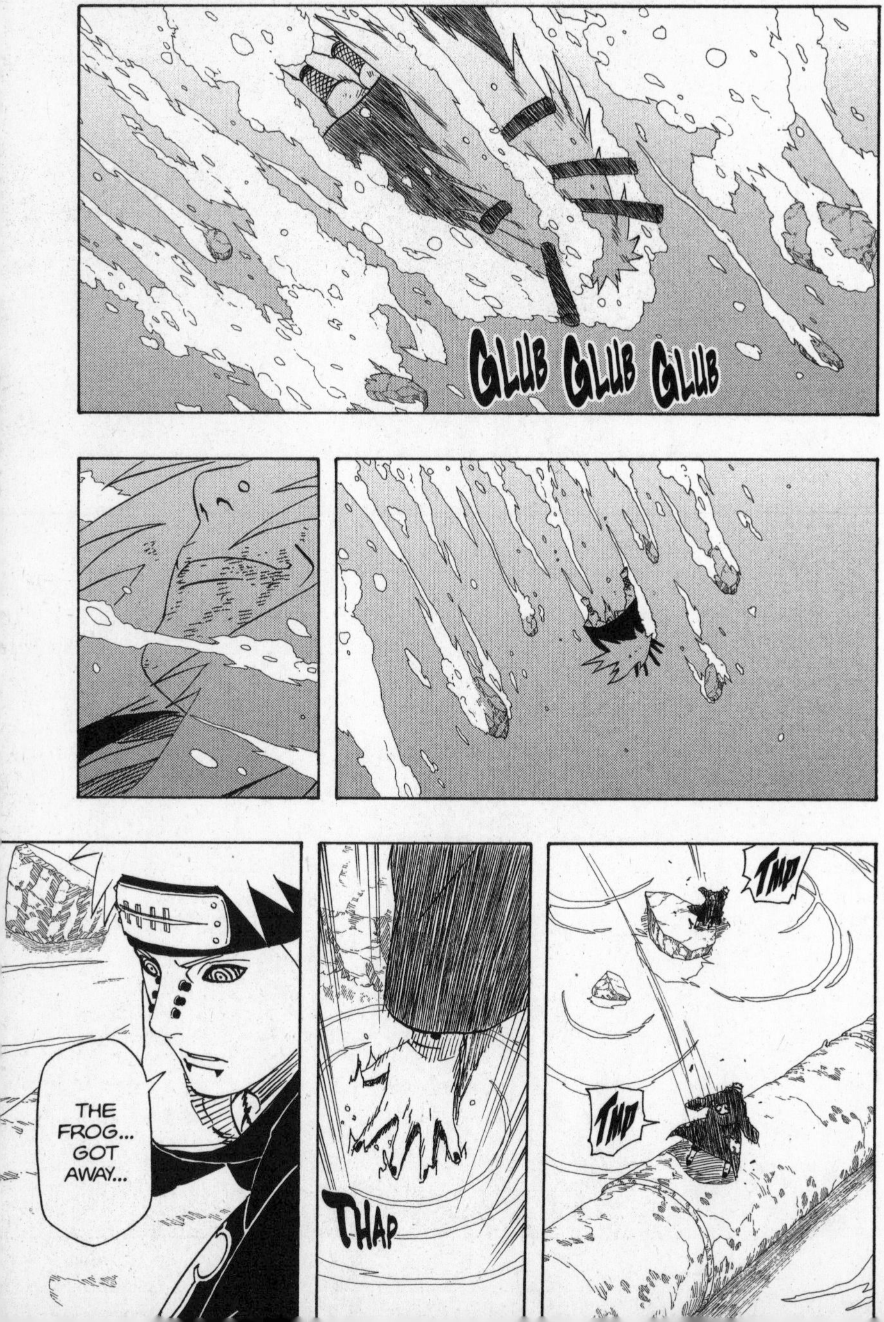
GLUB GLUB GLUB
TMP
TMP
THAP
THE FROG... GOT AWAY...

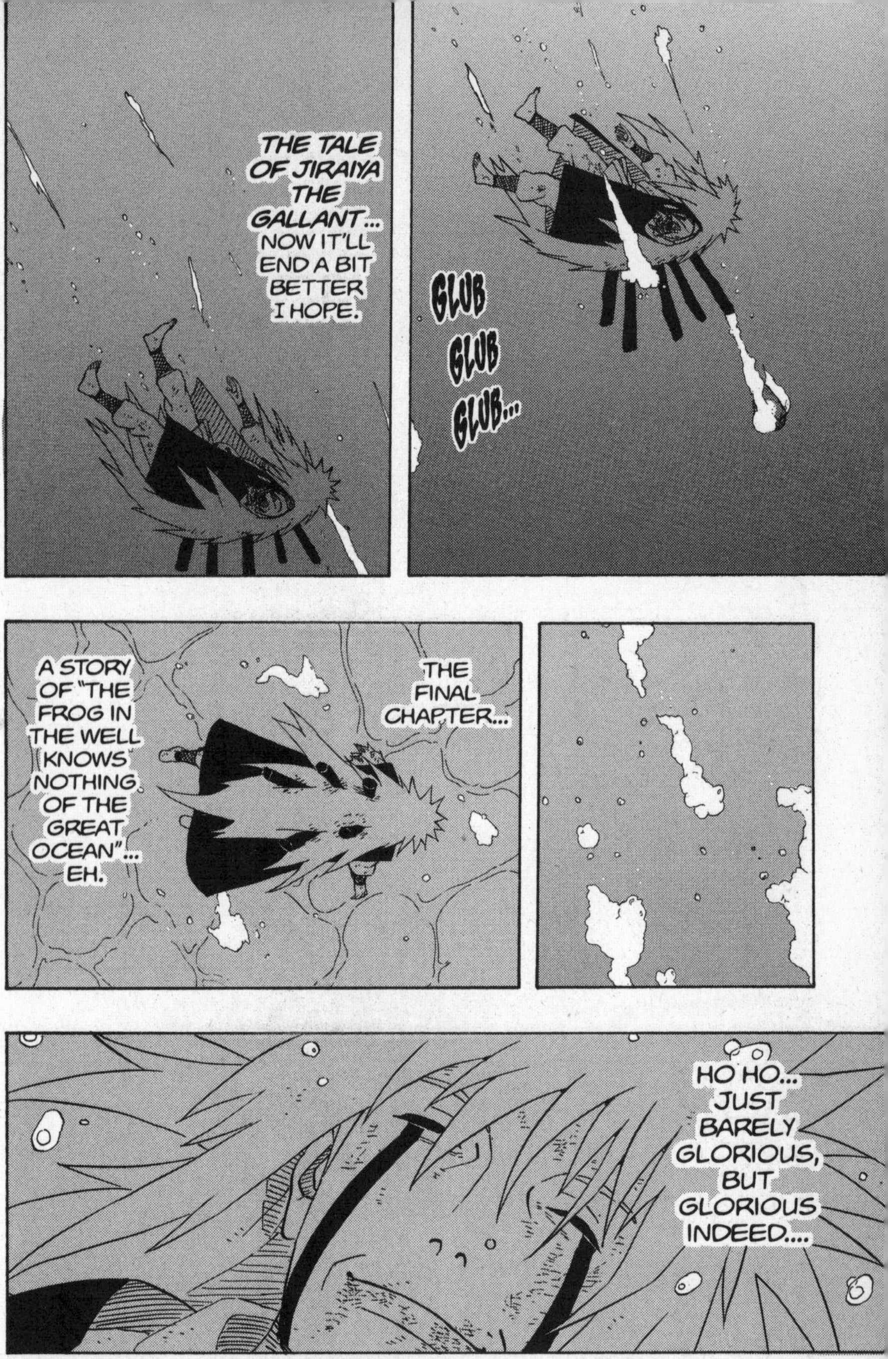
GLUB GLUB GLUB...
THE TALE OF JIRAIYA THE GALLANT... NOW IT'LL END A BIT BETTER I HOPE.
THE FINAL CHAPTER...
A STORY OF "THE FROG IN THE WELL KNOWS NOTHING OF THE GREAT OCEAN"... EH.
HO HO... JUST BARELY GLORIOUS, BUT GLORIOUS INDEED....

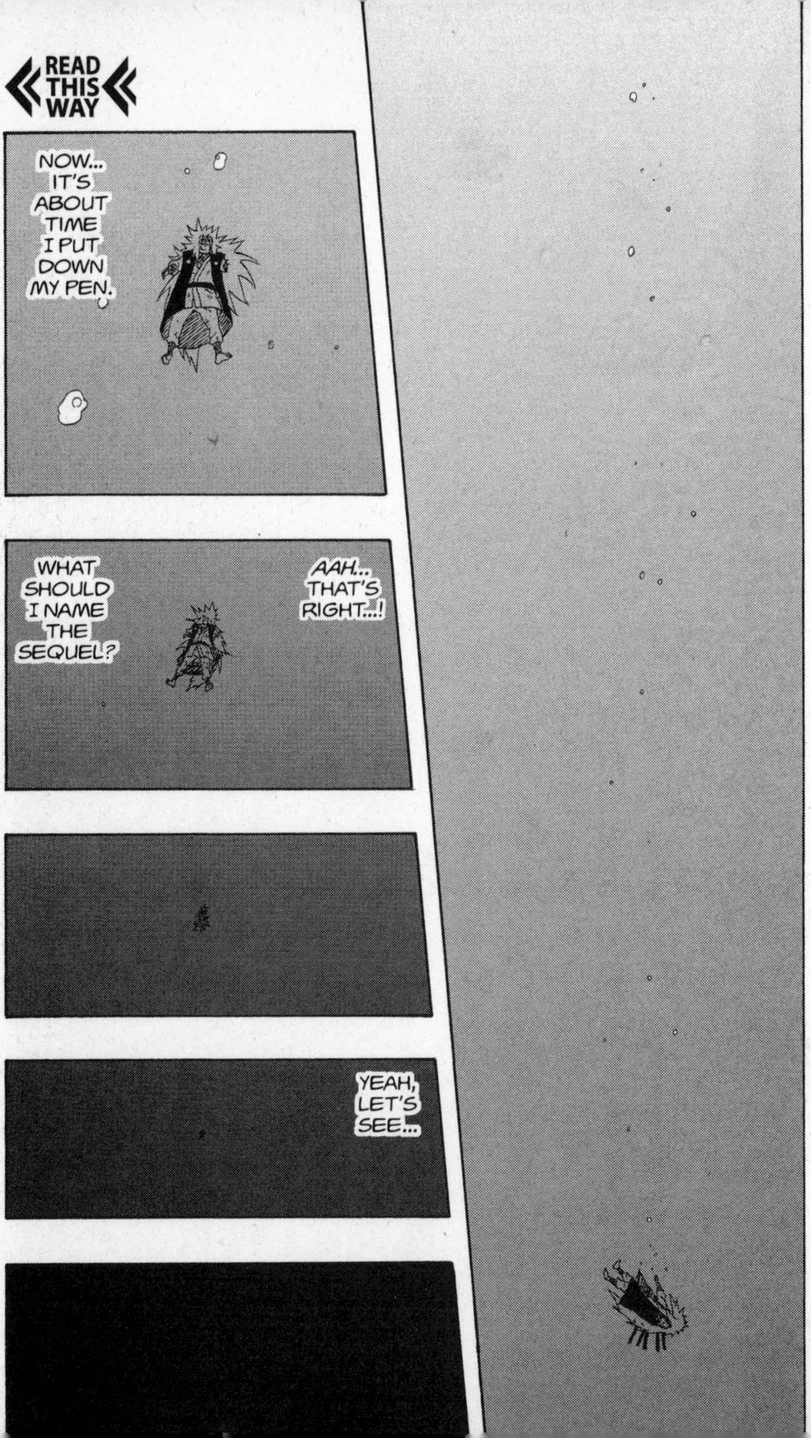
READ THIS WAY
NOW... IT'S ABOUT TIME I PUT DOWN MY PEN.
AAH... THAT'S RIGHT...!
WHAT SHOULD I NAME THE SEQUEL?
YEAH, LET'S SEE...

"THE
TALE OF
UZUMAKI
NARUTO"...

...YES...
THAT
HAS A
NICE
RING
TO IT...

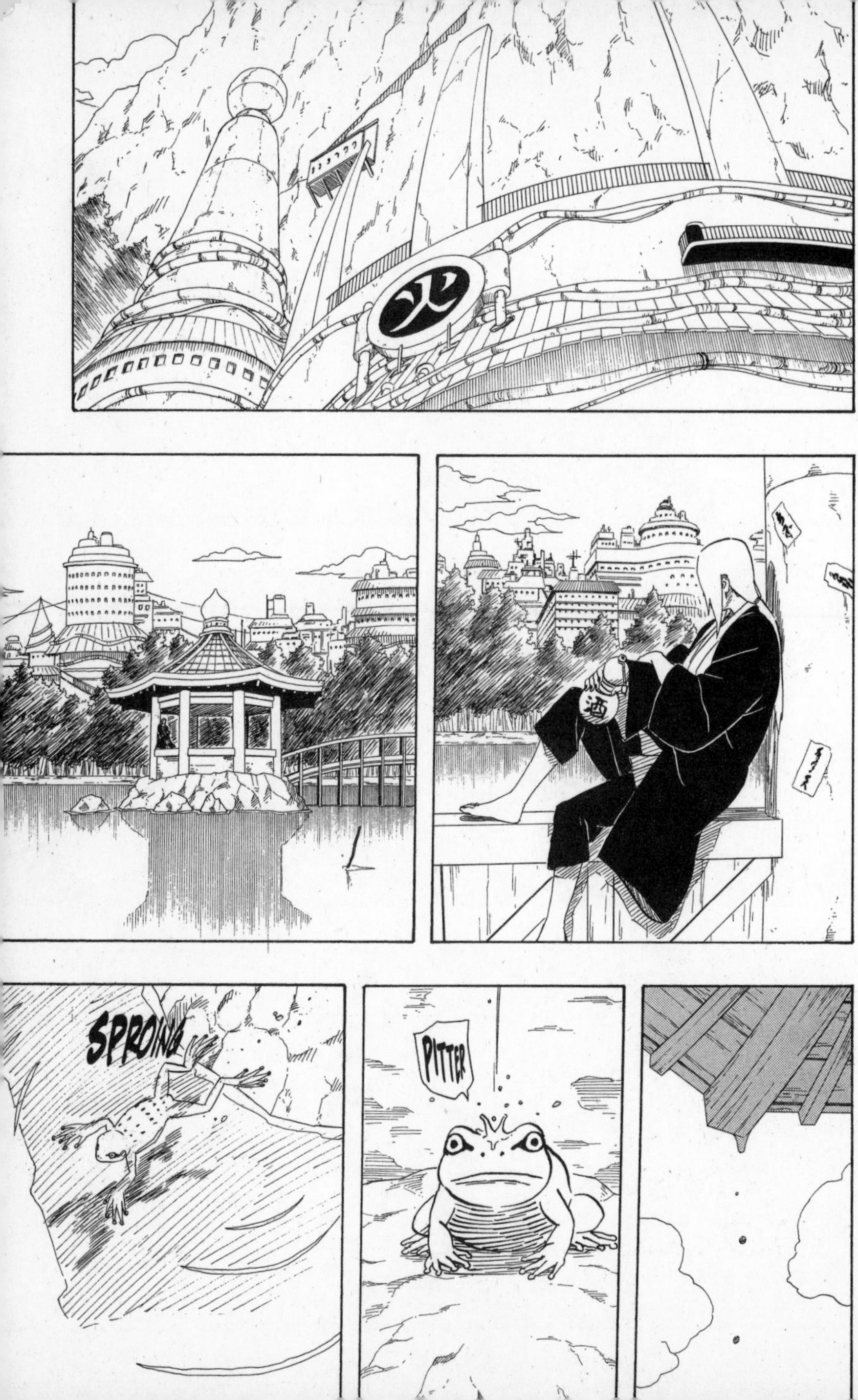
PITTER
SPROING

SPLUSH
...

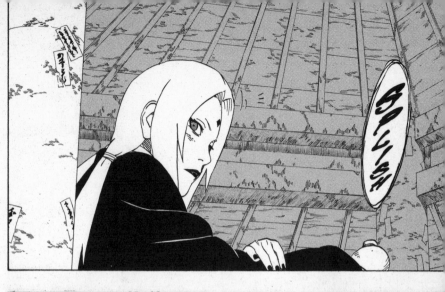

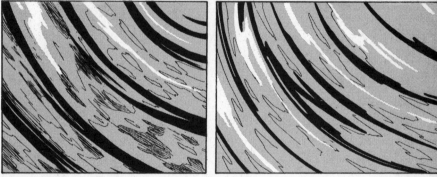

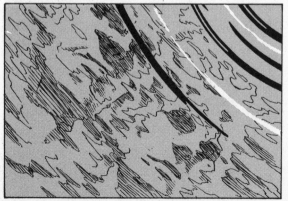

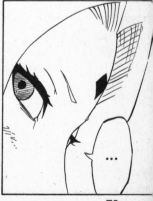

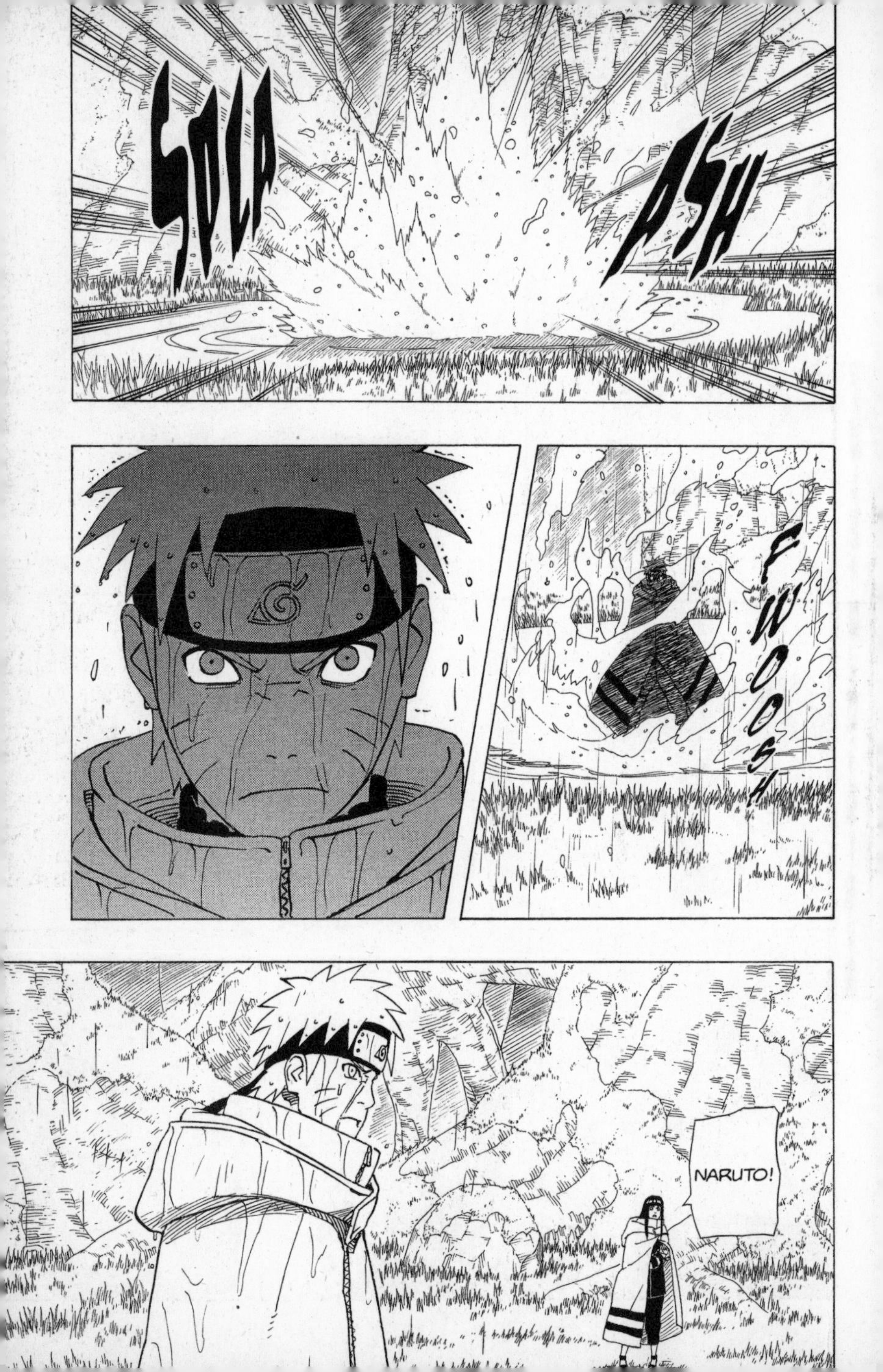
SPLA
ASH
FWOOSH!
NARUTO!

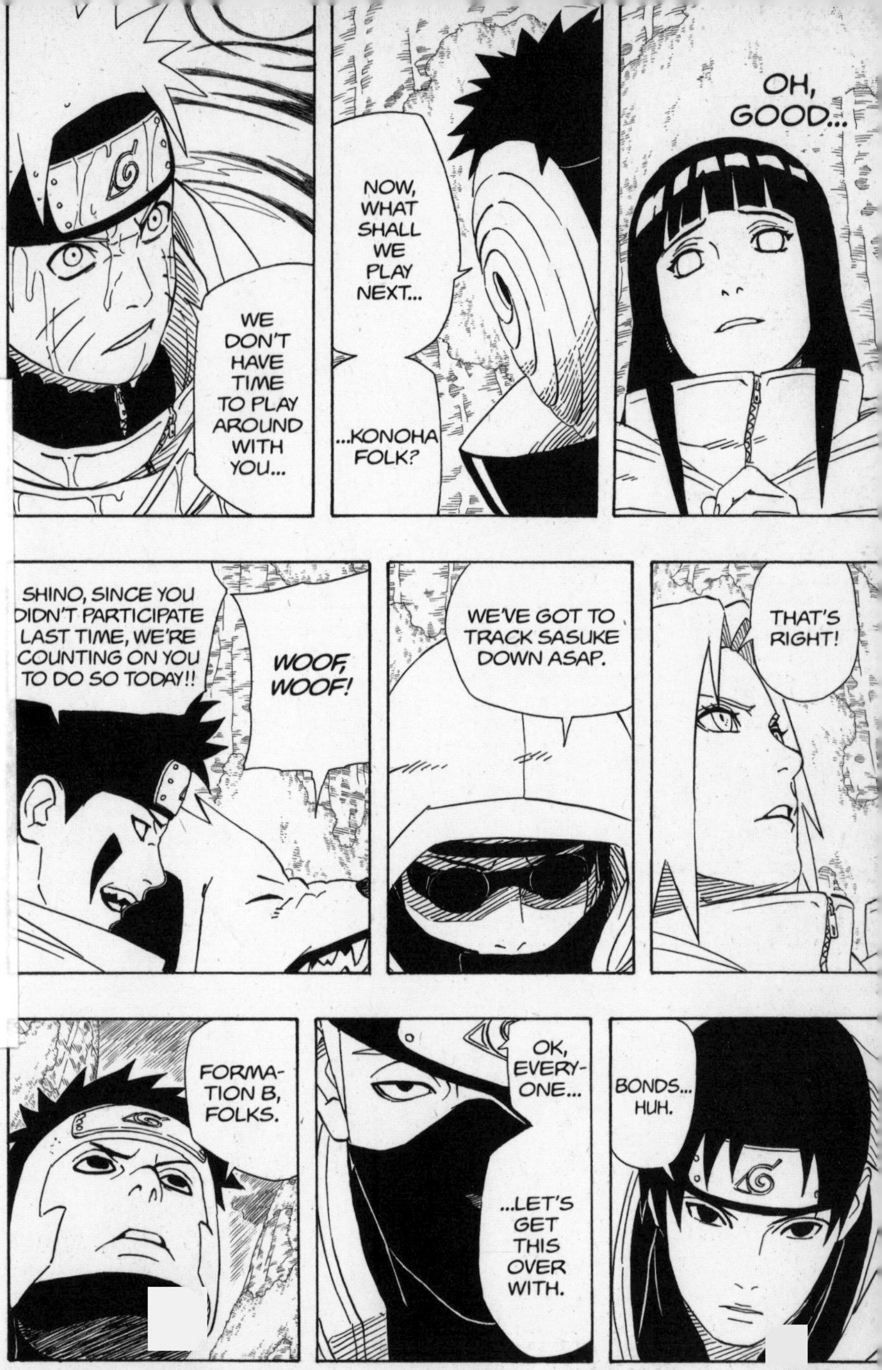
OH, GOOD...
NOW, WHAT SHALL WE PLAY NEXT...
...KONOHA FOLK?
WE DON'T HAVE TIME TO PLAY AROUND WITH YOU...
THAT'S RIGHT!
WE'VE GOT TO TRACK SASUKE DOWN ASAP.
SHINO, SINCE YOU DIDN'T PARTICIPATE LAST TIME, WE'RE COUNTING ON YOU TO DO SO TODAY!!
WOOF, WOOF!
BONDS... HUH.
OK, EVERY-ONE...
...LET'S GET THIS OVER WITH.
FORMA-TION B, FOLKS.

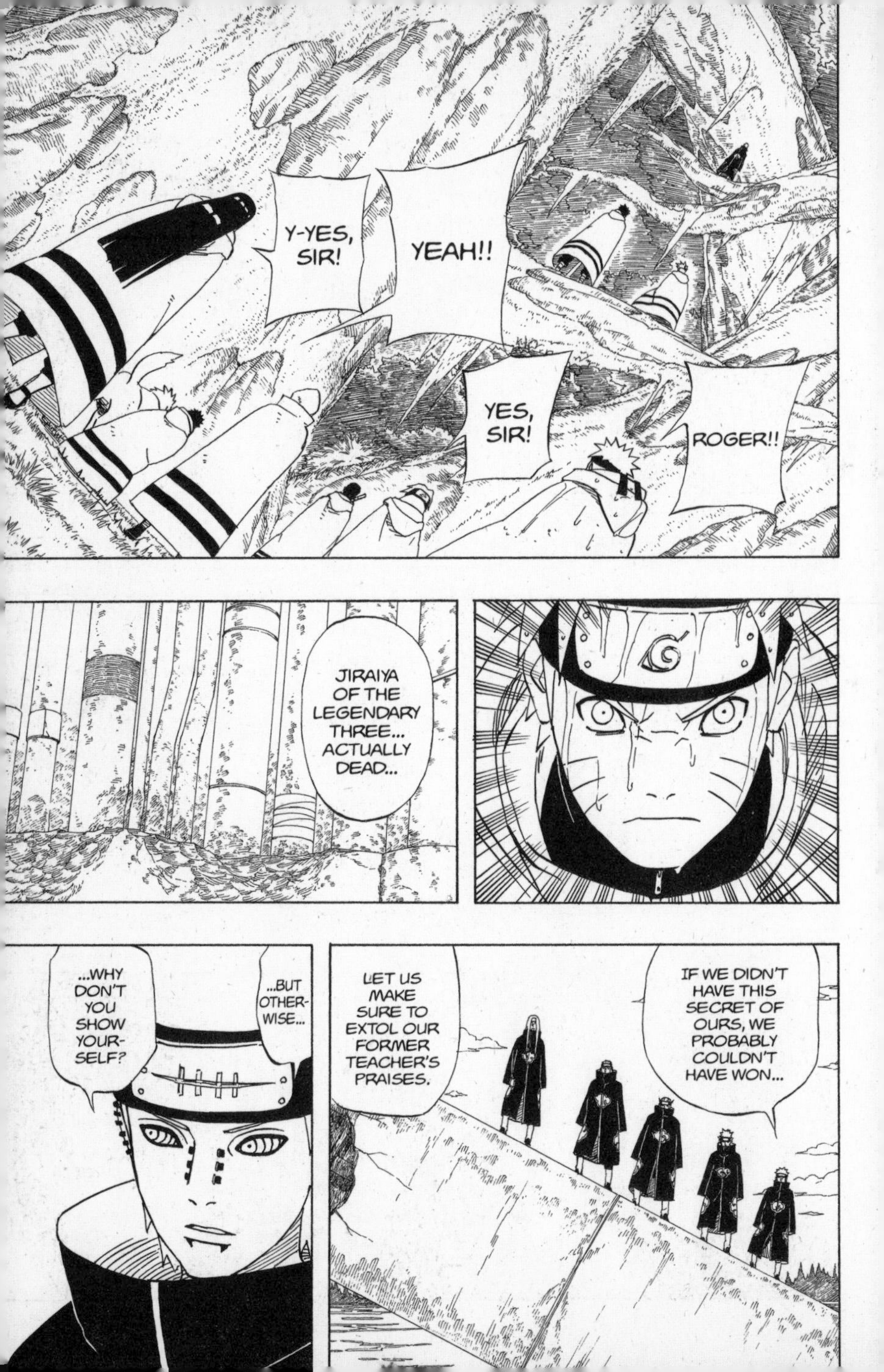
ROGER!!
YES, SIR!
YEAH!!
Y-YES, SIR!
JIRAIYA OF THE LEGENDARY THREE... ACTUALLY DEAD...
IF WE DIDN'T HAVE THIS SECRET OF OURS, WE PROBABLY COULDN'T HAVE WON...
LET US MAKE SURE TO EXTOL OUR FORMER TEACHER'S PRAISES.
...BUT OTHER-WISE...
...WHY DON'T YOU SHOW YOUR-SELF?

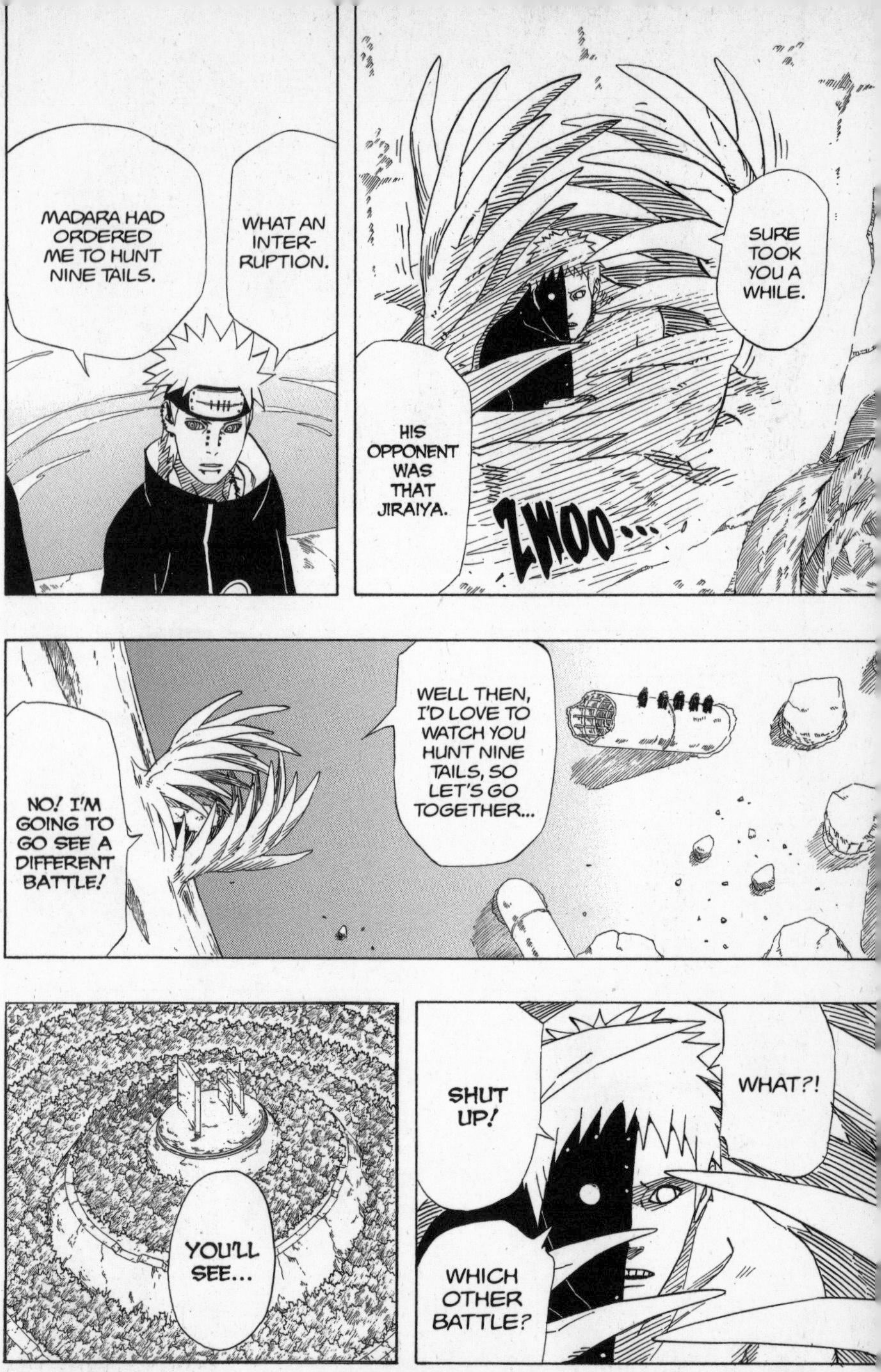
SURE TOOK YOU A WHILE.
HIS OPPONENT WAS THAT JIRAIYA.
ZWOO...
WHAT AN INTER-RUPTION.
MADARA HAD ORDERED ME TO HUNT NINE TAILS.
WELL THEN, I'D LOVE TO WATCH YOU HUNT NINE TAILS, SO LET'S GO TOGETHER...
NO! I'M GOING TO GO SEE A DIFFERENT BATTLE!
WHAT?!
SHUT UP!
WHICH OTHER BATTLE?
YOU'LL SEE...

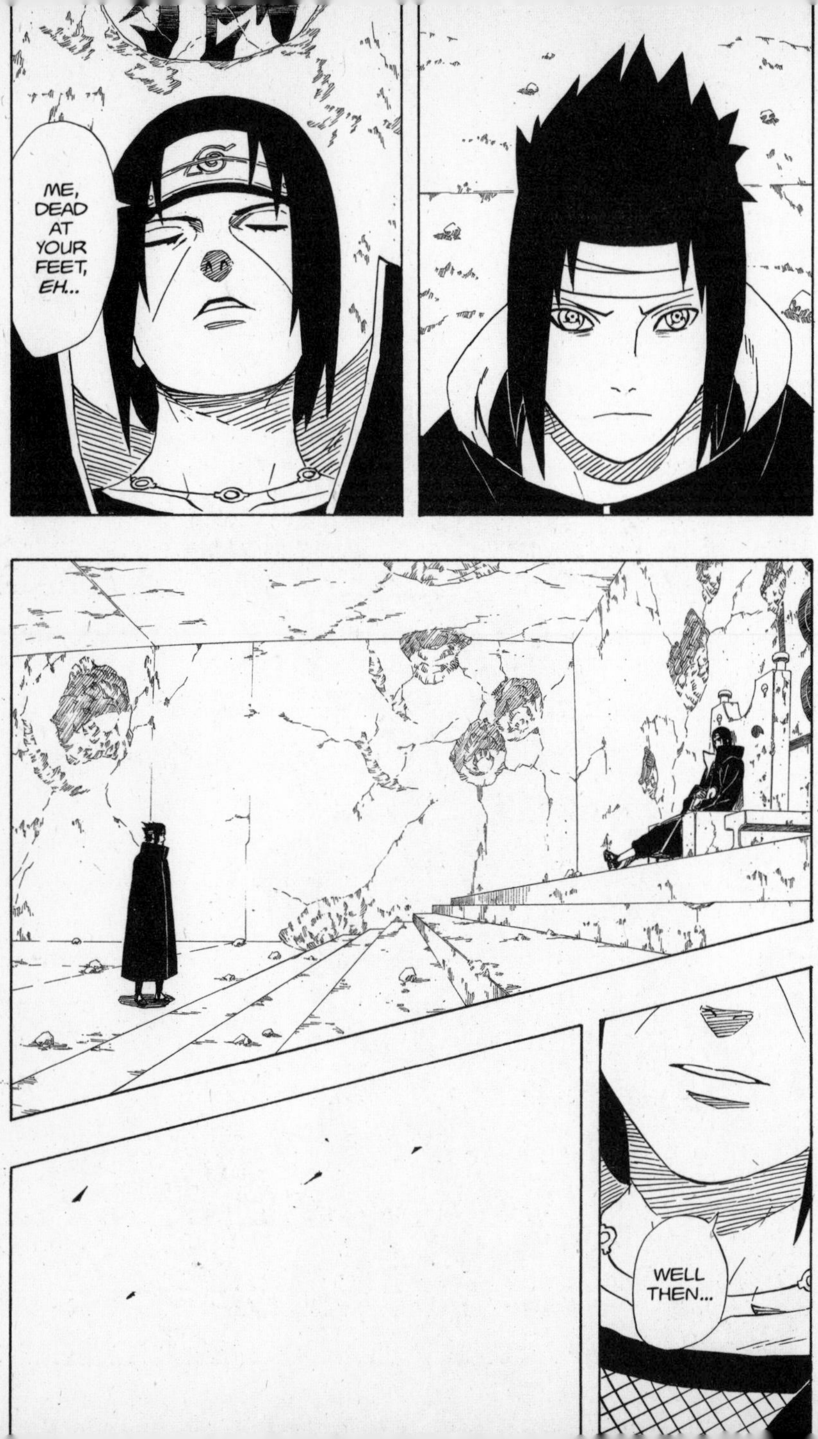
ME, DEAD AT YOUR FEET, EH...
WELL THEN...

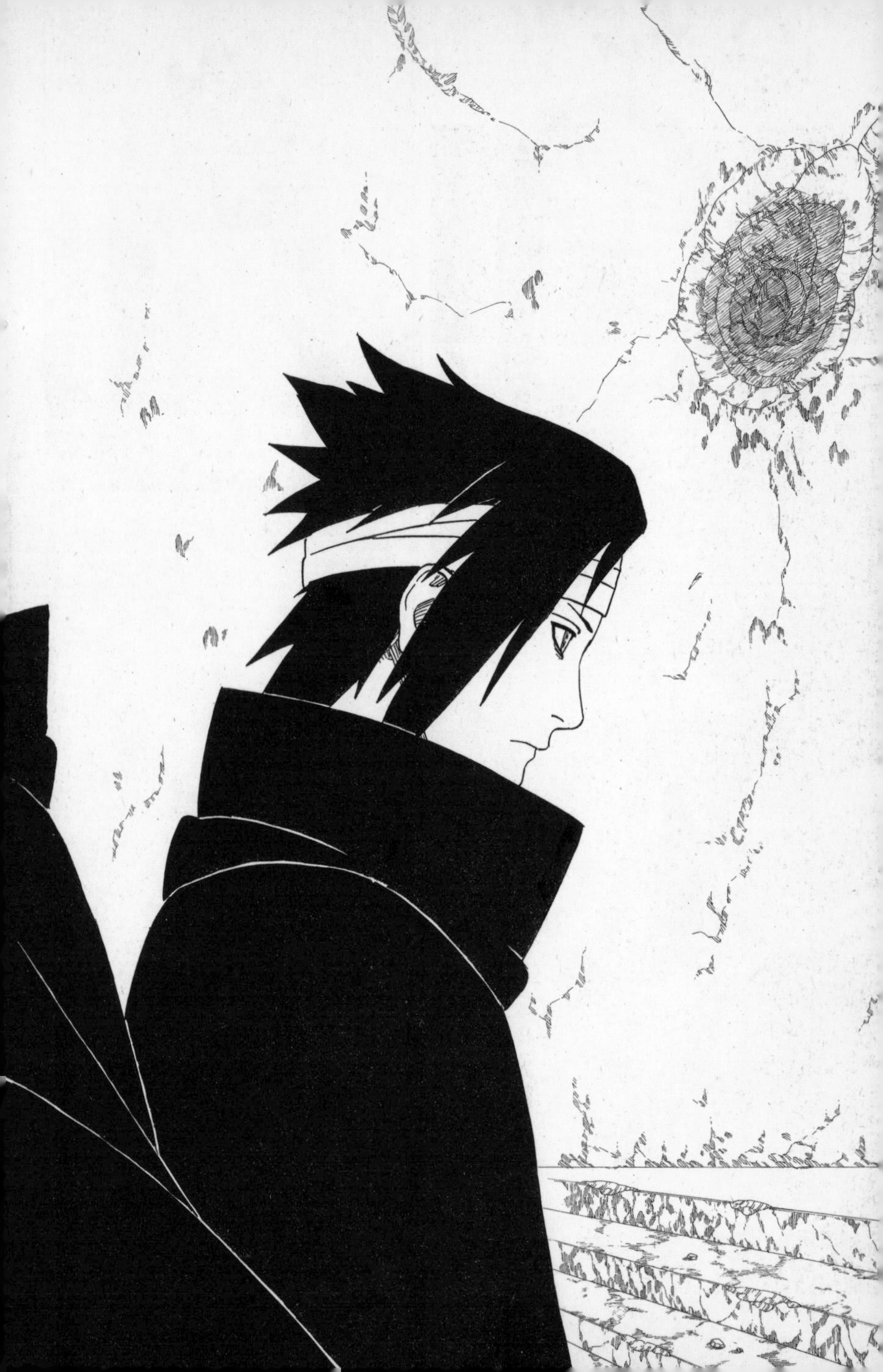

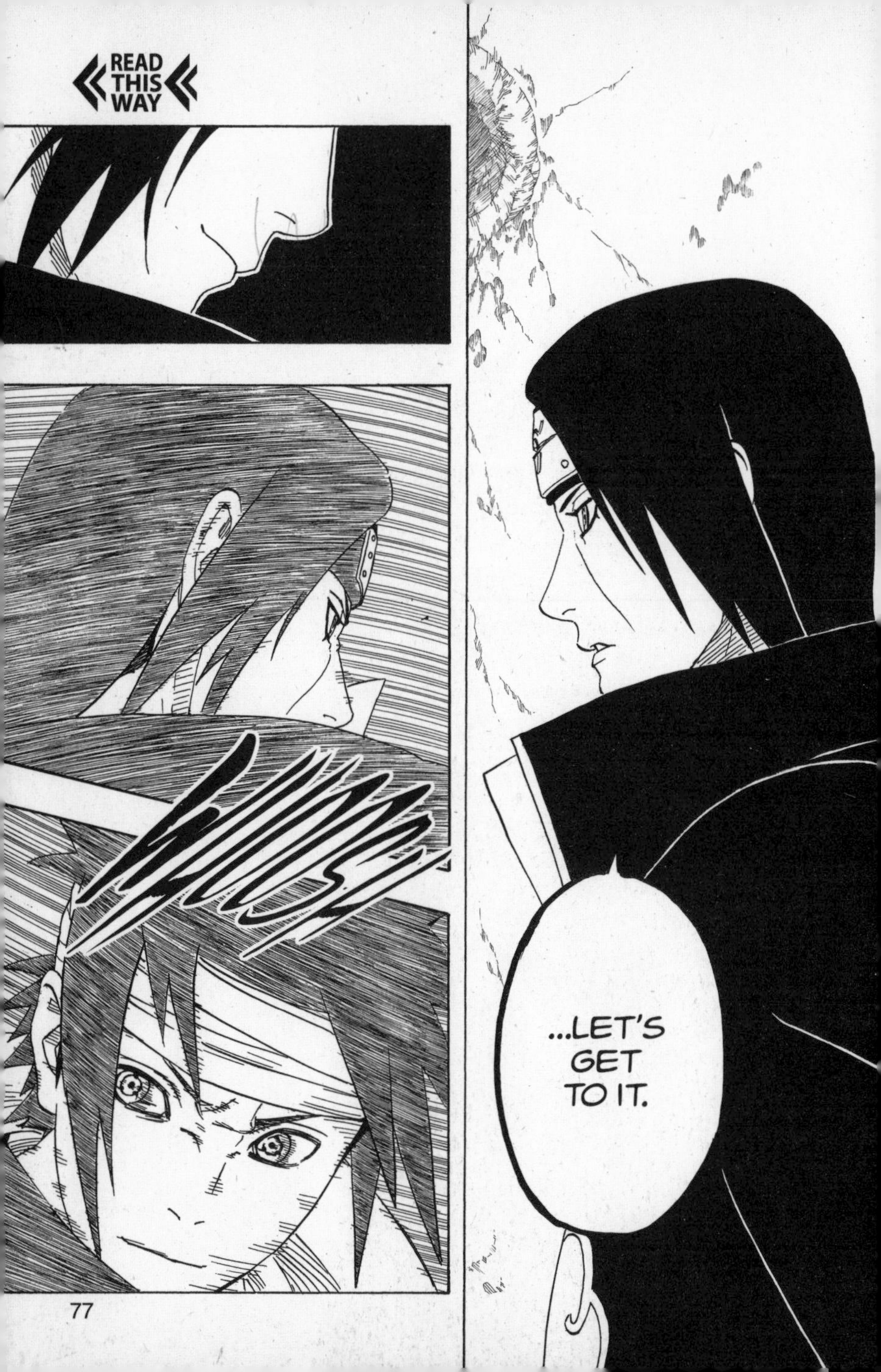
READ THIS WAY
...LET'S GET TO IT.
WHOOSH

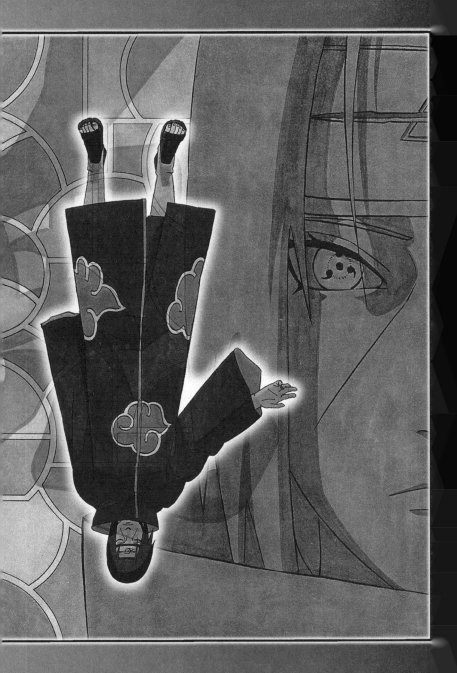

Number 384: Two Paths...

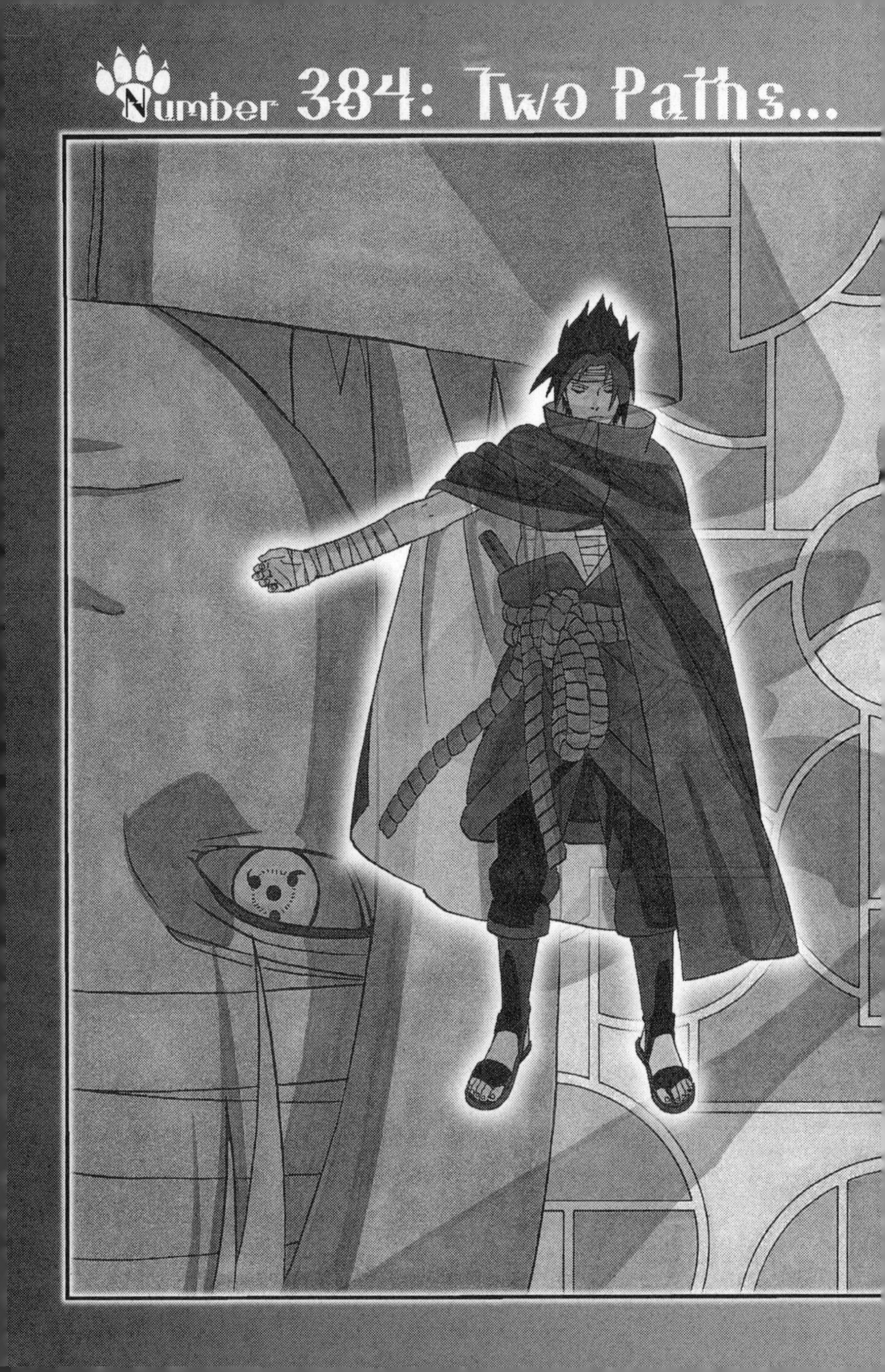

NARUTO

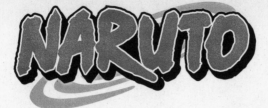

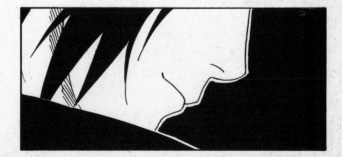

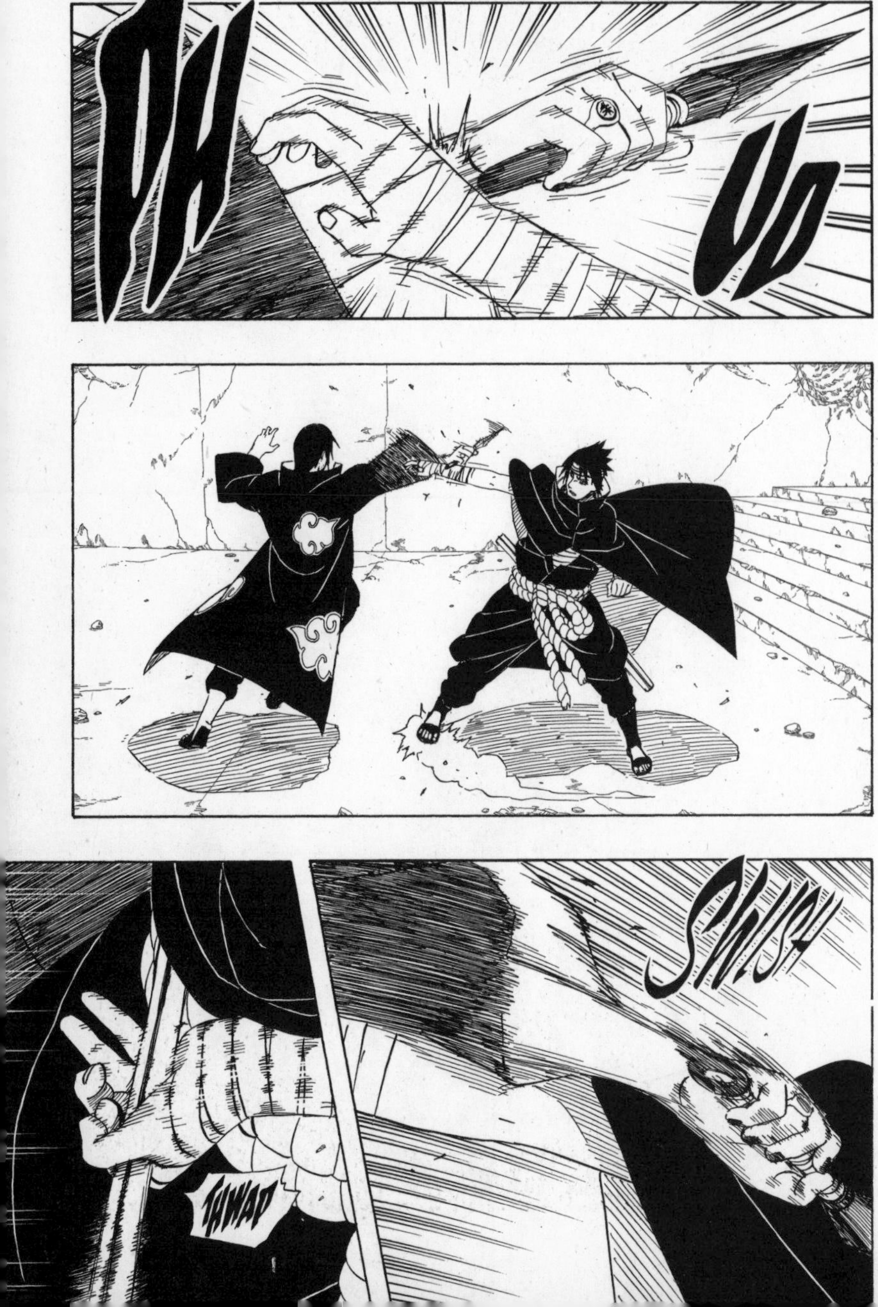
SWISH
THWAP

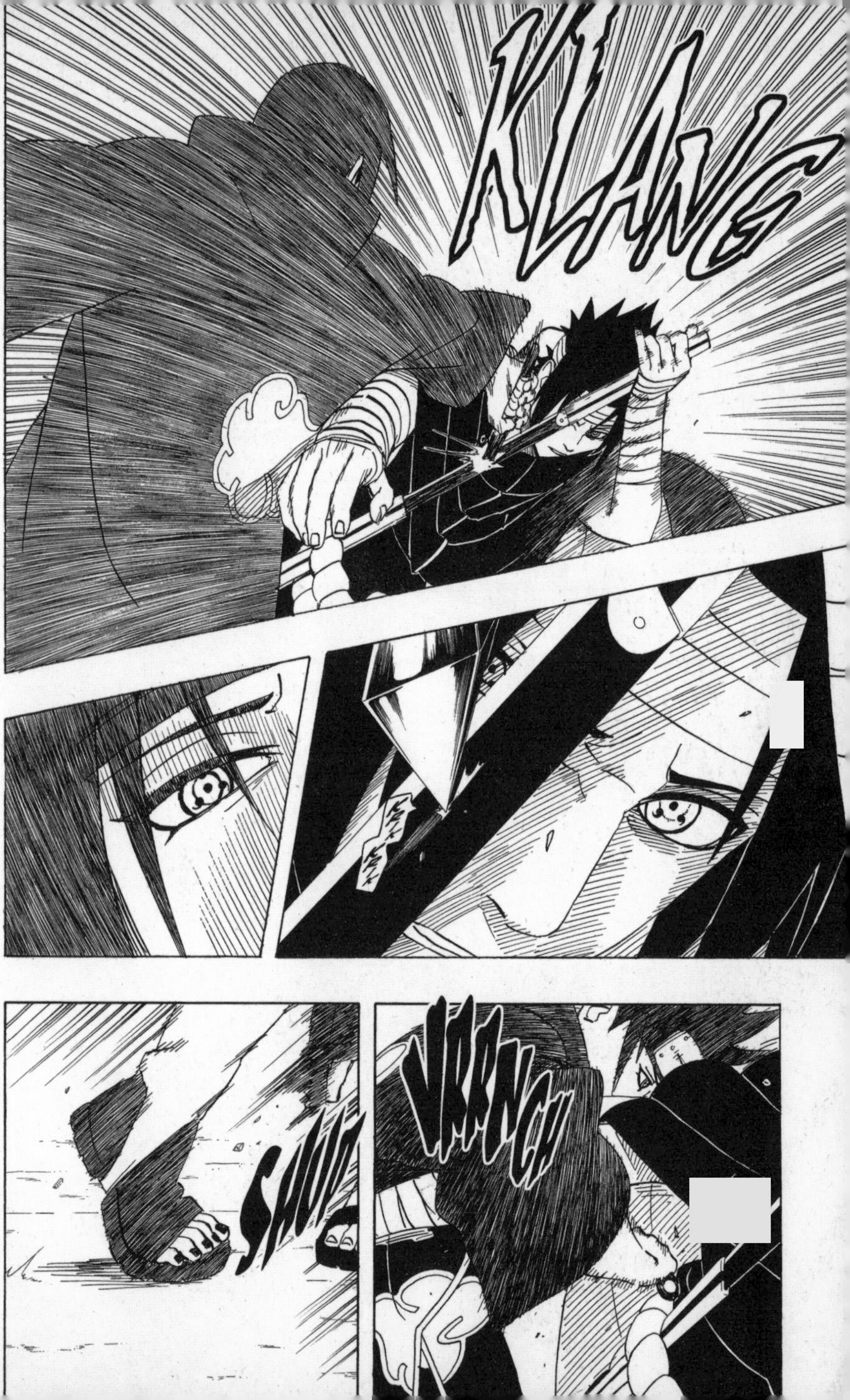
KLANG
VRRNCH

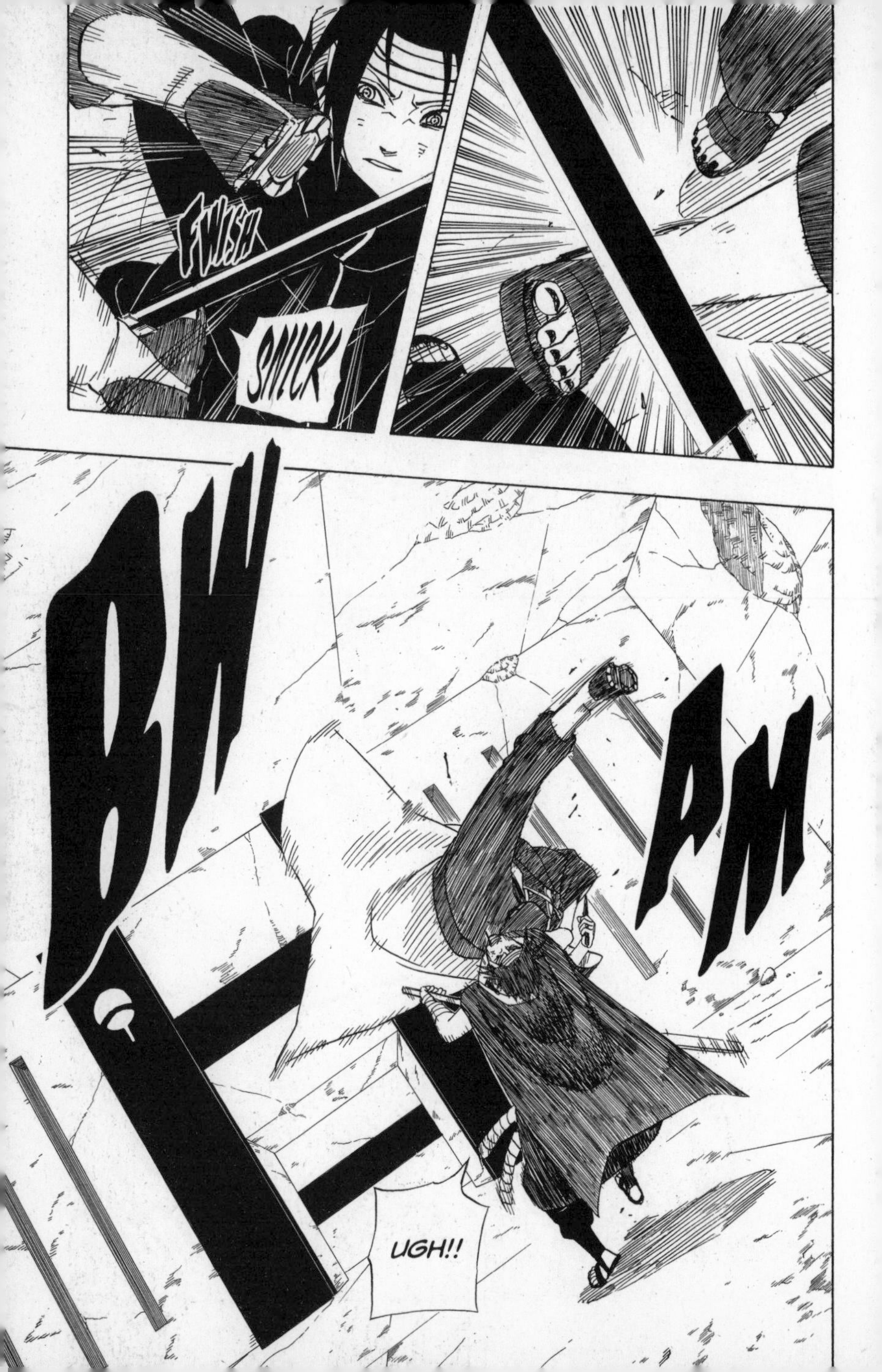
FWISH
SNICK
BA
AM
UGH!!

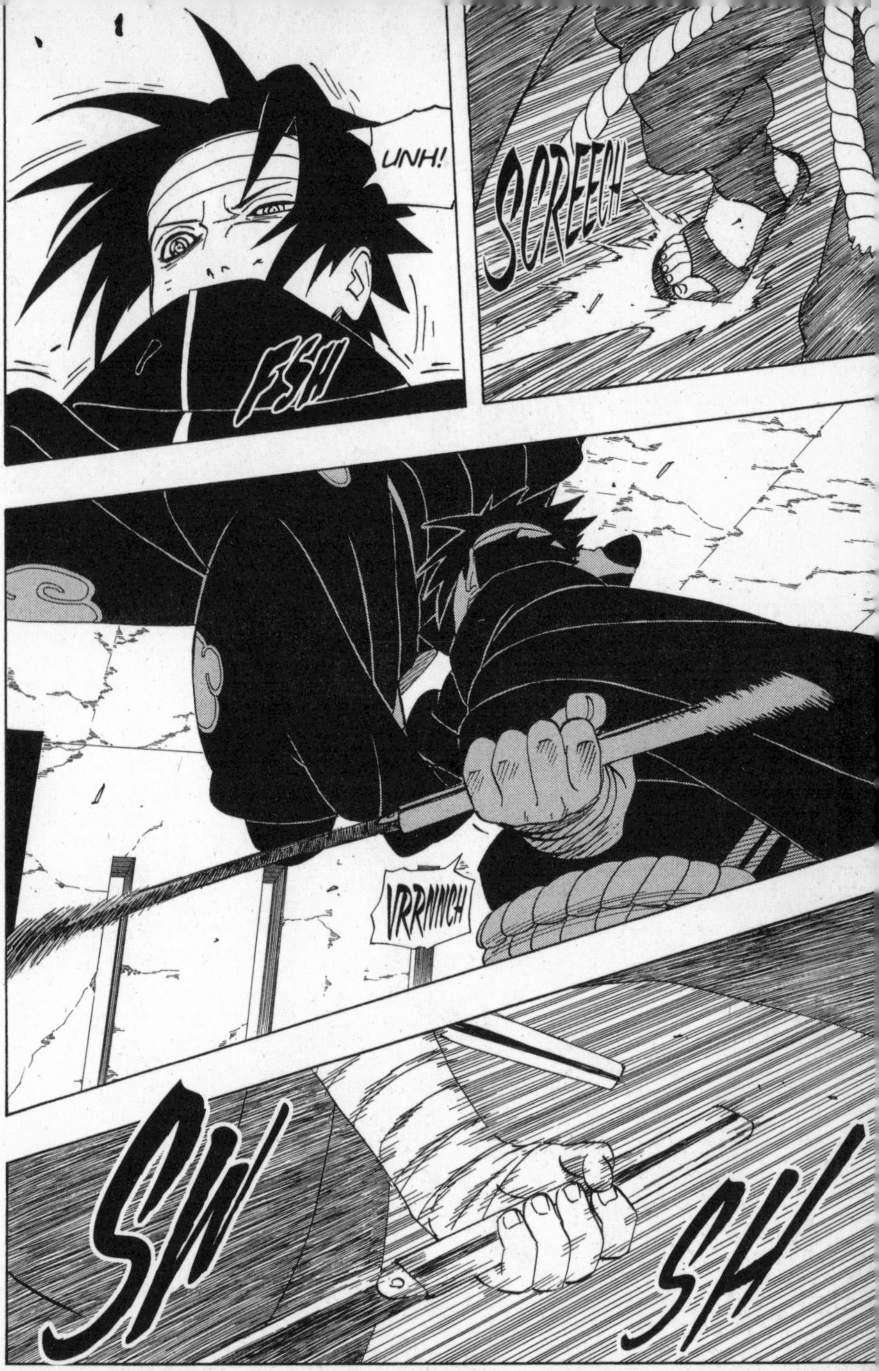
SCREECH
UNH!
FSH
VRRNNCH
SH
SH

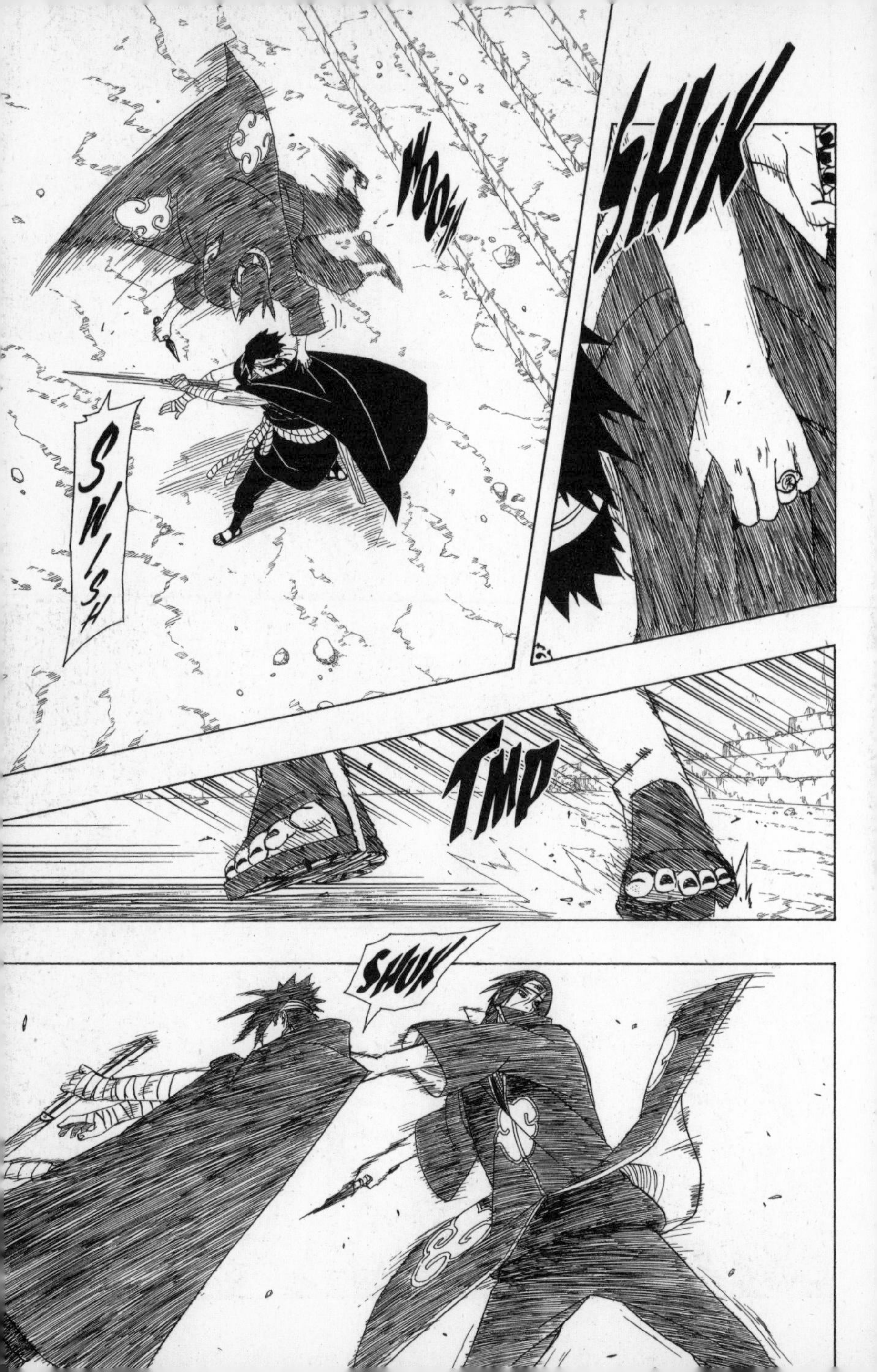
SHIK
WOOSH
SWISH
TMP
SHUK

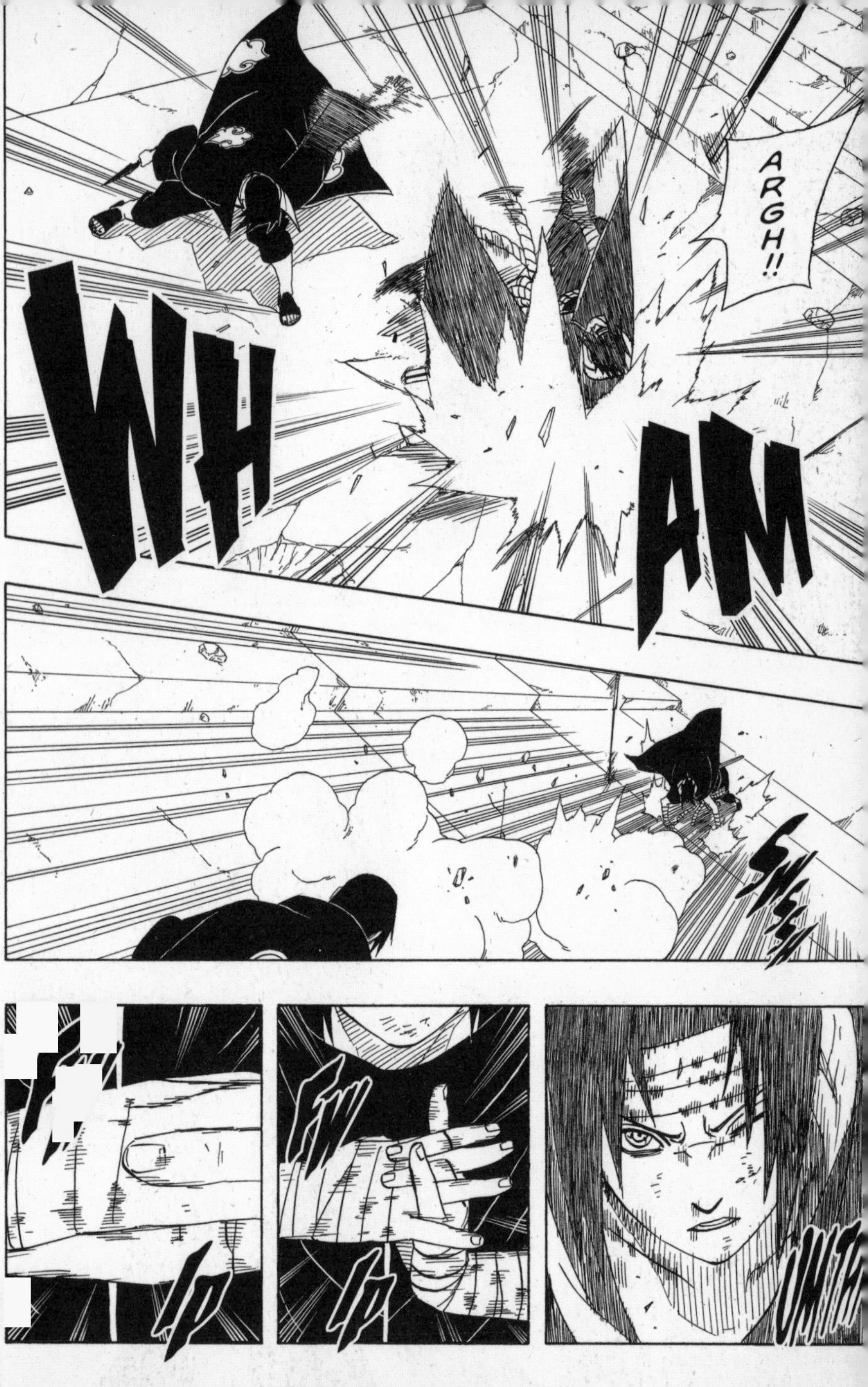
ARGH!!
WHAM

READ THIS WAY

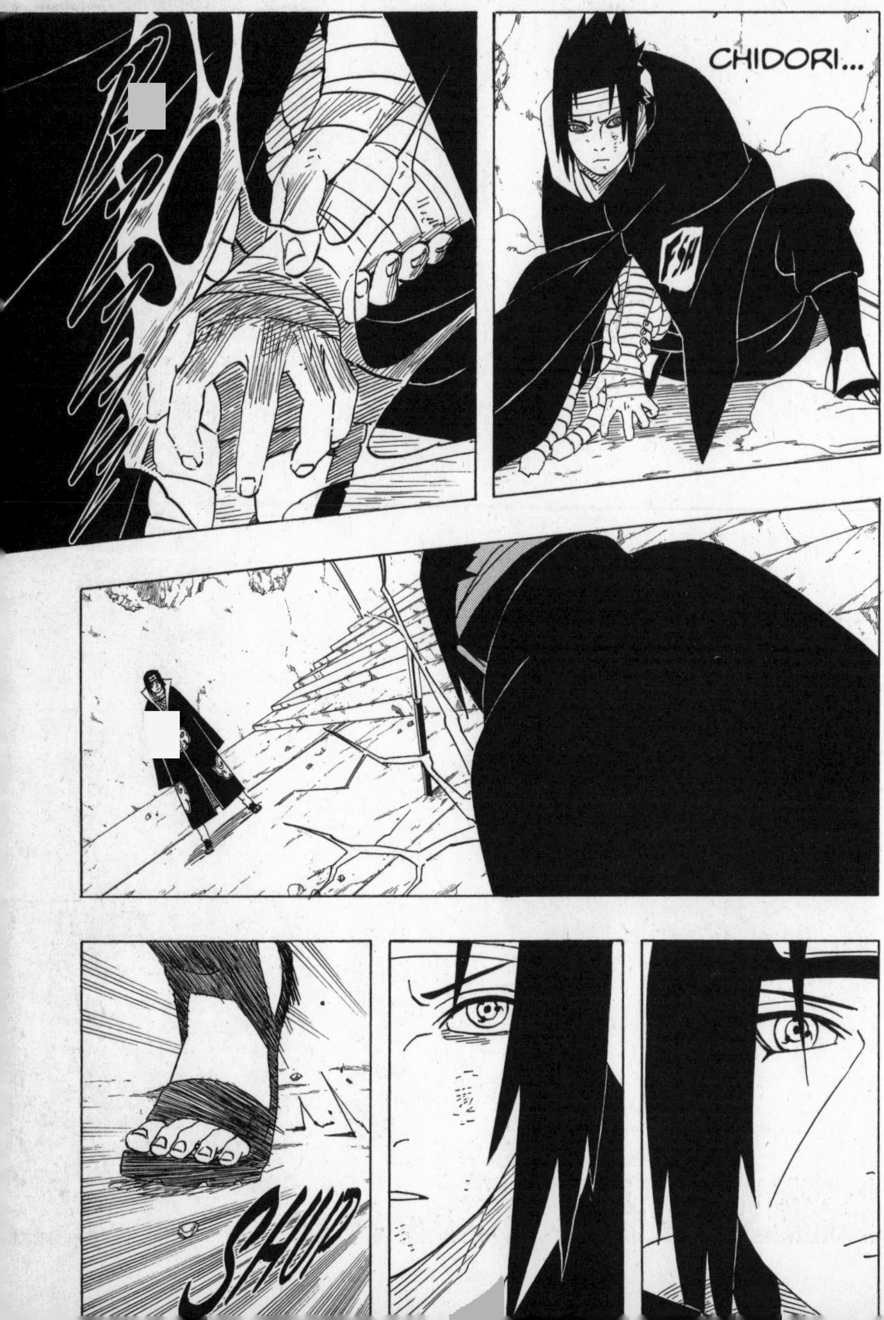
CHIDORI...
SHUP

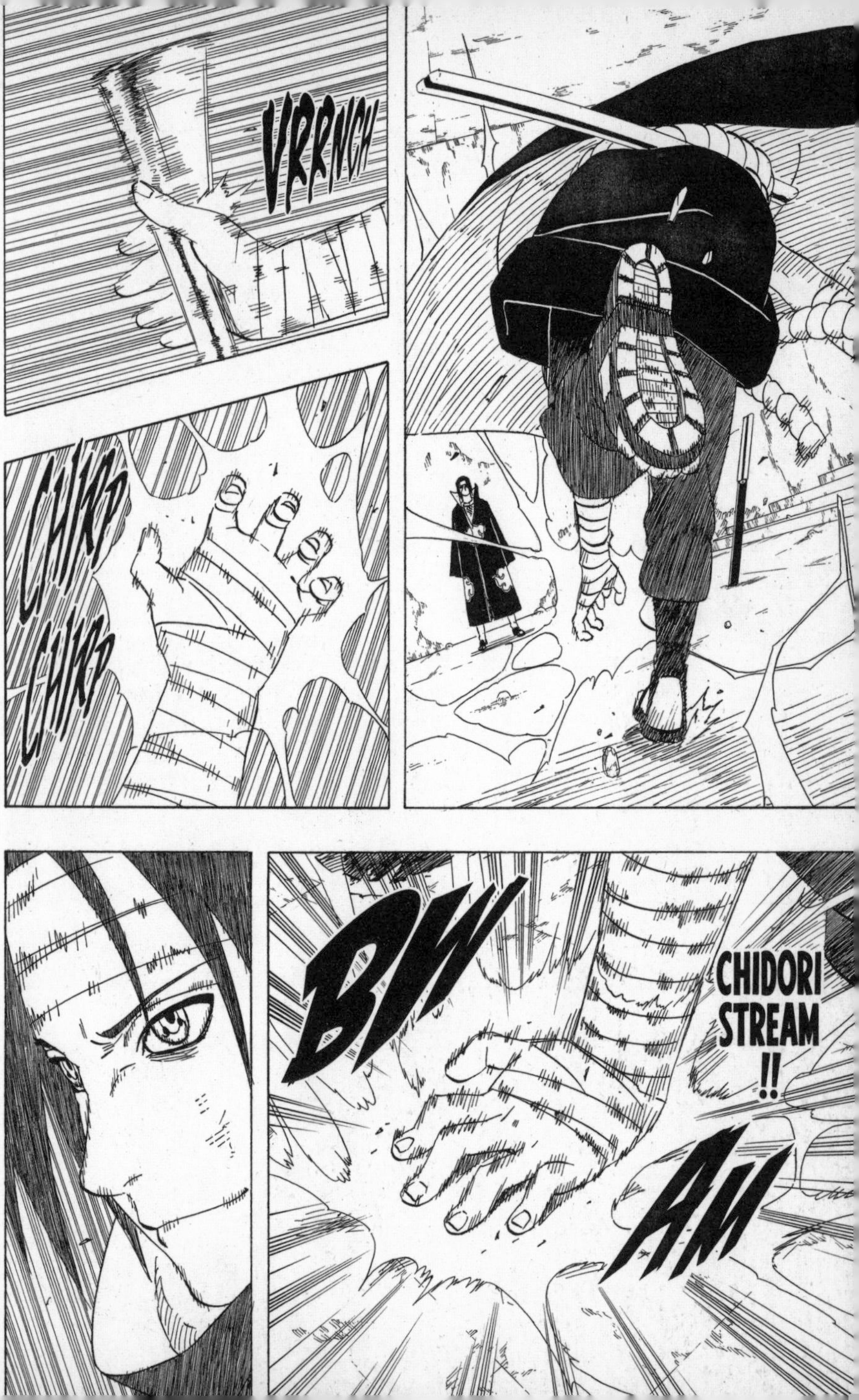
VRRNCH
CHIRP CHIRP
CHIDORI STREAM!!

READ THIS WAY

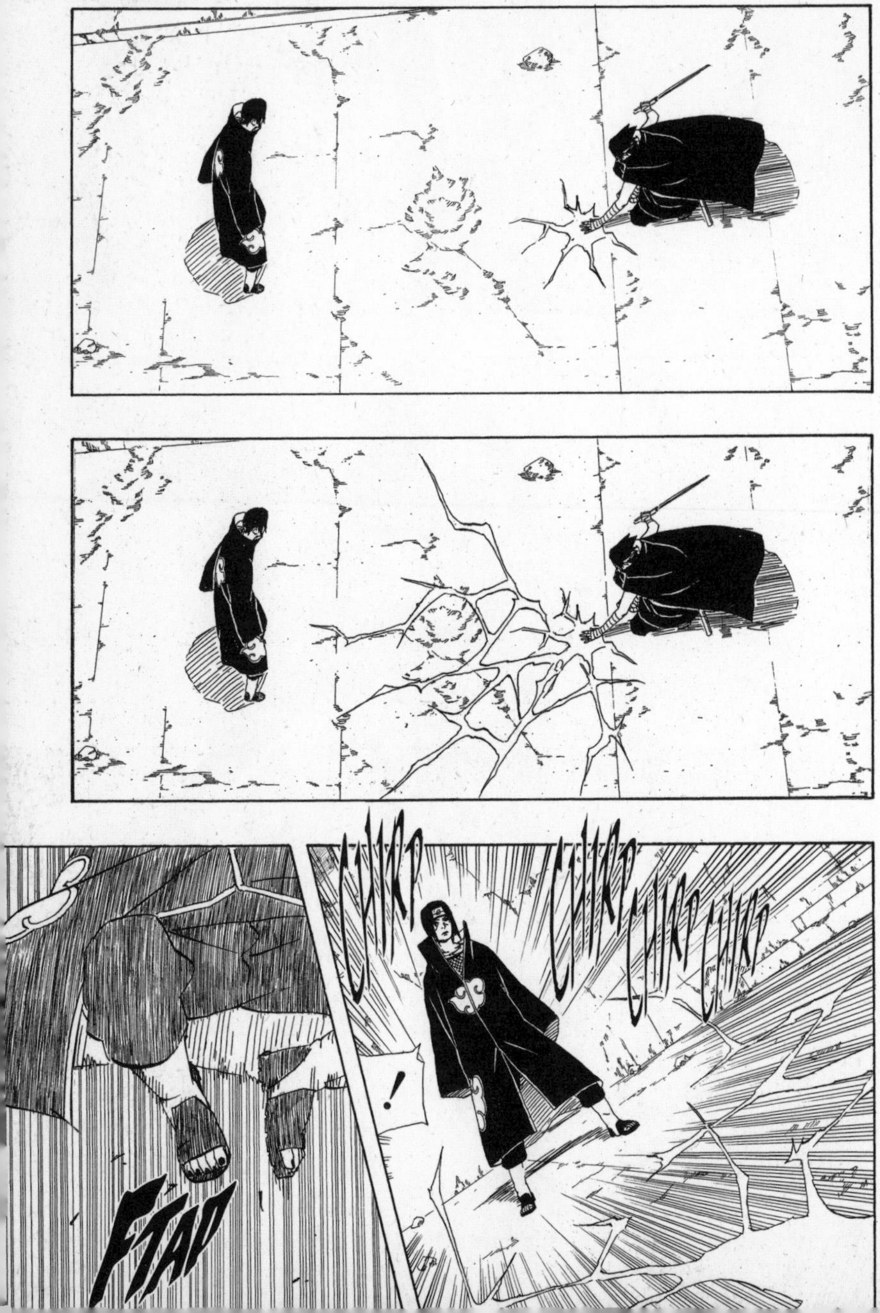
CHIRP
CHIRP
CHIRP
CHIRP
!
FTAP

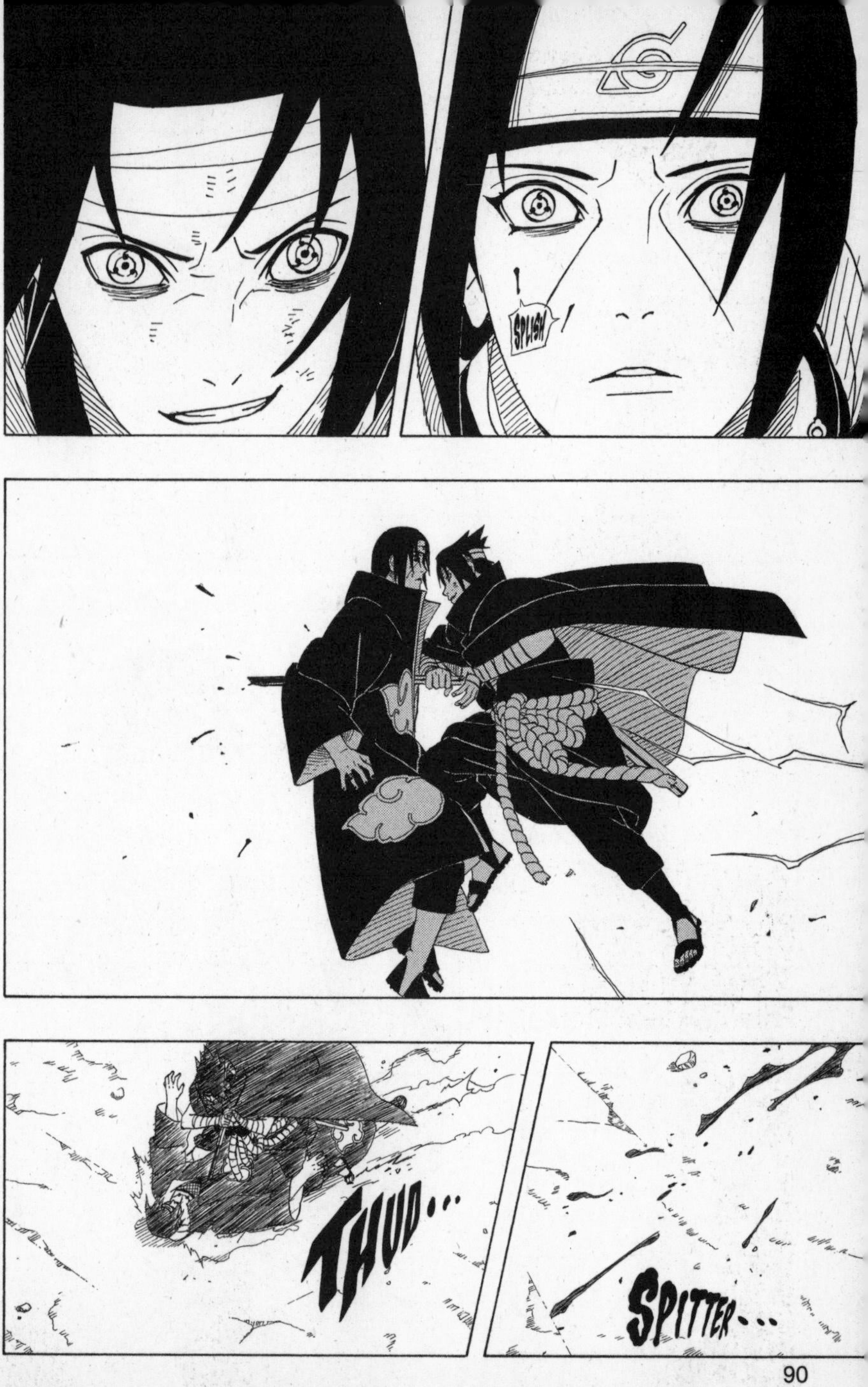
SPLISH
SPITTER...
THUD...

YOU'VE... GOTTEN STRONGER...

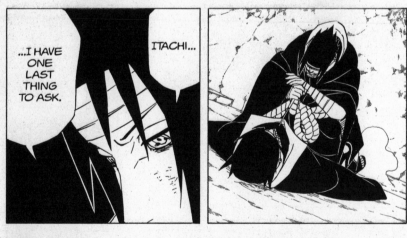

...I HAVE ONE LAST THING TO ASK.

ITACHI...

FSH...

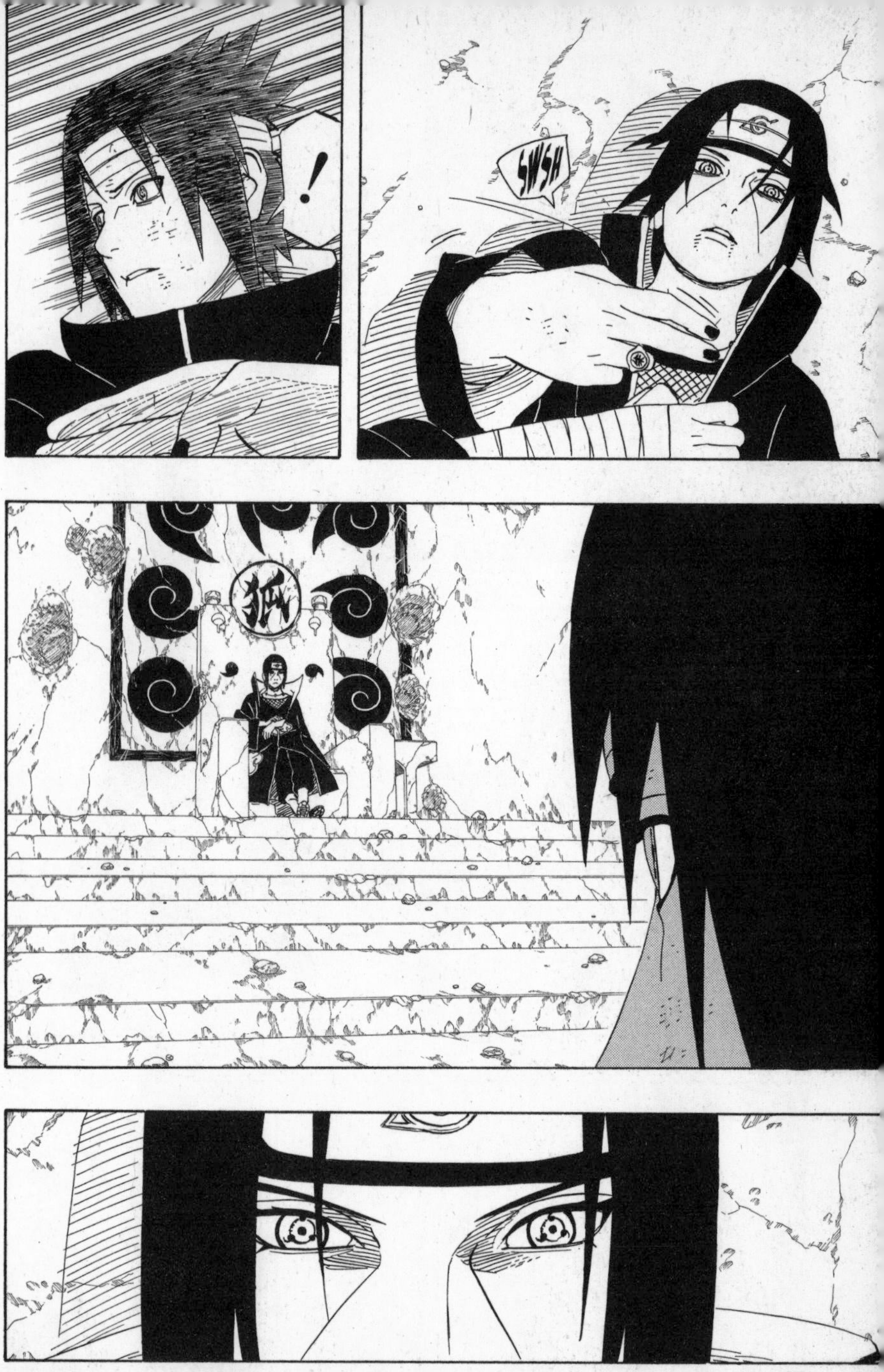
SWSH
!

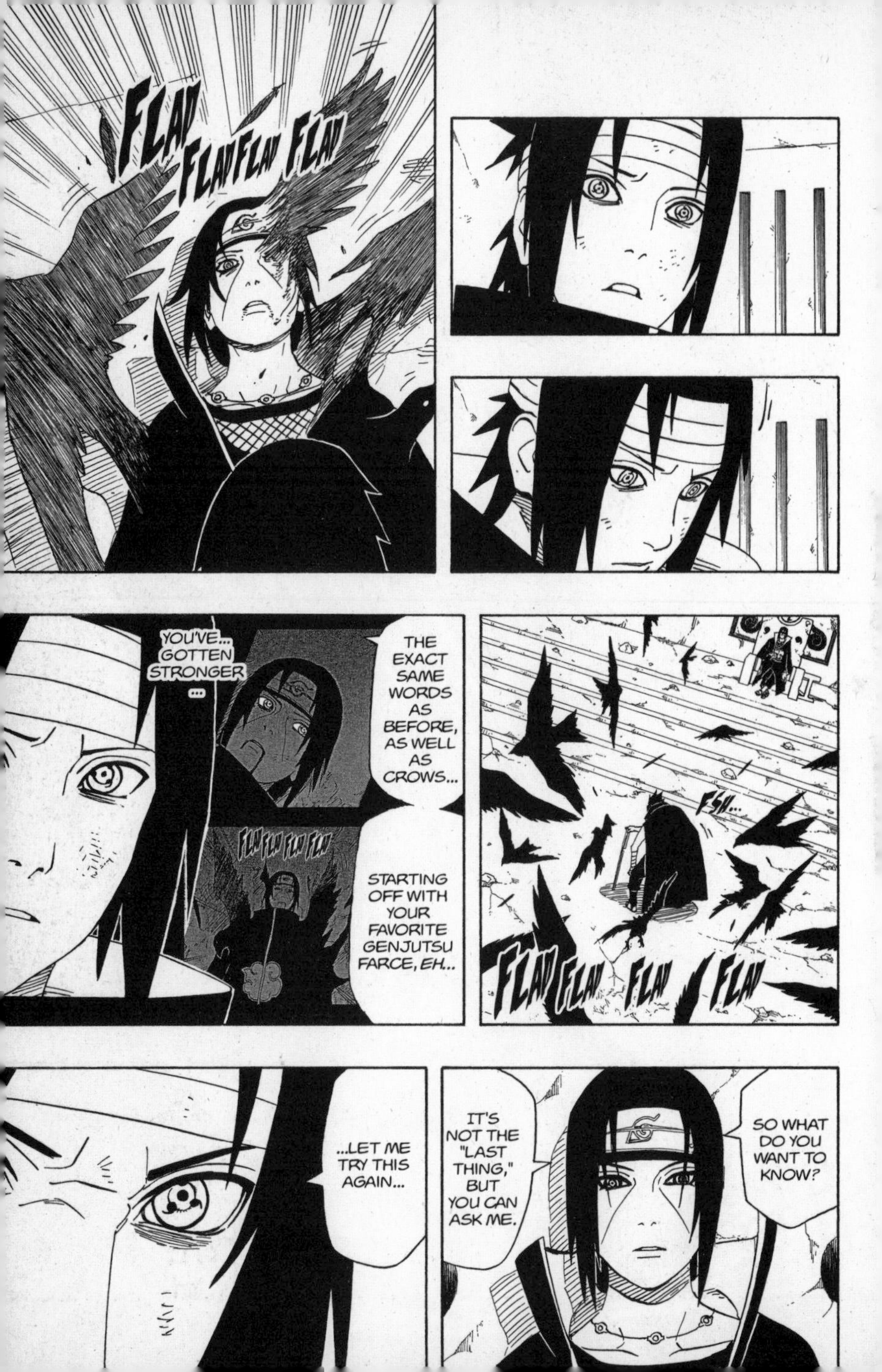
FLAP
FLAP FLAP FLAP
FSH...
FLAP FLAP FLAP FLAP
THE EXACT SAME WORDS AS BEFORE, AS WELL AS CROWS...
YOU'VE... GOTTEN STRONGER ...
FLAP FLAP FLAP FLAP
STARTING OFF WITH YOUR FAVORITE GENJUTSU FARCE, *EH*...
SO WHAT DO YOU WANT TO KNOW?
IT'S NOT THE "LAST THING," BUT YOU CAN ASK ME.
...LET ME TRY THIS AGAIN...

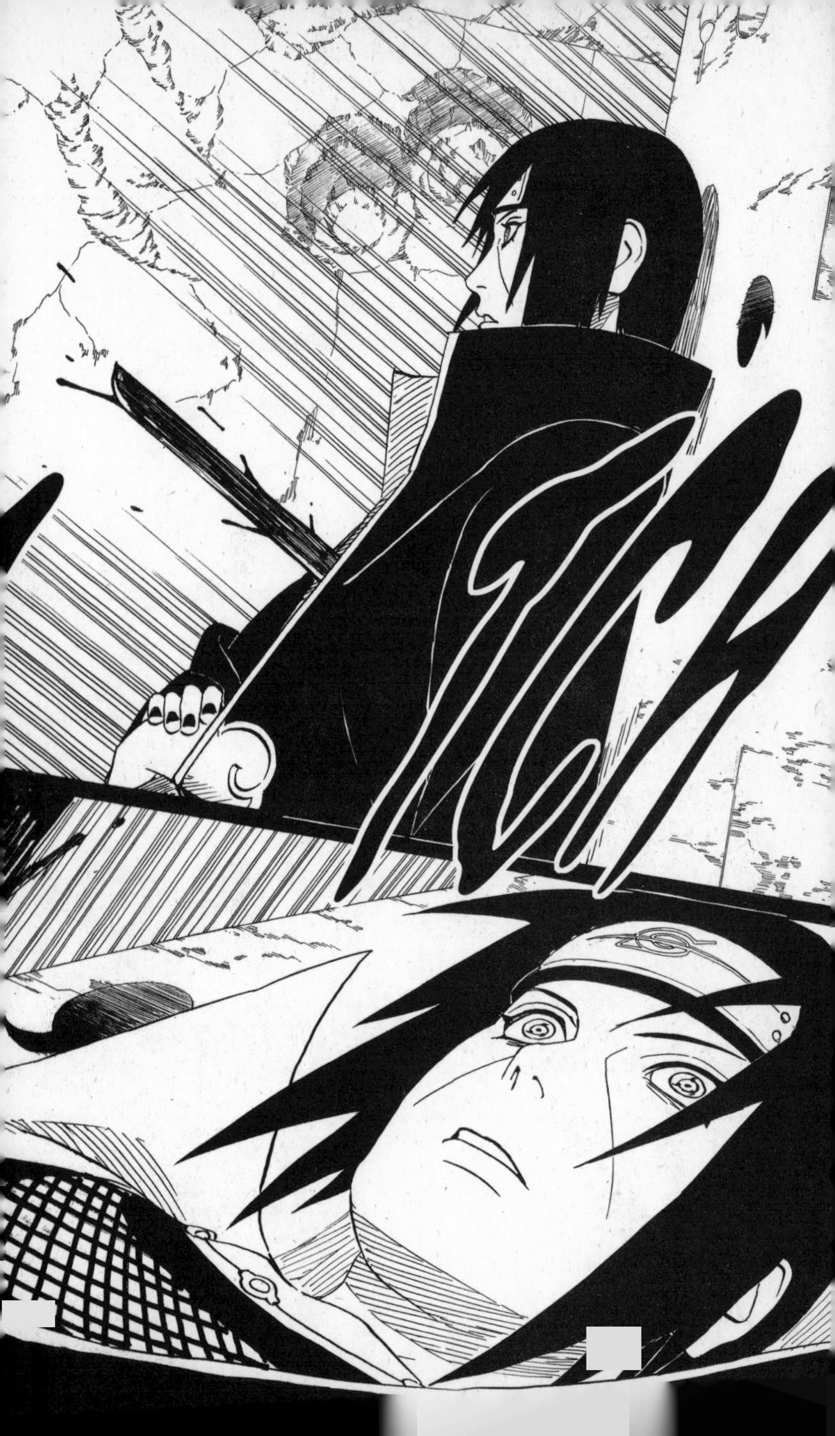

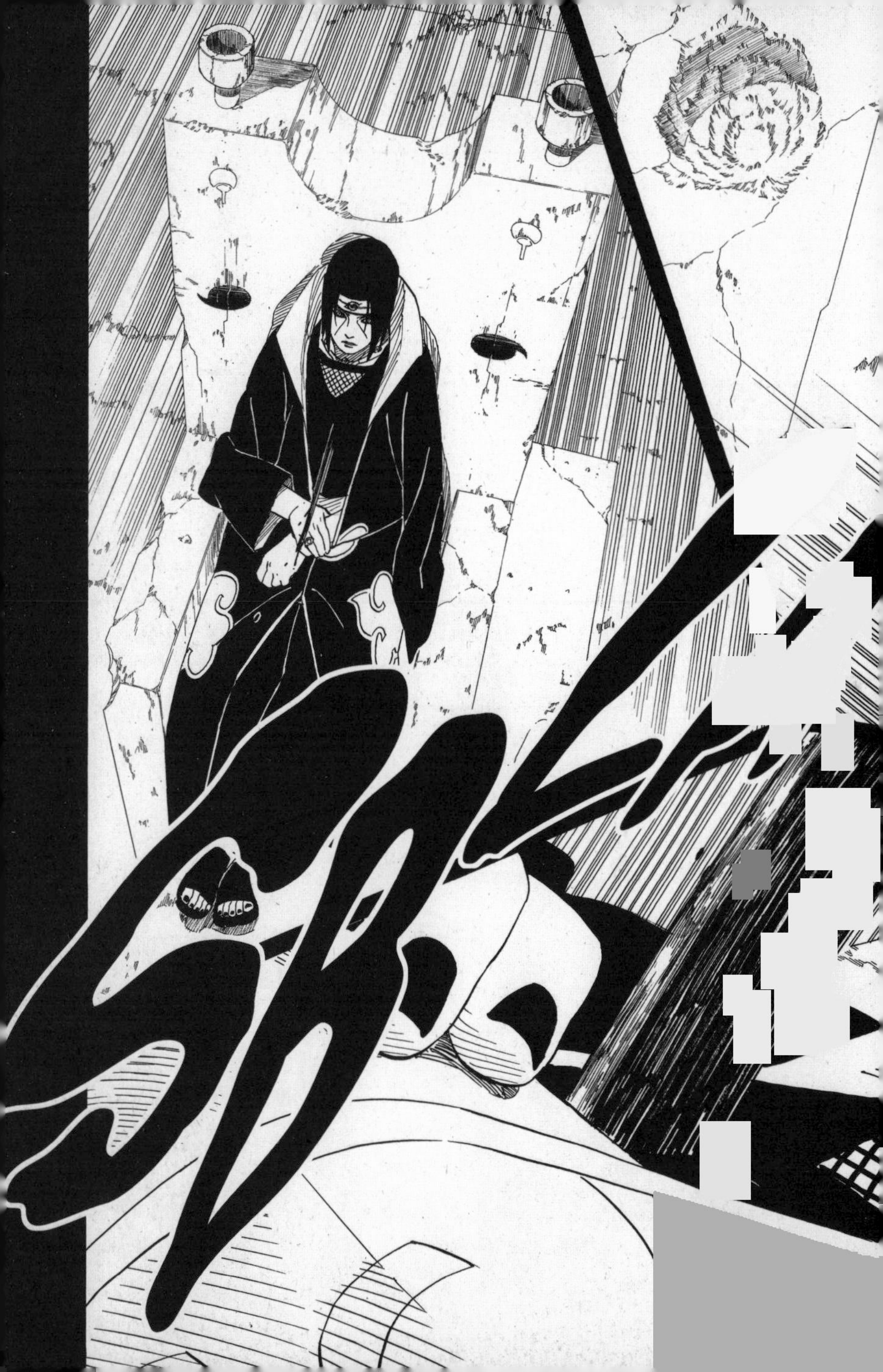

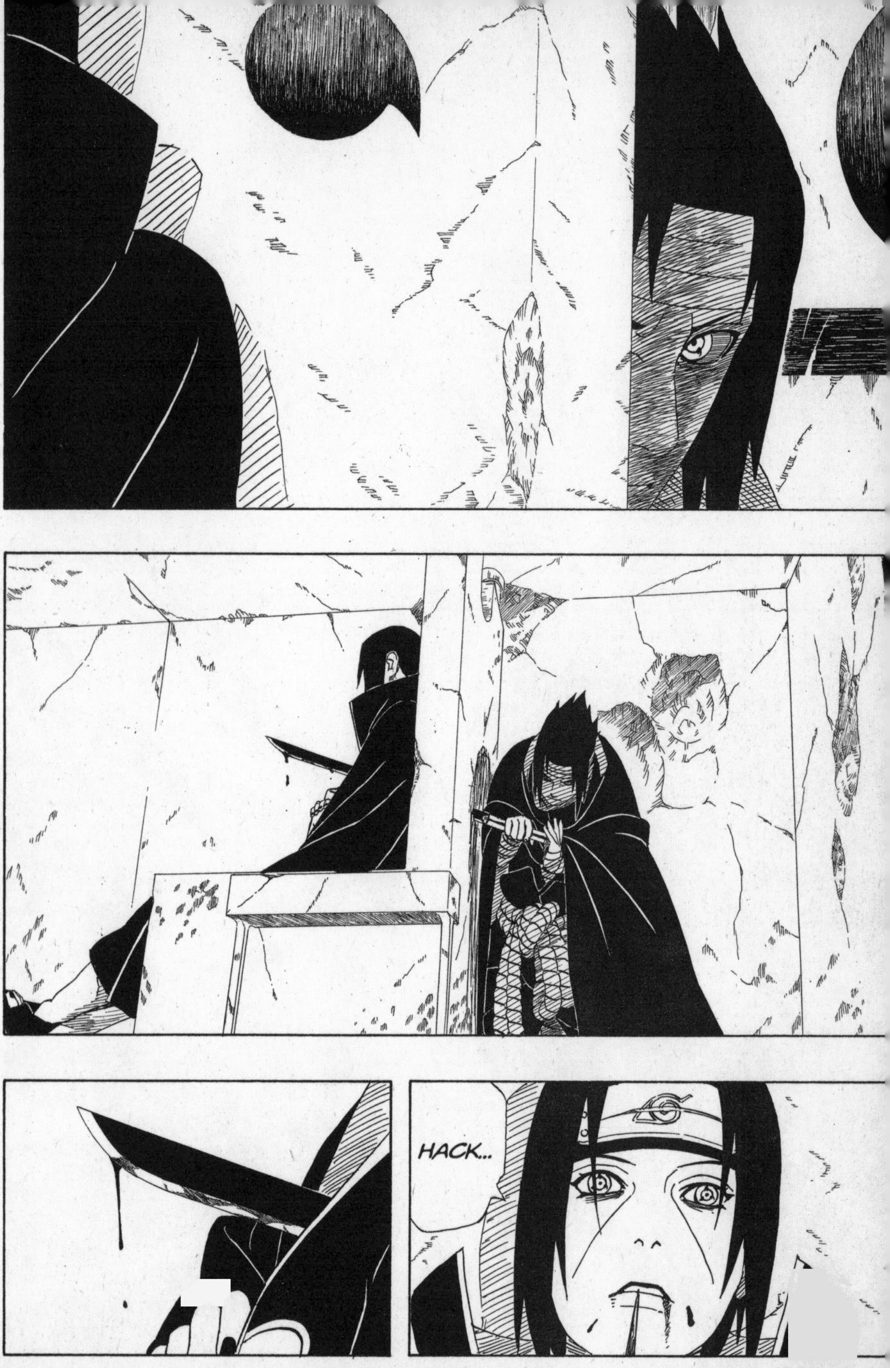
HACK...

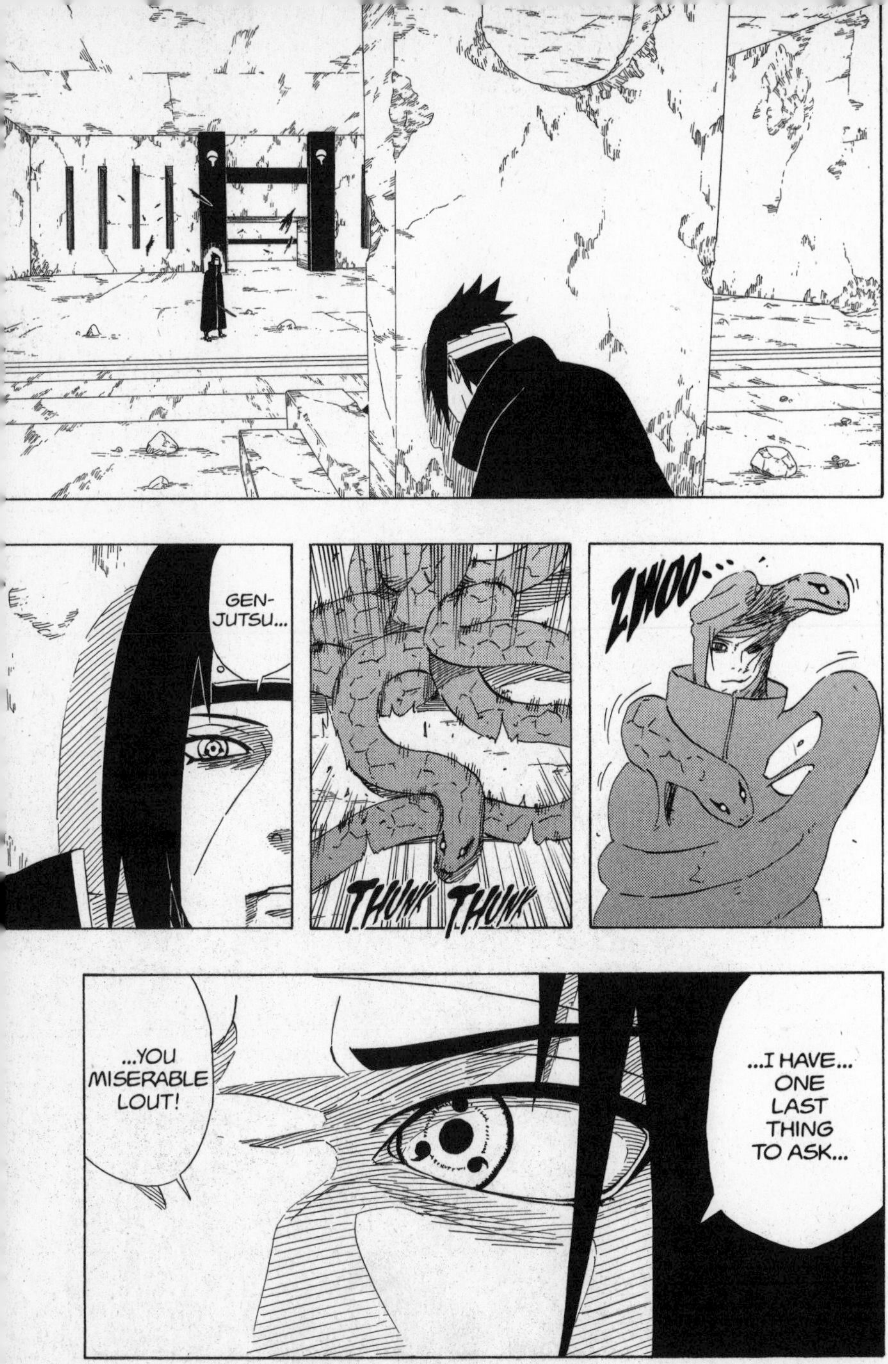
ZWOO...
THUNK THUNK
GEN-JUTSU...
...I HAVE... ONE LAST THING TO ASK...
...YOU MISERABLE LOUT!

NARUTO

Number 385: The Secret of the Mangekyo...!!

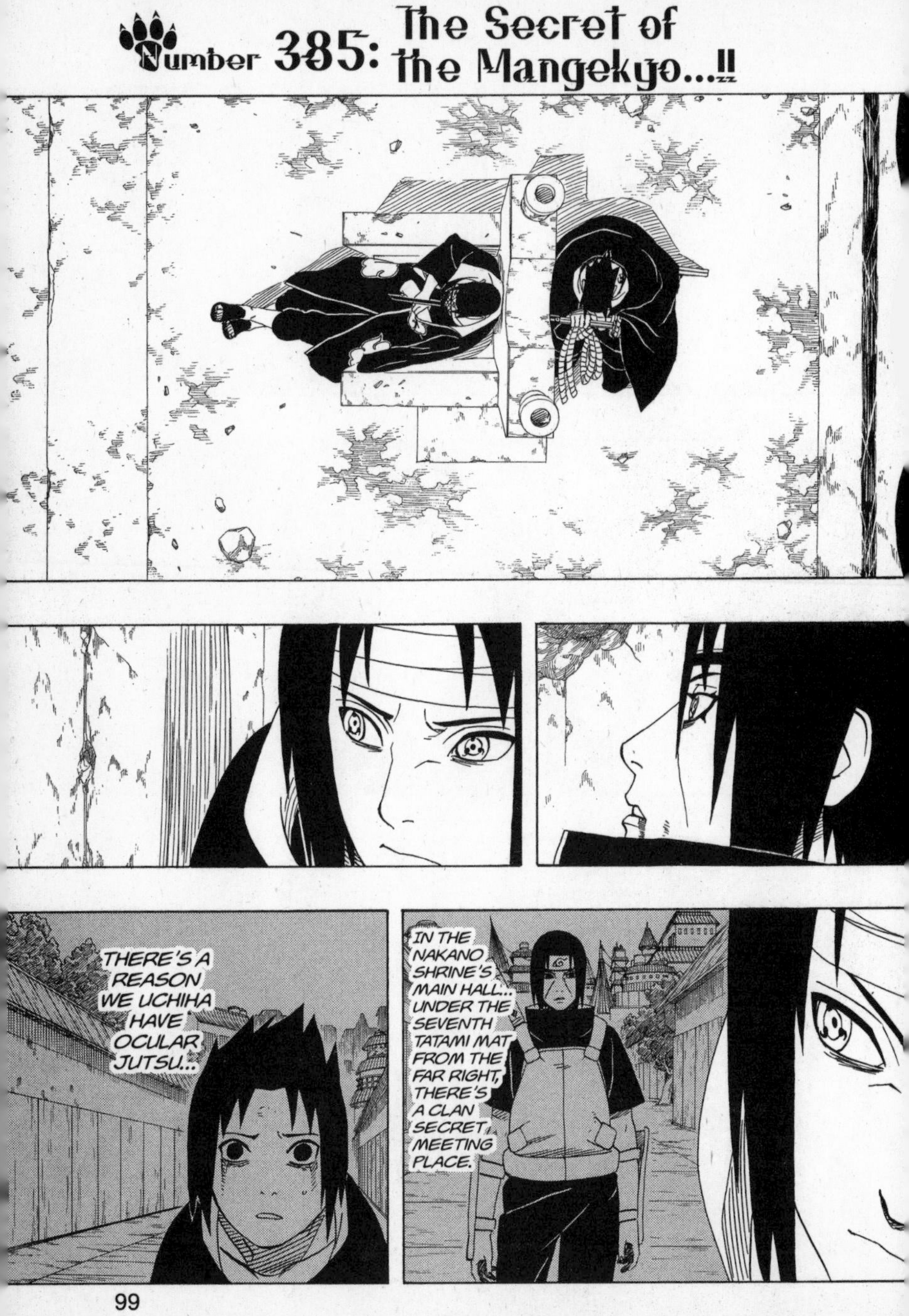

IN THE NAKANO SHRINE'S MAIN HALL... UNDER THE SEVENTH TATAMI MAT FROM THE FAR RIGHT, THERE'S A CLAN SECRET MEETING PLACE.
THERE'S A REASON WE UCHIHA HAVE OCULAR JUTSU...

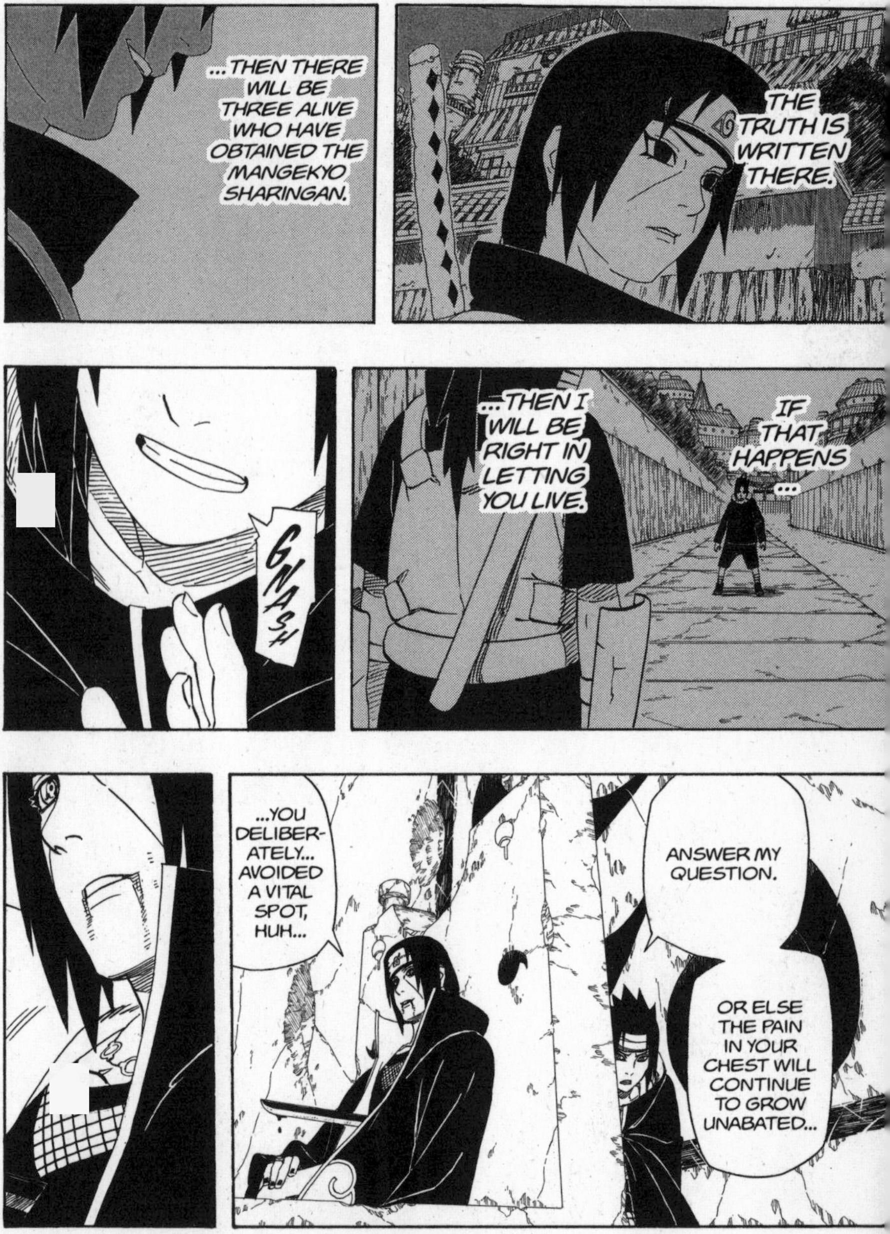
THE TRUTH IS WRITTEN THERE.
...THEN THERE WILL BE THREE ALIVE WHO HAVE OBTAINED THE MANGEKYO SHARINGAN.
IF THAT HAPPENS...
...THEN I WILL BE RIGHT IN LETTING YOU LIVE.
GNASH
ANSWER MY QUESTION.
OR ELSE THE PAIN IN YOUR CHEST WILL CONTINUE TO GROW UNABATED...
...YOU DELIBER-ATELY... AVOIDED A VITAL SPOT, HUH...

READ THIS WAY

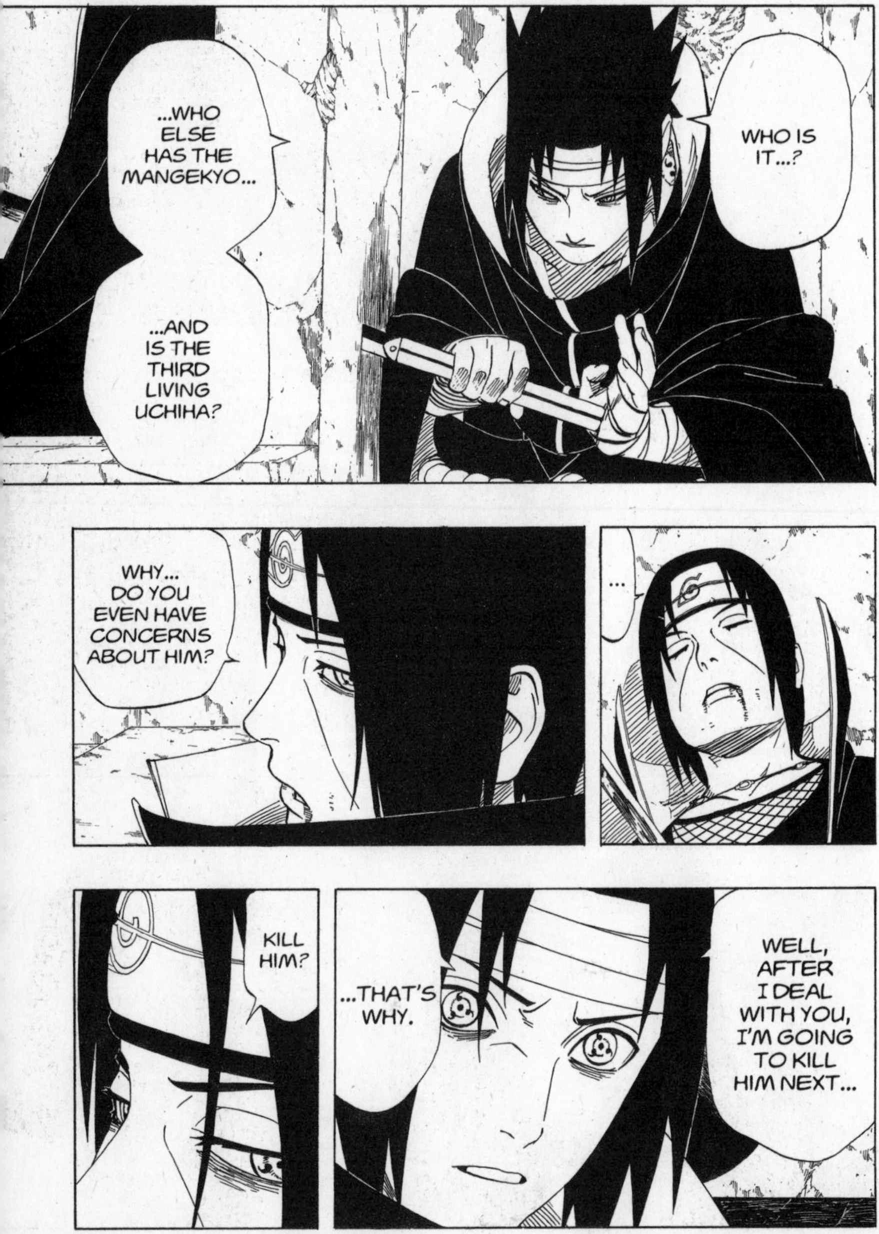
WHO IS IT...?
...WHO ELSE HAS THE MANGEKYO...
...AND IS THE THIRD LIVING UCHIHA?
...
WHY... DO YOU EVEN HAVE CONCERNS ABOUT HIM?
WELL, AFTER I DEAL WITH YOU, I'M GOING TO KILL HIM NEXT...
...THAT'S WHY.
KILL HIM?

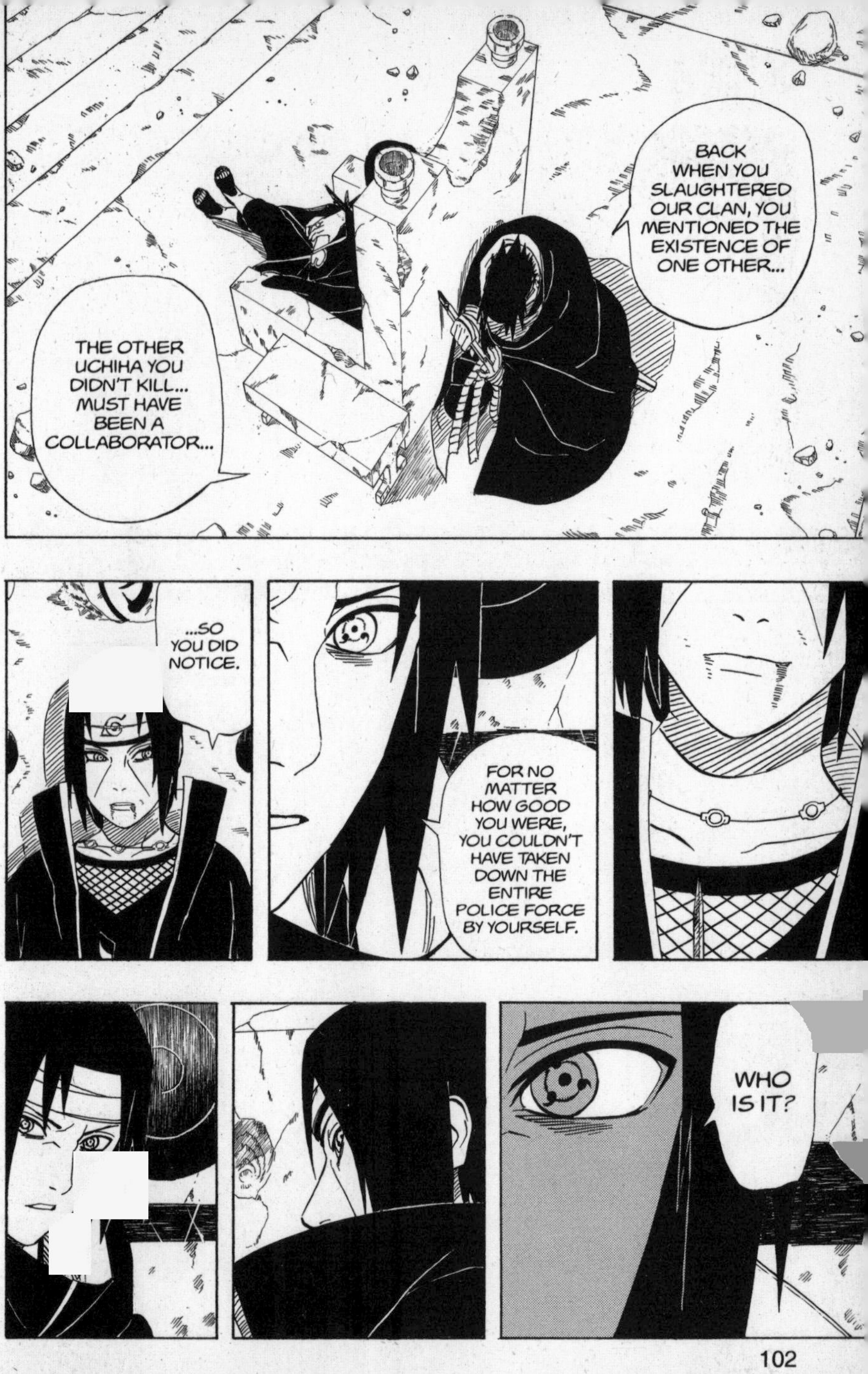
BACK WHEN YOU SLAUGHTERED OUR CLAN, YOU MENTIONED THE EXISTENCE OF ONE OTHER...
THE OTHER UCHIHA YOU DIDN'T KILL... MUST HAVE BEEN A COLLABORATOR...
FOR NO MATTER HOW GOOD YOU WERE, YOU COULDN'T HAVE TAKEN DOWN THE ENTIRE POLICE FORCE BY YOURSELF.
...SO YOU DID NOTICE.
WHO IS IT?

READ THIS WAY

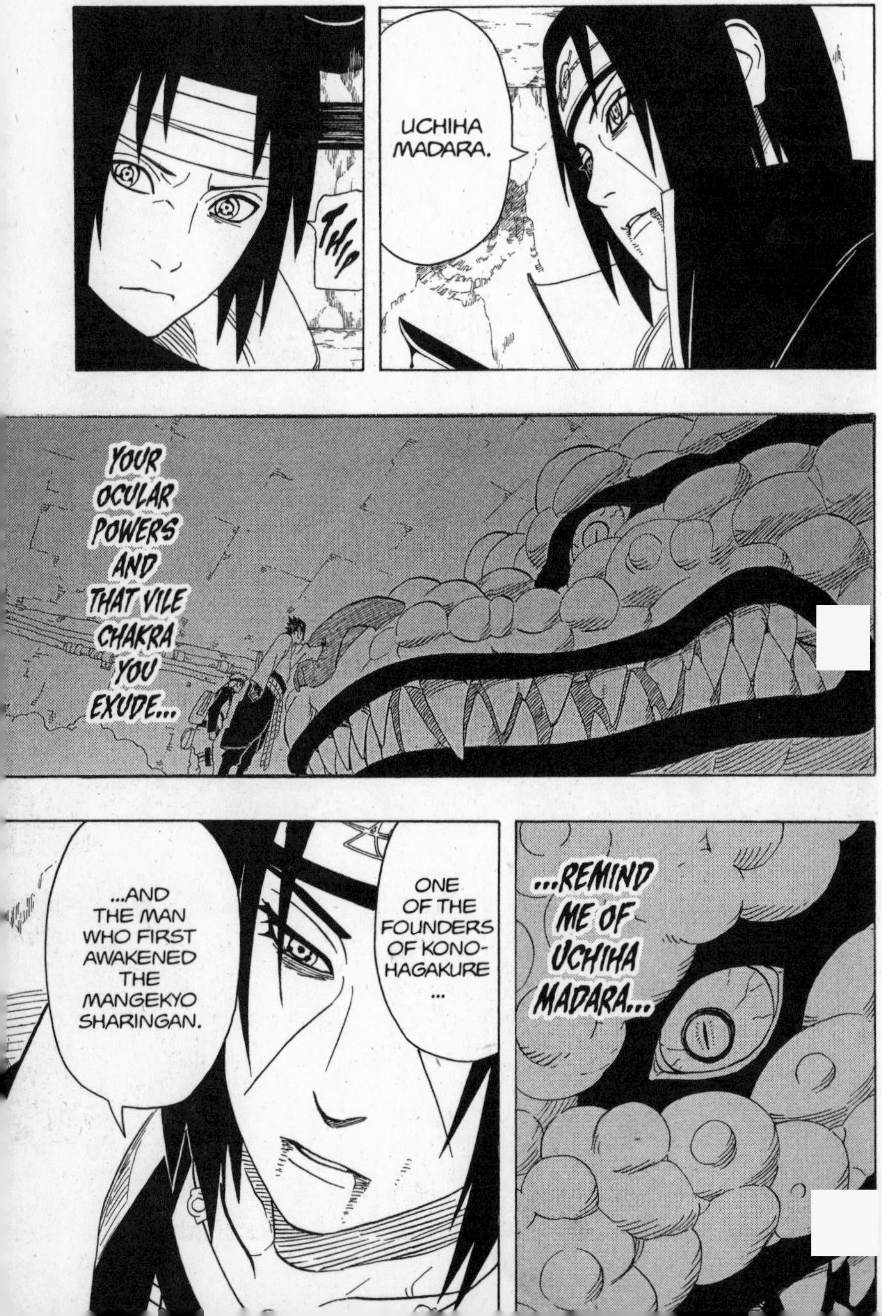
UCHIHA MADARA.
THIP
YOUR OCULAR POWERS AND THAT VILE CHAKRA YOU EXUDE...
...REMIND ME OF UCHIHA MADARA...
ONE OF THE FOUNDERS OF KONO-HAGAKURE ...
...AND THE MAN WHO FIRST AWAKENED THE MANGEKYO SHARINGAN.

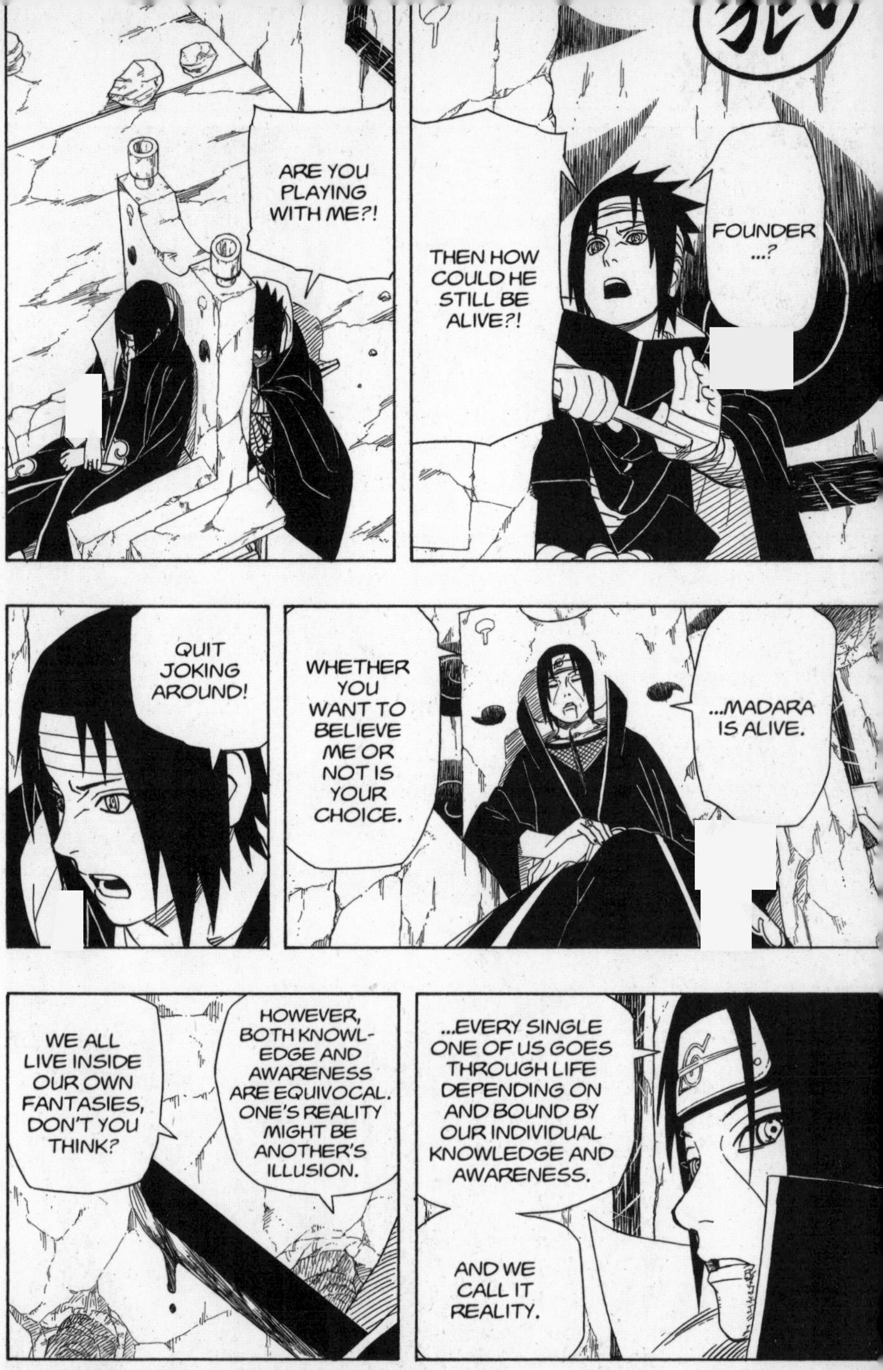
FOUNDER ...?
THEN HOW COULD HE STILL BE ALIVE?!
ARE YOU PLAYING WITH ME?!
...MADARA IS ALIVE.
WHETHER YOU WANT TO BELIEVE ME OR NOT IS YOUR CHOICE.
QUIT JOKING AROUND!
...EVERY SINGLE ONE OF US GOES THROUGH LIFE DEPENDING ON AND BOUND BY OUR INDIVIDUAL KNOWLEDGE AND AWARENESS.
AND WE CALL IT REALITY.
HOWEVER, BOTH KNOWL-EDGE AND AWARENESS ARE EQUIVOCAL. ONE'S REALITY MIGHT BE ANOTHER'S ILLUSION.
WE ALL LIVE INSIDE OUR OWN FANTASIES, DON'T YOU THINK?

READ THIS WAY

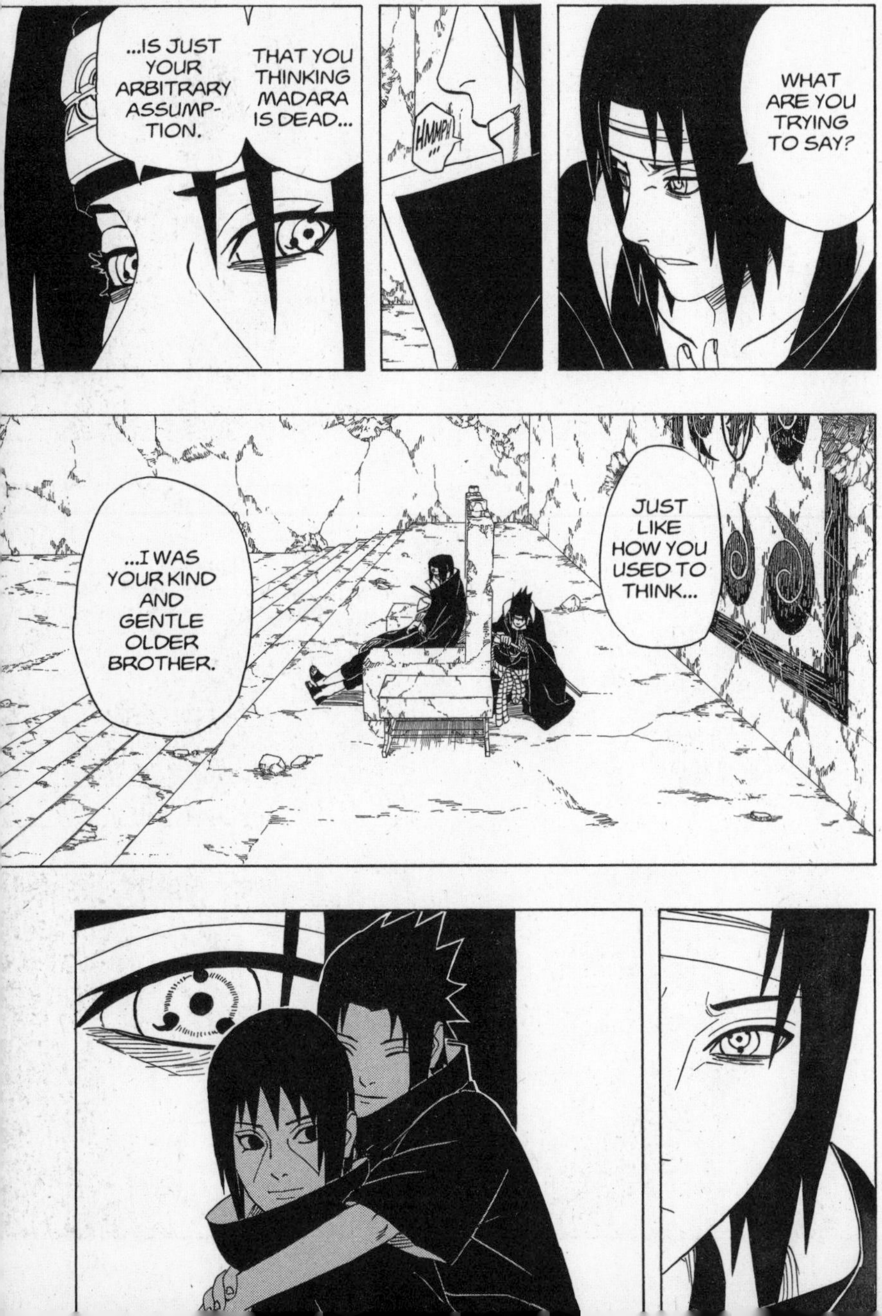
WHAT ARE YOU TRYING TO SAY?
HMMPH...
THAT YOU THINKING MADARA IS DEAD...
...IS JUST YOUR ARBITRARY ASSUMP-TION.
JUST LIKE HOW YOU USED TO THINK...
...I WAS YOUR KIND AND GENTLE OLDER BROTHER.

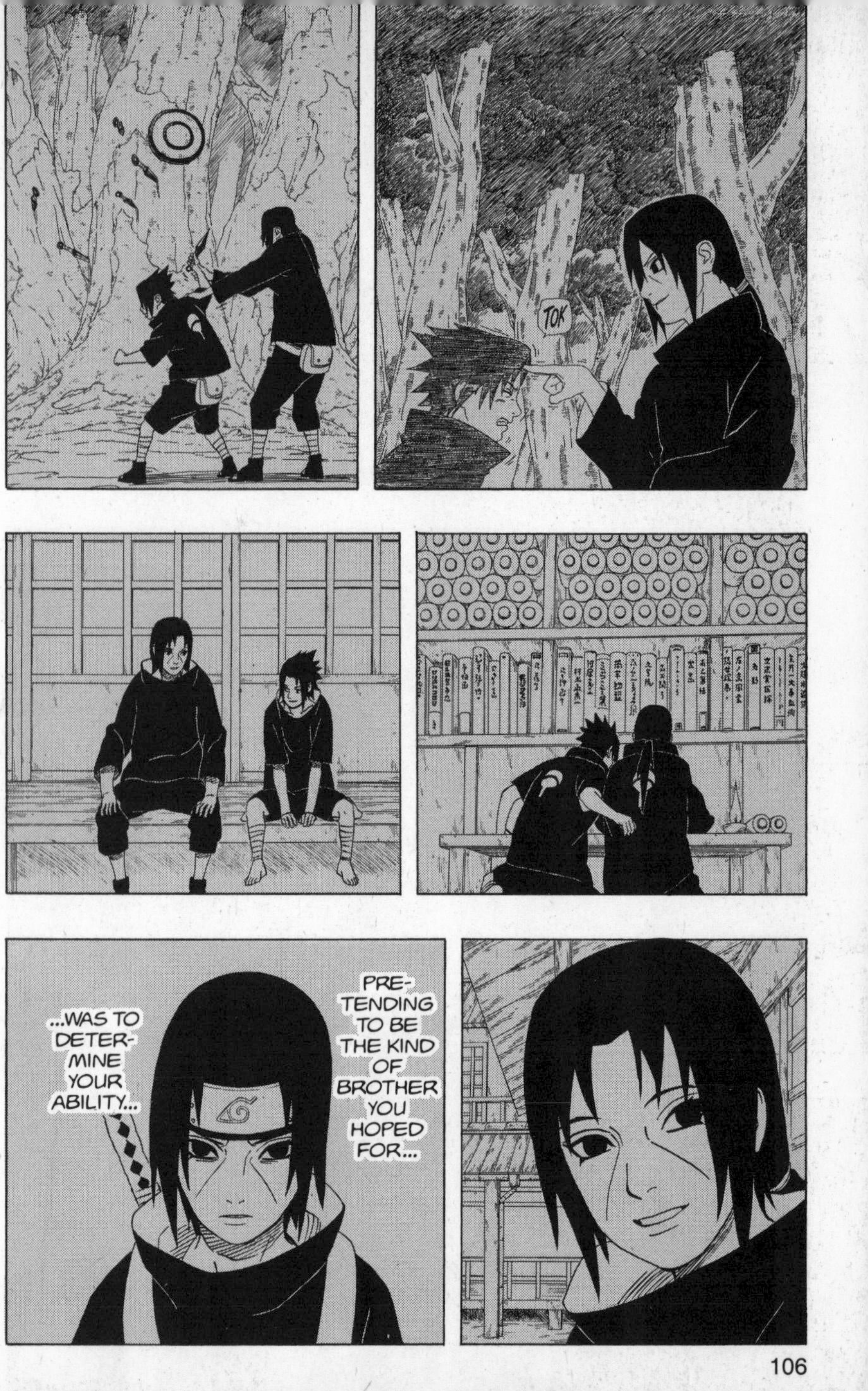
TOK
PRE-
TENDING
TO BE
THE KIND
OF
BROTHER
YOU
HOPED
FOR...
...WAS TO
DETER-
MINE
YOUR
ABILITY...

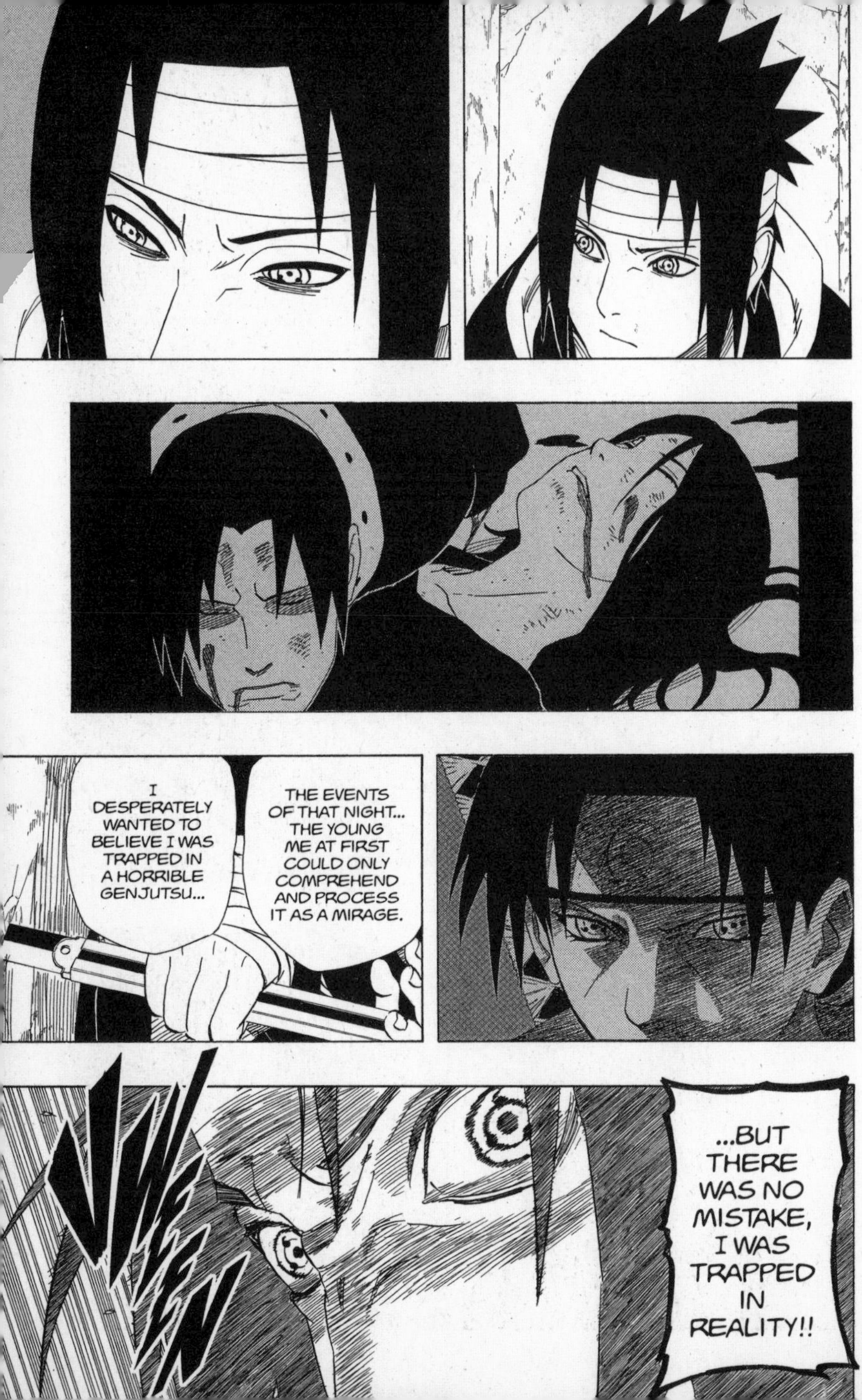
THE EVENTS OF THAT NIGHT... THE YOUNG ME AT FIRST COULD ONLY COMPREHEND AND PROCESS IT AS A MIRAGE.
I DESPERATELY WANTED TO BELIEVE I WAS TRAPPED IN A HORRIBLE GENJUTSU...
...BUT THERE WAS NO MISTAKE, I WAS TRAPPED IN REALITY!!

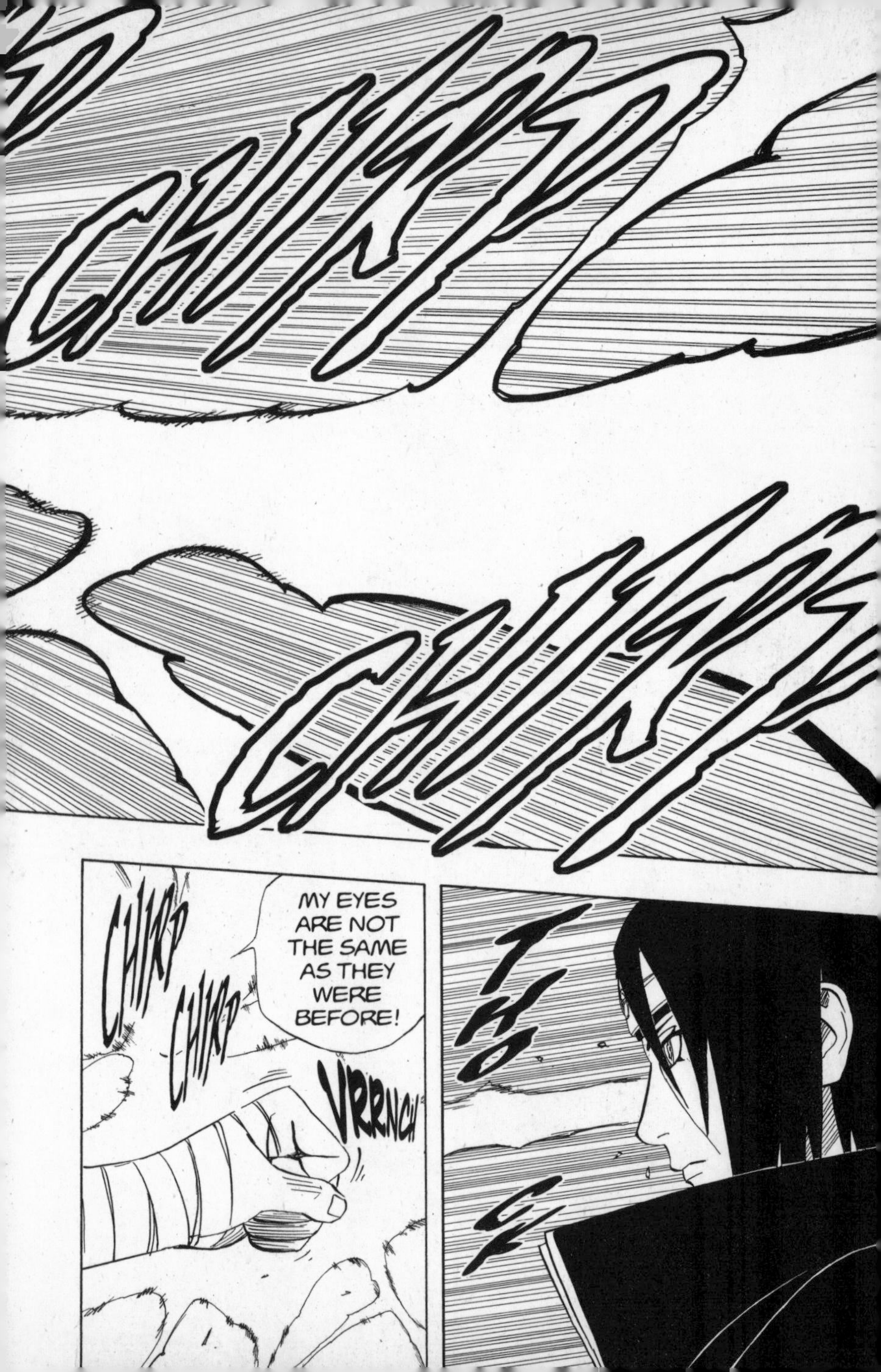
CHIRP
CHIRP
MY EYES ARE NOT THE SAME AS THEY WERE BEFORE!
CHIRP
CHIRP
VRRNCH

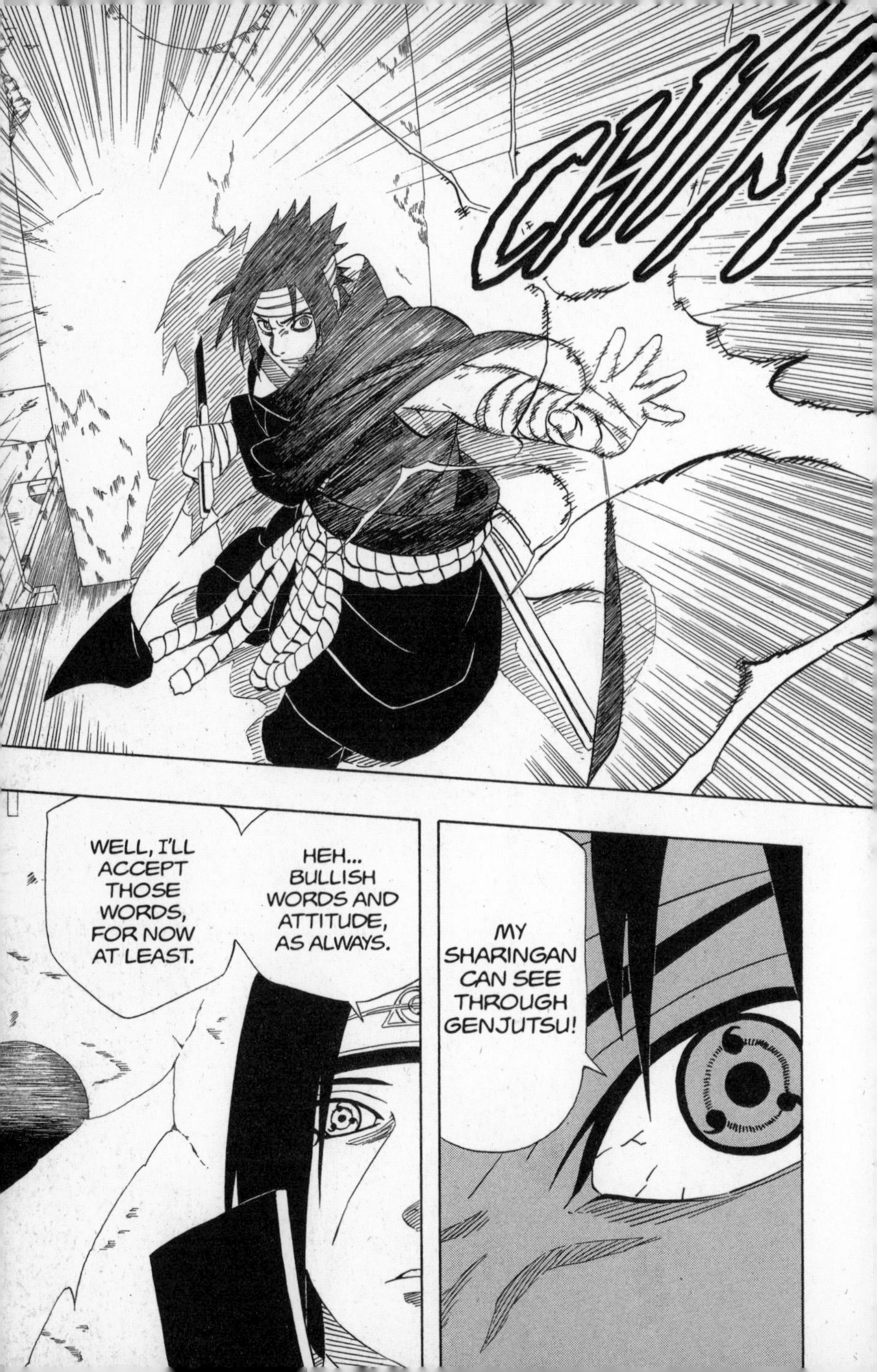
MY SHARINGAN CAN SEE THROUGH GENJUTSU!
HEH... BULLISH WORDS AND ATTITUDE, AS ALWAYS.
WELL, I'LL ACCEPT THOSE WORDS, FOR NOW AT LEAST.

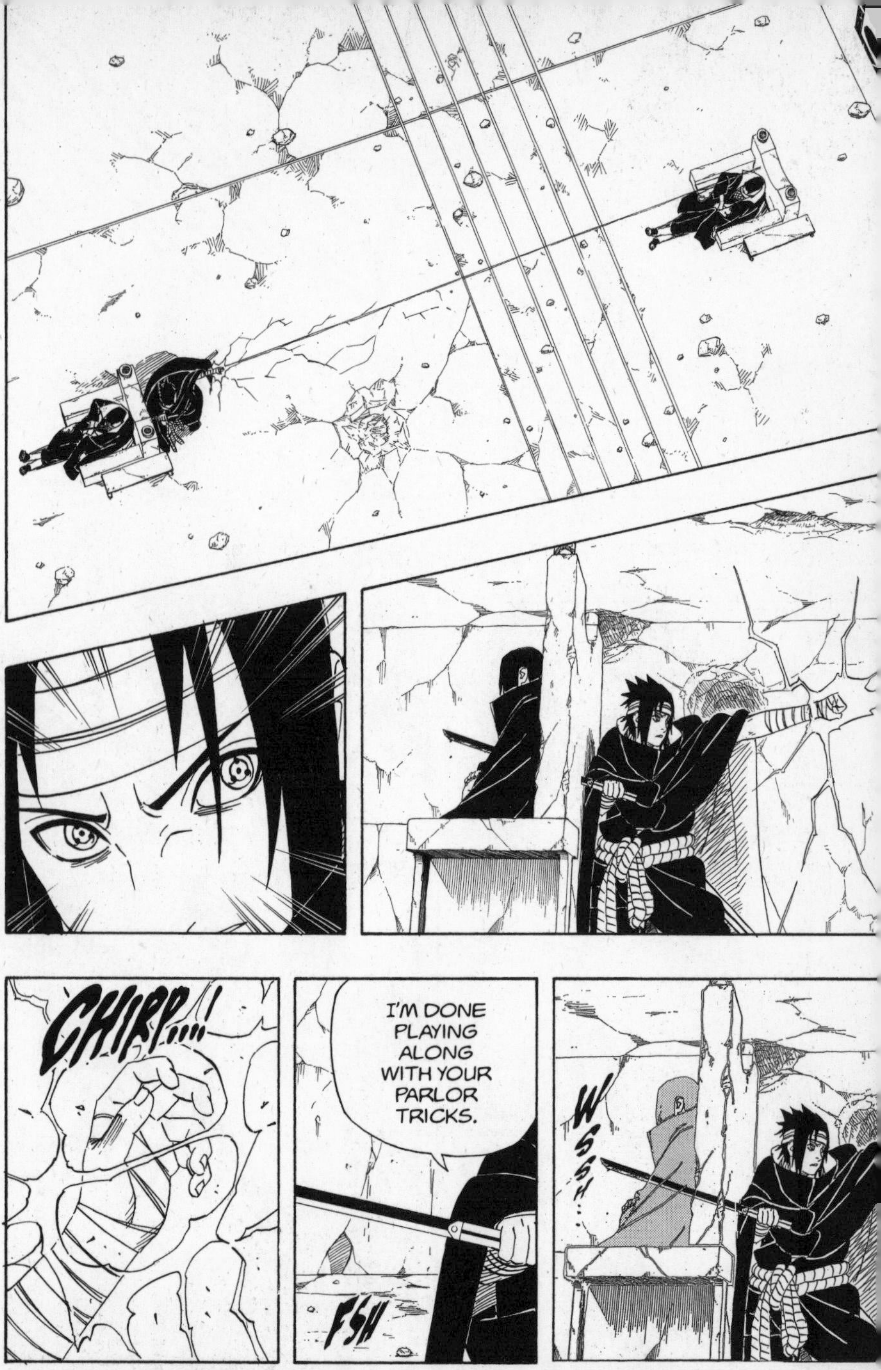
WSSH...
I'M DONE PLAYING ALONG WITH YOUR PARLOR TRICKS.
FSH
CHIRP....!

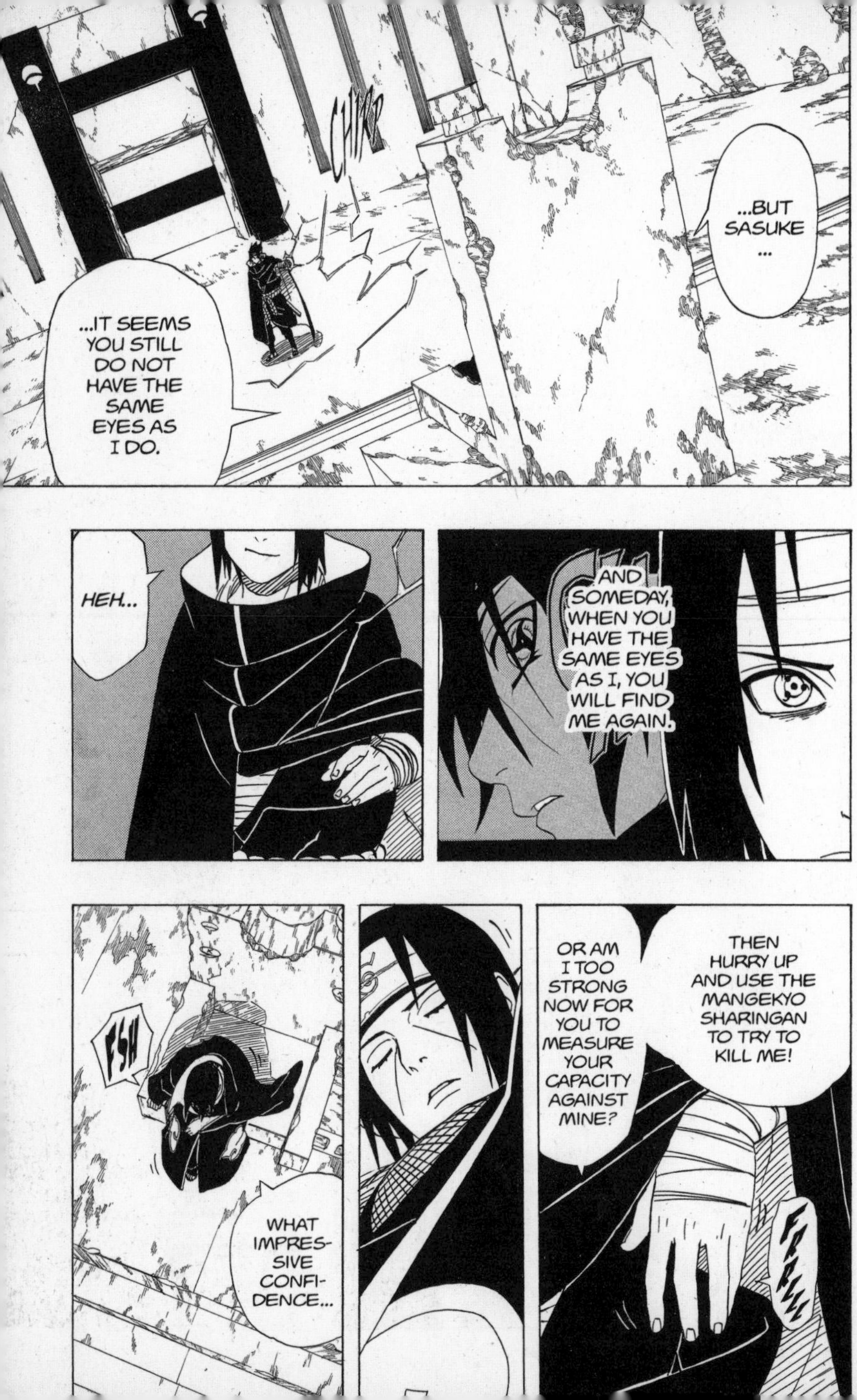
CHIRP
...BUT SASUKE ...
...IT SEEMS YOU STILL DO NOT HAVE THE SAME EYES AS I DO.
AND SOMEDAY, WHEN YOU HAVE THE SAME EYES AS I, YOU WILL FIND ME AGAIN.
HEH...
THEN HURRY UP AND USE THE MANGEKYO SHARINGAN TO TRY TO KILL ME!
OR AM I TOO STRONG NOW FOR YOU TO MEASURE YOUR CAPACITY AGAINST MINE?
FSH
WHAT IMPRES-SIVE CONFI-DENCE...

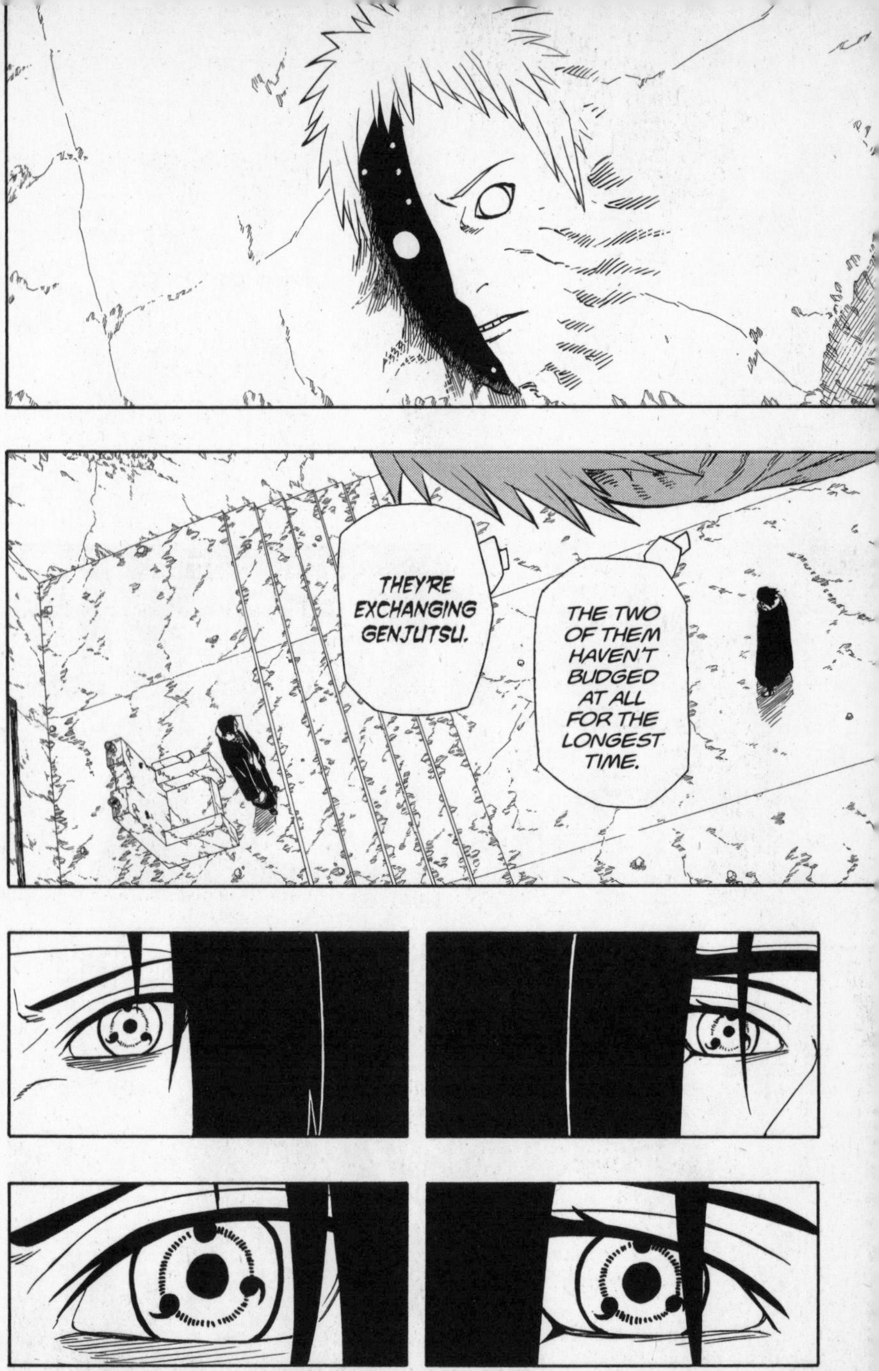
THE TWO OF THEM HAVEN'T BUDGED AT ALL FOR THE LONGEST TIME.
THEY'RE EXCHANGING GENJUTSU.

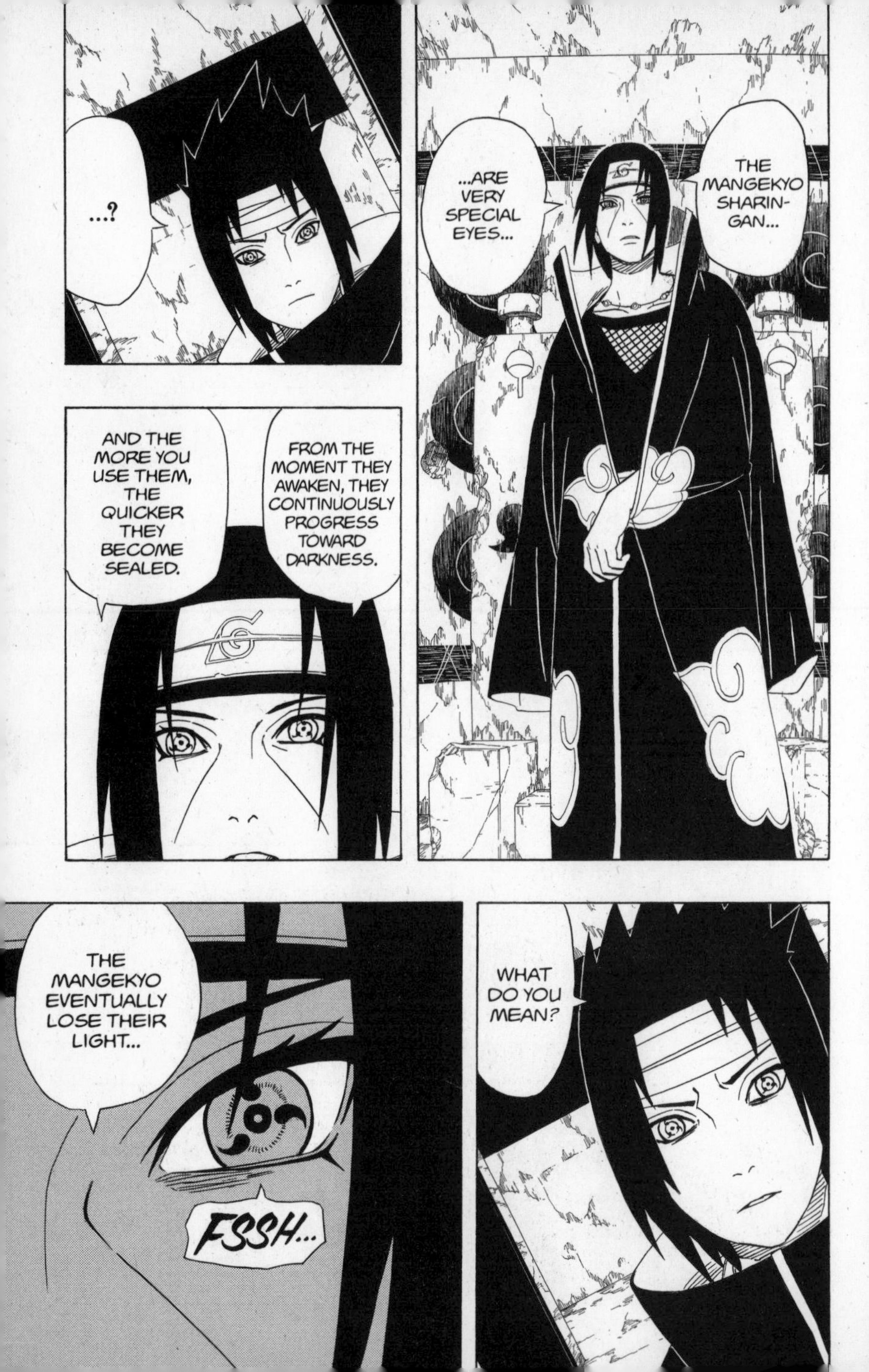
THE MANGEKYO SHARINGAN...
...ARE VERY SPECIAL EYES...
...?
FROM THE MOMENT THEY AWAKEN, THEY CONTINUOUSLY PROGRESS TOWARD DARKNESS.
AND THE MORE YOU USE THEM, THE QUICKER THEY BECOME SEALED.
WHAT DO YOU MEAN?
THE MANGEKYO EVENTUALLY LOSE THEIR LIGHT...
FSSH...

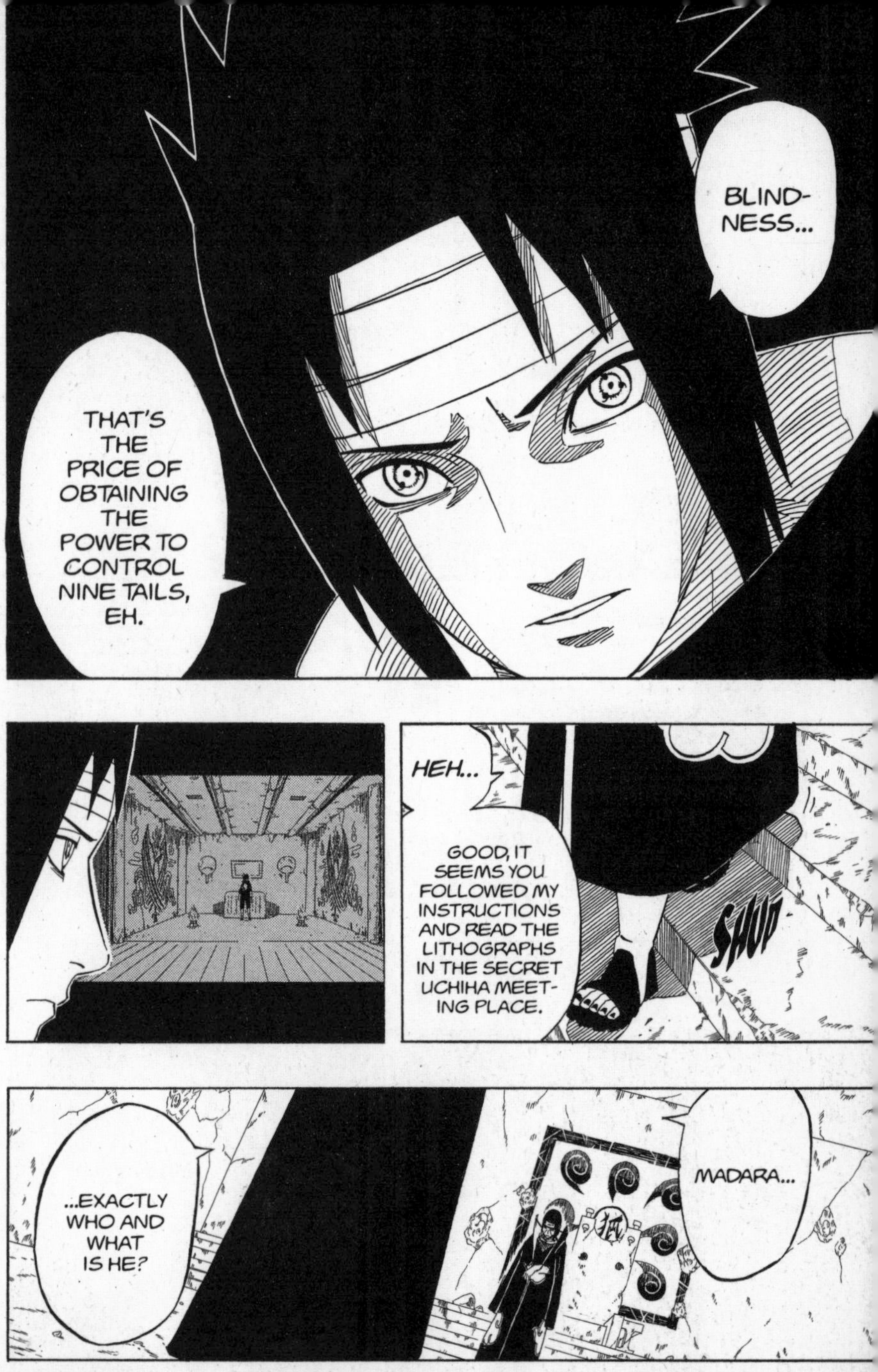
BLIND-NESS...
THAT'S THE PRICE OF OBTAINING THE POWER TO CONTROL NINE TAILS, EH.
HEH...
GOOD, IT SEEMS YOU FOLLOWED MY INSTRUCTIONS AND READ THE LITHOGRAPHS IN THE SECRET UCHIHA MEET-ING PLACE.
SHUP
MADARA...
...EXACTLY WHO AND WHAT IS HE?

READ THIS WAY

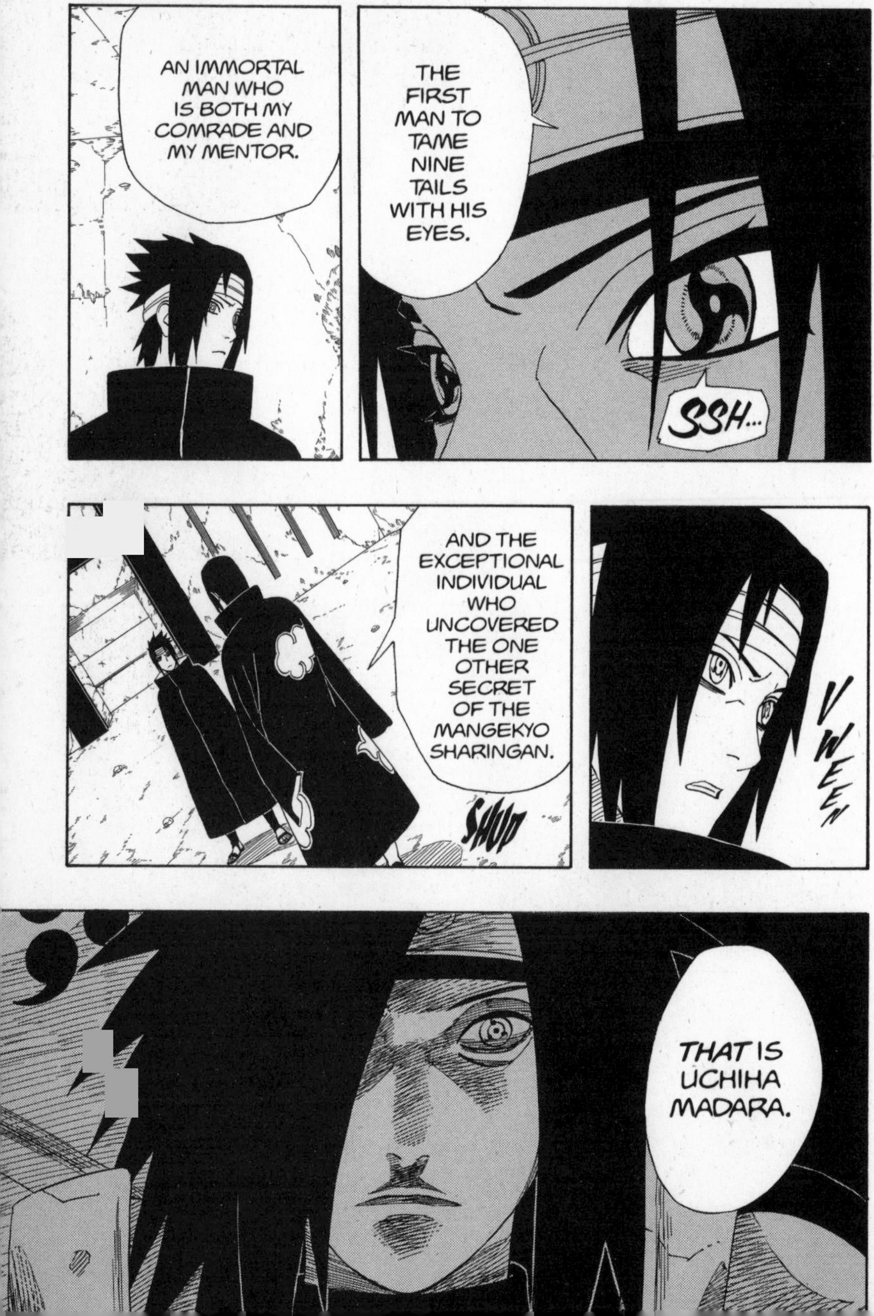
THE FIRST MAN TO TAME NINE TAILS WITH HIS EYES.
SSH...
AN IMMORTAL MAN WHO IS BOTH MY COMRADE AND MY MENTOR.
VWEEN
AND THE EXCEPTIONAL INDIVIDUAL WHO UNCOVERED THE ONE OTHER SECRET OF THE MANGEKYO SHARINGAN.
SHUP
THAT IS UCHIHA MADARA.

NARUTO

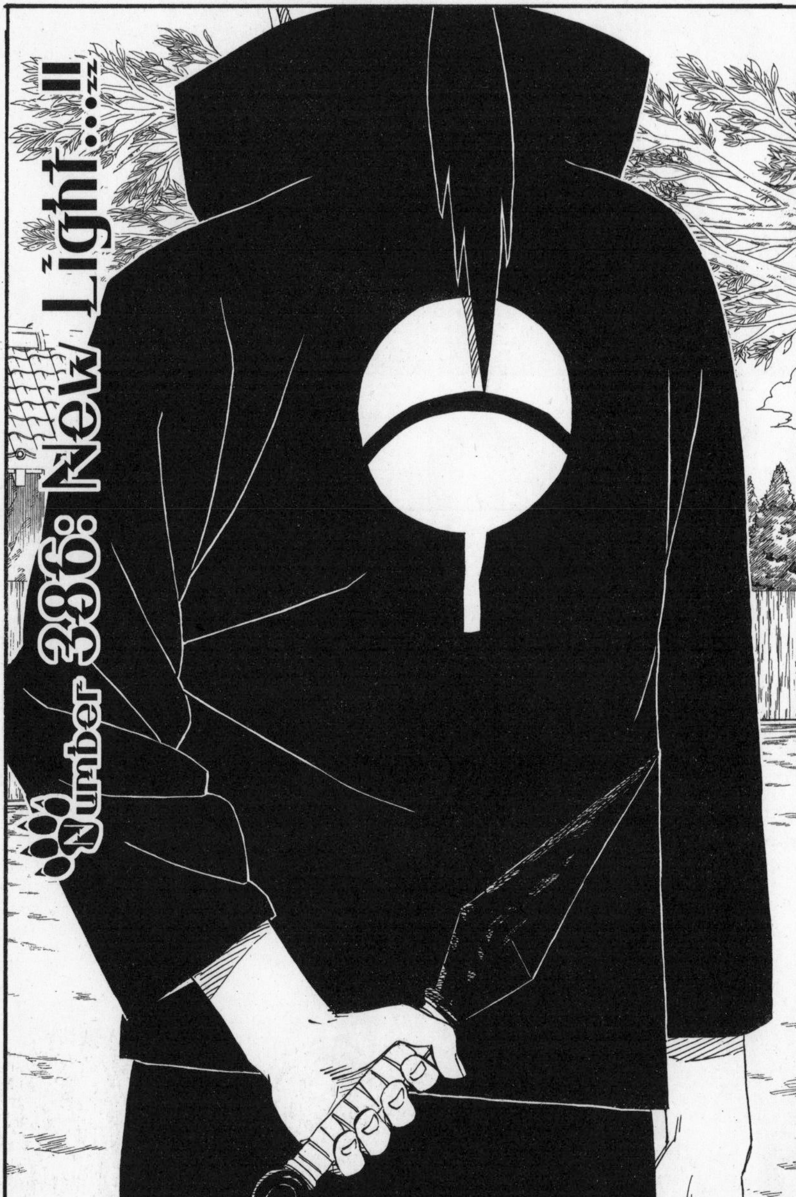
Number 386: New Light…!!

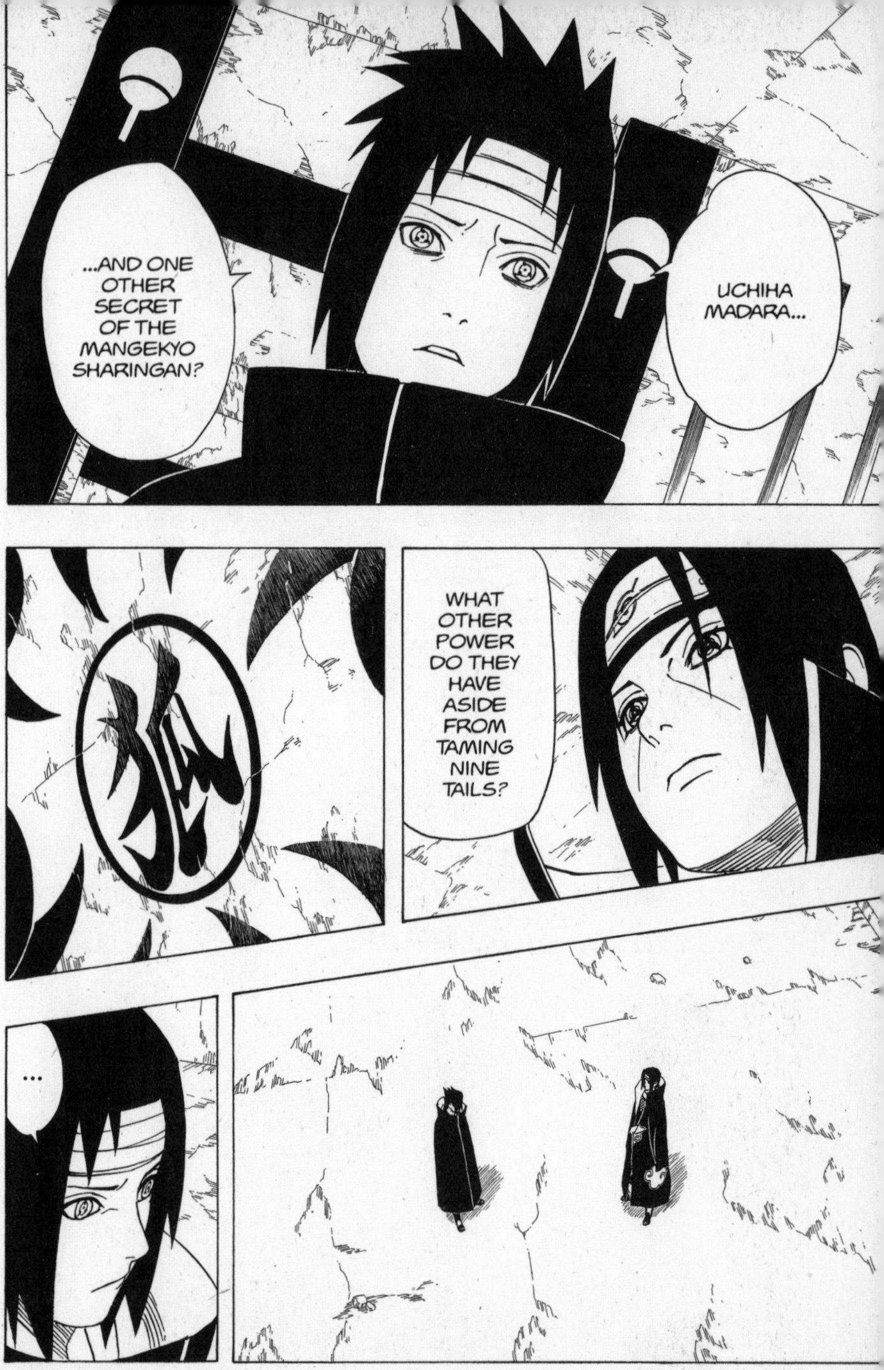
UCHIHA MADARA...
...AND ONE OTHER SECRET OF THE MANGEKYO SHARINGAN?
WHAT OTHER POWER DO THEY HAVE ASIDE FROM TAMING NINE TAILS?
...

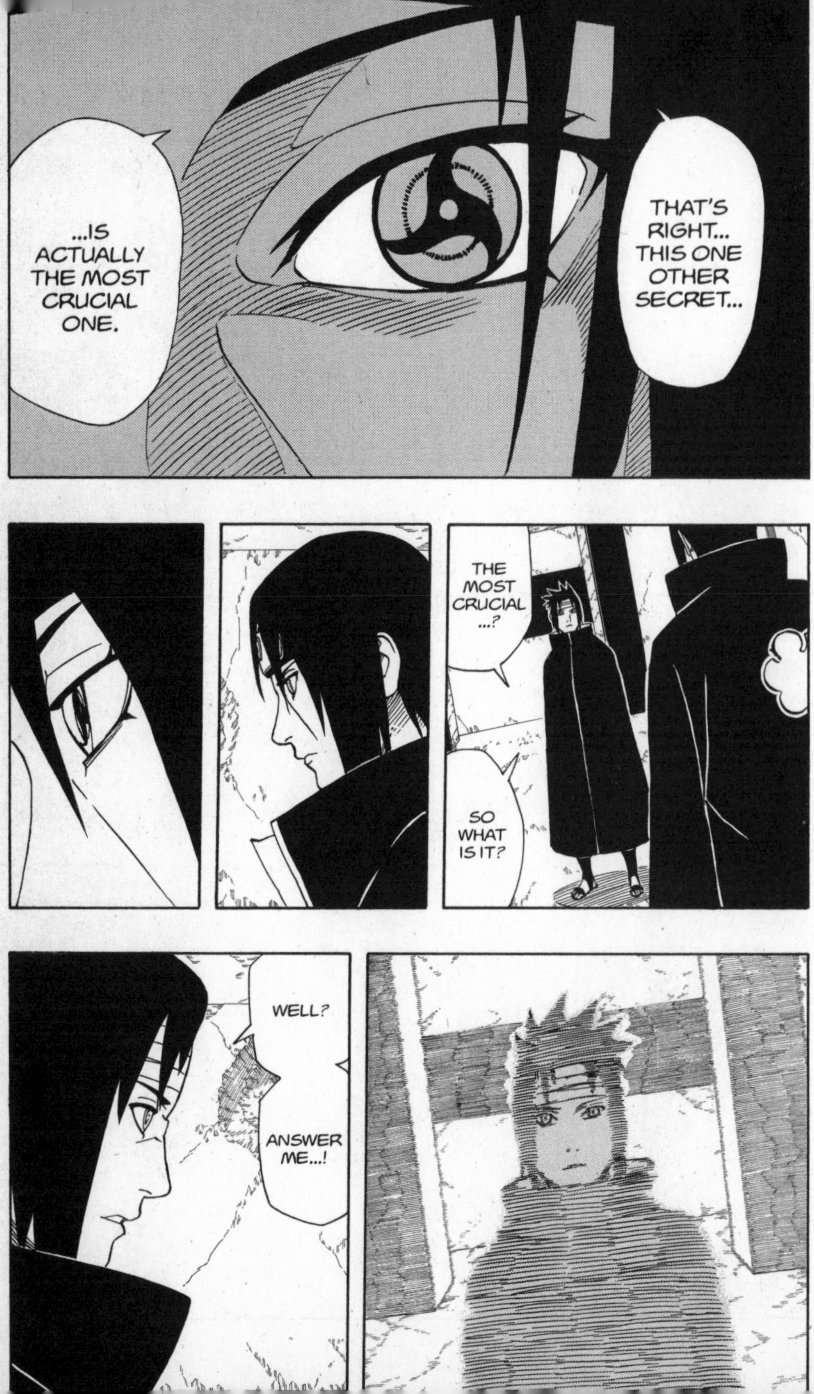
THAT'S RIGHT... THIS ONE OTHER SECRET...
...IS ACTUALLY THE MOST CRUCIAL ONE.
THE MOST CRUCIAL ...?
SO WHAT IS IT?
WELL?
ANSWER ME...!

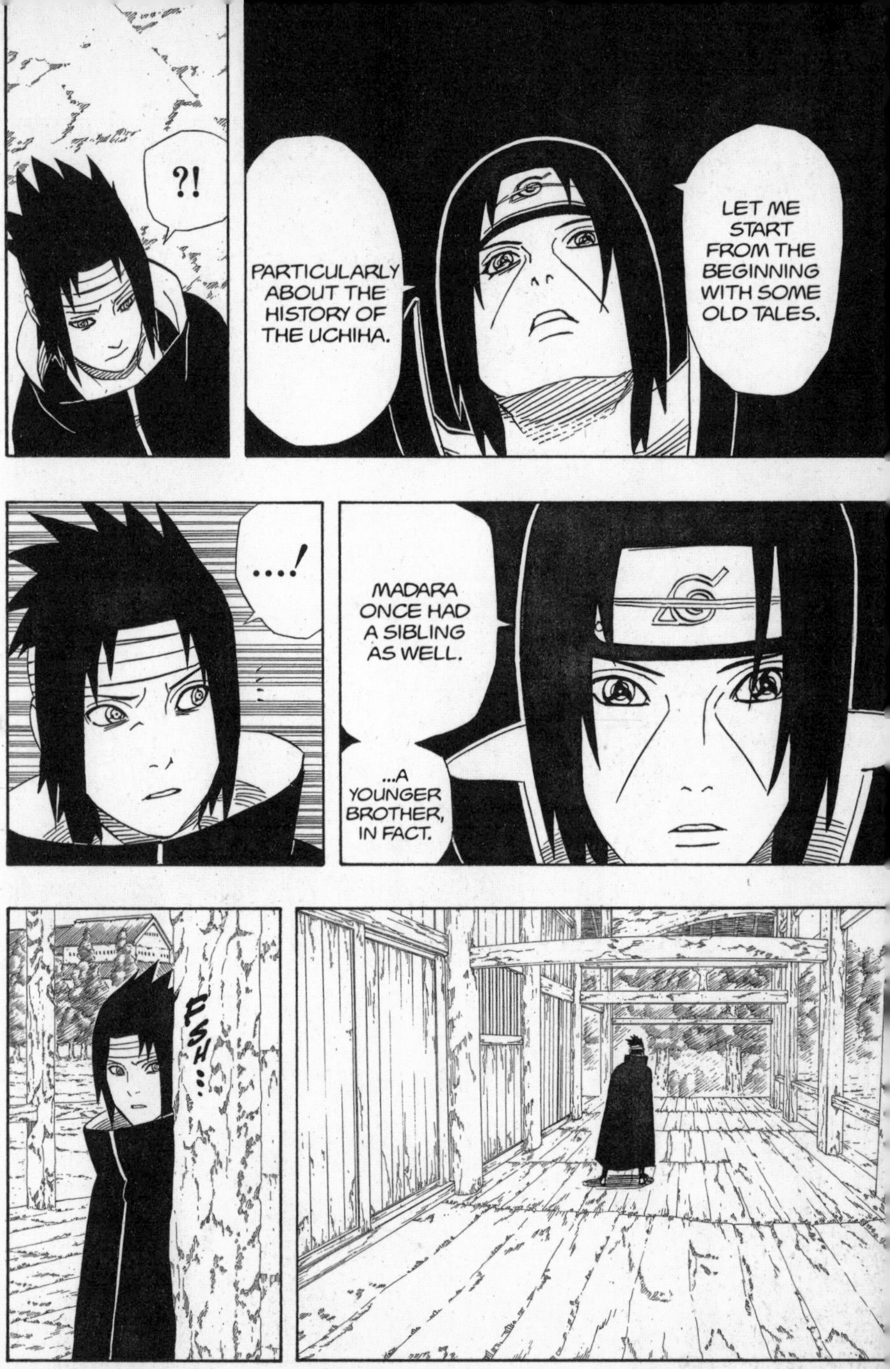
LET ME START FROM THE BEGINNING WITH SOME OLD TALES.
PARTICULARLY ABOUT THE HISTORY OF THE UCHIHA.
?!
MADARA ONCE HAD A SIBLING AS WELL.
...A YOUNGER BROTHER, IN FACT.
....!
FSH...

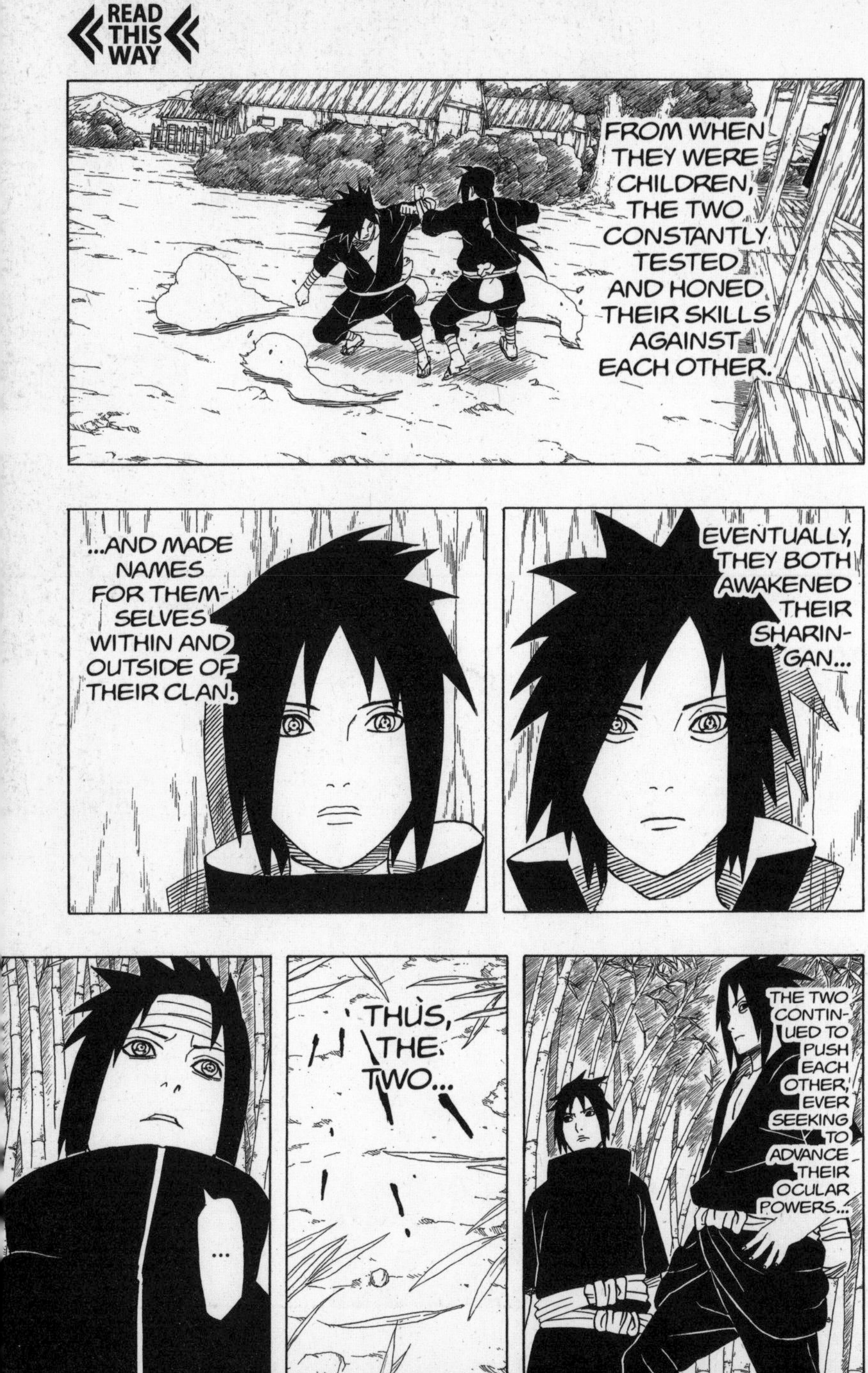
READ THIS WAY
FROM WHEN THEY WERE CHILDREN, THE TWO CONSTANTLY TESTED AND HONED THEIR SKILLS AGAINST EACH OTHER.
EVENTUALLY, THEY BOTH AWAKENED THEIR SHARIN-GAN...
...AND MADE NAMES FOR THEM-SELVES WITHIN AND OUTSIDE OF THEIR CLAN.
THE TWO CONTIN-UED TO PUSH EACH OTHER, EVER SEEKING TO ADVANCE THEIR OCULAR POWERS...
THUS, THE TWO...
...

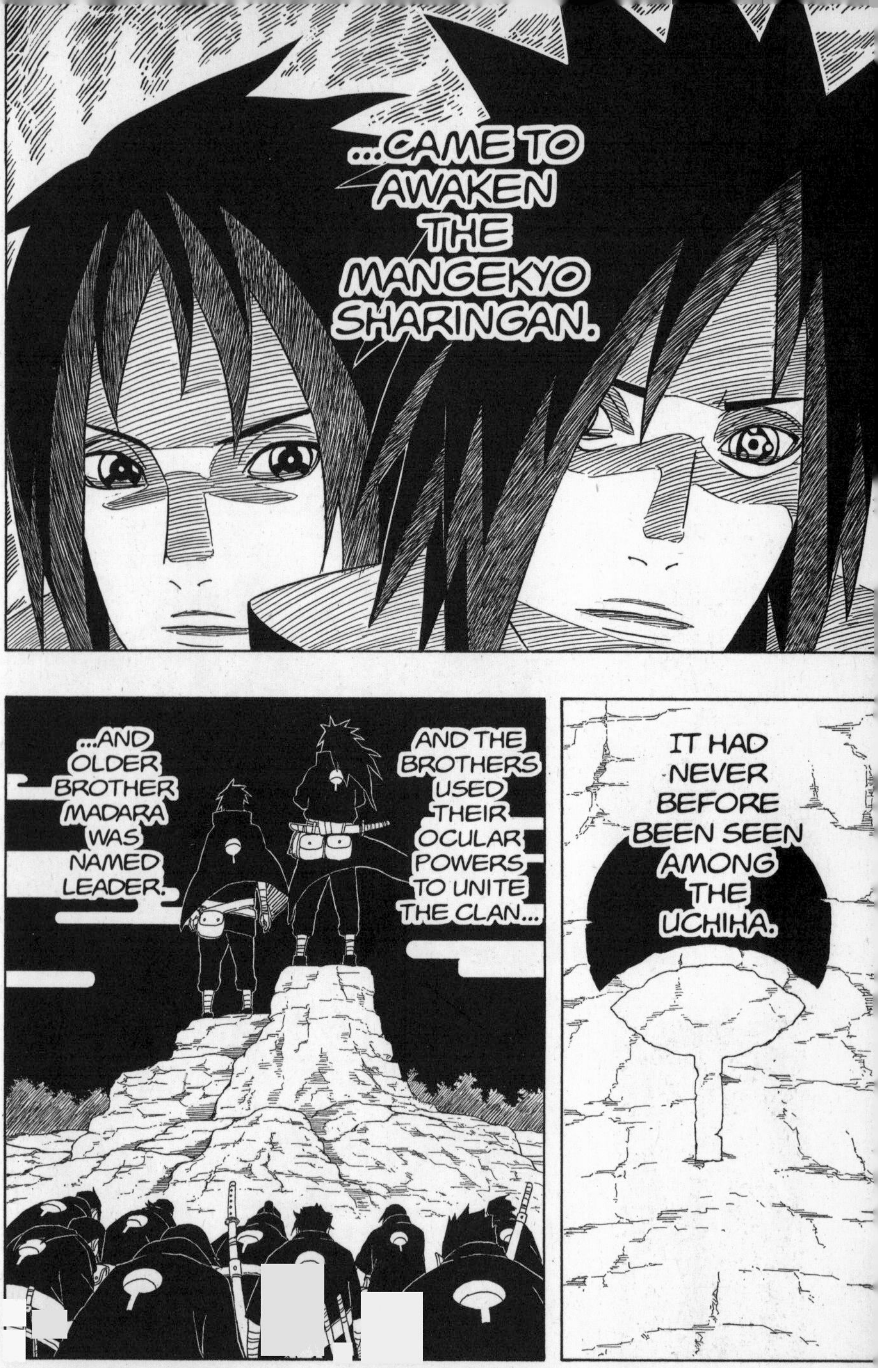
...CAME TO AWAKEN THE MANGEKYO SHARINGAN.
IT HAD NEVER BEFORE BEEN SEEN AMONG THE UCHIHA.
AND THE BROTHERS USED THEIR OCULAR POWERS TO UNITE THE CLAN...
...AND OLDER BROTHER MADARA WAS NAMED LEADER.

READ THIS WAY

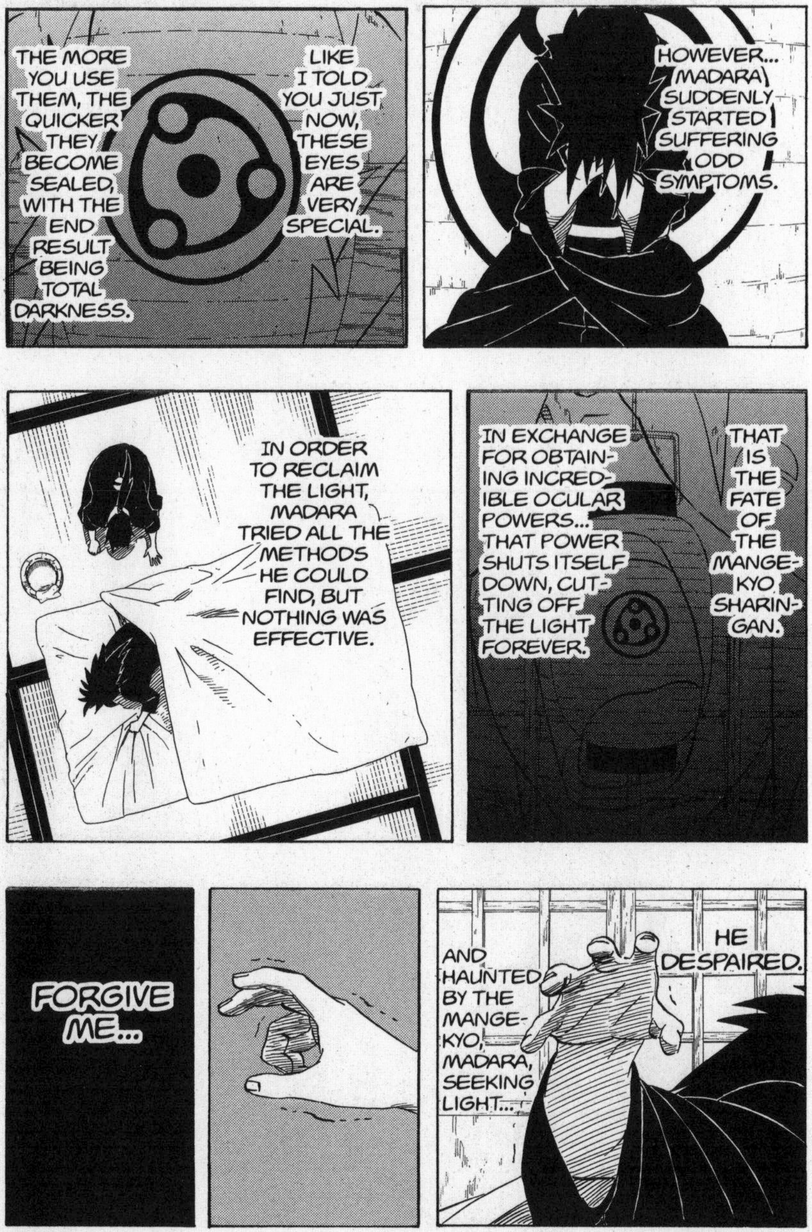
HOWEVER... MADARA SUDDENLY STARTED SUFFERING ODD SYMPTOMS.
LIKE I TOLD YOU JUST NOW, THESE EYES ARE VERY SPECIAL.
THE MORE YOU USE THEM, THE QUICKER THEY BECOME SEALED, WITH THE END RESULT BEING TOTAL DARKNESS.
THAT IS THE FATE OF THE MANGE-KYO SHARIN-GAN.
IN EXCHANGE FOR OBTAIN-ING INCRED-IBLE OCULAR POWERS... THAT POWER SHUTS ITSELF DOWN, CUT-TING OFF THE LIGHT FOREVER.
IN ORDER TO RECLAIM THE LIGHT, MADARA TRIED ALL THE METHODS HE COULD FIND, BUT NOTHING WAS EFFECTIVE.
HE DESPAIRED.
AND HAUNTED BY THE MANGE-KYO, MADARA, SEEKING LIGHT...
FORGIVE ME...

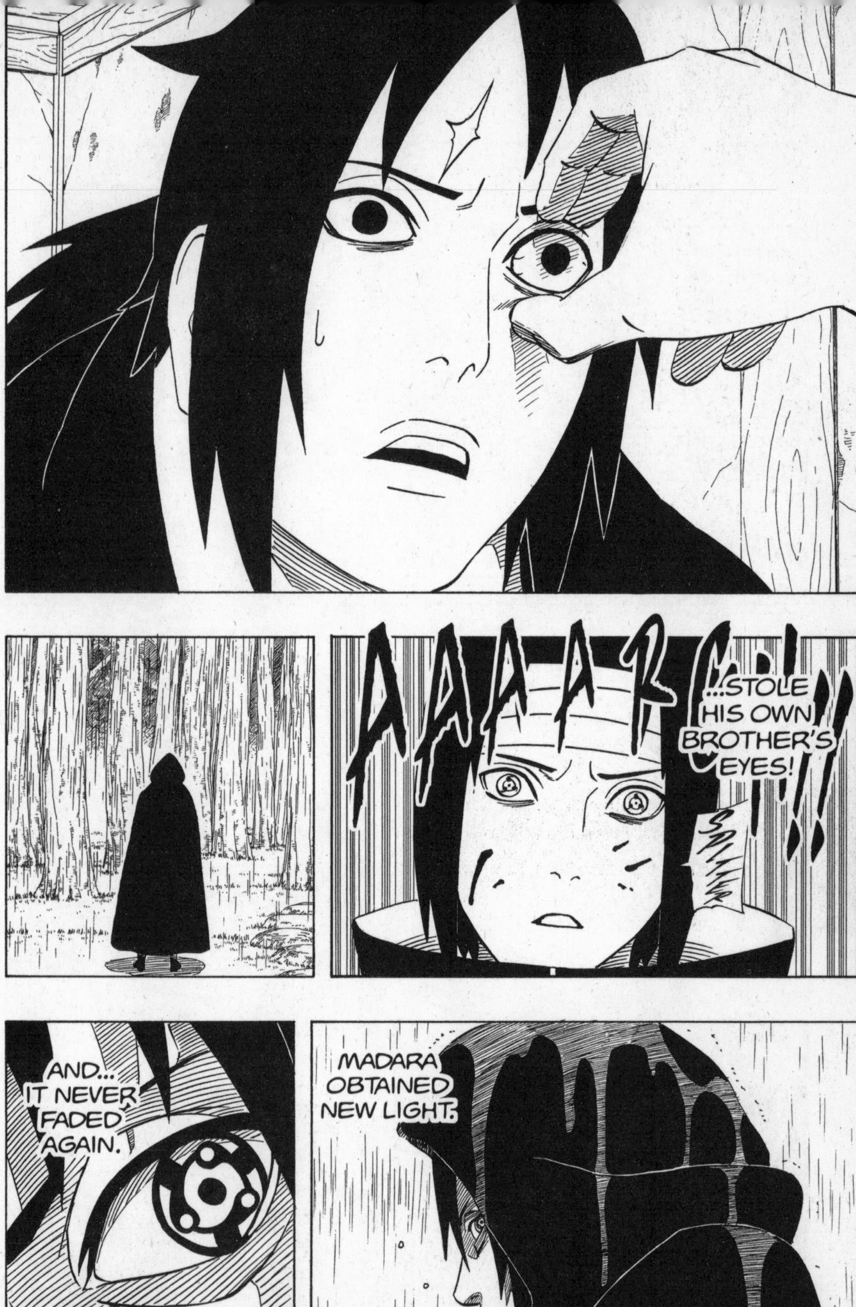
AAAARG
...STOLE HIS OWN BROTHER'S EYES!
MADARA OBTAINED NEW LIGHT.
AND... IT NEVER FADED AGAIN.

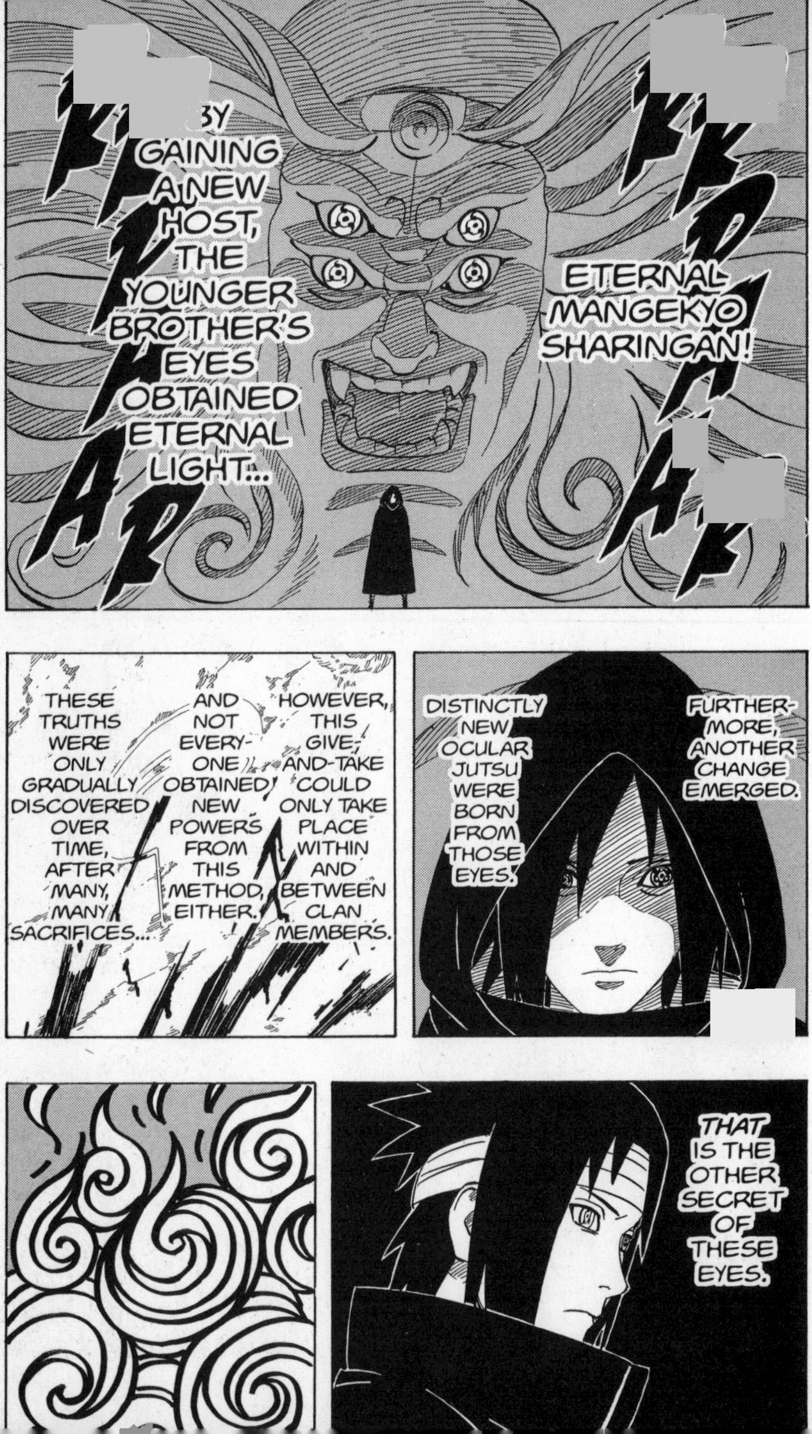
BY GAINING A NEW HOST, THE YOUNGER BROTHER'S EYES OBTAINED ETERNAL LIGHT...
ETERNAL MANGEKYO SHARINGAN!
FURTHERMORE, ANOTHER CHANGE EMERGED.
DISTINCTLY NEW OCULAR JUTSU WERE BORN FROM THOSE EYES.
HOWEVER, THIS GIVE-AND-TAKE COULD ONLY TAKE PLACE WITHIN AND BETWEEN CLAN MEMBERS.
AND NOT EVERYONE OBTAINED NEW POWERS FROM THIS METHOD, EITHER.
THESE TRUTHS WERE ONLY GRADUALLY DISCOVERED OVER TIME, AFTER MANY, MANY SACRIFICES...
THAT IS THE OTHER SECRET OF THESE EYES.

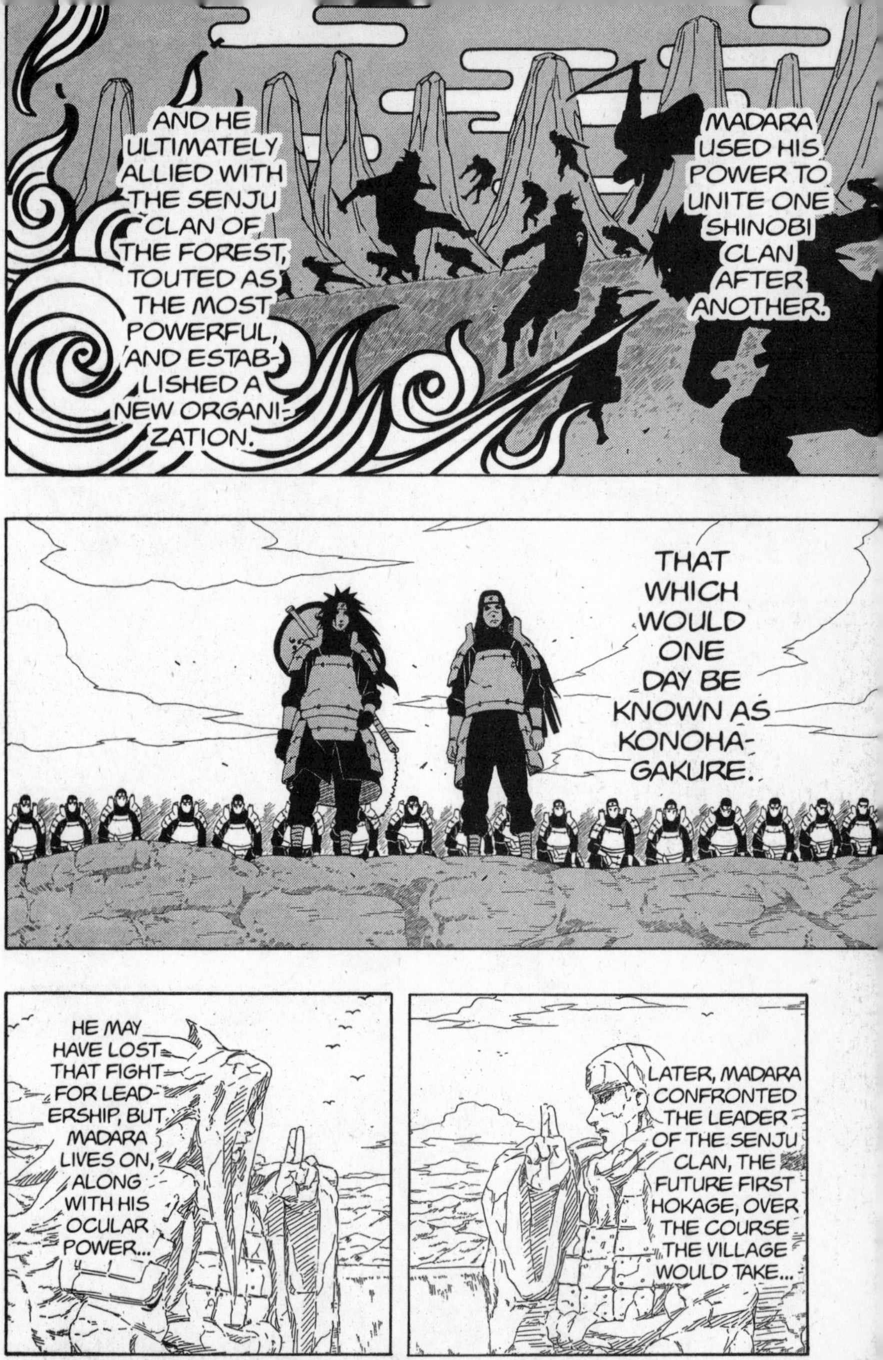
MADARA USED HIS POWER TO UNITE ONE SHINOBI CLAN AFTER ANOTHER.
AND HE ULTIMATELY ALLIED WITH THE SENJU CLAN OF THE FOREST, TOUTED AS THE MOST POWERFUL, AND ESTAB-LISHED A NEW ORGANI-ZATION.
THAT WHICH WOULD ONE DAY BE KNOWN AS KONOHA-GAKURE.
LATER, MADARA CONFRONTED THE LEADER OF THE SENJU CLAN, THE FUTURE FIRST HOKAGE, OVER THE COURSE THE VILLAGE WOULD TAKE...
HE MAY HAVE LOST THAT FIGHT FOR LEAD-ERSHIP, BUT MADARA LIVES ON, ALONG WITH HIS OCULAR POWER...

READ THIS WAY

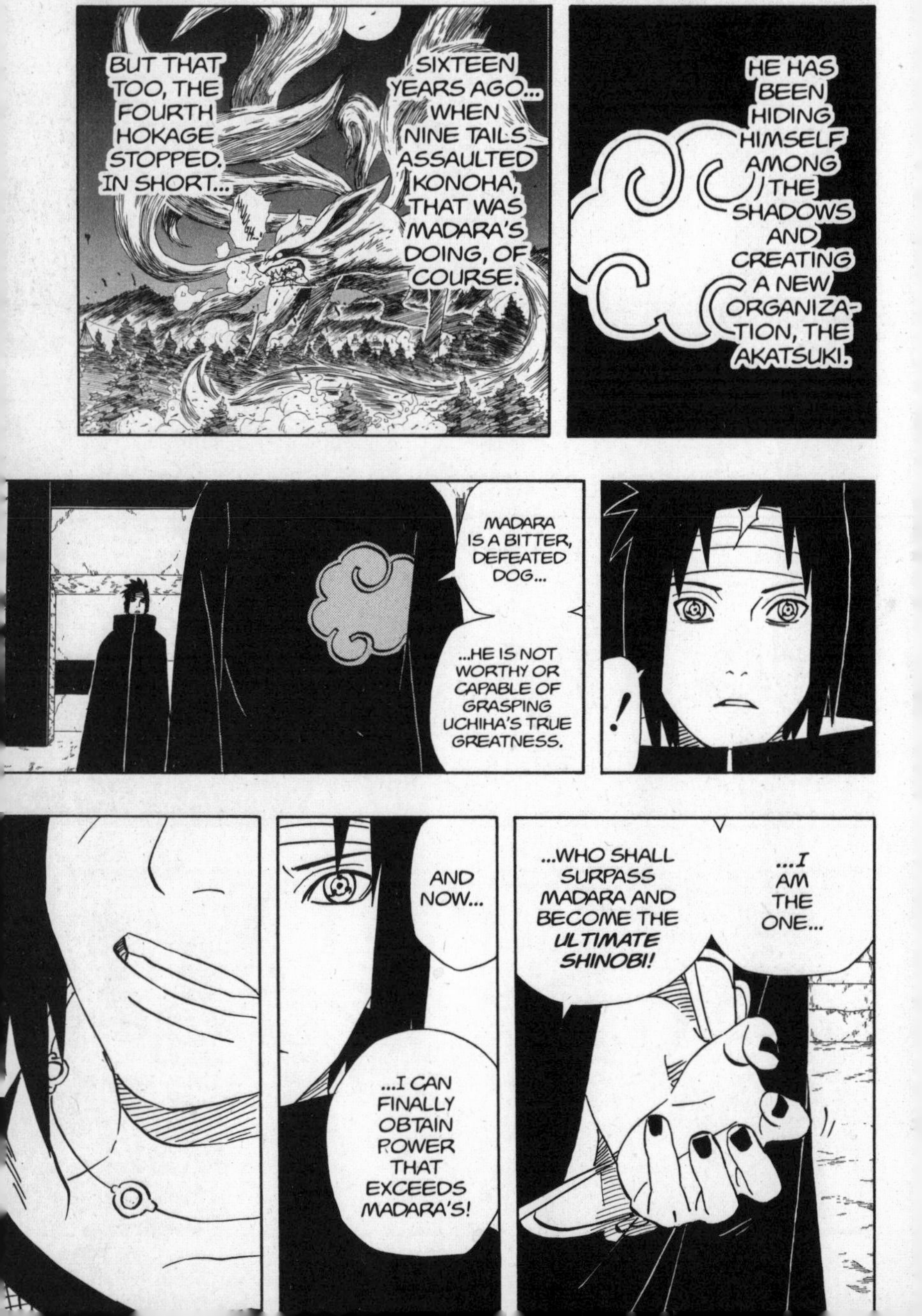
HE HAS BEEN HIDING HIMSELF AMONG THE SHADOWS AND CREATING A NEW ORGANIZATION, THE AKATSUKI.
SIXTEEN YEARS AGO... WHEN NINE TAILS ASSAULTED KONOHA, THAT WAS MADARA'S DOING, OF COURSE.
BUT THAT TOO, THE FOURTH HOKAGE STOPPED. IN SHORT...
!
MADARA IS A BITTER, DEFEATED DOG...
...HE IS NOT WORTHY OR CAPABLE OF GRASPING UCHIHA'S TRUE GREATNESS.
...I AM THE ONE...
...WHO SHALL SURPASS MADARA AND BECOME THE *ULTIMATE SHINOBI!*
AND NOW...
...I CAN FINALLY OBTAIN POWER THAT EXCEEDS MADARA'S!

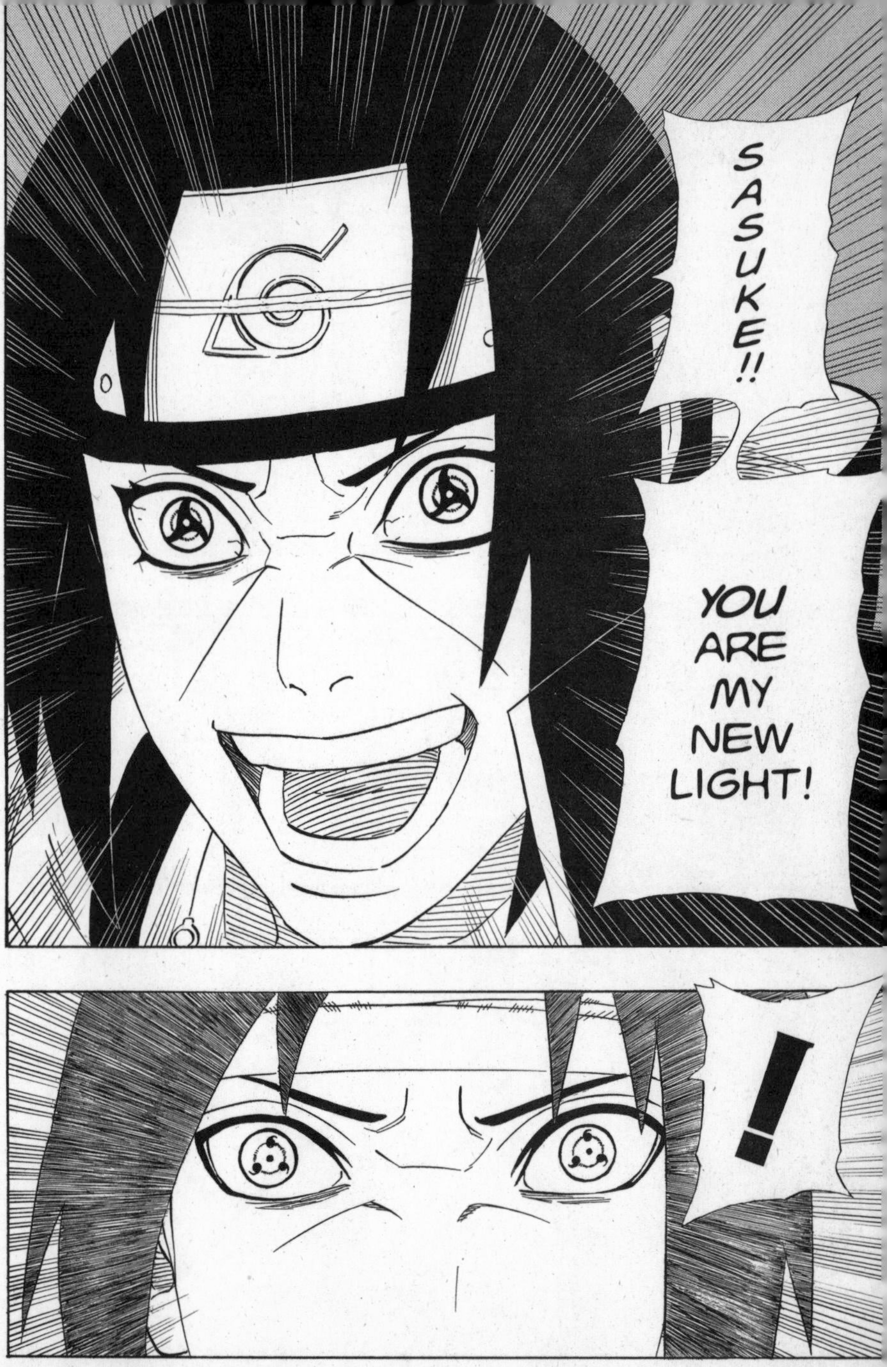
SASUKE!!
YOU ARE MY NEW LIGHT!
!

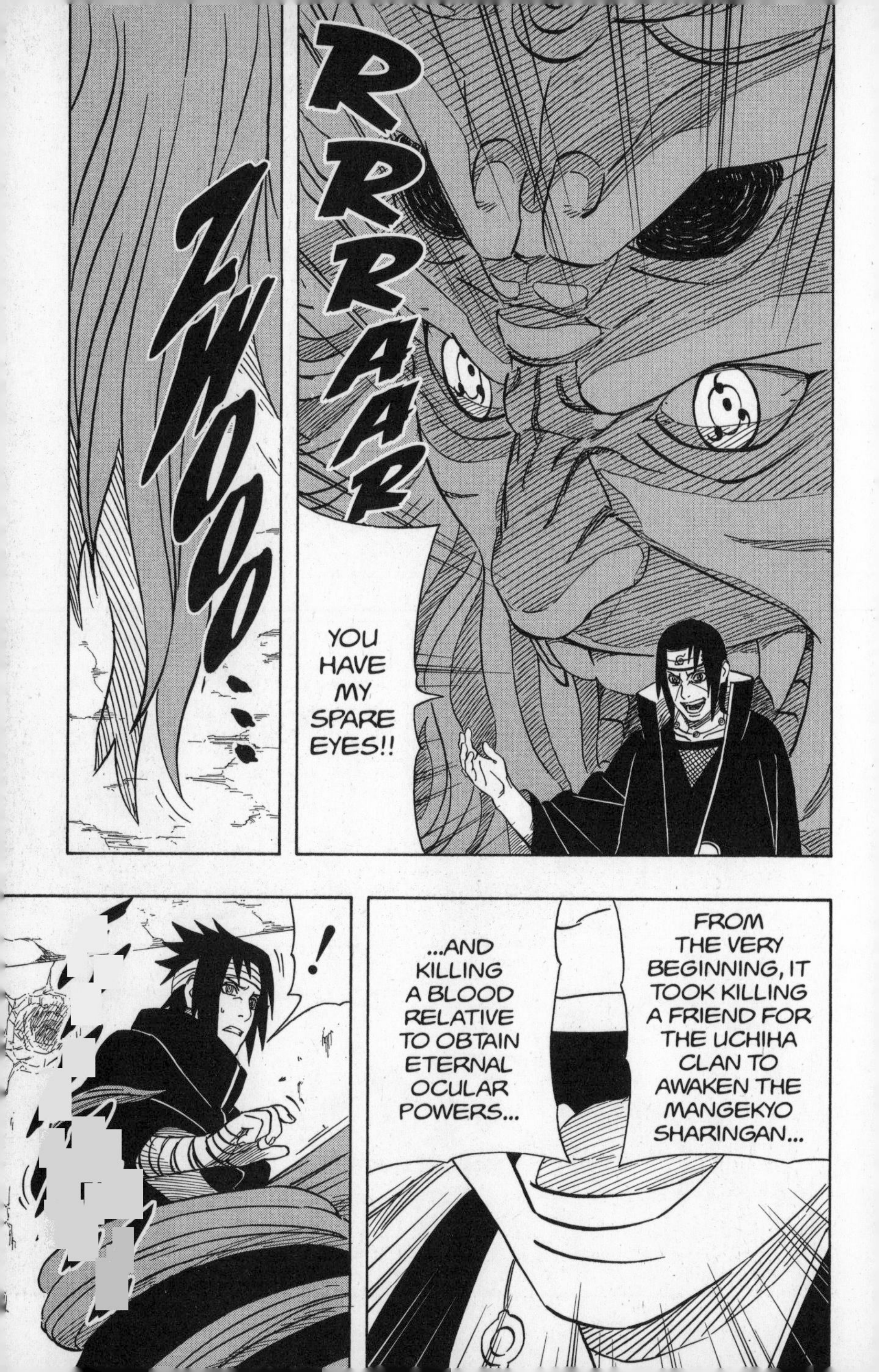
RRRAR
YOU HAVE MY SPARE EYES!!
ZWOOO
FROM THE VERY BEGINNING, IT TOOK KILLING A FRIEND FOR THE UCHIHA CLAN TO AWAKEN THE MANGEKYO SHARINGAN...
...AND KILLING A BLOOD RELATIVE TO OBTAIN ETERNAL OCULAR POWERS...
!

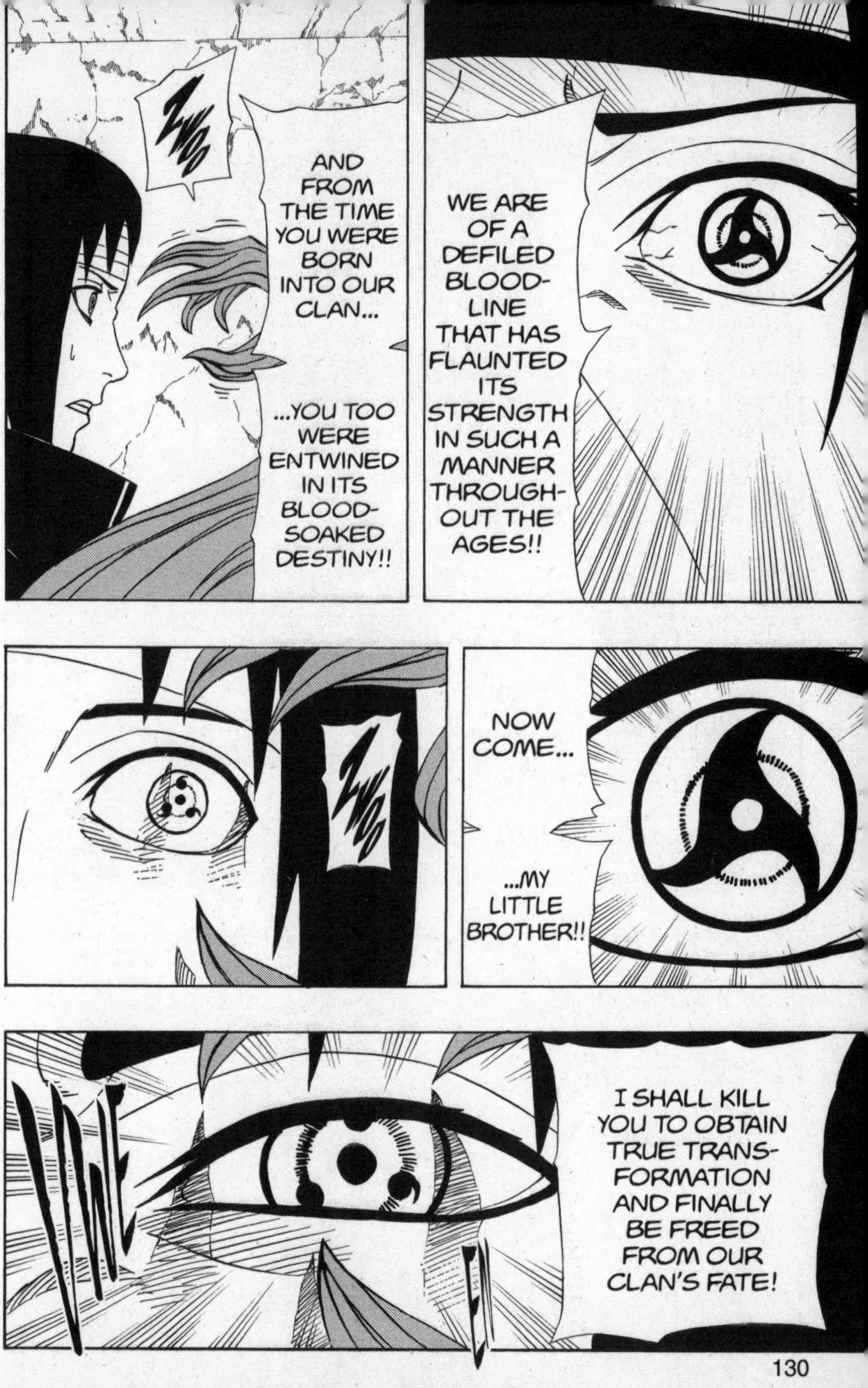
WE ARE OF A DEFILED BLOOD-LINE THAT HAS FLAUNTED ITS STRENGTH IN SUCH A MANNER THROUGH-OUT THE AGES!!
AND FROM THE TIME YOU WERE BORN INTO OUR CLAN...
...YOU TOO WERE ENTWINED IN ITS BLOOD-SOAKED DESTINY!!
NOW COME...
...MY LITTLE BROTHER!!
I SHALL KILL YOU TO OBTAIN TRUE TRANS-FORMATION AND FINALLY BE FREED FROM OUR CLAN'S FATE!

READ THIS WAY

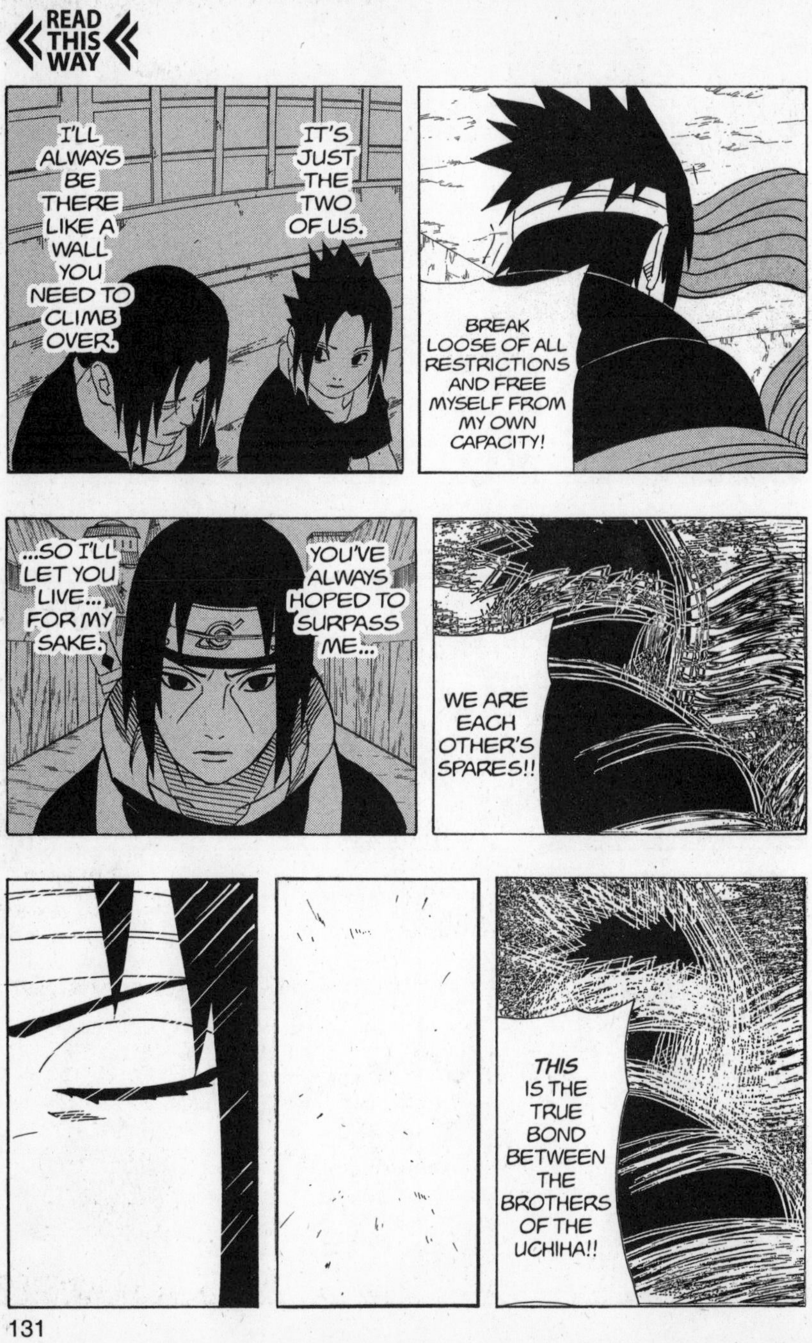
BREAK LOOSE OF ALL RESTRICTIONS AND FREE MYSELF FROM MY OWN CAPACITY!
IT'S JUST THE TWO OF US.
I'LL ALWAYS BE THERE LIKE A WALL YOU NEED TO CLIMB OVER.
WE ARE EACH OTHER'S SPARES!!
YOU'VE ALWAYS HOPED TO SURPASS ME...
...SO I'LL LET YOU LIVE... FOR MY SAKE.
THIS IS THE TRUE BOND BETWEEN THE BROTHERS OF THE UCHIHA!!

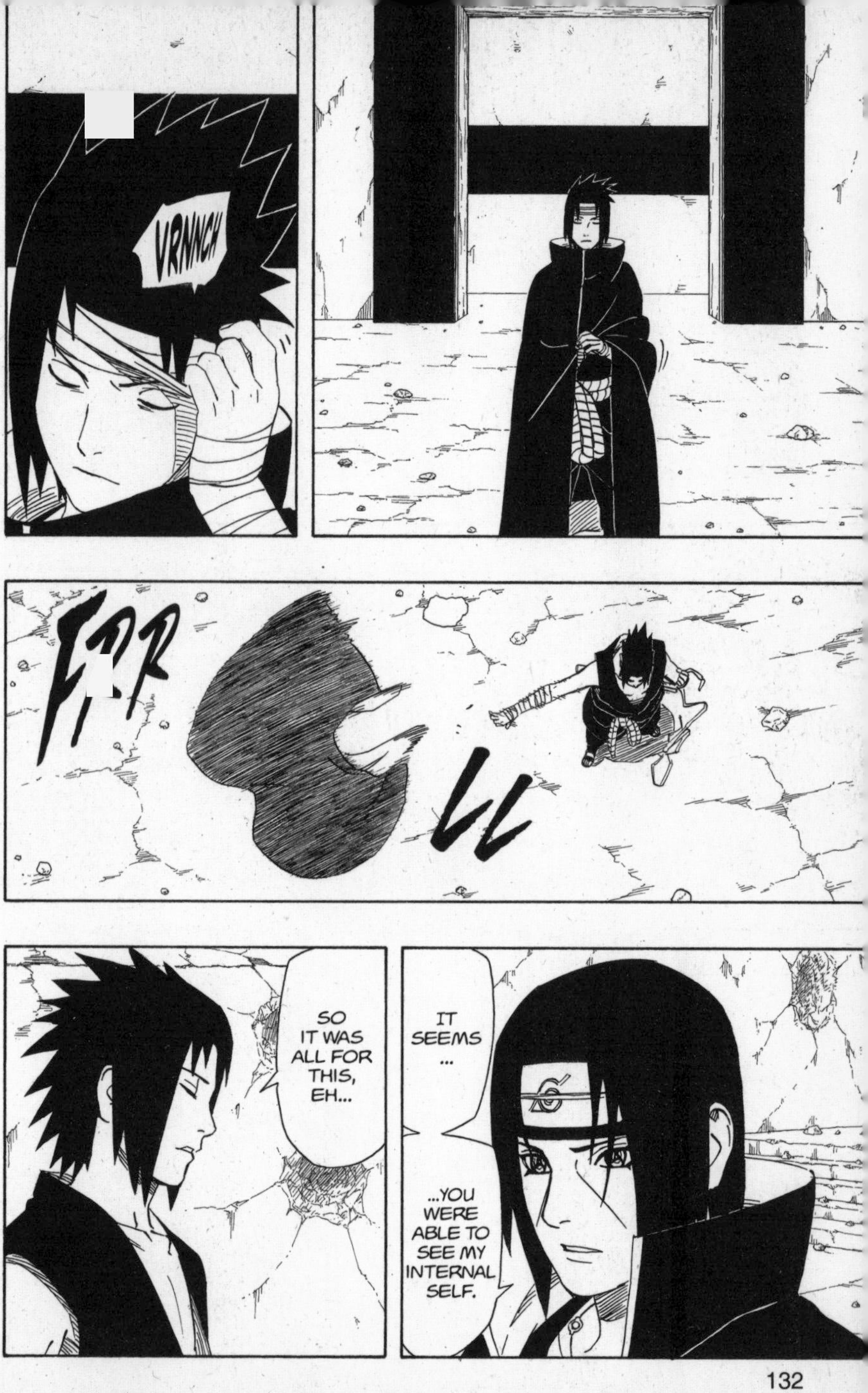
VRNNCH
IT SEEMS...
...YOU WERE ABLE TO SEE MY INTERNAL SELF.
SO IT WAS ALL FOR THIS, EH...

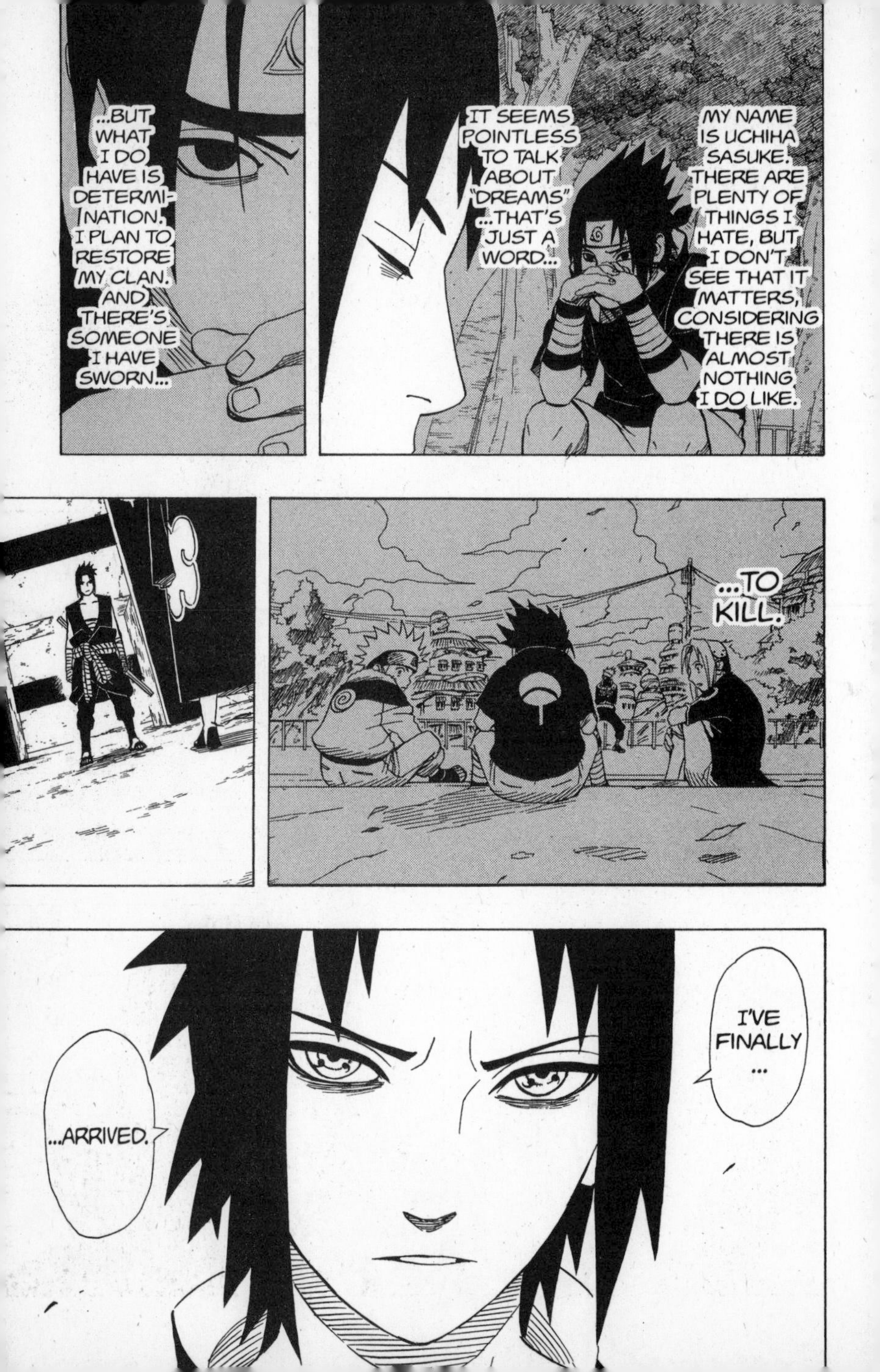
MY NAME IS UCHIHA SASUKE. THERE ARE PLENTY OF THINGS I HATE, BUT I DON'T SEE THAT IT MATTERS, CONSIDERING THERE IS ALMOST NOTHING I DO LIKE.
IT SEEMS POINTLESS TO TALK ABOUT "DREAMS" ...THAT'S JUST A WORD...
...BUT WHAT I DO HAVE IS DETERMINATION. I PLAN TO RESTORE MY CLAN. AND, THERE'S SOMEONE I HAVE SWORN...
...TO KILL.
I'VE FINALLY ...
...ARRIVED.

NARUTO

Number 387: Reality...!!

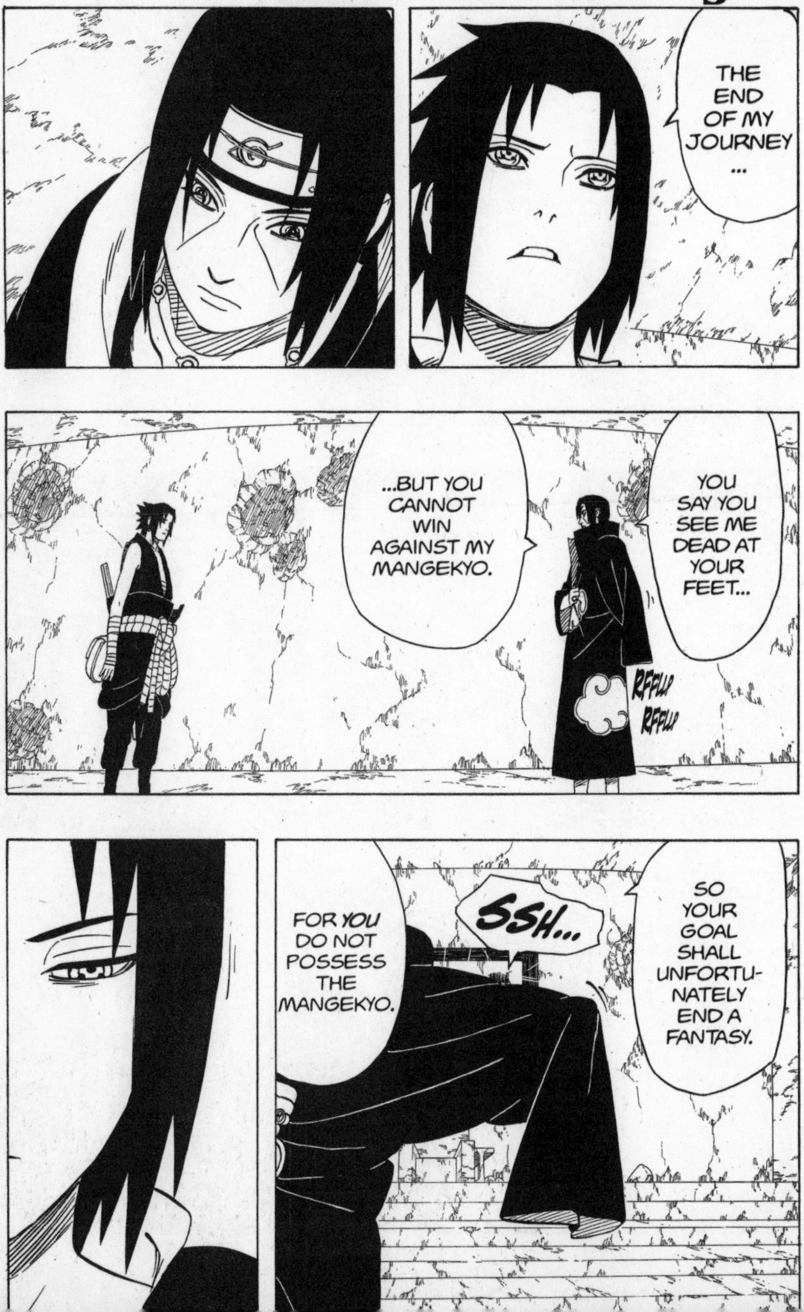
THE END OF MY JOURNEY ...
YOU SAY YOU SEE ME DEAD AT YOUR FEET...
...BUT YOU CANNOT WIN AGAINST MY MANGEKYO.
RFFLLP RFFLLP
SO YOUR GOAL SHALL UNFORTUNATELY END A FANTASY.
SSH...
FOR YOU DO NOT POSSESS THE MANGEKYO.

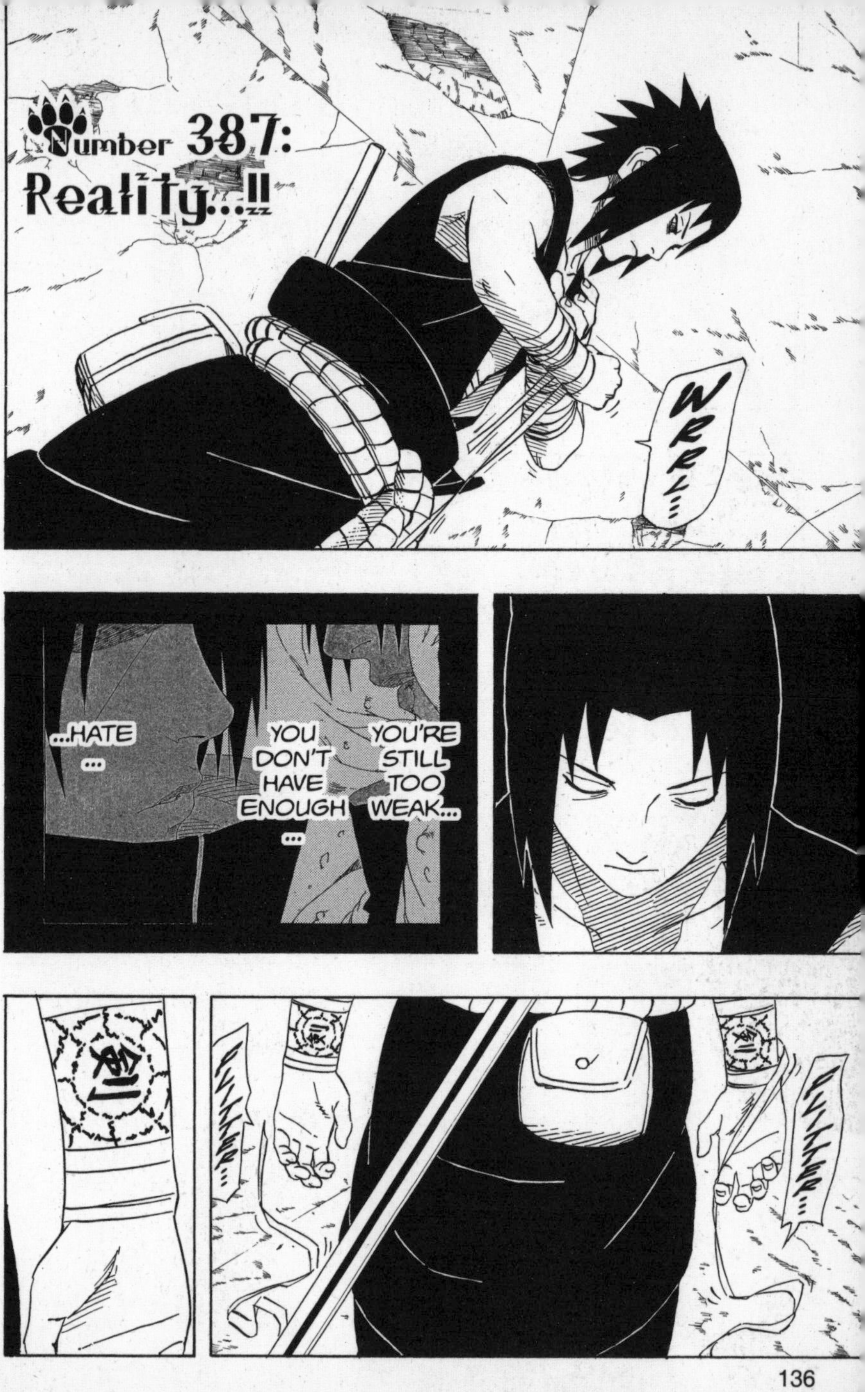
Number 387: Reality...!!
WRRL...
YOU'RE STILL TOO WEAK...
YOU DON'T HAVE ENOUGH ...
...HATE ...
QUIVVER...
QUIVVER...

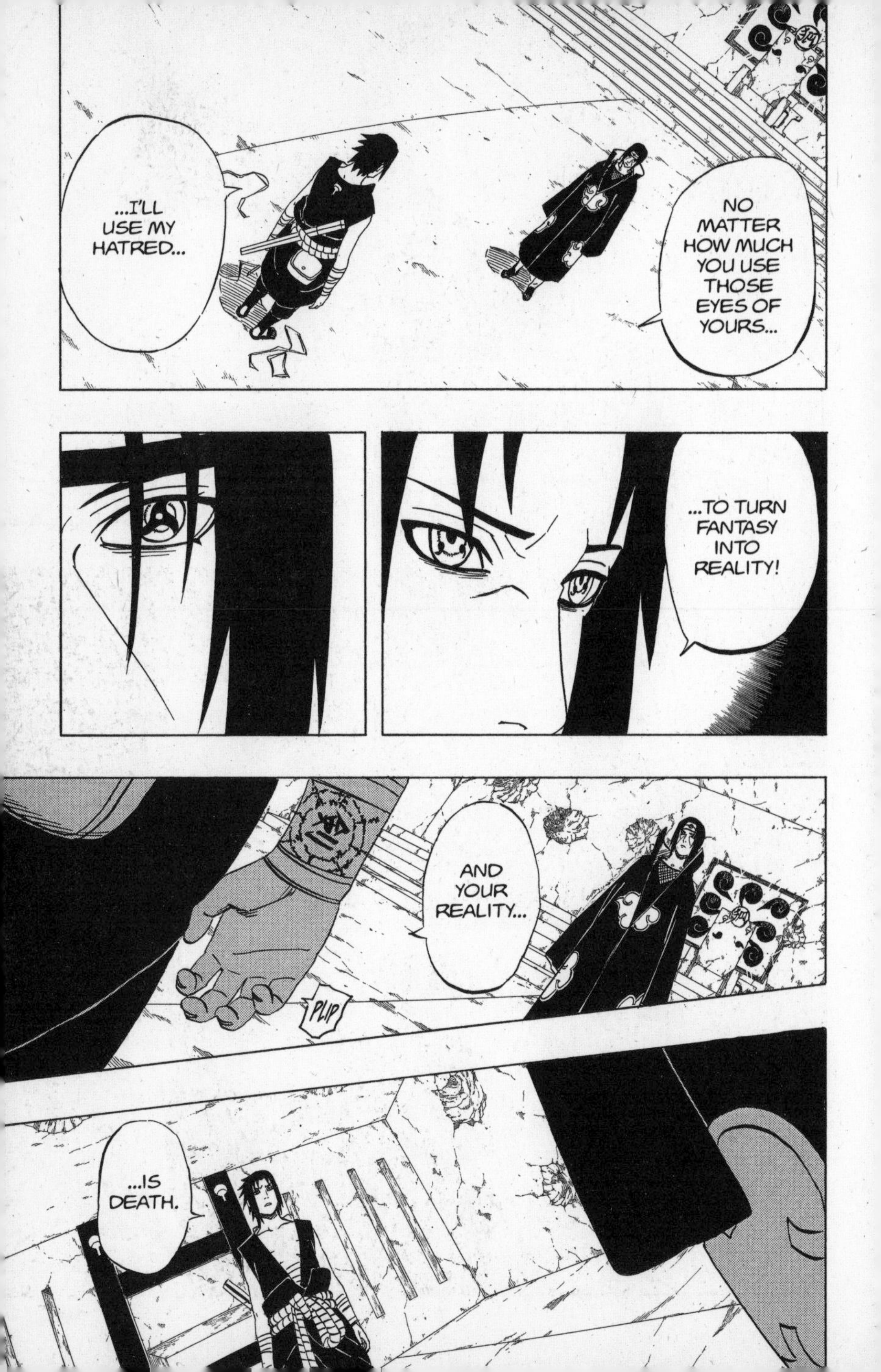
NO MATTER HOW MUCH YOU USE THOSE EYES OF YOURS...
...I'LL USE MY HATRED...
...TO TURN FANTASY INTO REALITY!
AND YOUR REALITY...
PLIP
...IS DEATH.

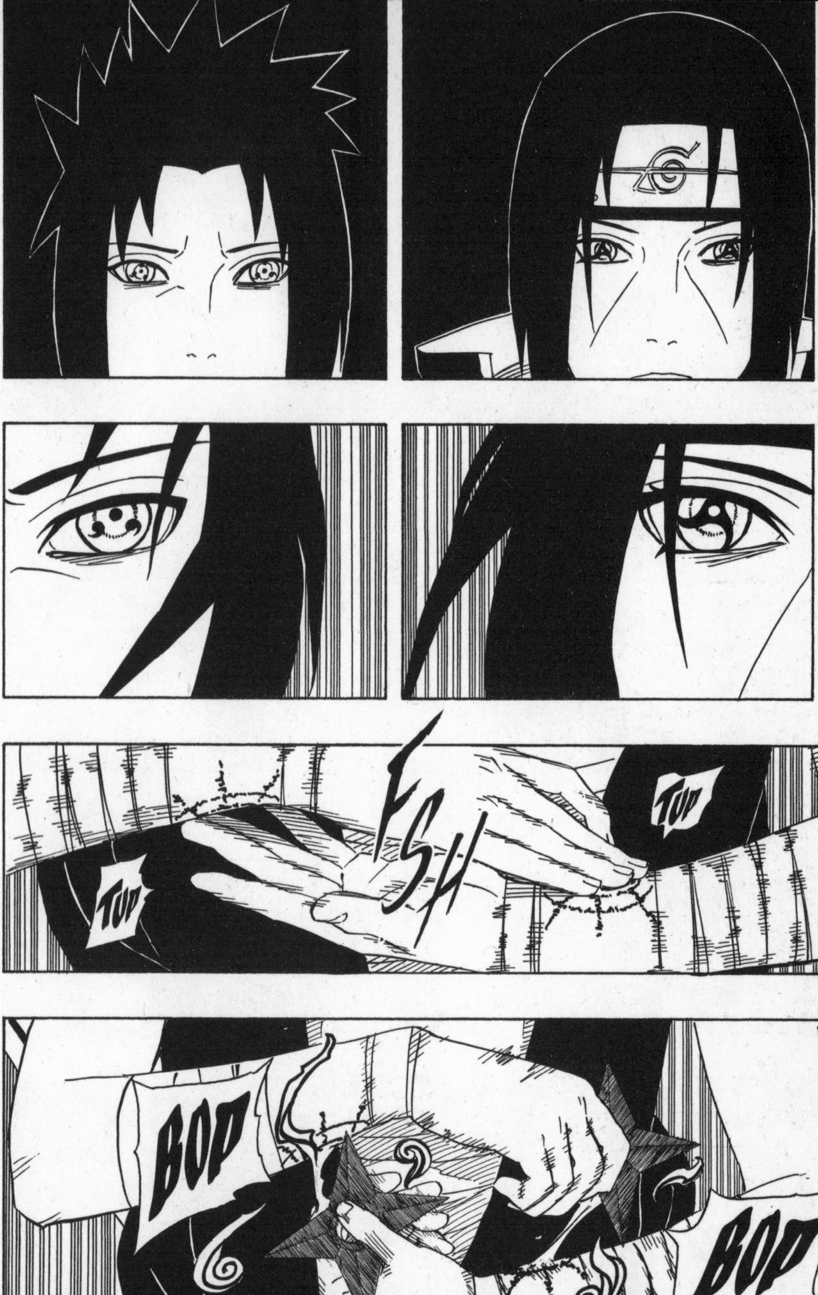
TUP
FSH
TUP
BOP
BOP

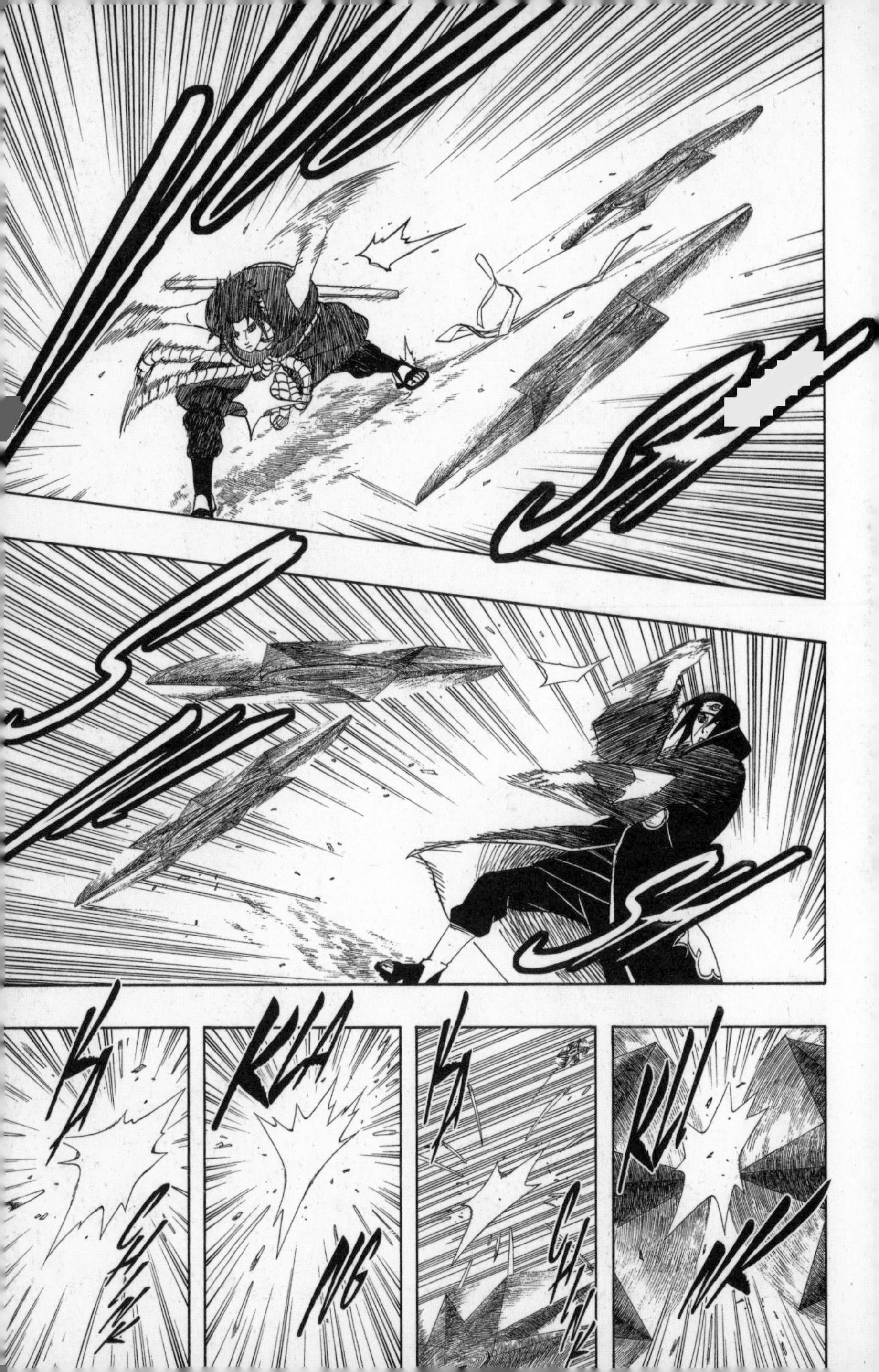
KLINK
KACHINK
KLANG
KACHINK

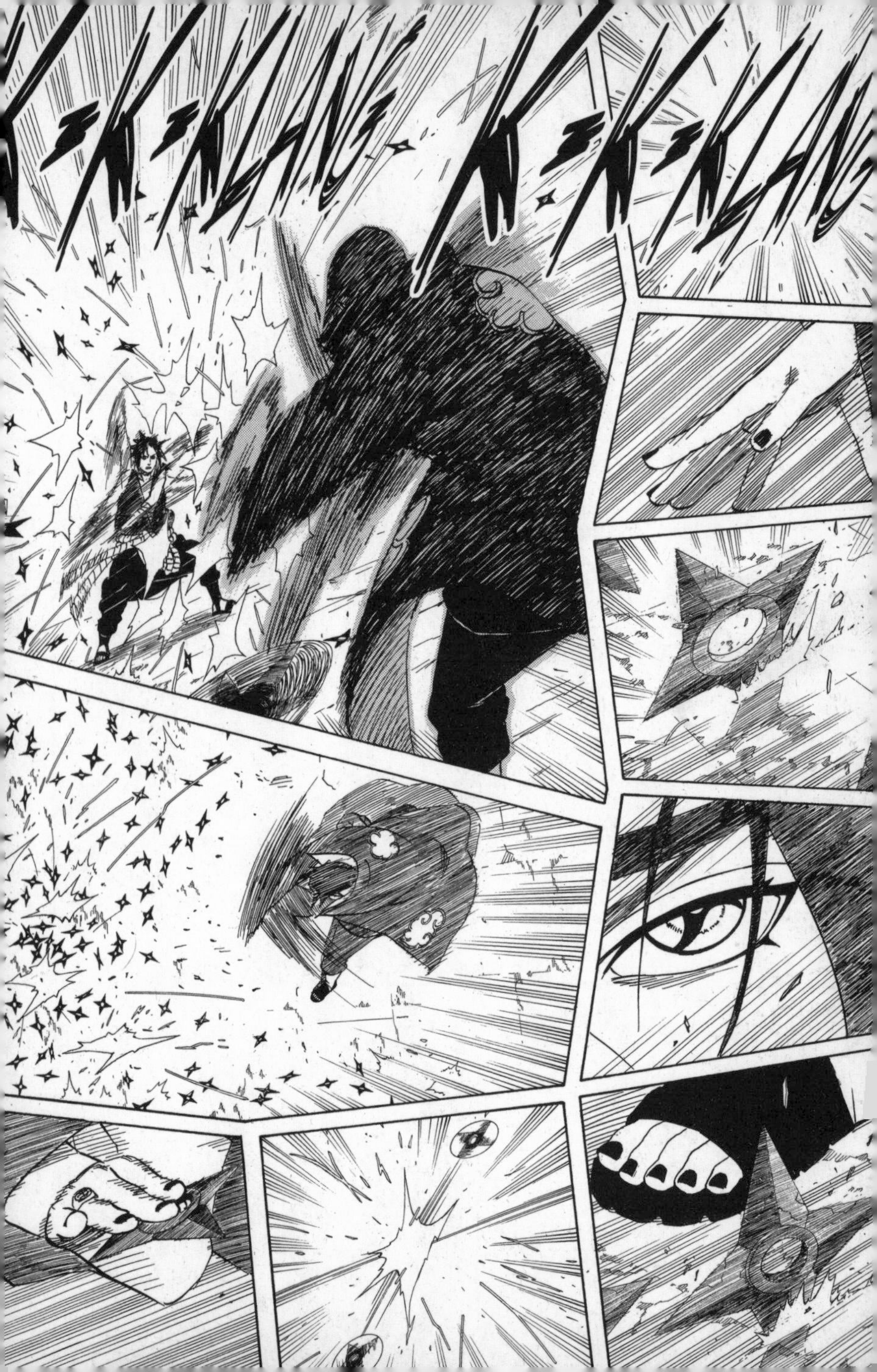

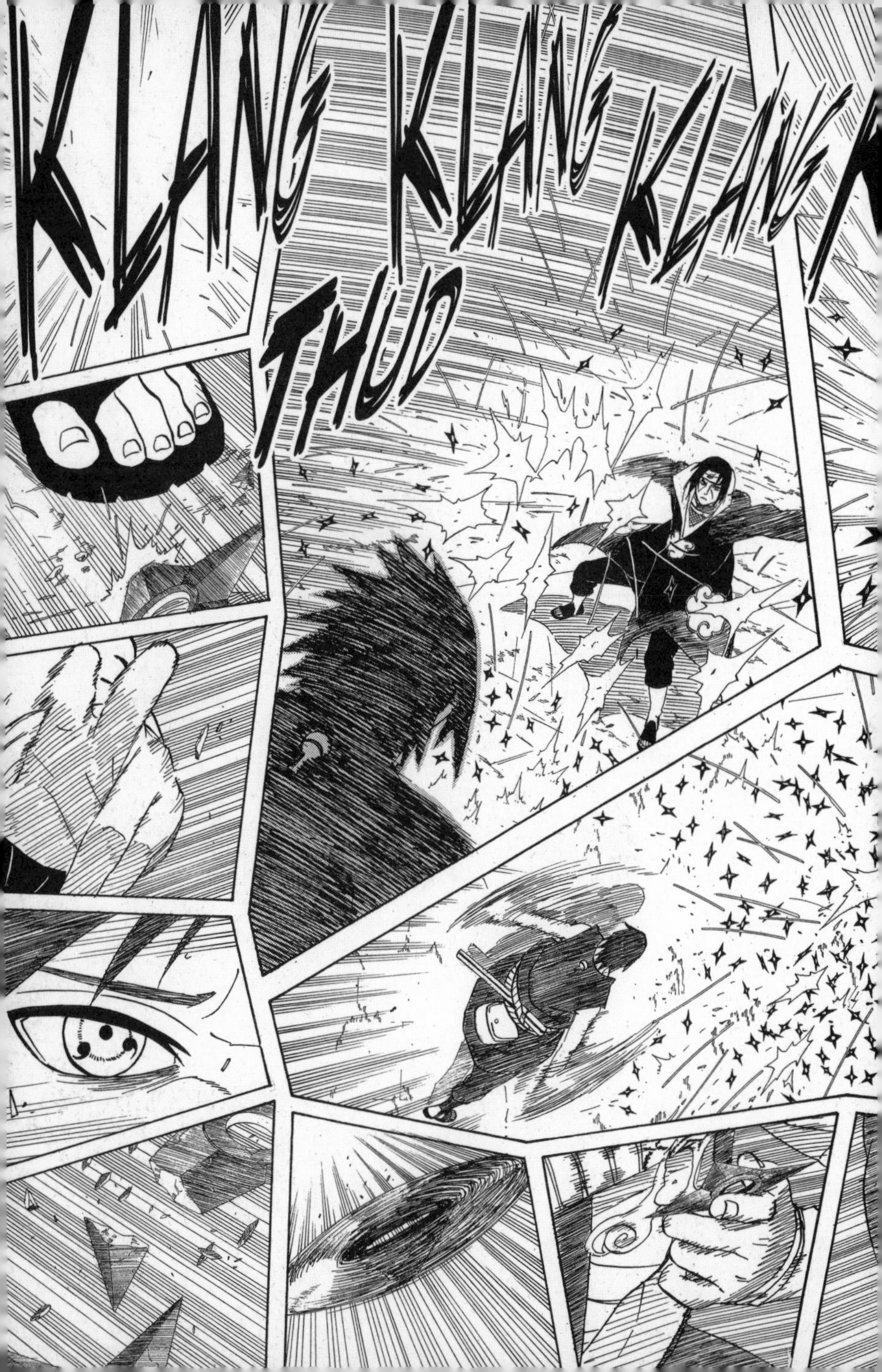
KLANG KLANG KLANG K
THUD

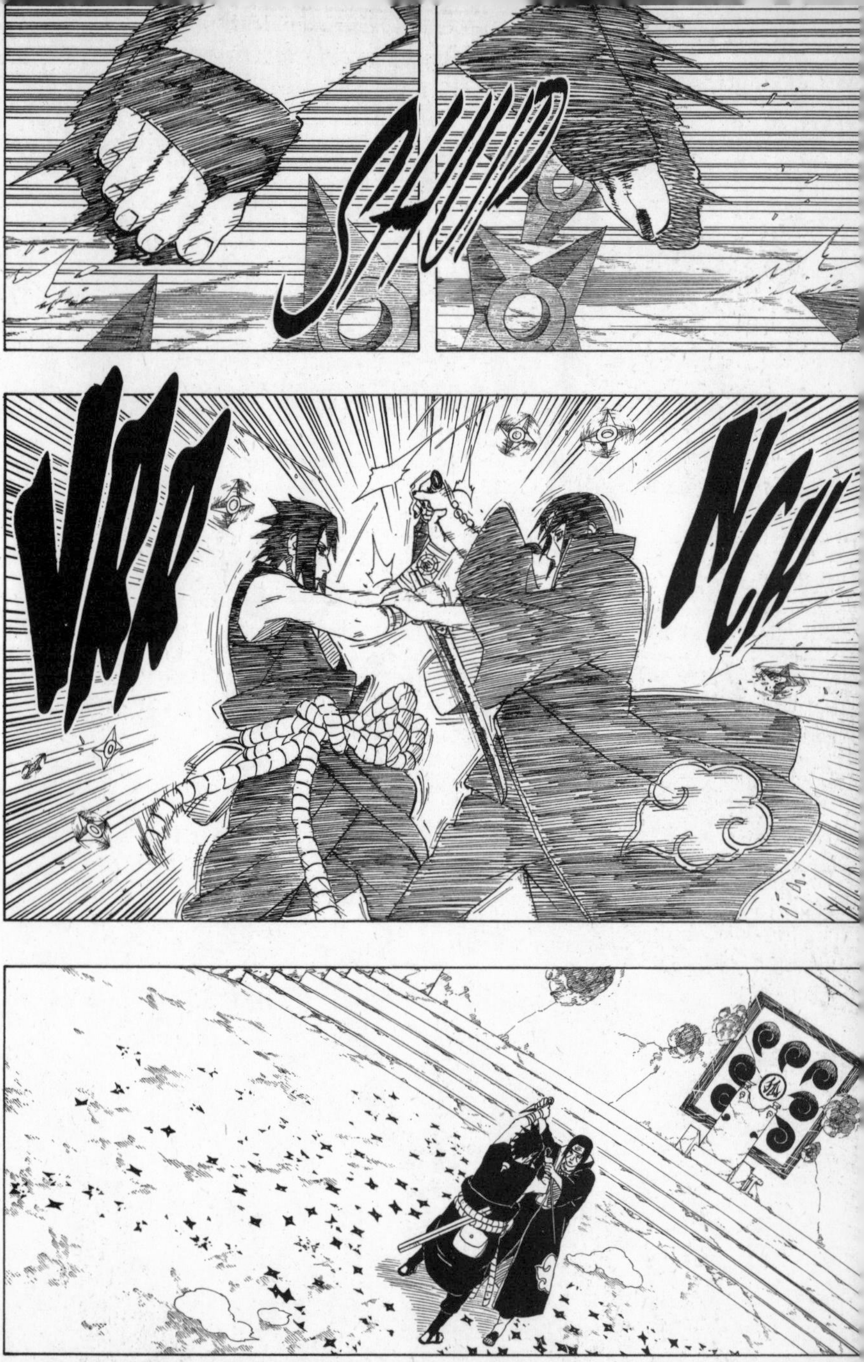
SHUP
NCH

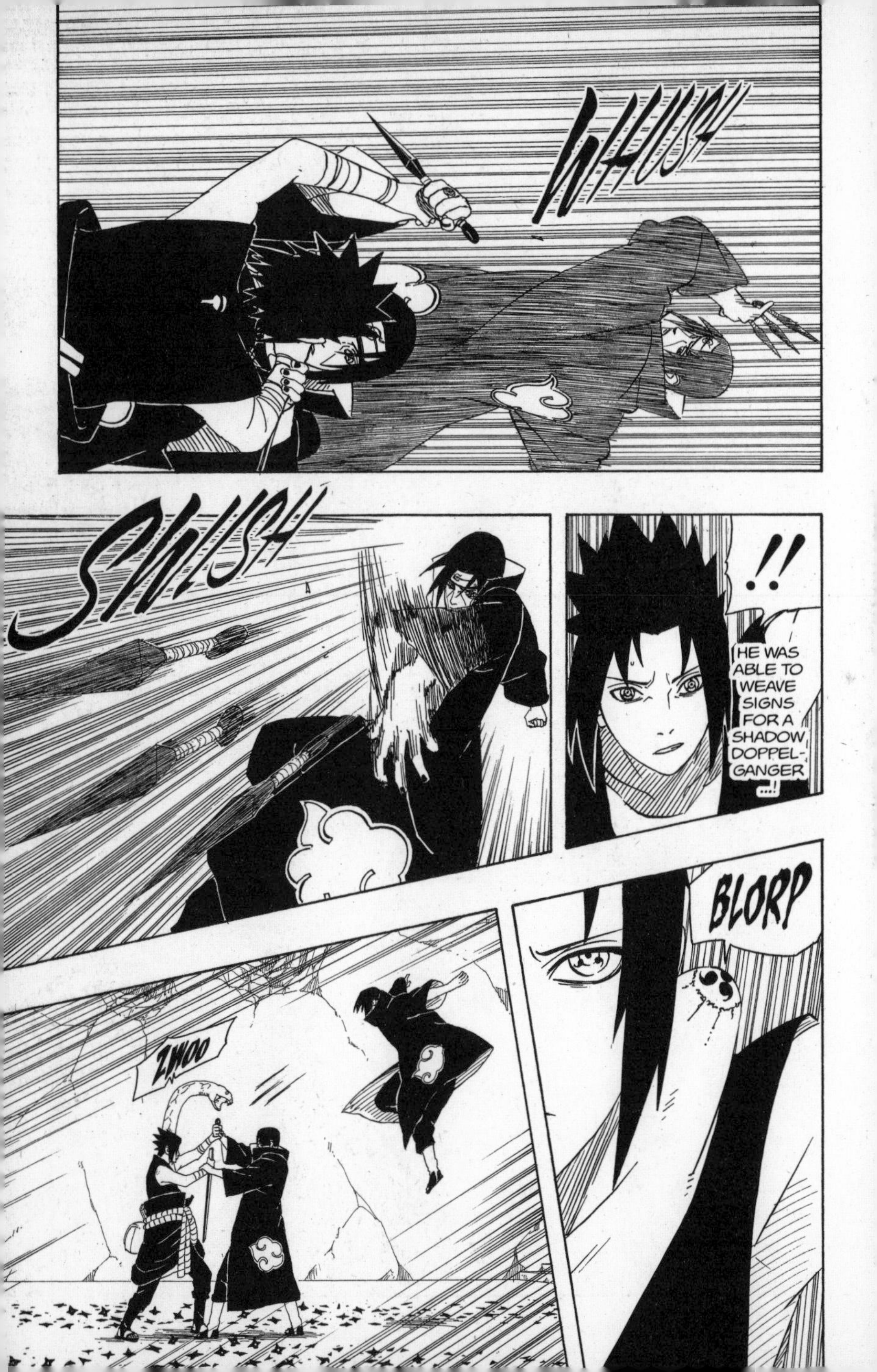
WHUSH
!!
HE WAS ABLE TO WEAVE SIGNS FOR A SHADOW DOPPEL-GANGER ...!
SWISH
BLORP
ZWOO

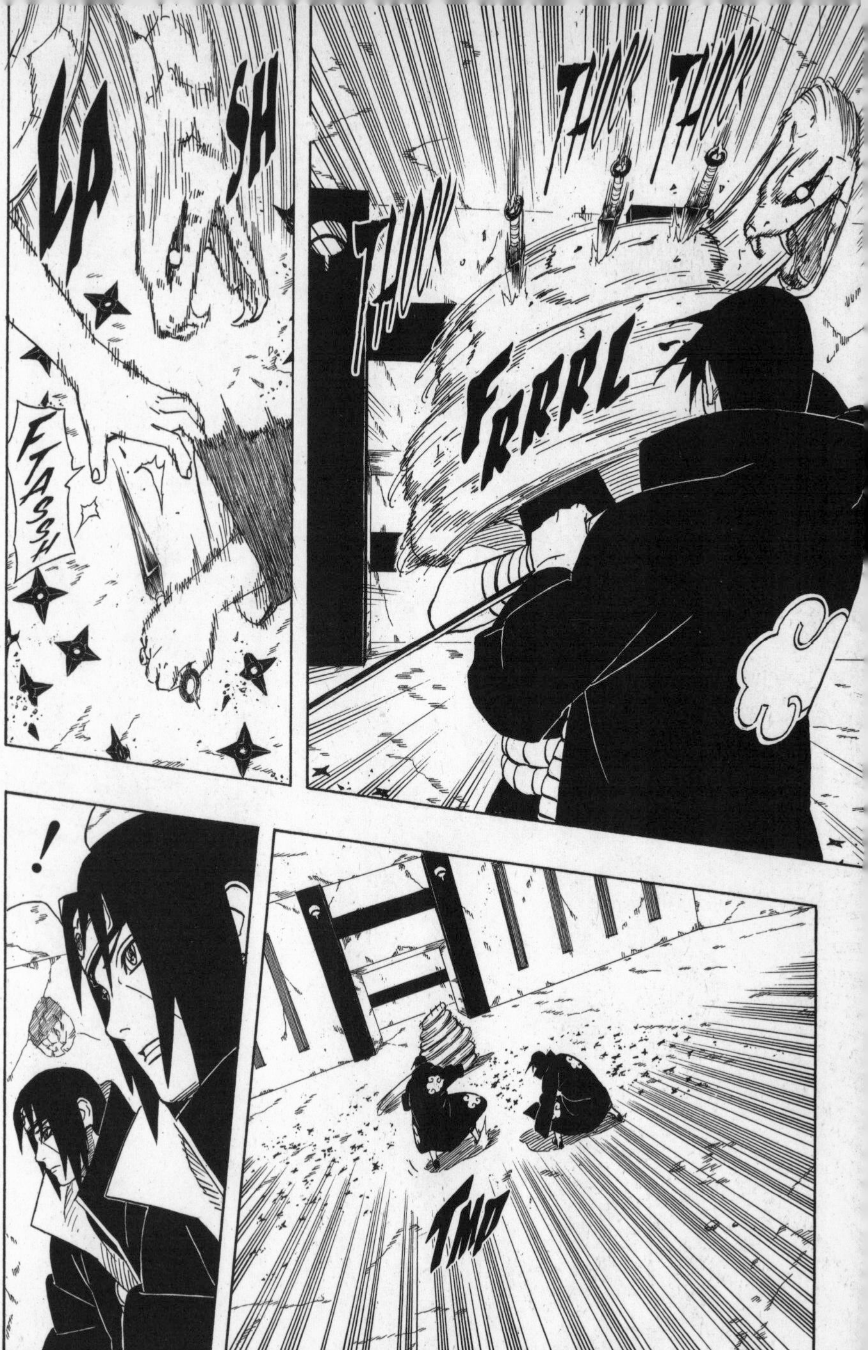
THUCK THUCK
THUCK
FRRRL
FTASSH
THD
!

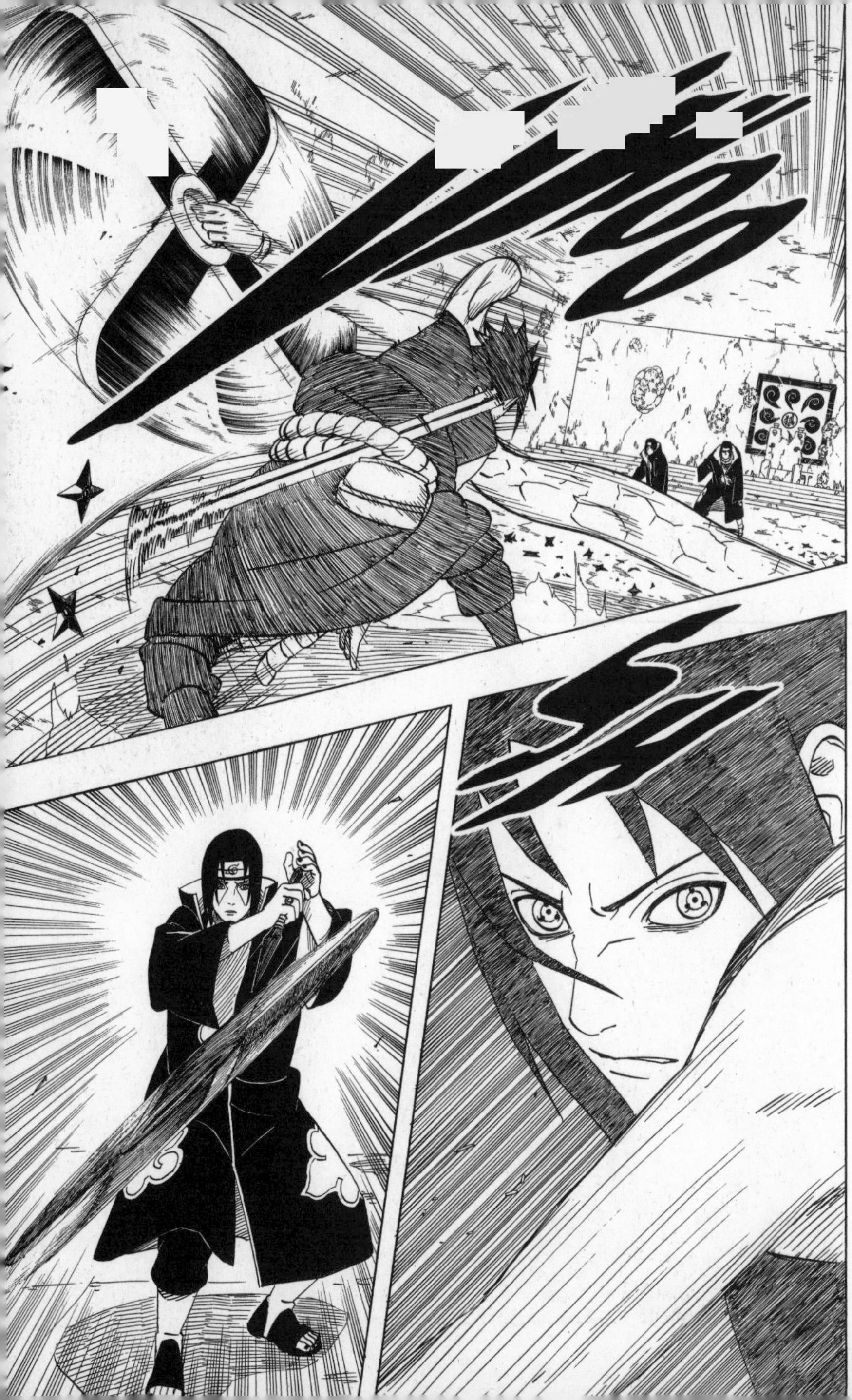

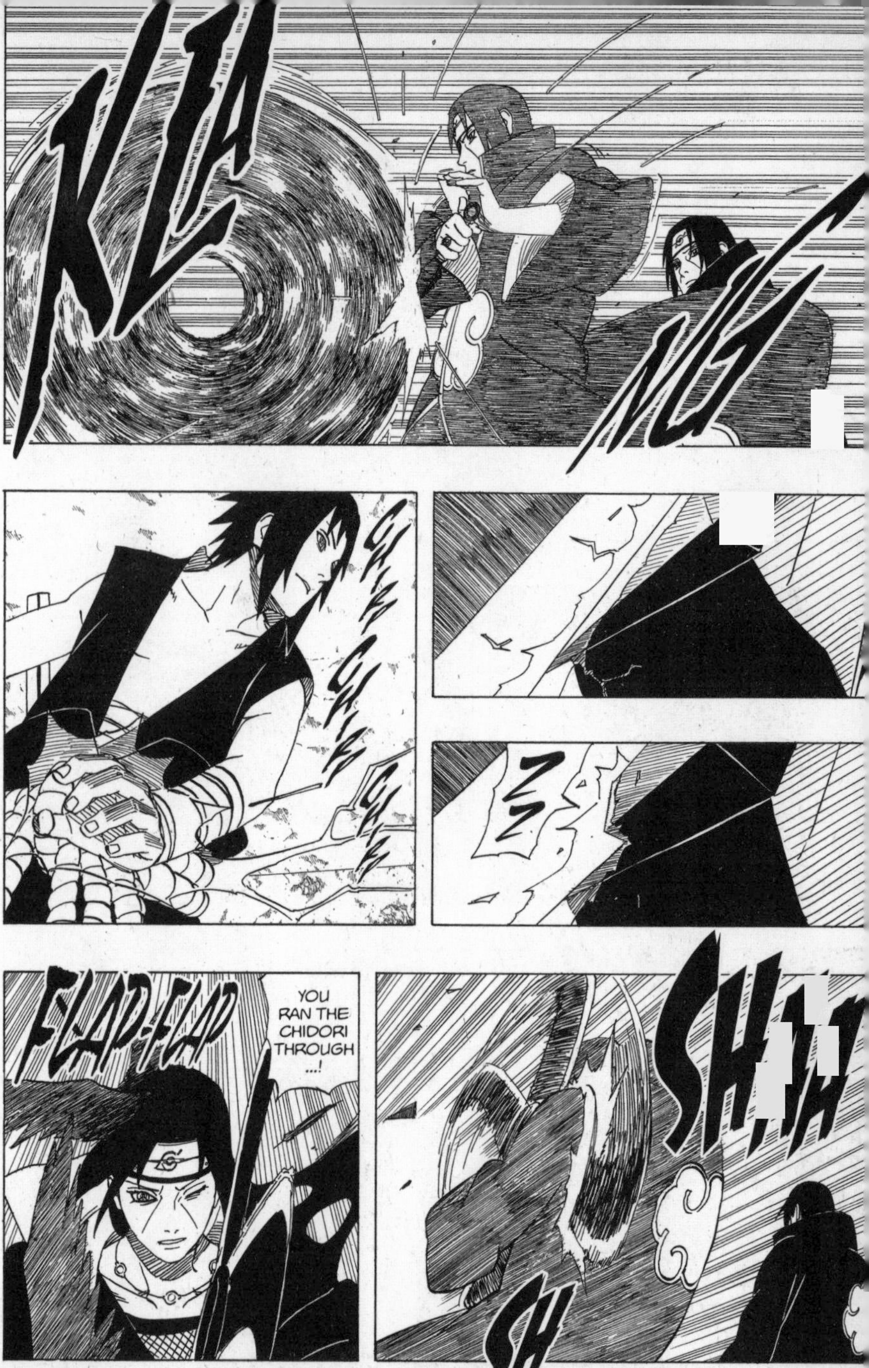
KZA
CHW CHW CHW
SH
FLAP-FLAP
YOU RAN THE CHIDORI THROUGH ...!

READ THIS WAY

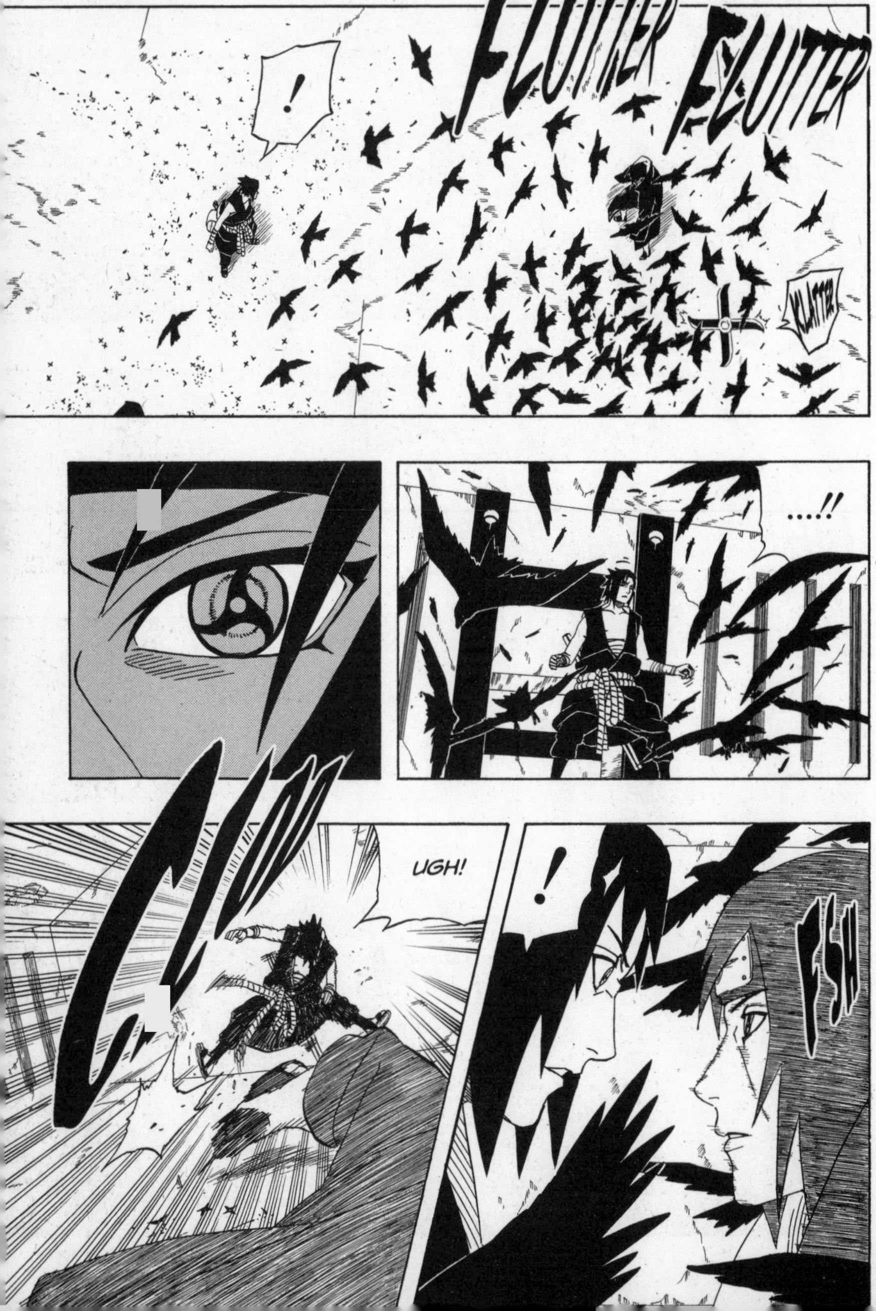
FLUTTER FLUTTER
KLATTER
!
....!!
!
FSH
UGH!

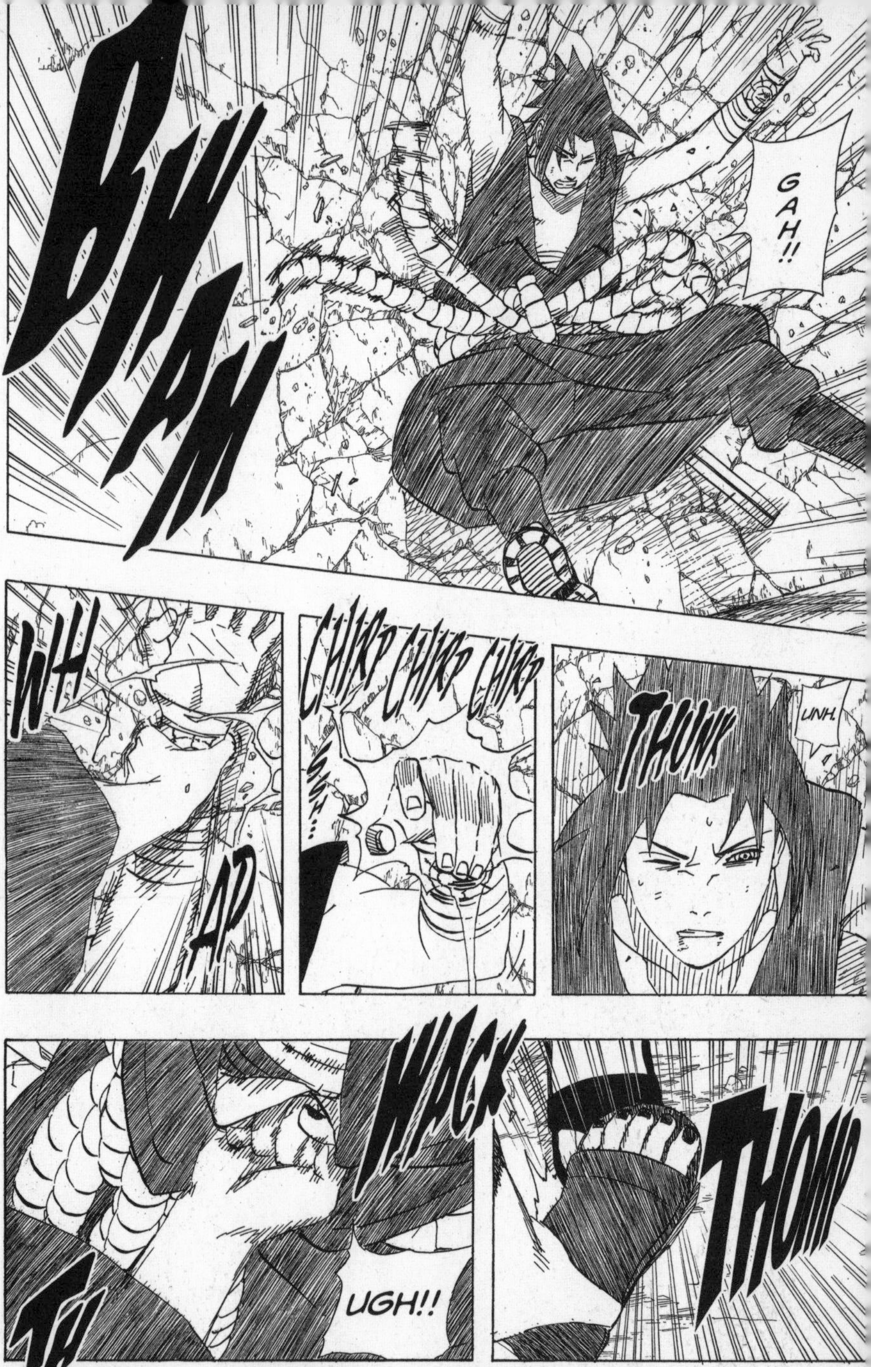
GAH!!
BWAM
UNH.
THUNK
CHIRP CHIRP CHIRP
SSSH...
WHAP
THOMP
WHACK
UGH!!

READ THIS WAY

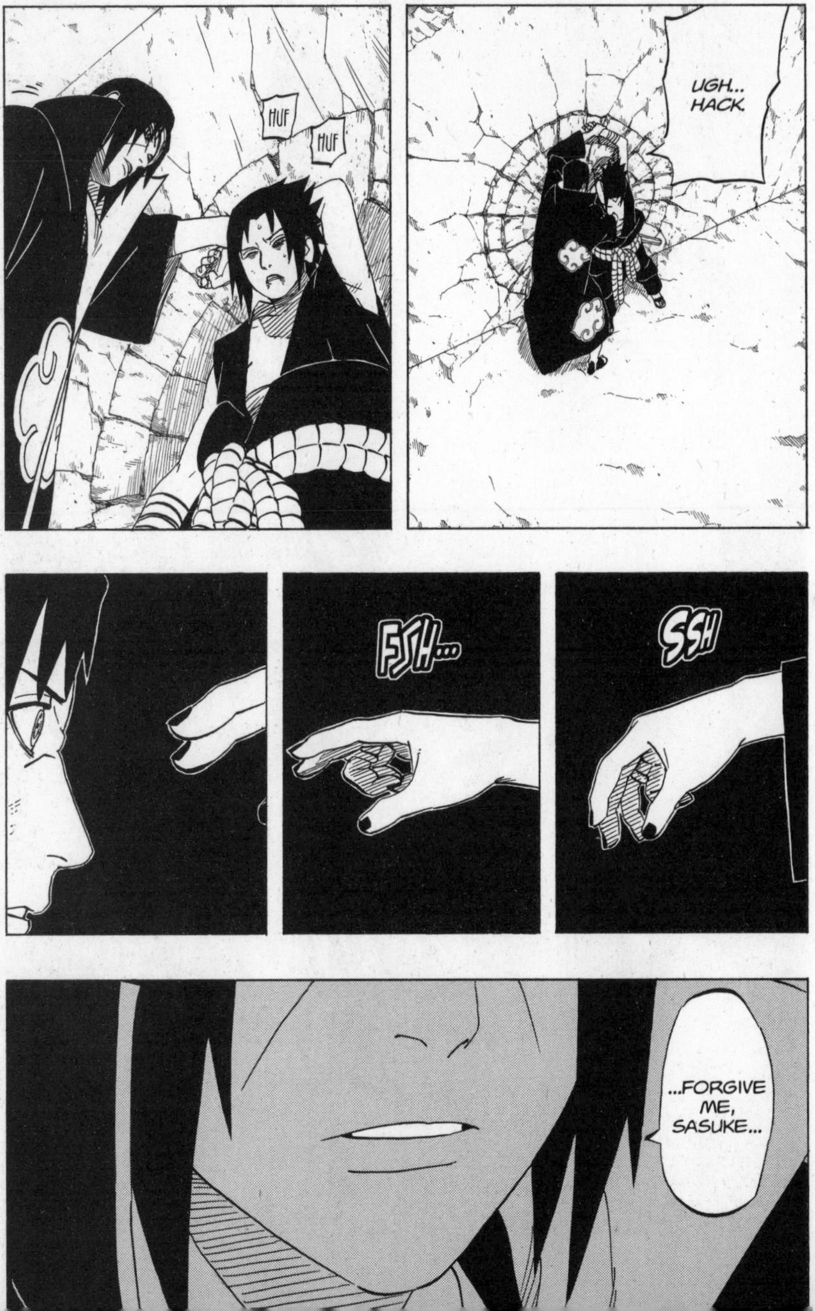
UGH... HACK.
HUF
HUF
SSH
FSH...
...FORGIVE ME, SASUKE...

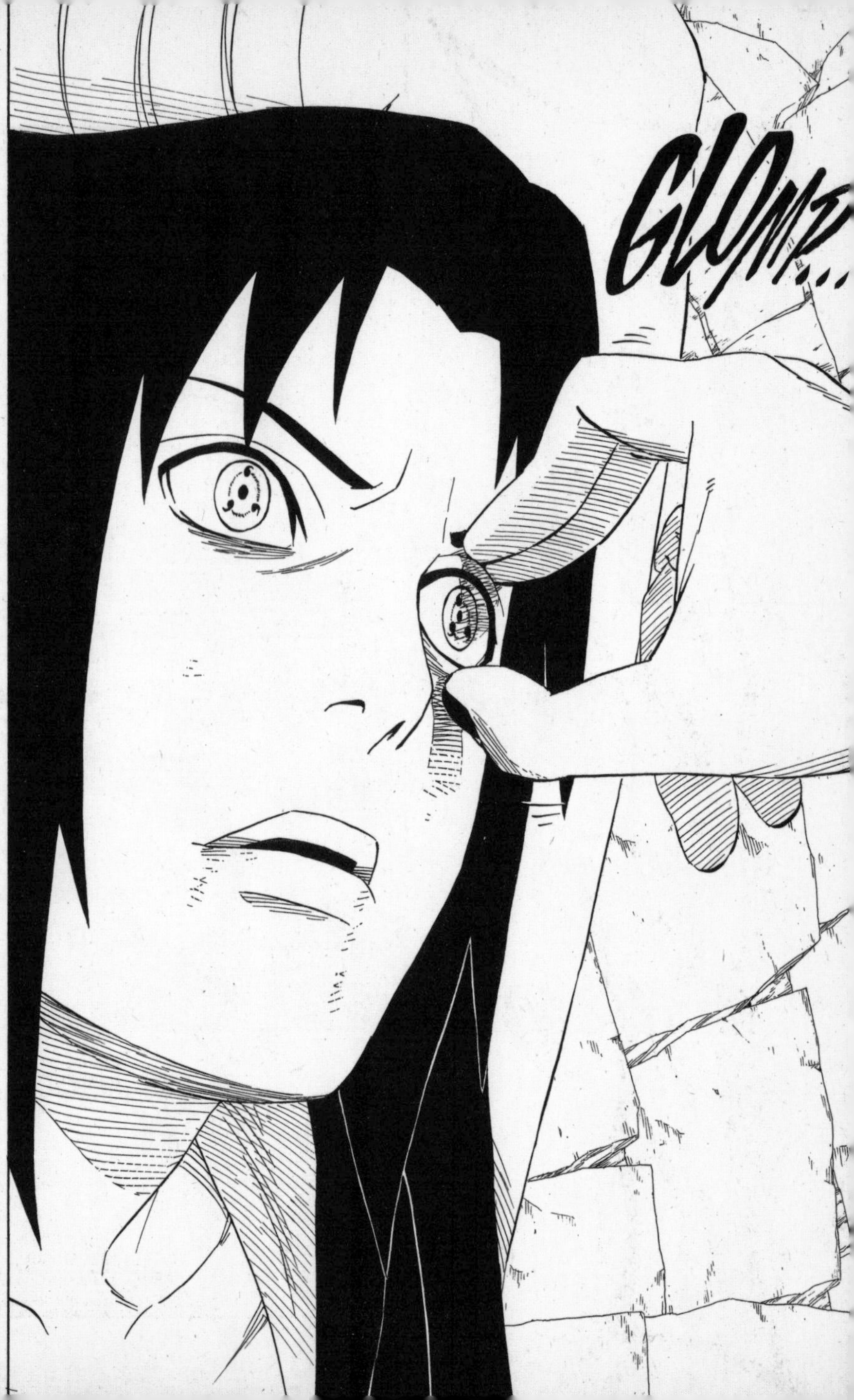
GLOMP...

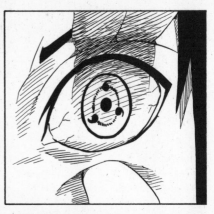

THIS
IS MY
REALITY...

...GIVE
ME
YOUR
LIGHT!

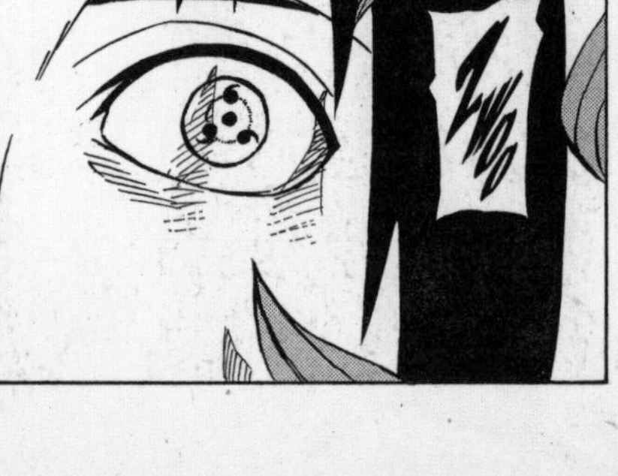
ZWOO

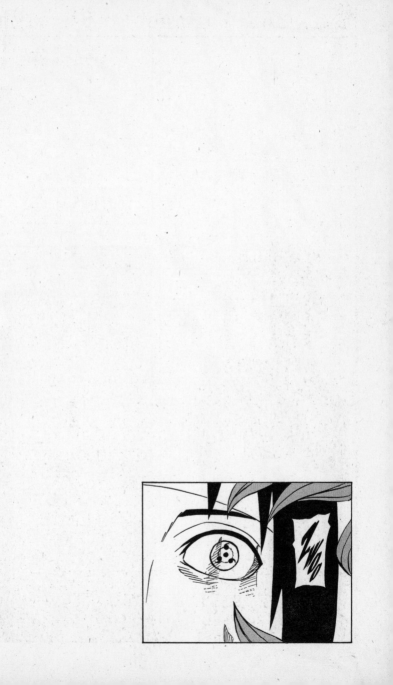

Number 388: Variance of Strength...!!

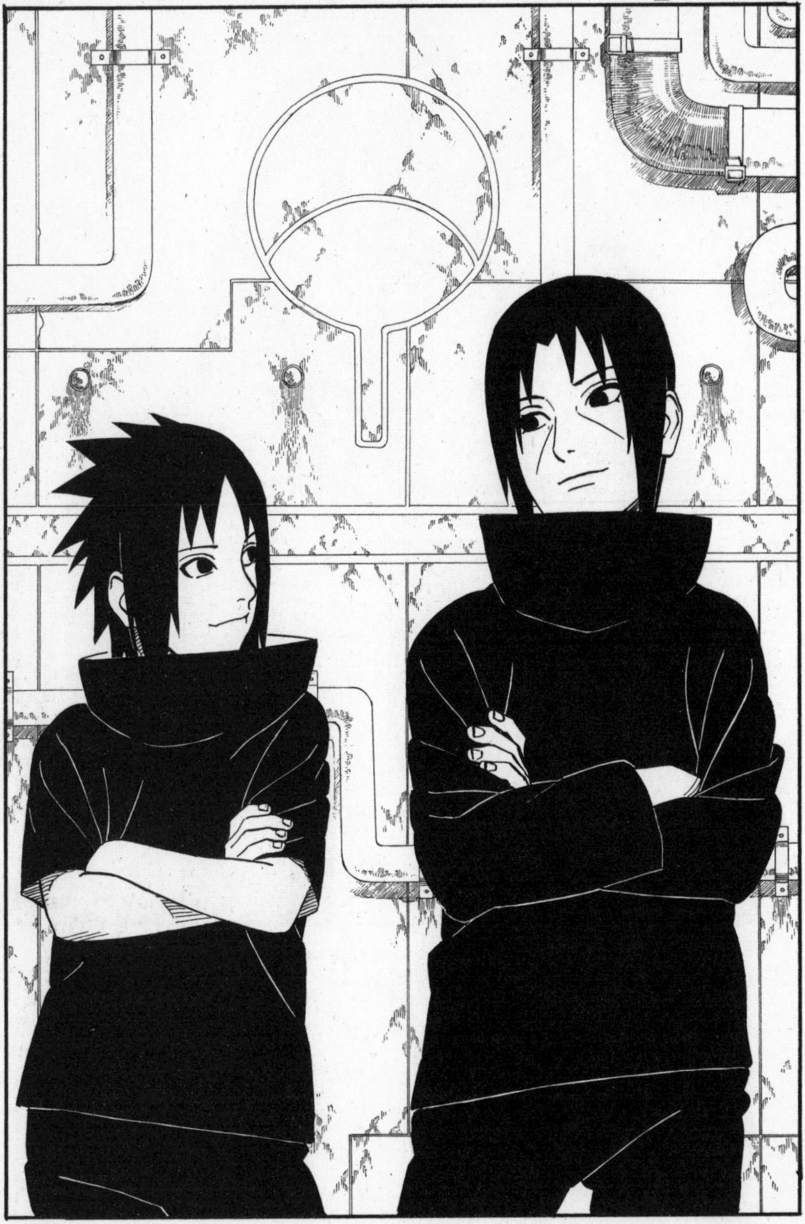

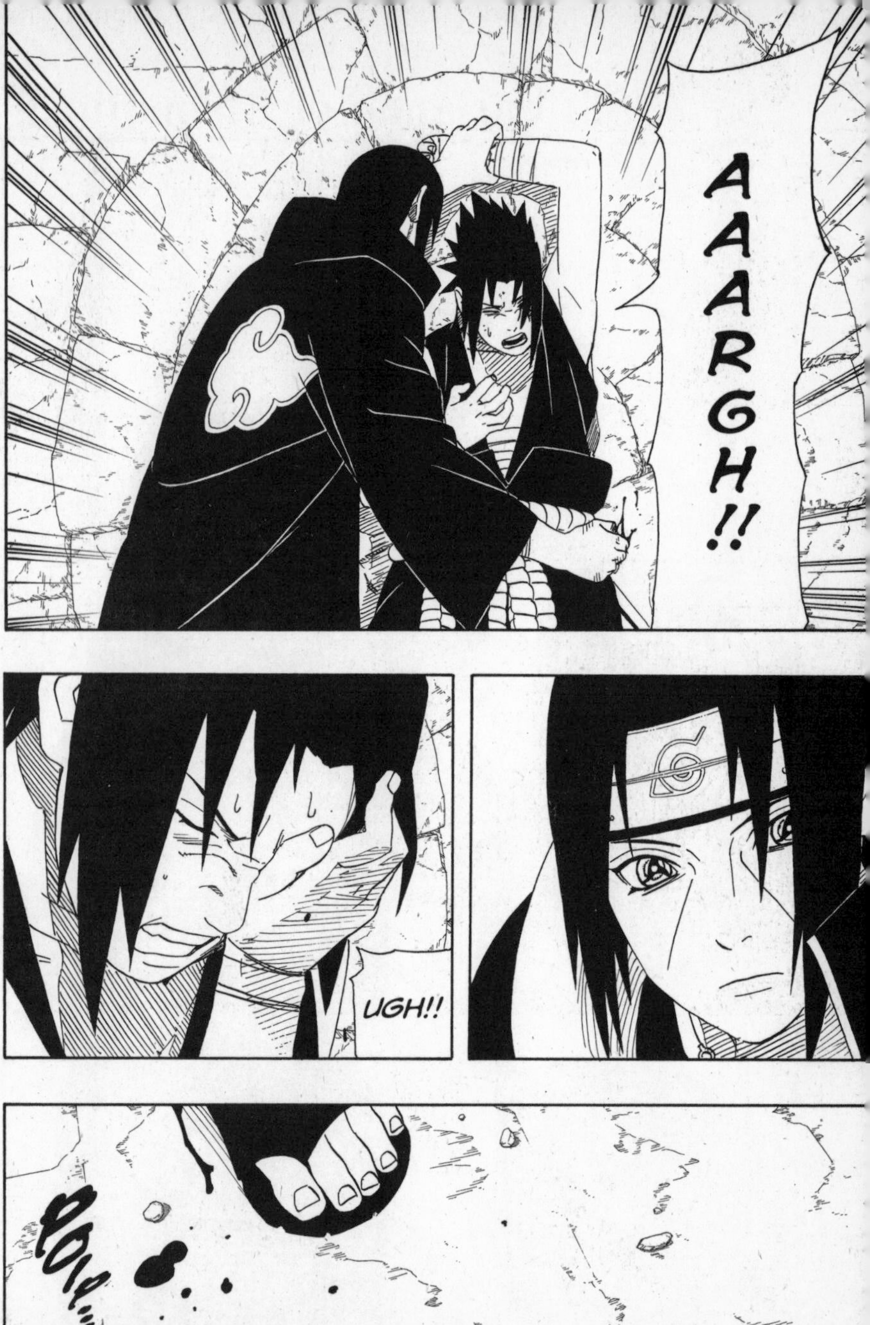
AAARGH!!
UGH!!

I TOLD YOU.

YOU WON'T WIN. I HAVE THE MANGEKYO AND YOU DO NOT!

!

GGH... AAH— UNH...

SSH

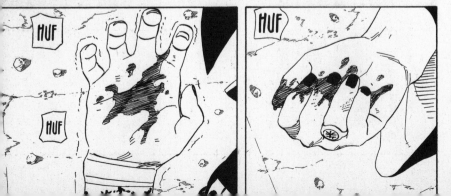

HUF

HUF

HUF

HUF

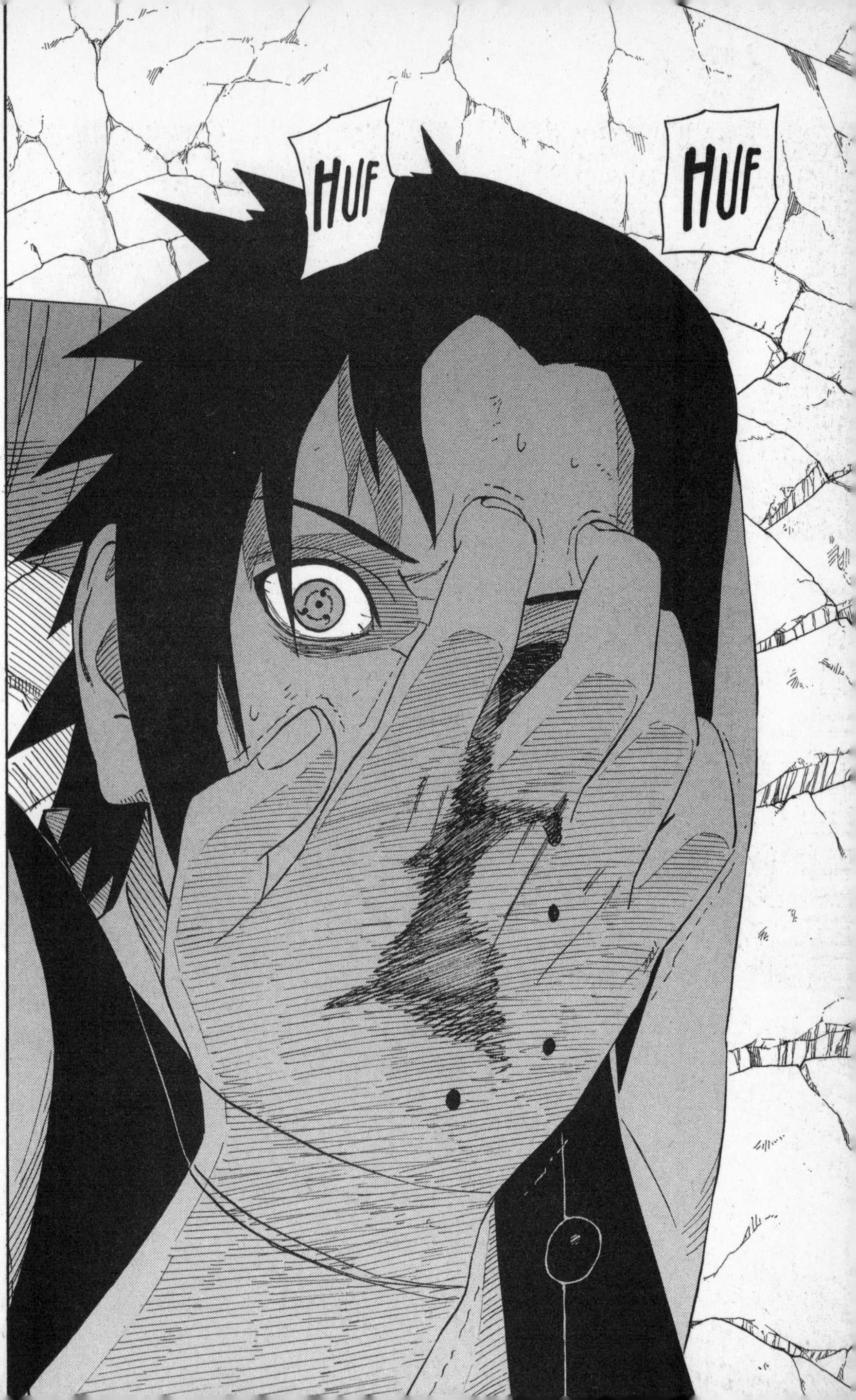
HUF
HUF

READ THIS WAY

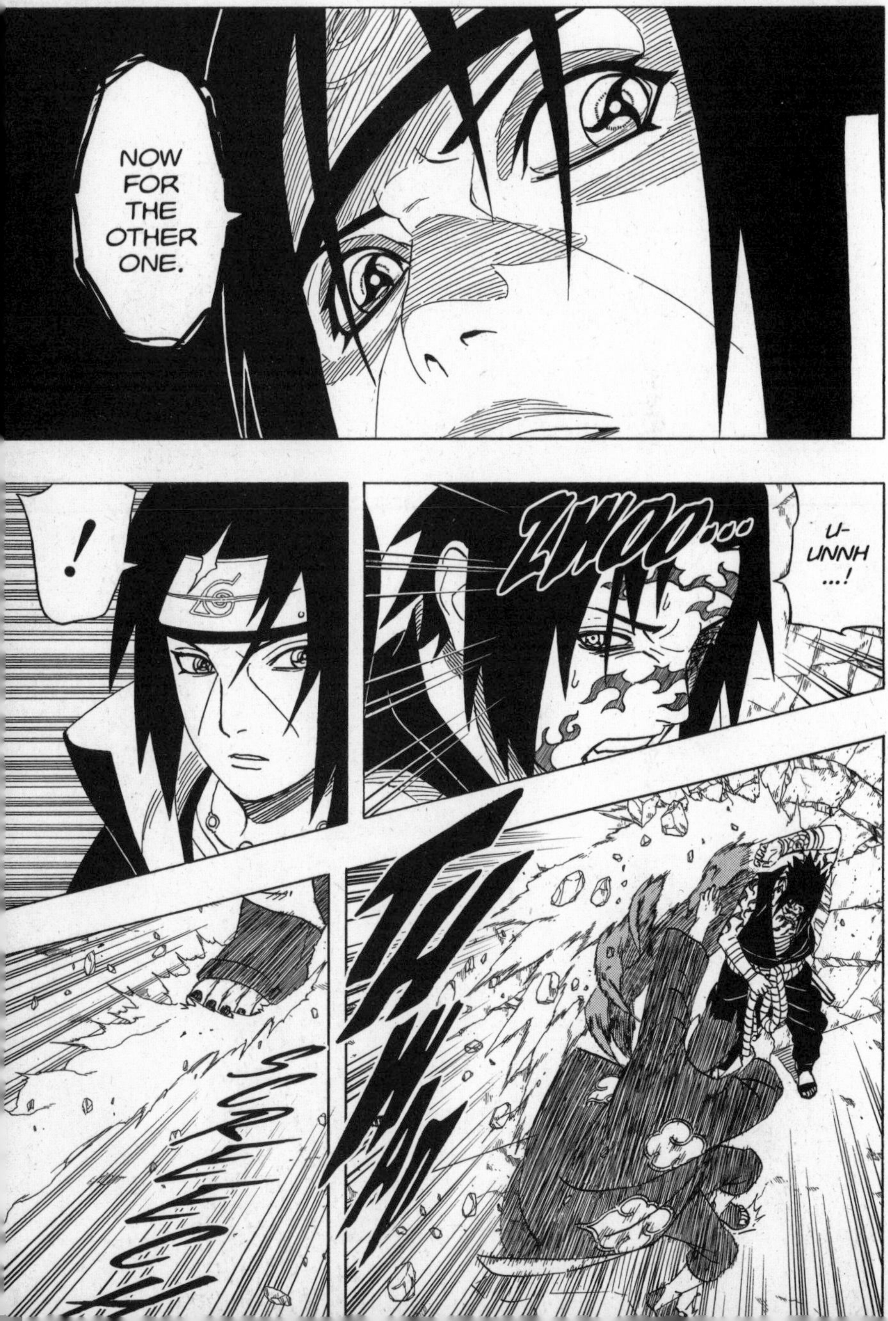
NOW FOR THE OTHER ONE.
ZWOO...
U-UNNH...!
!

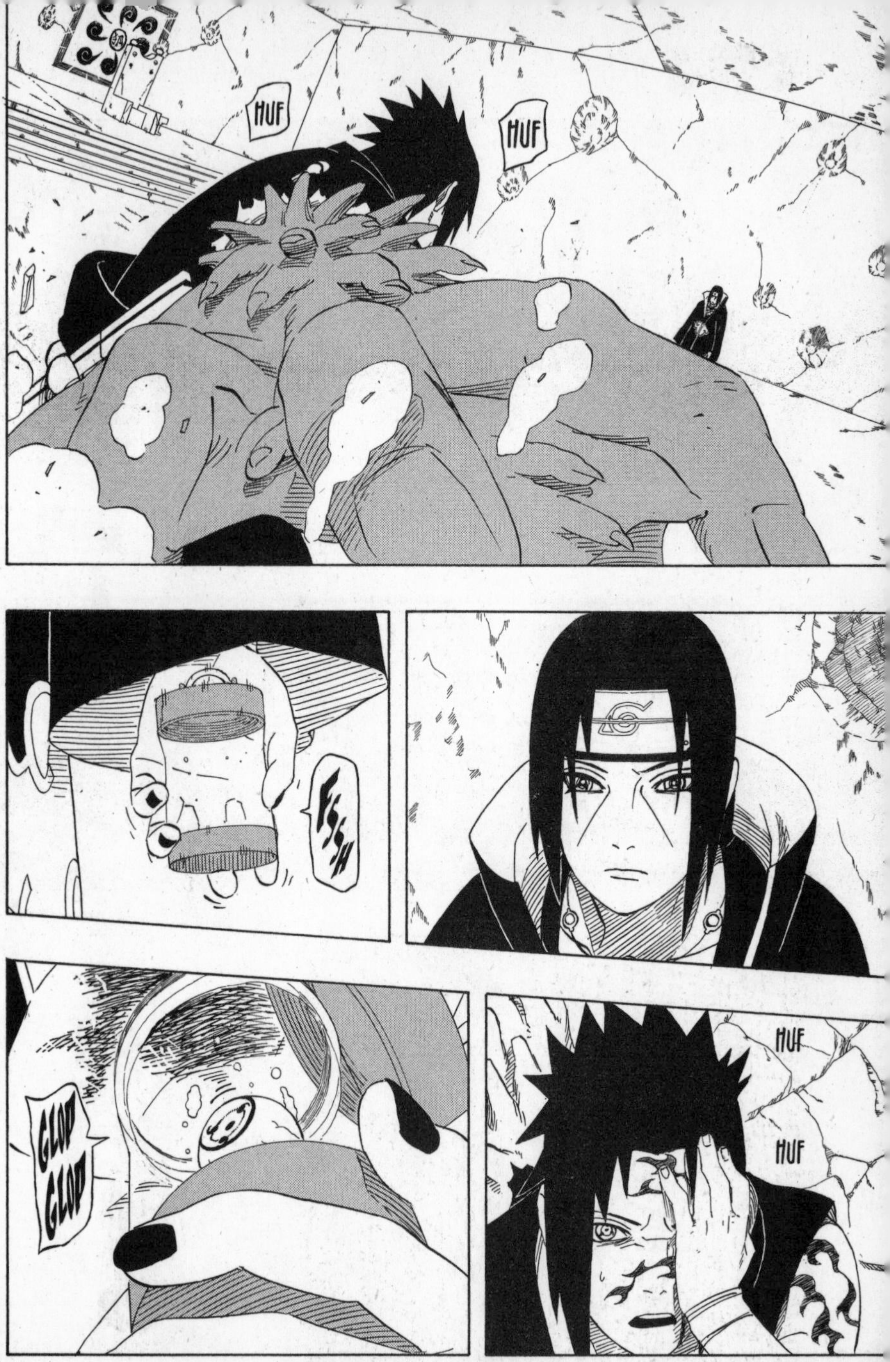
HUF
HUF
FSSH
HUF
HUF
GLOP GLOP

READ THIS WAY

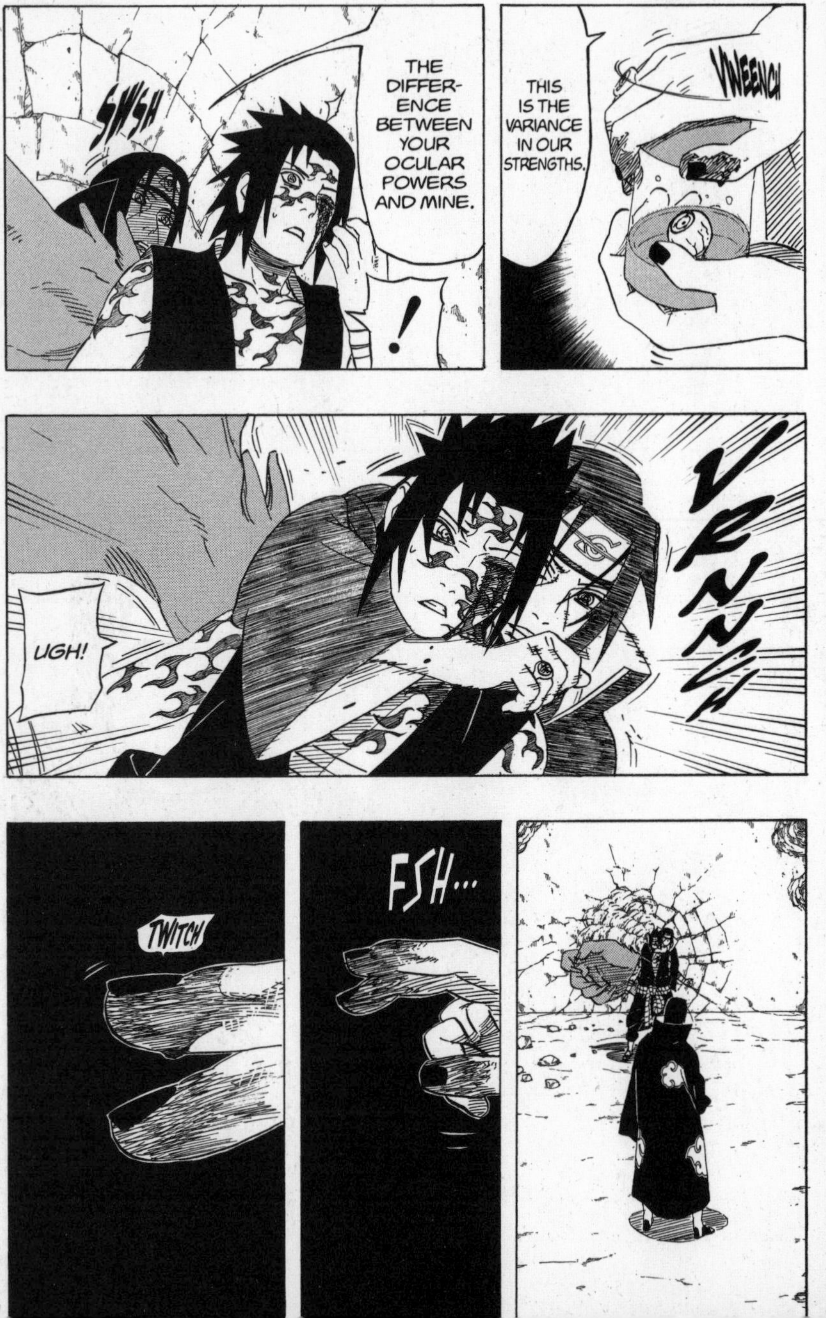
VWEENCH
THIS IS THE VARIANCE IN OUR STRENGTHS.
THE DIFFERENCE BETWEEN YOUR OCULAR POWERS AND MINE.
SWSH
!
VRNNCH
UGH!
FSH...
TWITCH

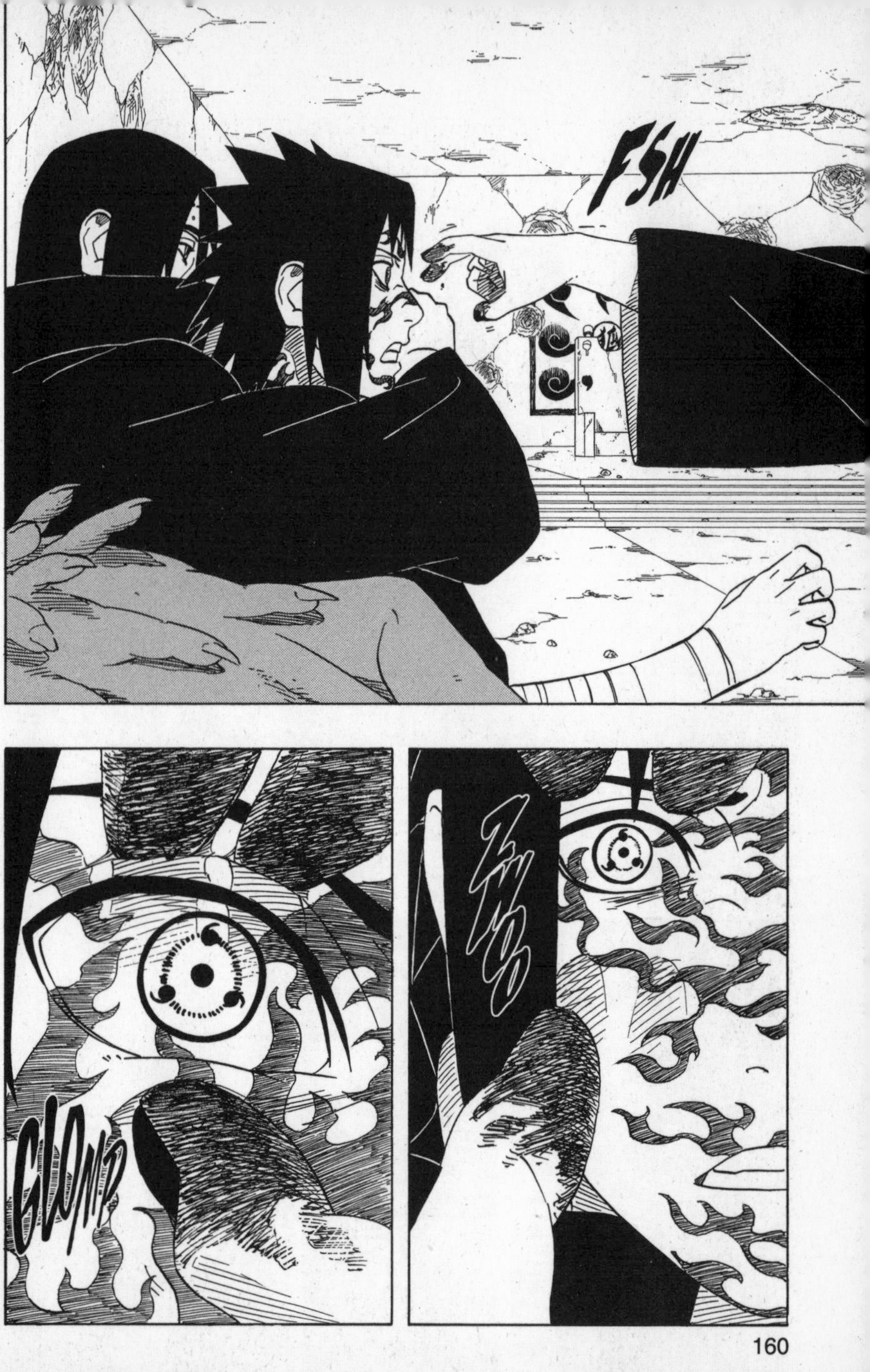
FSH
ZWOO
GLOMP

READ THIS WAY

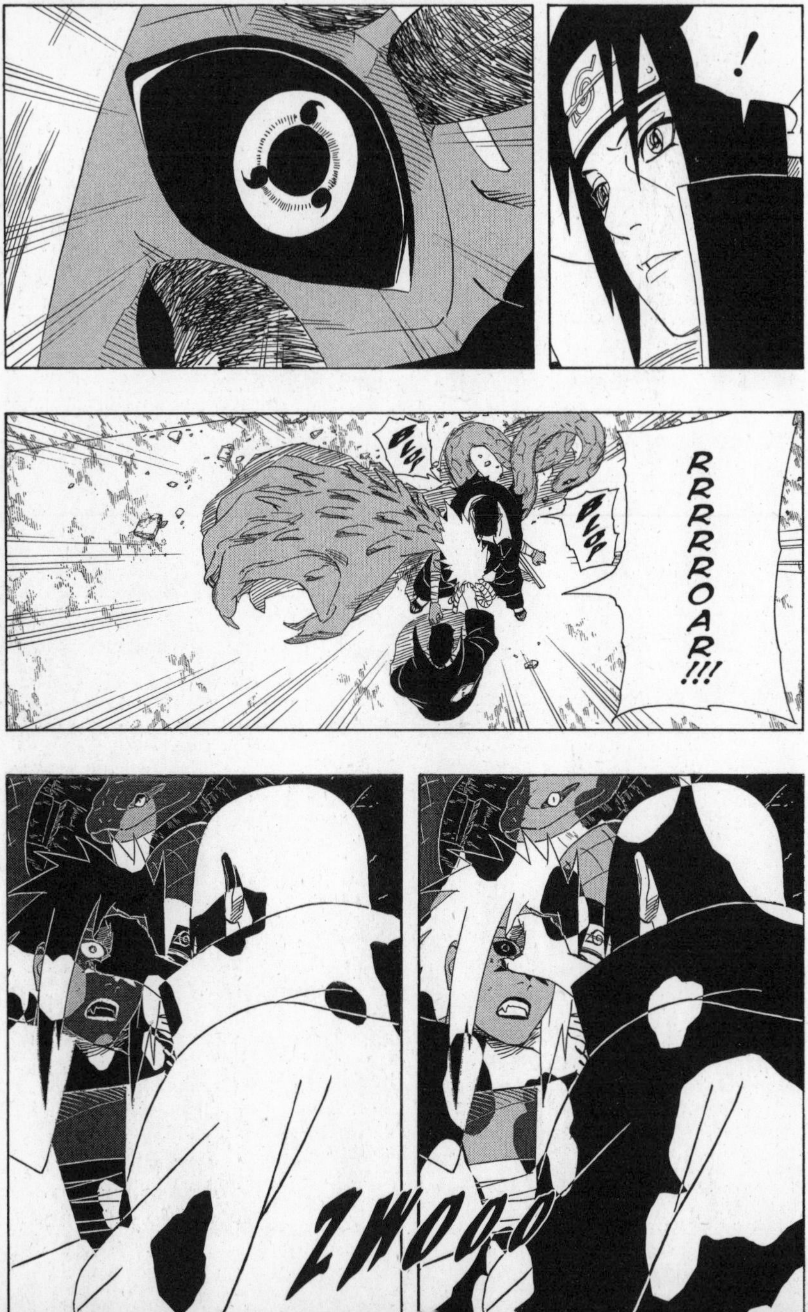
!
RRRRROAR!!!
BLOP
BLOP
ZWOOO

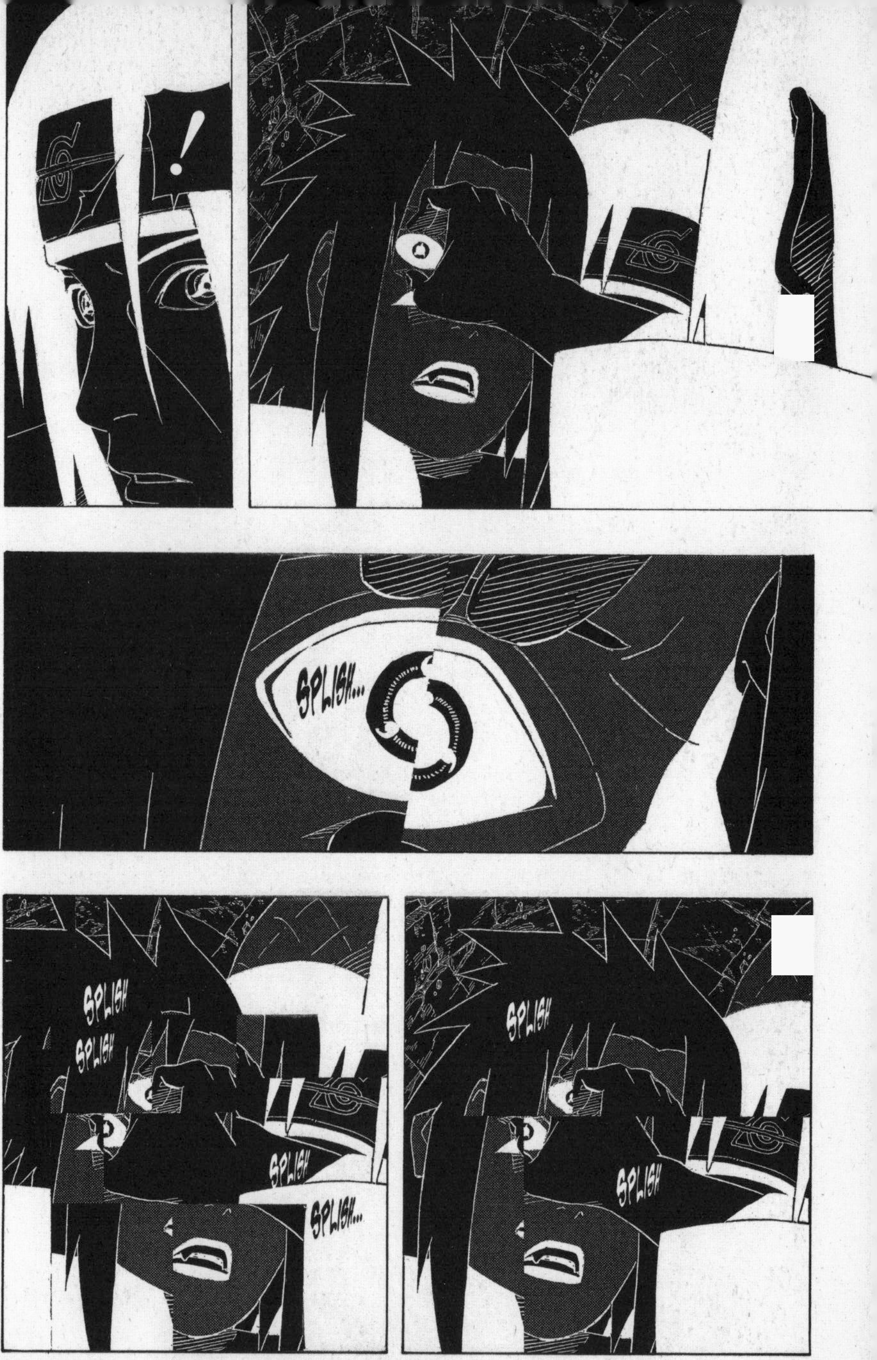
!
SPLISH...
SPLISH
SPLISH
SPLISH
SPLISH
SPLISH
SPLISH...

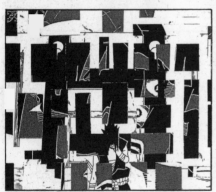

HUF

SSH

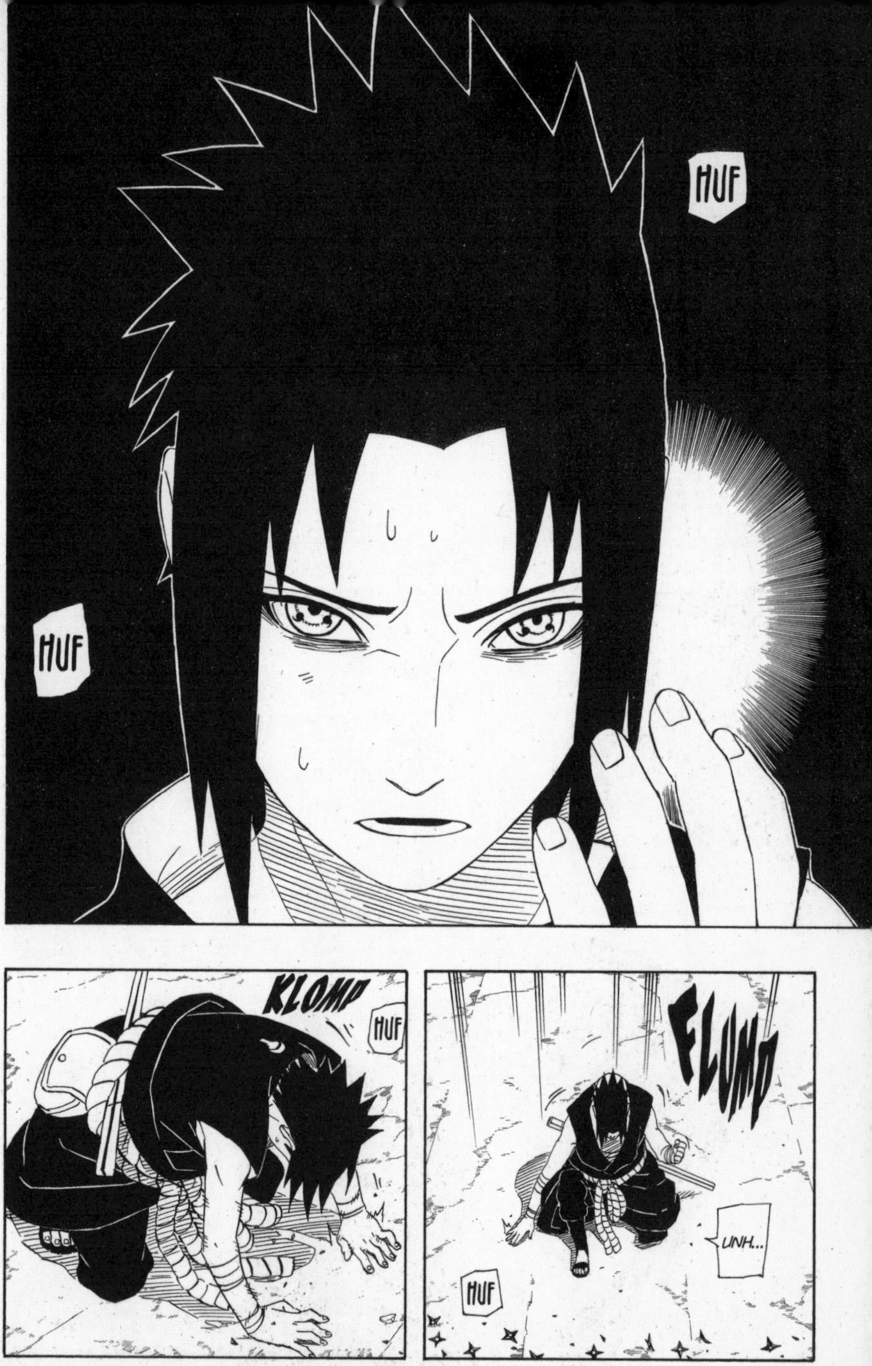
HUF
HUF
FLUMP
UNH...
HUF
KLOMP
HUF

READ THIS WAY

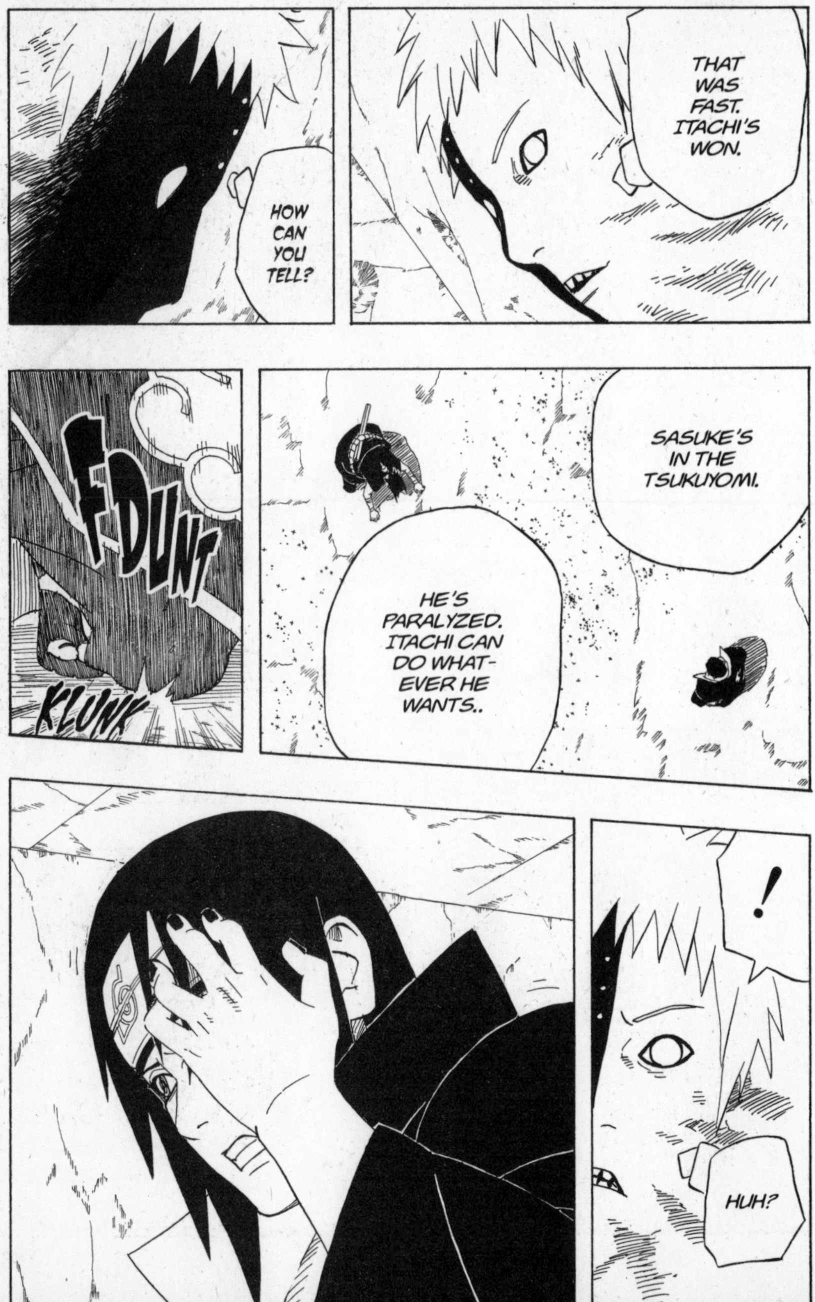
THAT WAS FAST. ITACHI'S WON.
HOW CAN YOU TELL?
SASUKE'S IN THE TSUKUYOMI.
HE'S PARALYZED. ITACHI CAN DO WHAT-EVER HE WANTS..
F-DUNT
KLUNK
!
HUH?

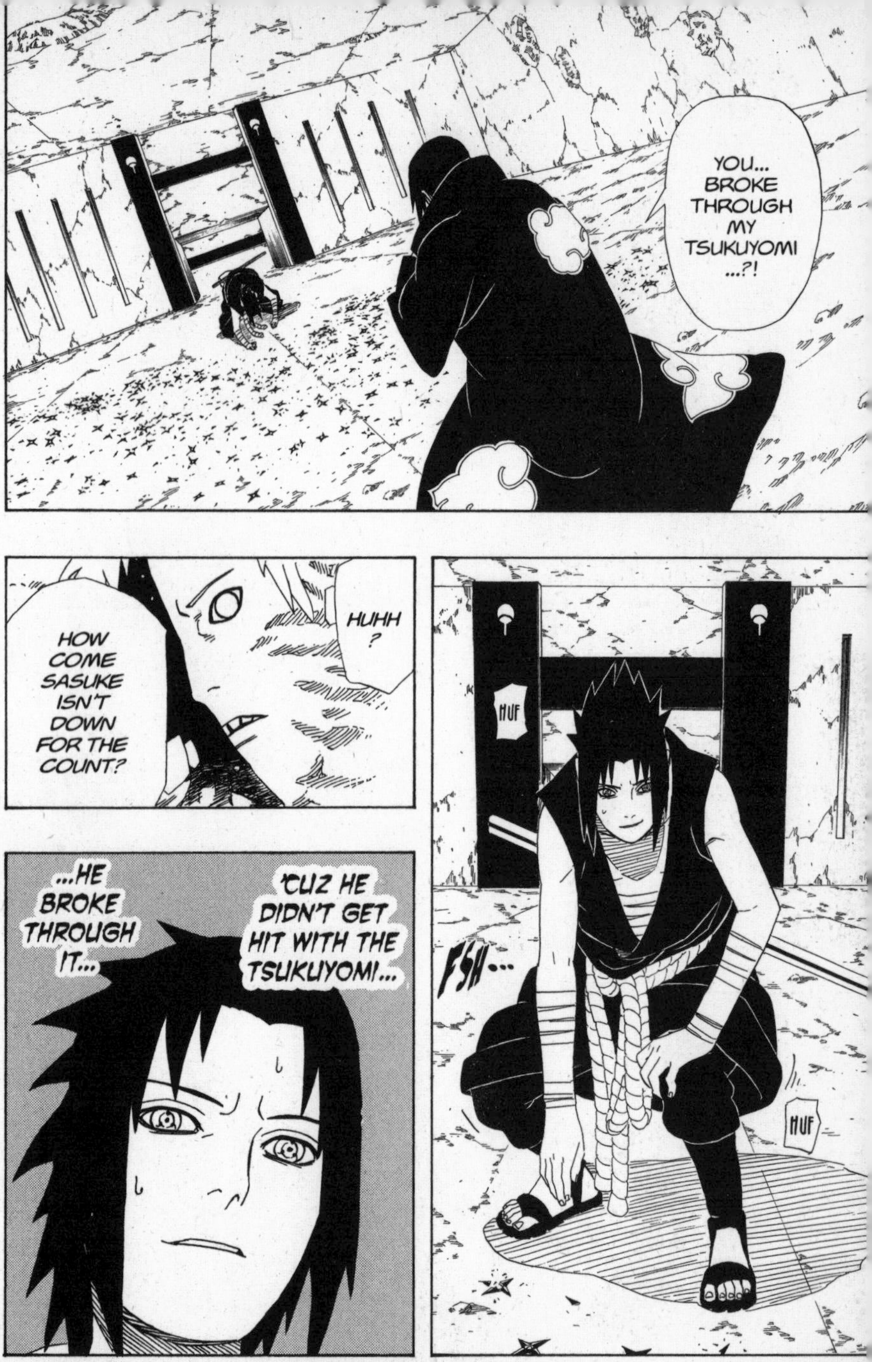
YOU... BROKE THROUGH MY TSUKUYOMI ...?!
HUF
FSH...
HUF
HUHH ?
HOW COME SASUKE ISN'T DOWN FOR THE COUNT?
'CUZ HE DIDN'T GET HIT WITH THE TSUKUYOMI...
...HE BROKE THROUGH IT...

READ THIS WAY

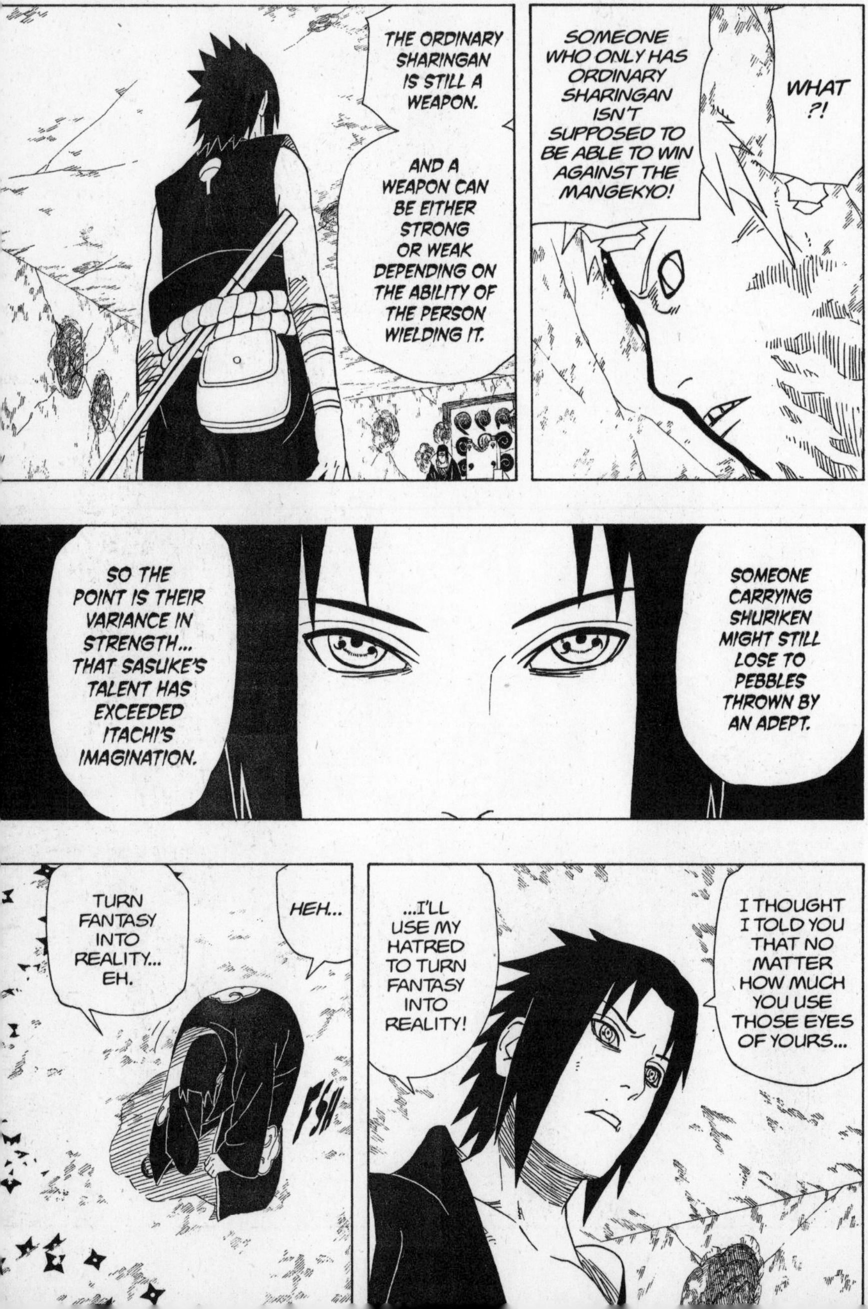
WHAT?!
SOMEONE WHO ONLY HAS ORDINARY SHARINGAN ISN'T SUPPOSED TO BE ABLE TO WIN AGAINST THE MANGEKYO!
THE ORDINARY SHARINGAN IS STILL A WEAPON.
AND A WEAPON CAN BE EITHER STRONG OR WEAK DEPENDING ON THE ABILITY OF THE PERSON WIELDING IT.
SOMEONE CARRYING SHURIKEN MIGHT STILL LOSE TO PEBBLES THROWN BY AN ADEPT.
SO THE POINT IS THEIR VARIANCE IN STRENGTH... THAT SASUKE'S TALENT HAS EXCEEDED ITACHI'S IMAGINATION.
I THOUGHT I TOLD YOU THAT NO MATTER HOW MUCH YOU USE THOSE EYES OF YOURS...
...I'LL USE MY HATRED TO TURN FANTASY INTO REALITY!
HEH...
TURN FANTASY INTO REALITY... EH.
FSH

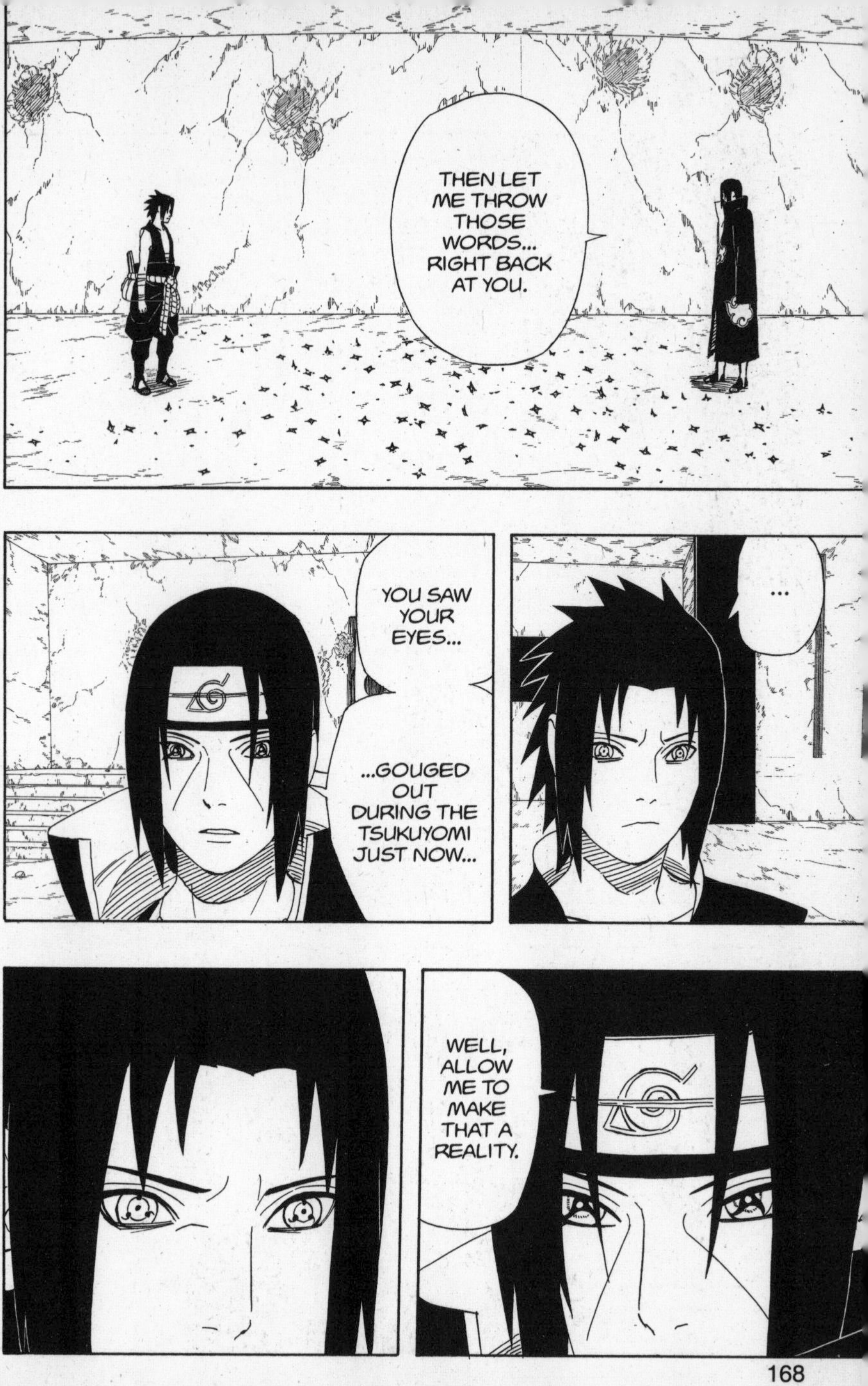
THEN LET ME THROW THOSE WORDS... RIGHT BACK AT YOU.
...
YOU SAW YOUR EYES...
...GOUGED OUT DURING THE TSUKUYOMI JUST NOW...
WELL, ALLOW ME TO MAKE THAT A REALITY.

READ THIS WAY

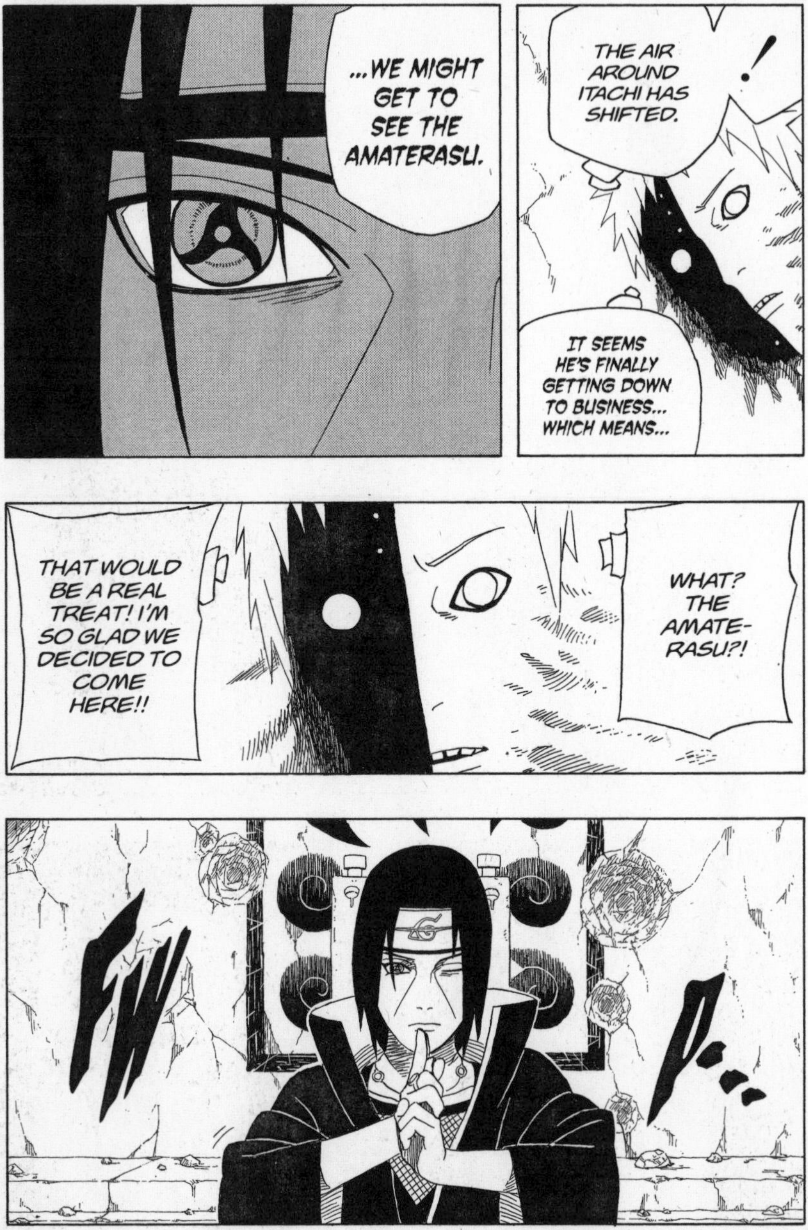
THE AIR AROUND ITACHI HAS SHIFTED.
!
IT SEEMS HE'S FINALLY GETTING DOWN TO BUSINESS... WHICH MEANS...
...WE MIGHT GET TO SEE THE AMATERASU.
WHAT? THE AMATE-RASU?!
THAT WOULD BE A REAL TREAT! I'M SO GLAD WE DECIDED TO COME HERE!!

NARUTO

Number 389: Sasuke's Flow!!

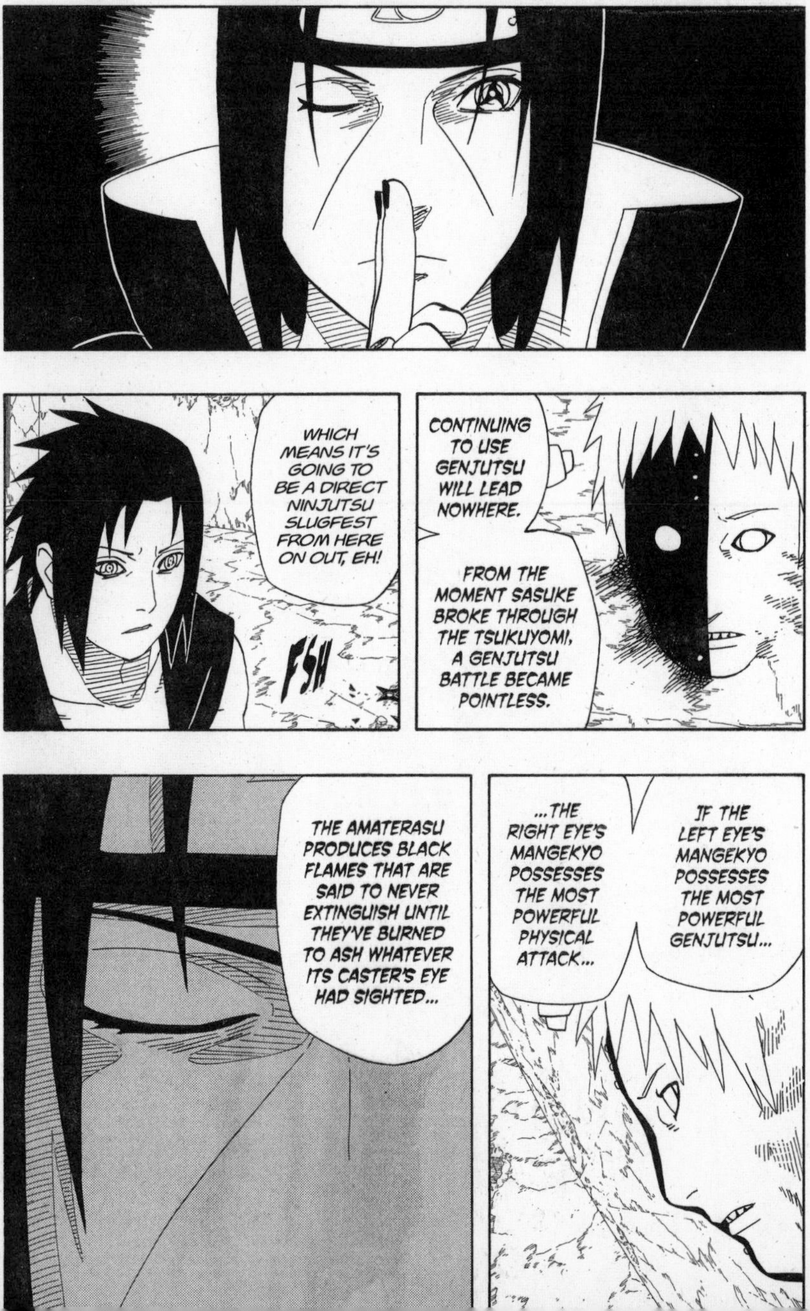
CONTINUING TO USE GENJUTSU WILL LEAD NOWHERE.
FROM THE MOMENT SASUKE BROKE THROUGH THE TSUKUYOMI, A GENJUTSU BATTLE BECAME POINTLESS.
WHICH MEANS IT'S GOING TO BE A DIRECT NINJUTSU SLUGFEST FROM HERE ON OUT, EH!
FSH
IF THE LEFT EYE'S MANGEKYO POSSESSES THE MOST POWERFUL GENJUTSU...
...THE RIGHT EYE'S MANGEKYO POSSESSES THE MOST POWERFUL PHYSICAL ATTACK...
THE AMATERASU PRODUCES BLACK FLAMES THAT ARE SAID TO NEVER EXTINGUISH UNTIL THEY'VE BURNED TO ASH WHATEVER ITS CASTER'S EYE HAD SIGHTED...

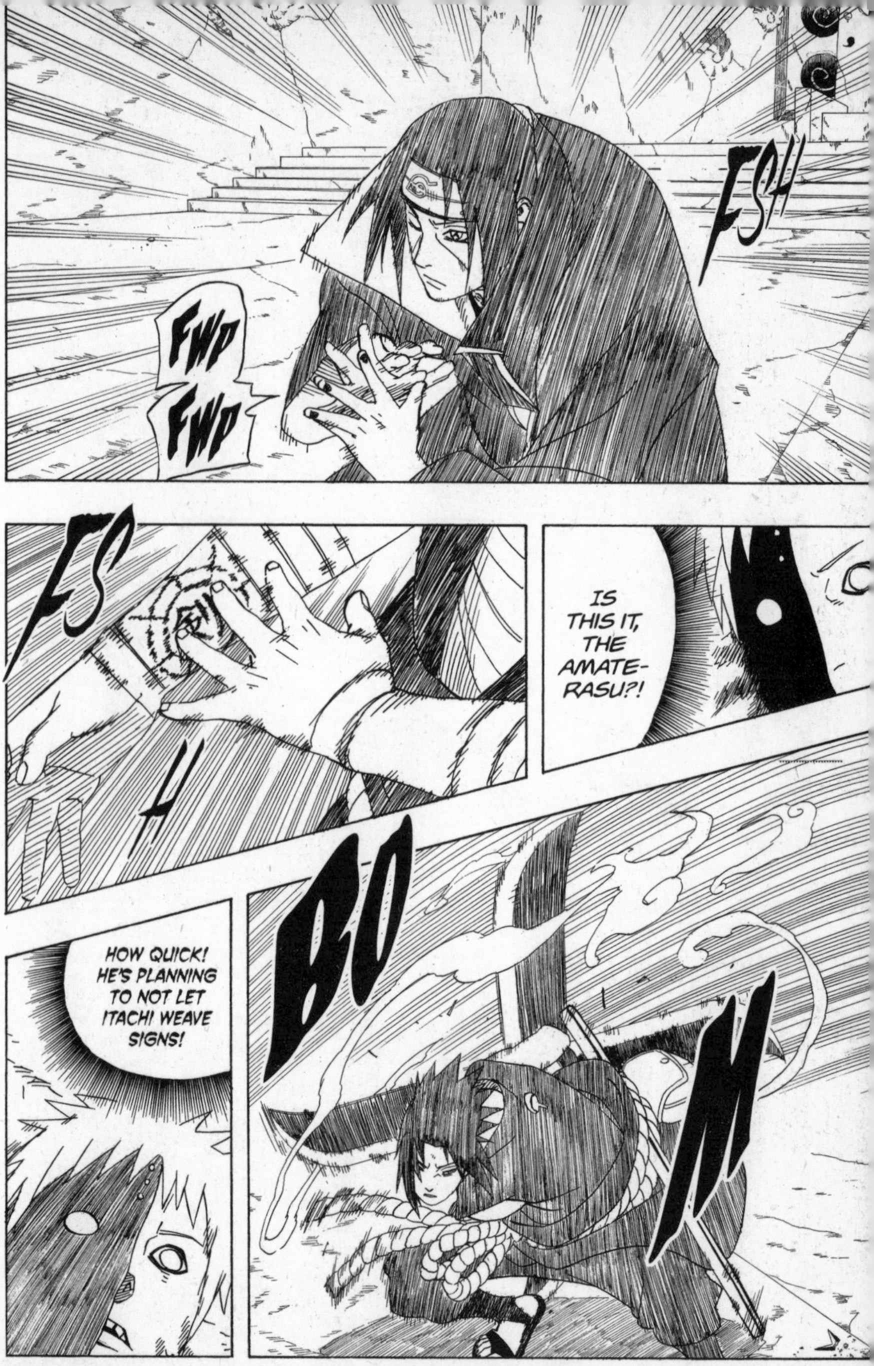
FSH
FWP FWP
IS THIS IT, THE AMATERASU?!
FSH
BOM
HOW QUICK! HE'S PLANNING TO NOT LET ITACHI WEAVE SIGNS!

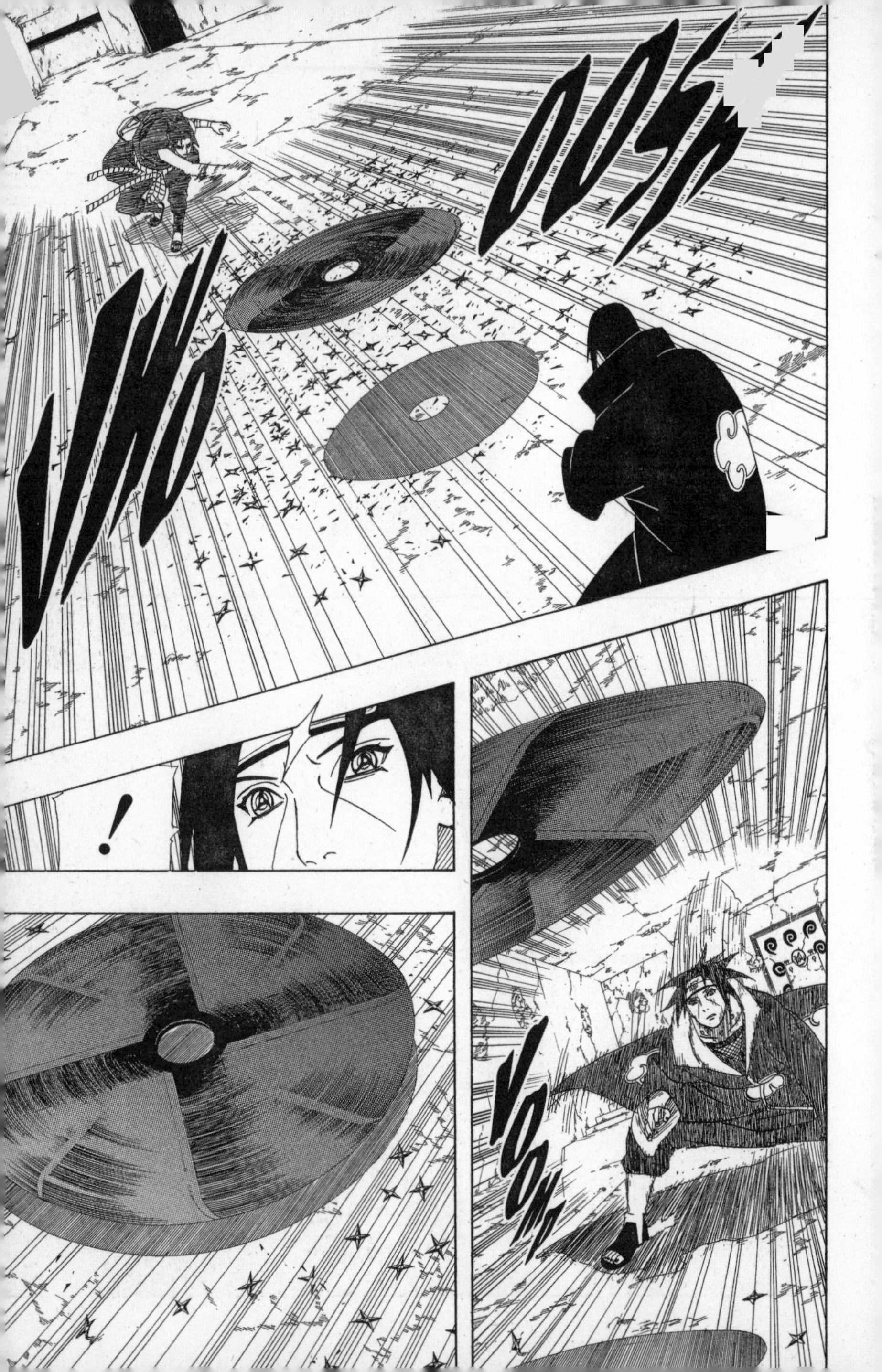
VOOSH
!

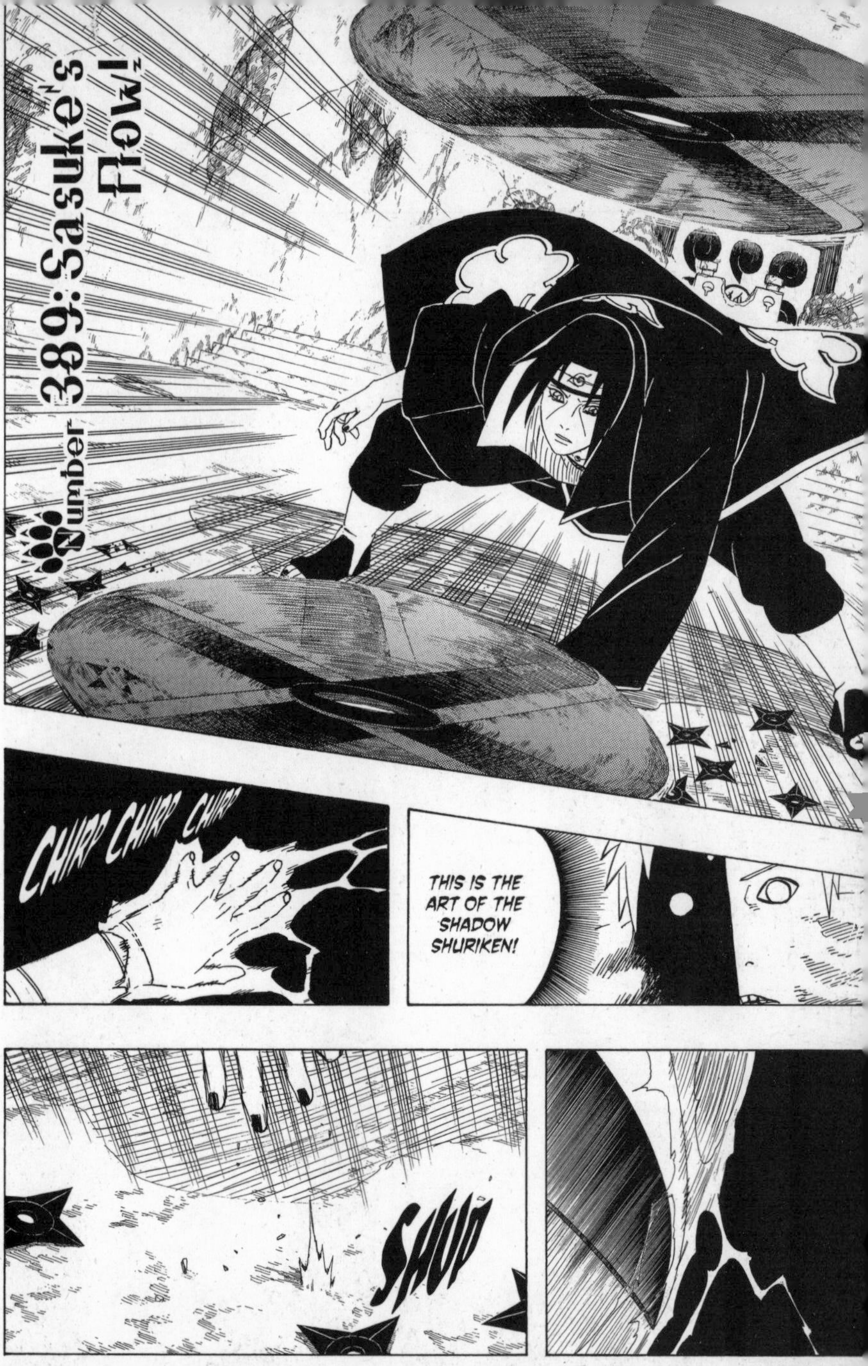
Number 389: Sasuke's Flow!
THIS IS THE ART OF THE SHADOW SHURIKEN!
CHIRP CHIRP CHIRP
SHUP

READ THIS WAY

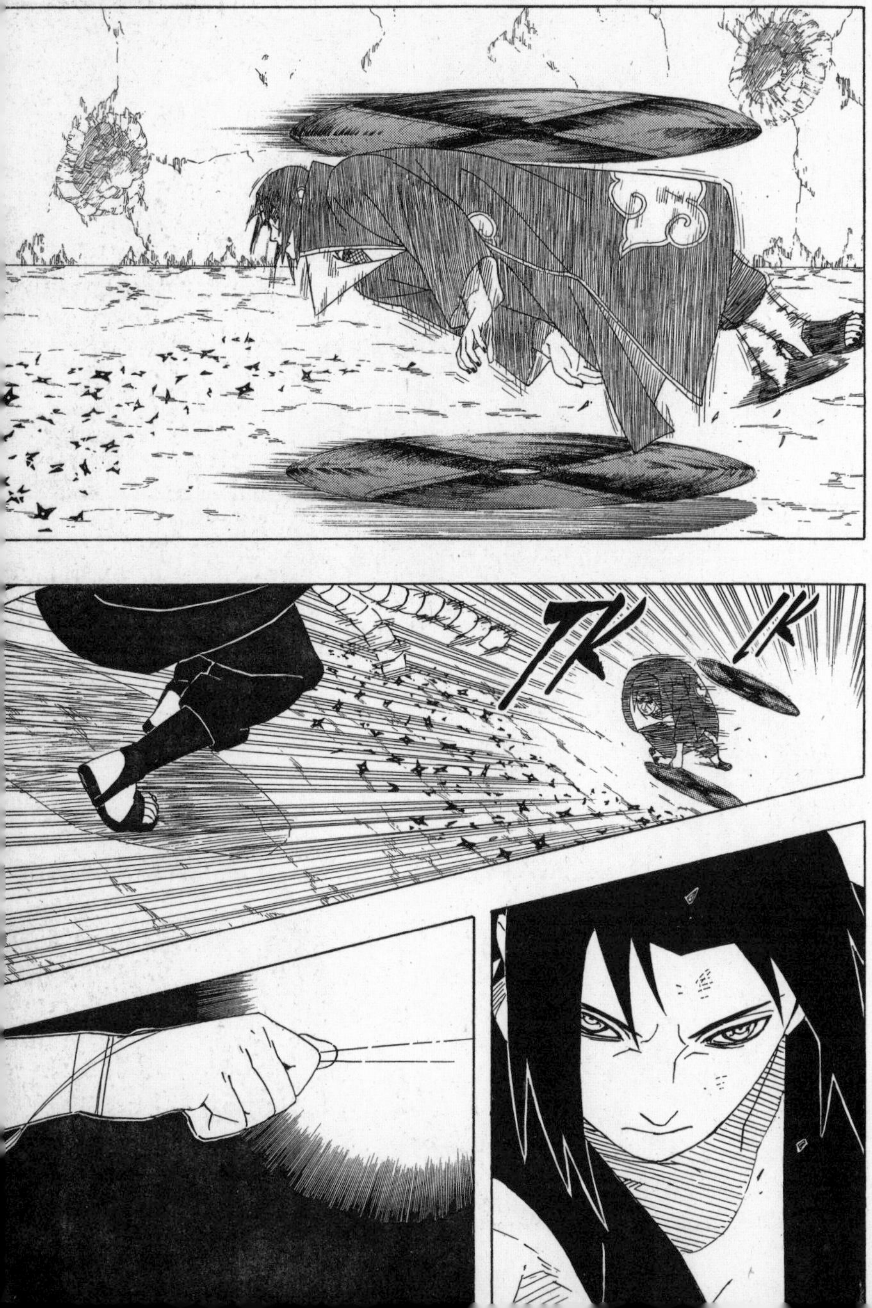
TKK

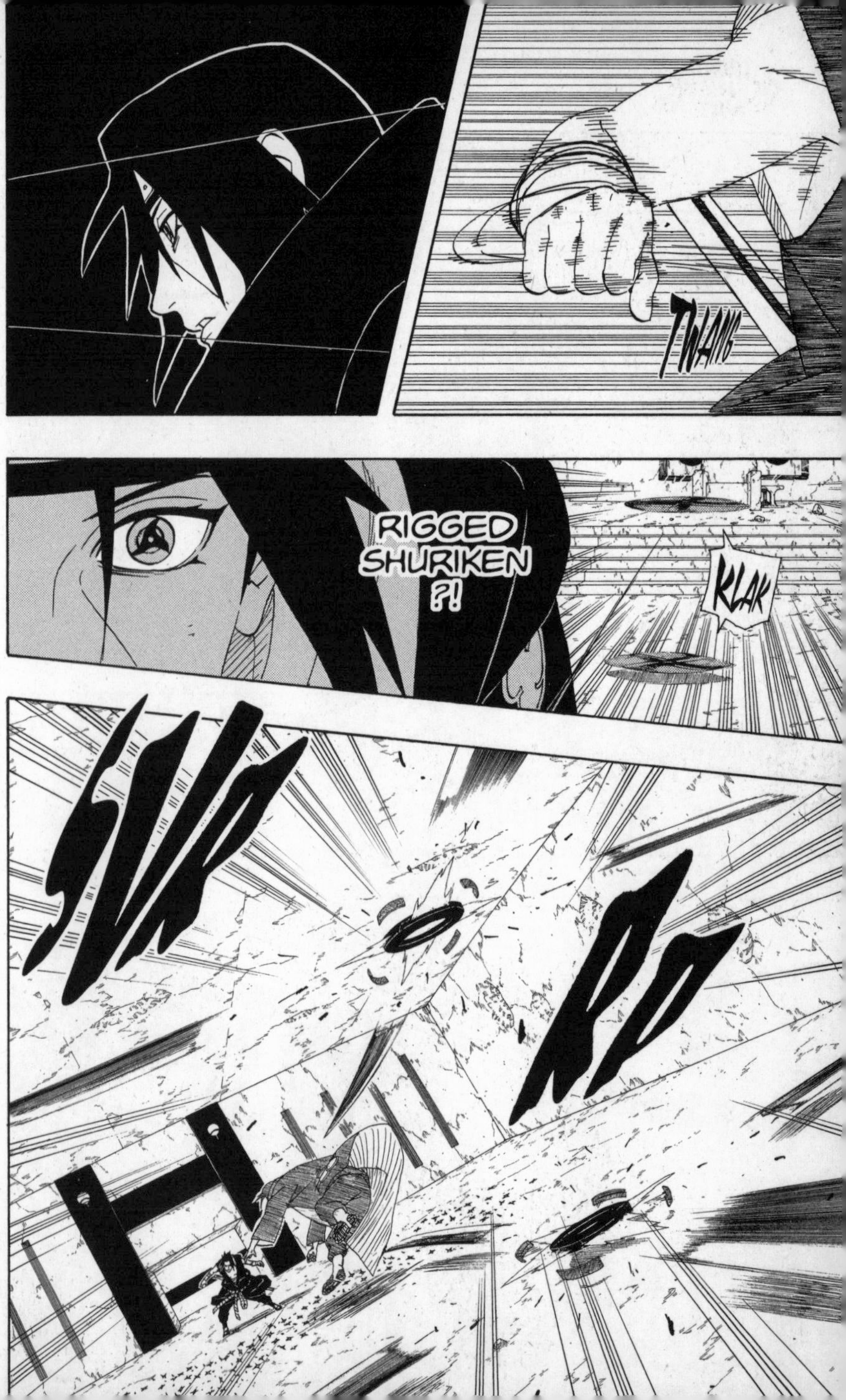
TWANG
KLAK
RIGGED SHURIKEN ?!

READ THIS WAY

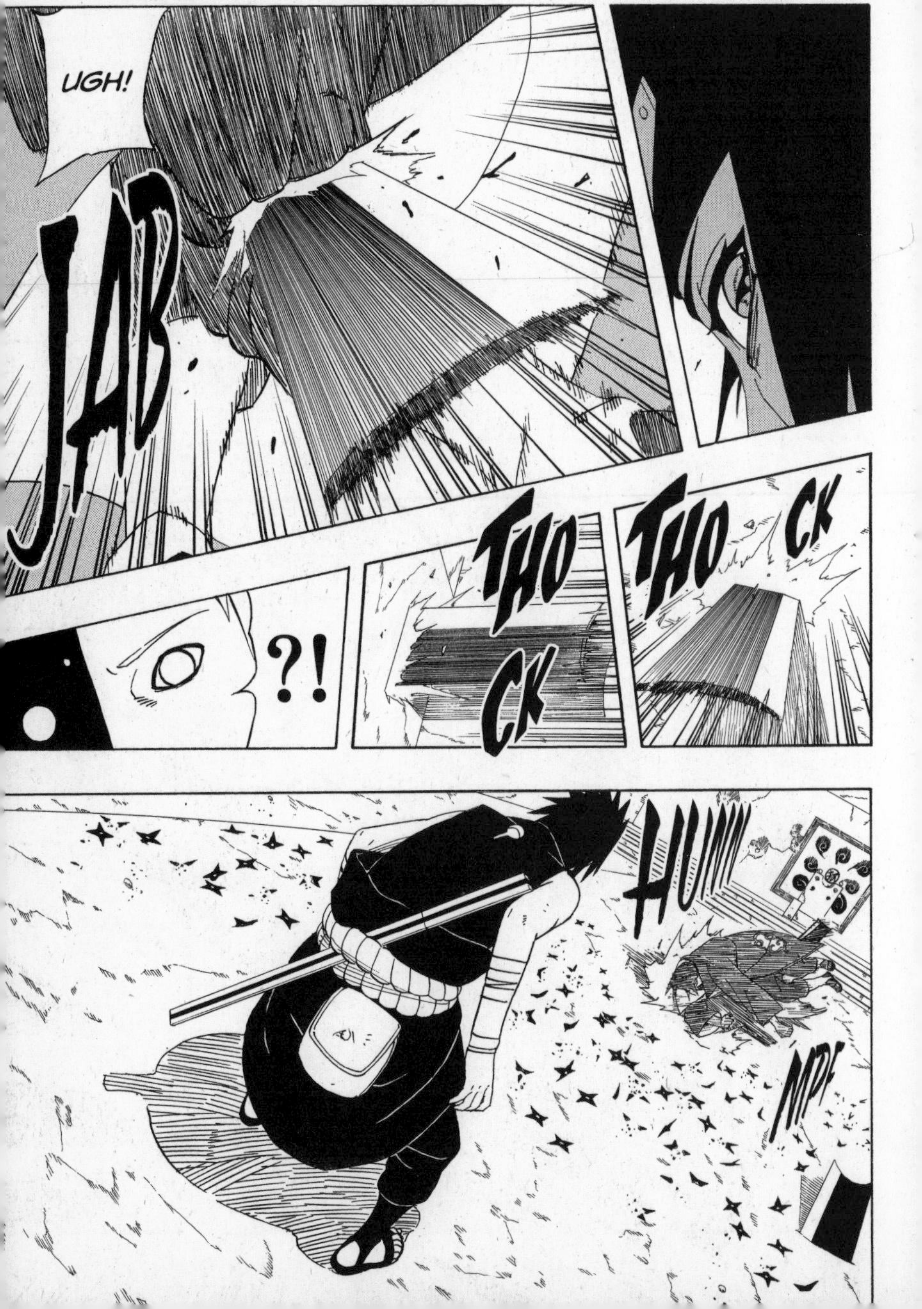
UGH!
JAB
THOCK
THOCK
?!

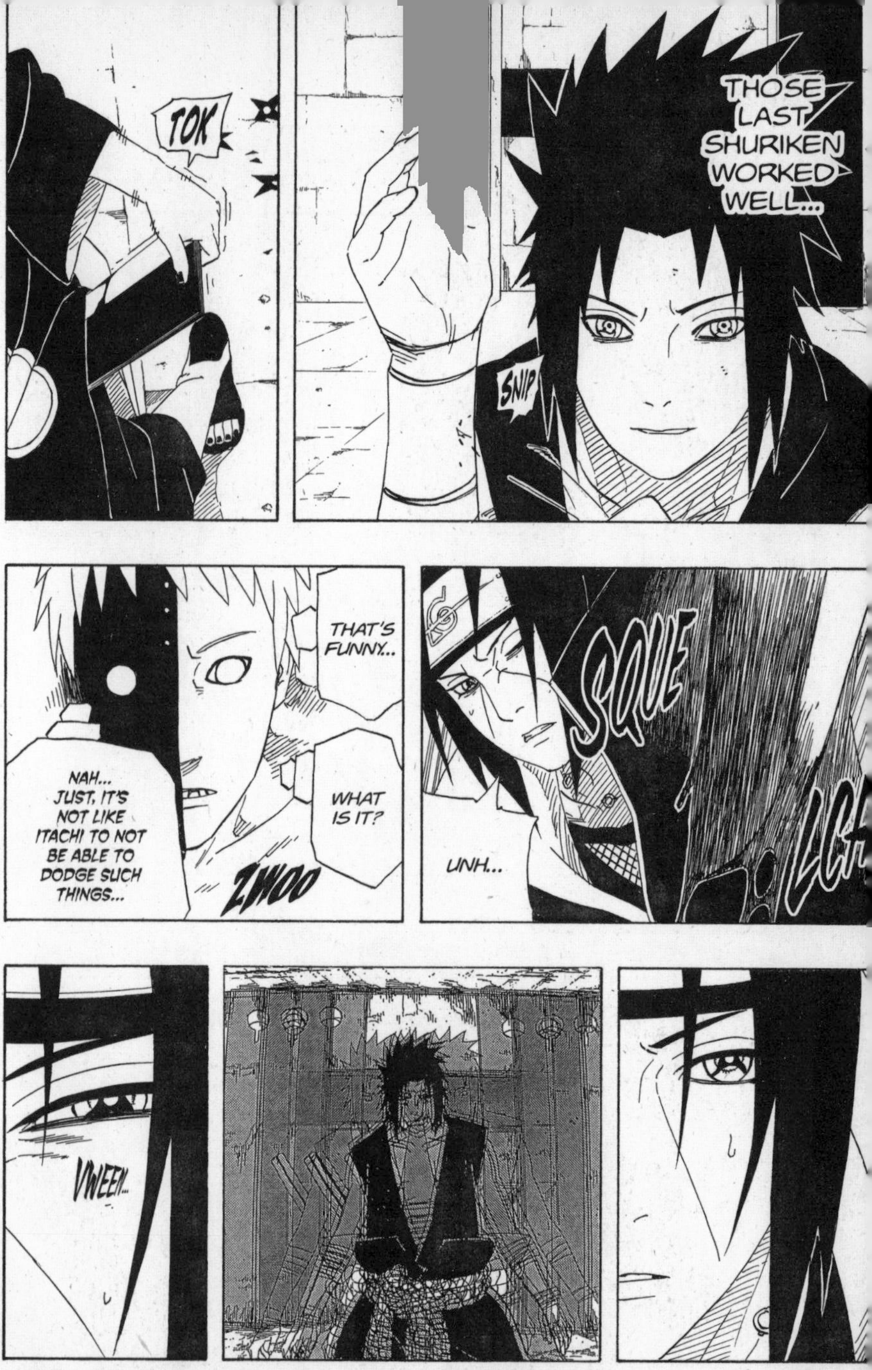
THOSE LAST SHURIKEN WORKED WELL...
SNIP
TOK
SQUE
LCH
UNH...
THAT'S FUNNY...
WHAT IS IT?
NAH... JUST, IT'S NOT LIKE ITACHI TO NOT BE ABLE TO DODGE SUCH THINGS...
ZWOO
VWEEN...

READ THIS WAY

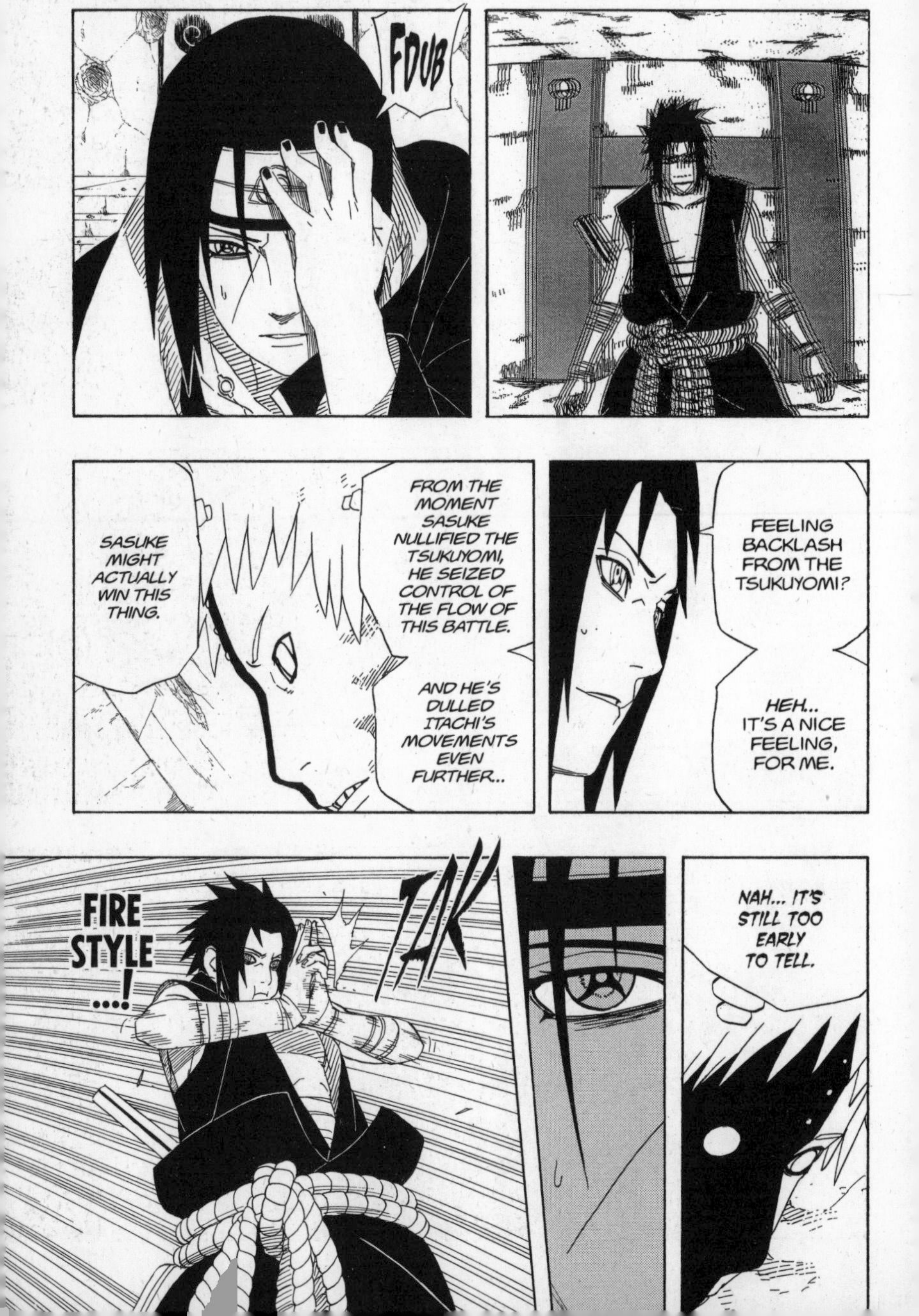
FDUB
FEELING BACKLASH FROM THE TSUKUYOMI?
HEH... IT'S A NICE FEELING, FOR ME.
FROM THE MOMENT SASUKE NULLIFIED THE TSUKUYOMI, HE SEIZED CONTROL OF THE FLOW OF THIS BATTLE.
AND HE'S DULLED ITACHI'S MOVEMENTS EVEN FURTHER...
SASUKE MIGHT ACTUALLY WIN THIS THING.
NAH... IT'S STILL TOO EARLY TO TELL.
TAK
FIRE STYLE ....!

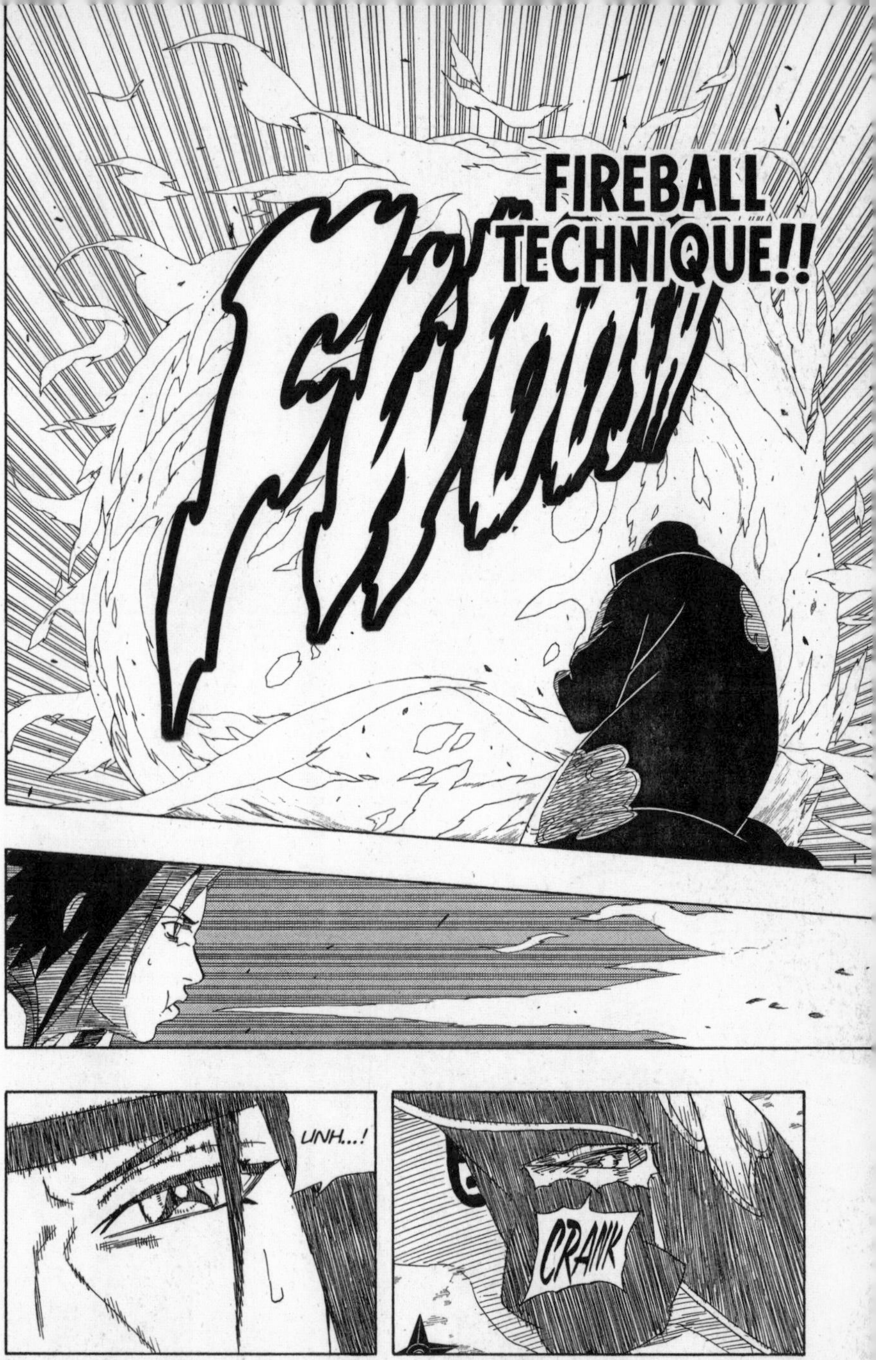
FIREBALL TECHNIQUE!!
CRANK
UNH...!

READ THIS WAY

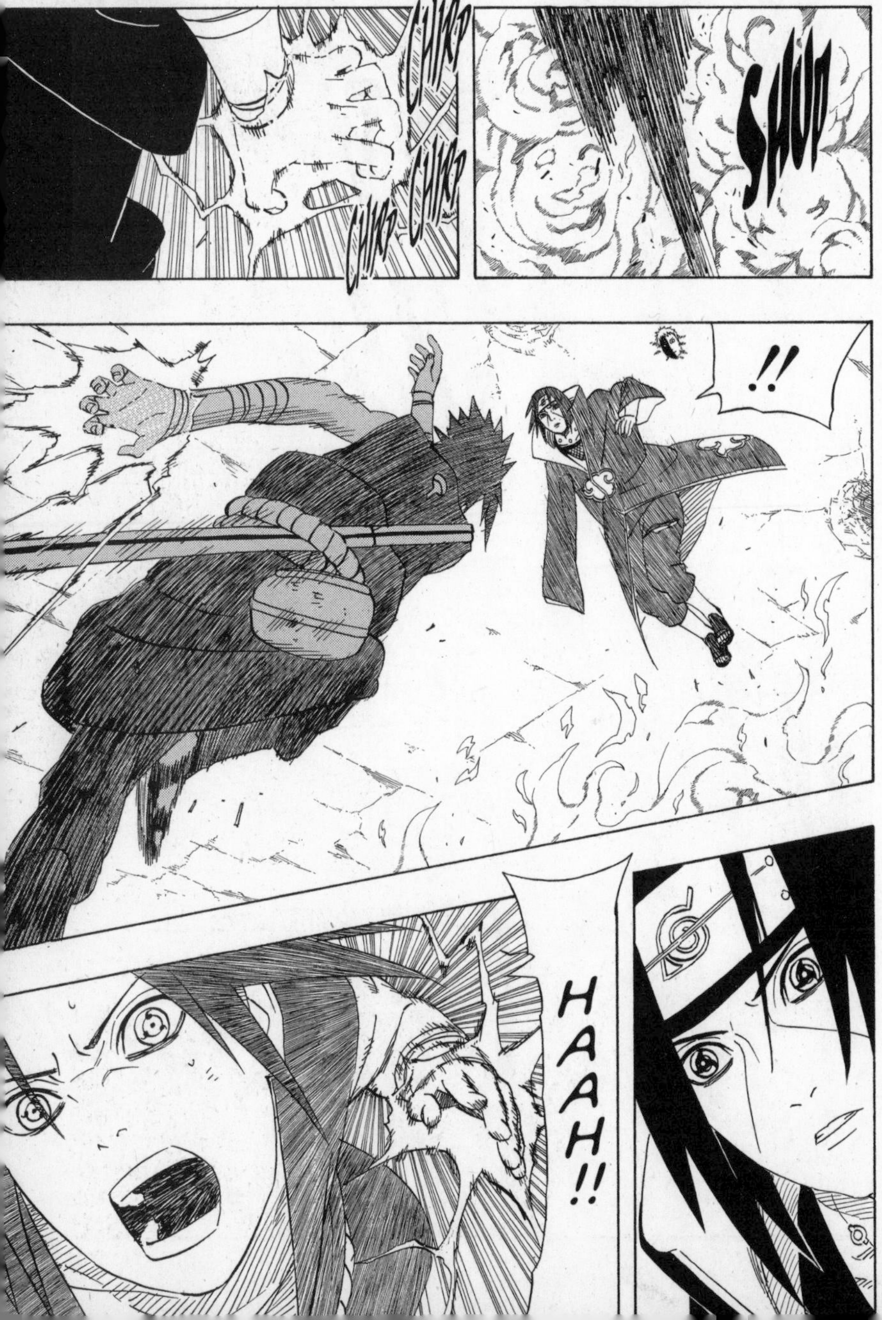
SHUP
CHIRP CHIRP CHIRP CHIRP
!!
HAAAH!!

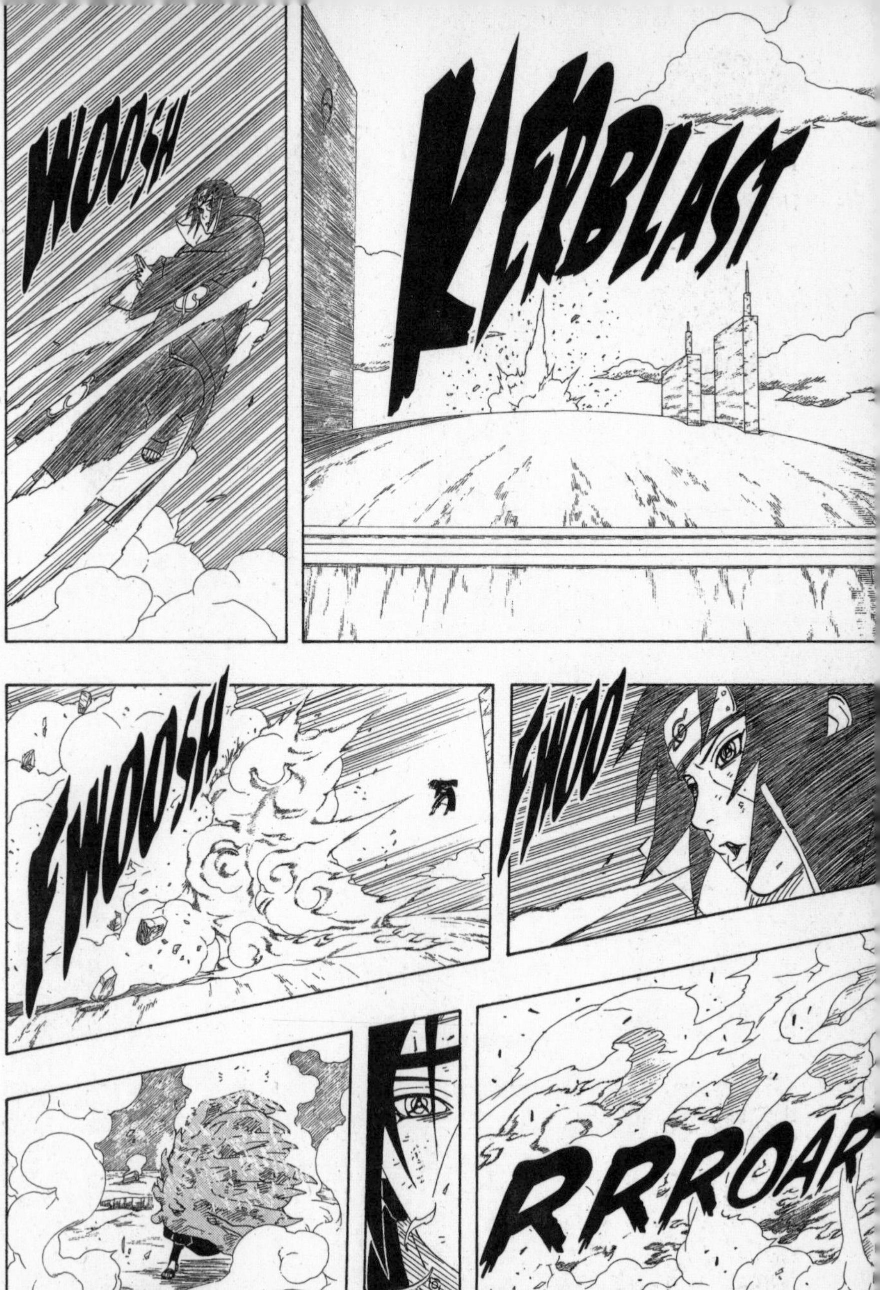
KERBLAST
WHOOSH
FWOO
FWOOSH
RRROAR

READ THIS WAY

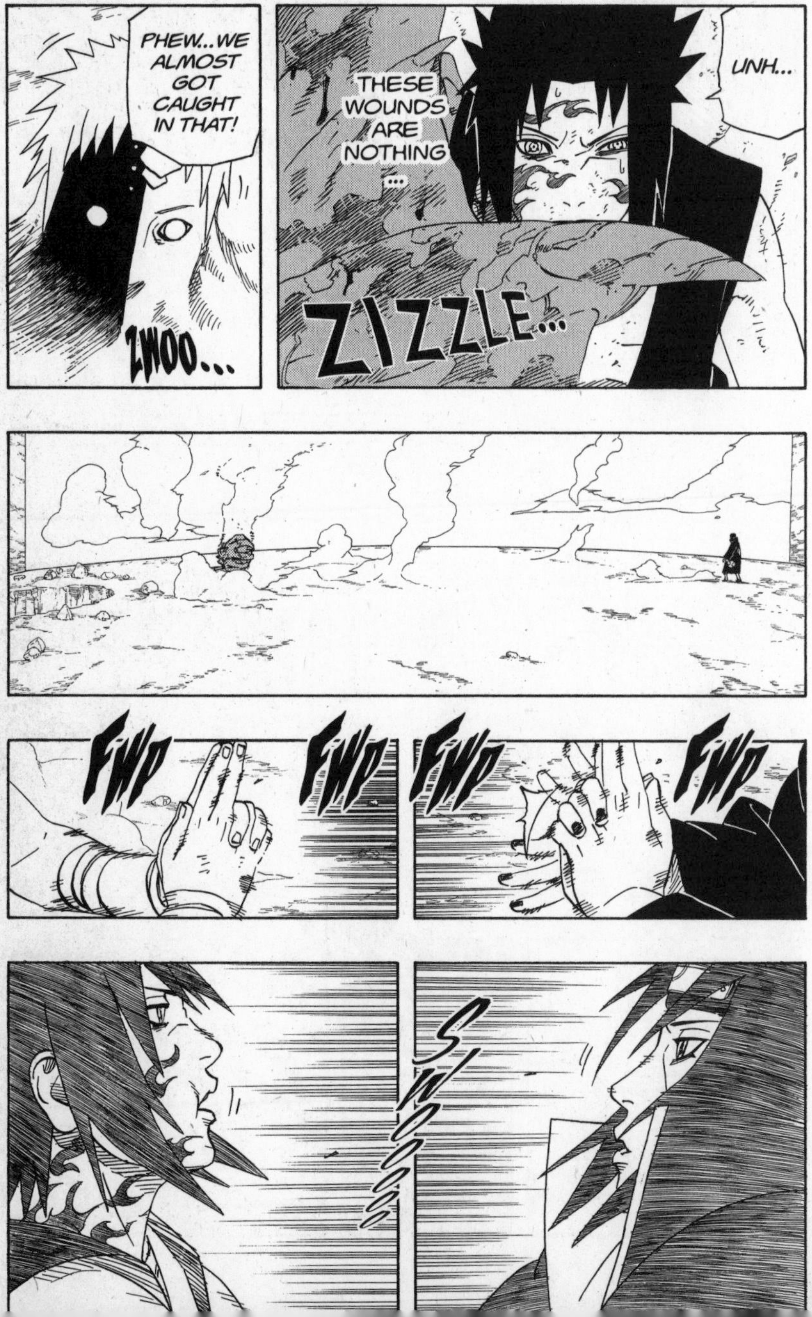
UNH...
THESE WOUNDS ARE NOTHING...
ZIZZLE...
PHEW...WE ALMOST GOT CAUGHT IN THAT!
ZWOO...
FWP
FWP
FWP
FWP
SWOOOOOO

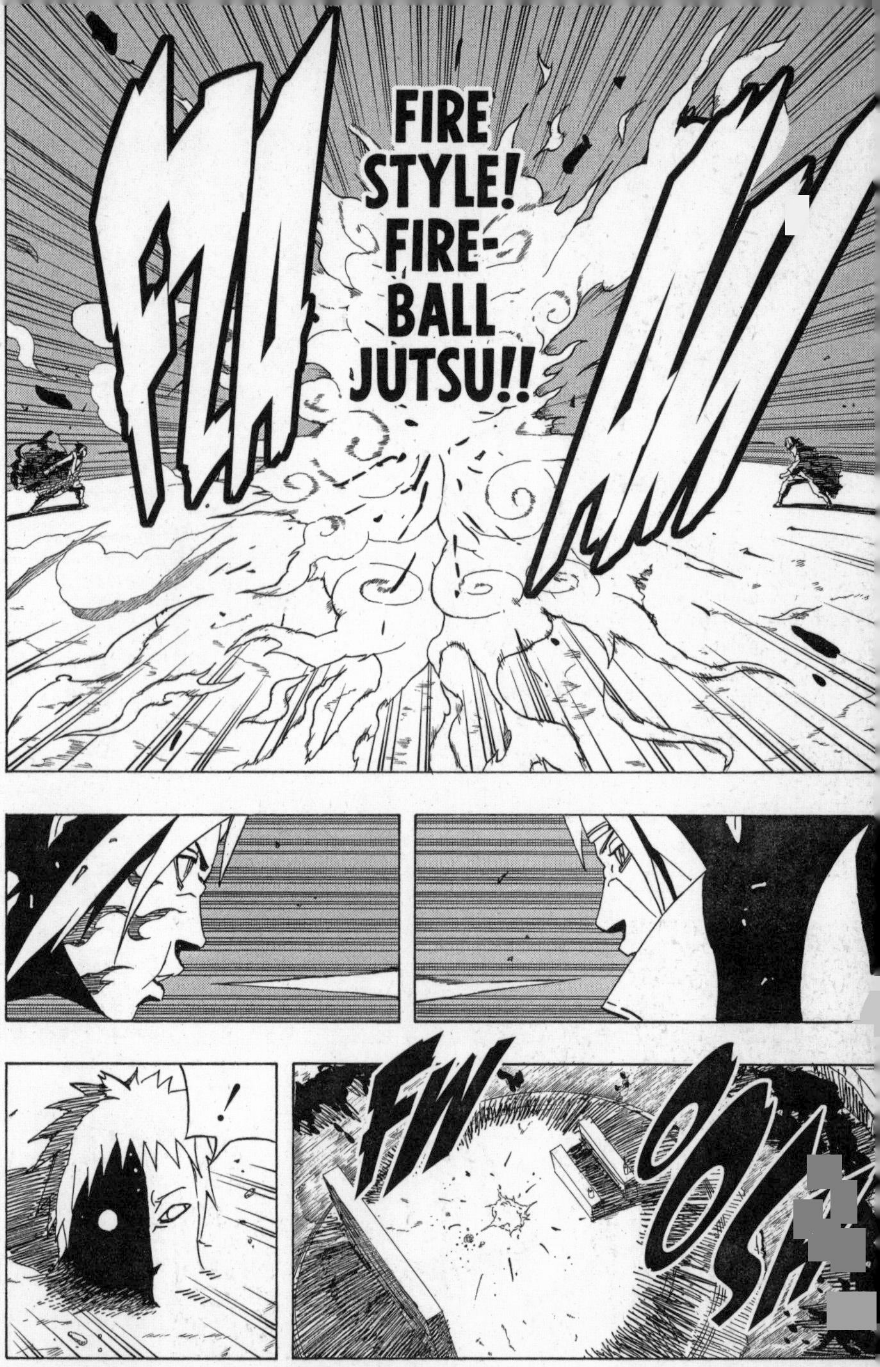
FIRE STYLE! FIRE-BALL JUTSU!!
FW
!

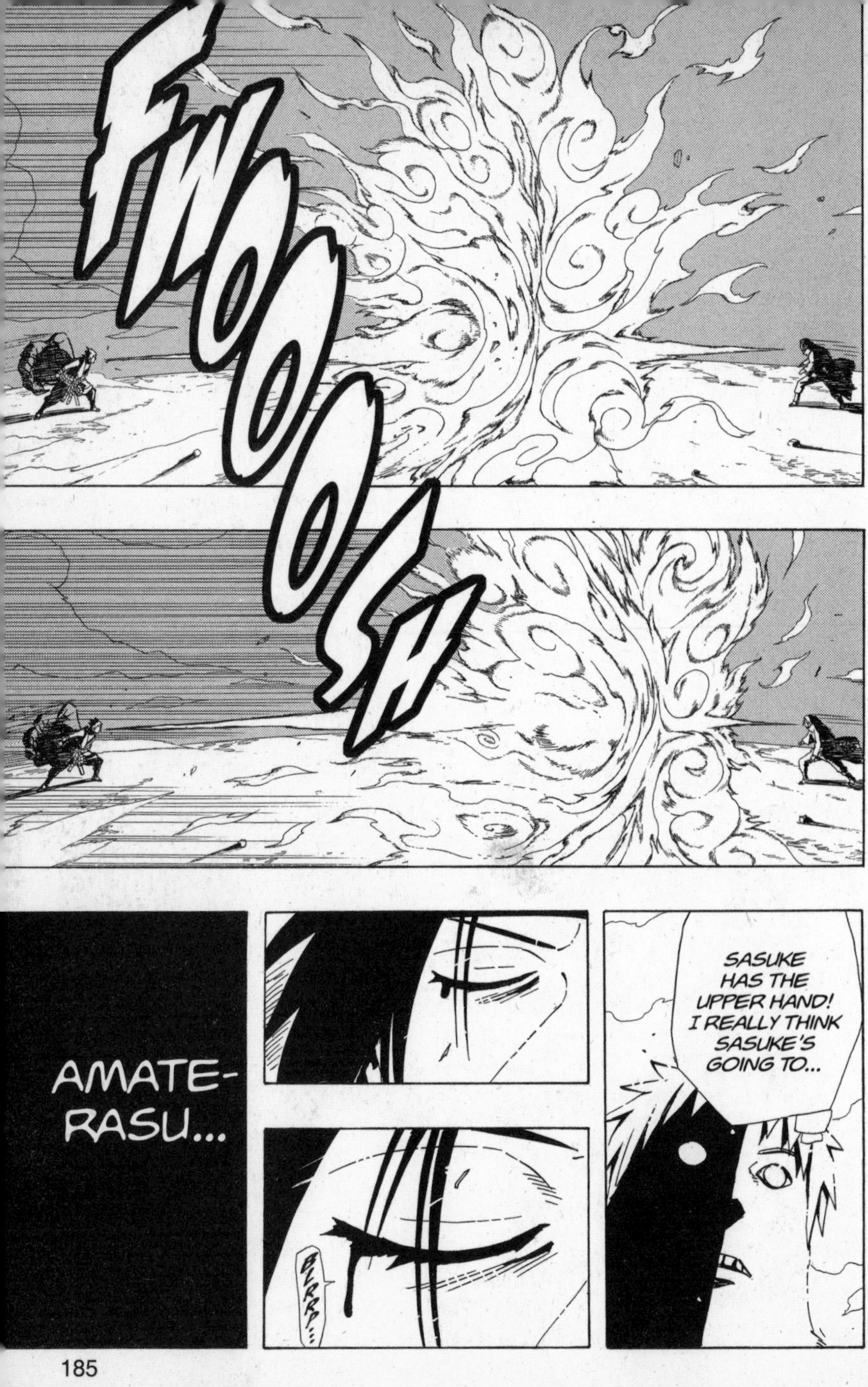
FWOOOOOSH
SASUKE HAS THE UPPER HAND! I REALLY THINK SASUKE'S GOING TO...
BLRRP...
AMATE-RASU...

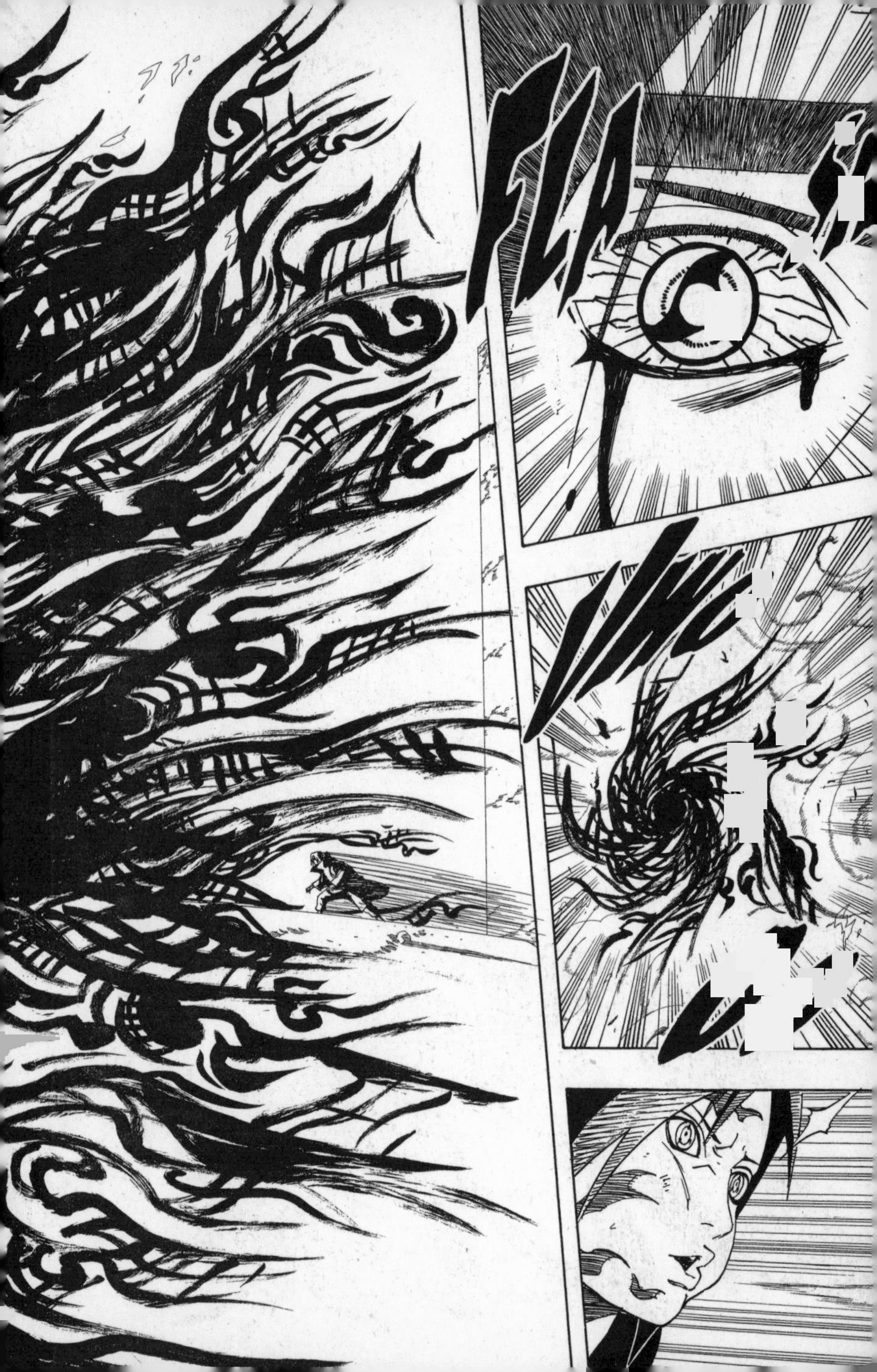
FLA

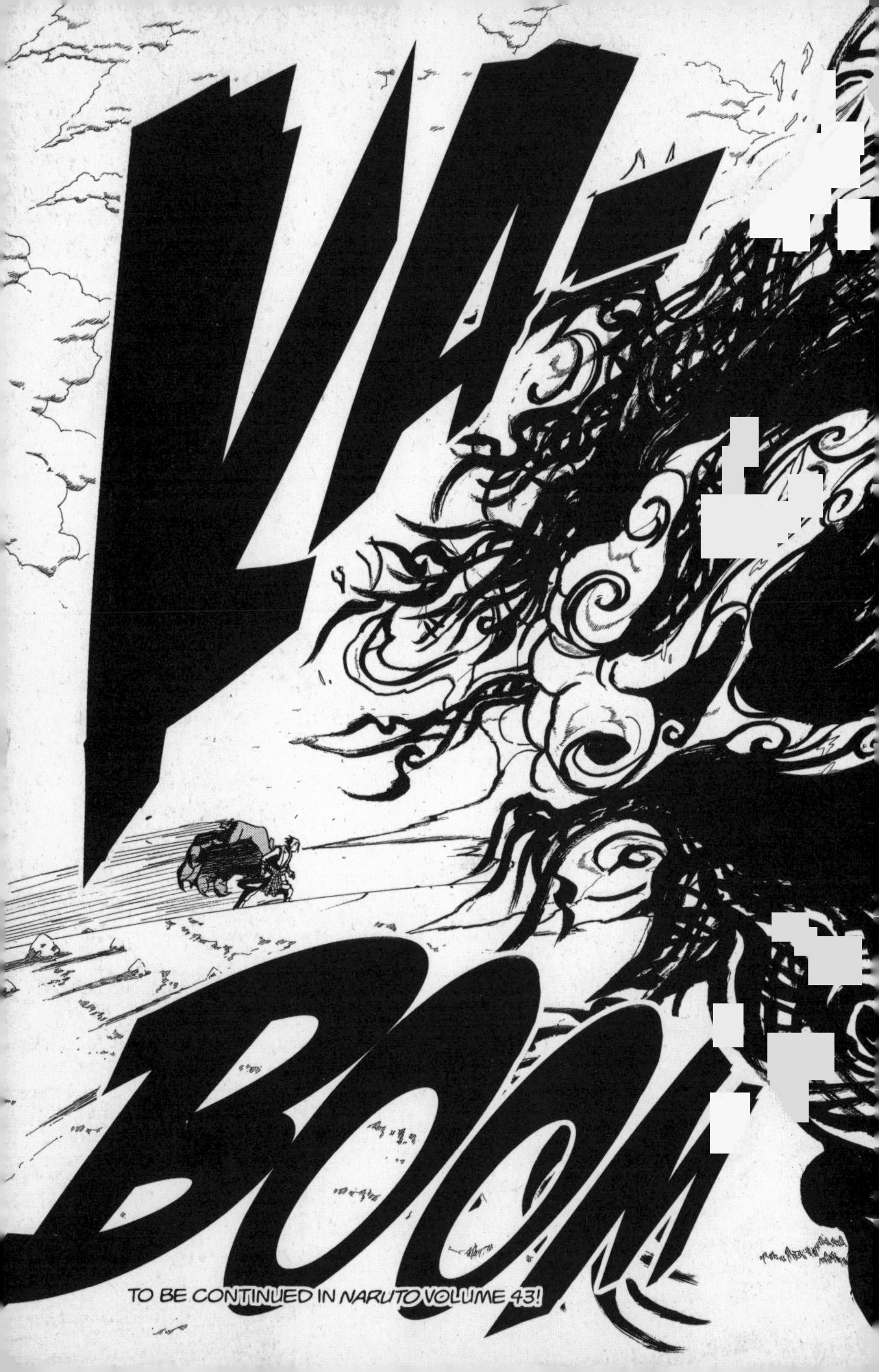
BOOM
TO BE CONTINUED IN NARUTO VOLUME 43!

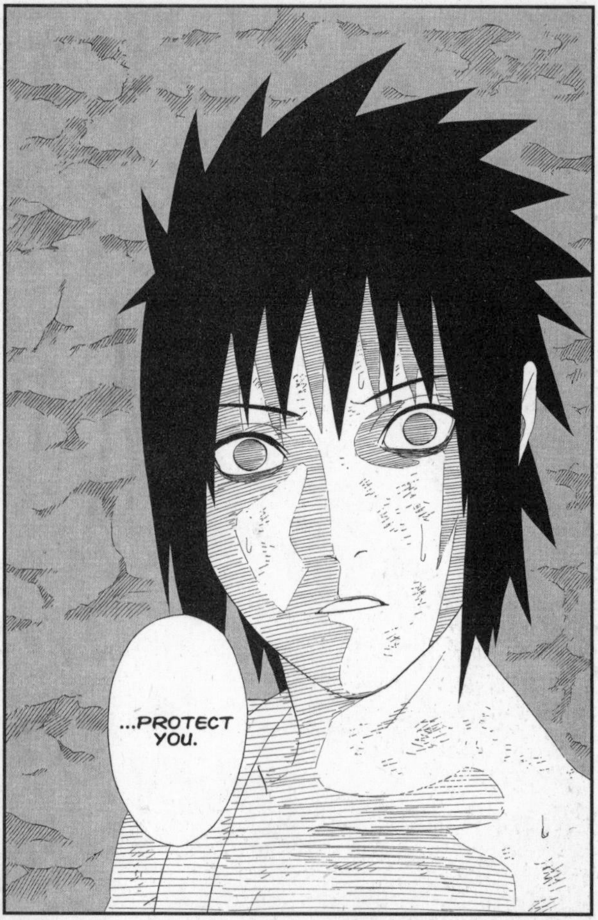
...PROTECT YOU.

IN THE NEXT VOLUME...

THE MAN WITH THE TRUTH

The time has come for the secrets of the Uchiha to be told. What Sasuke finally finds out about his family's damaged past will rock Naruto's former teammate to the core of his existence. Prepare for the ultimate reveal. It's time to change the world of Naruto forever!

AVAILABLE MAY 2009!

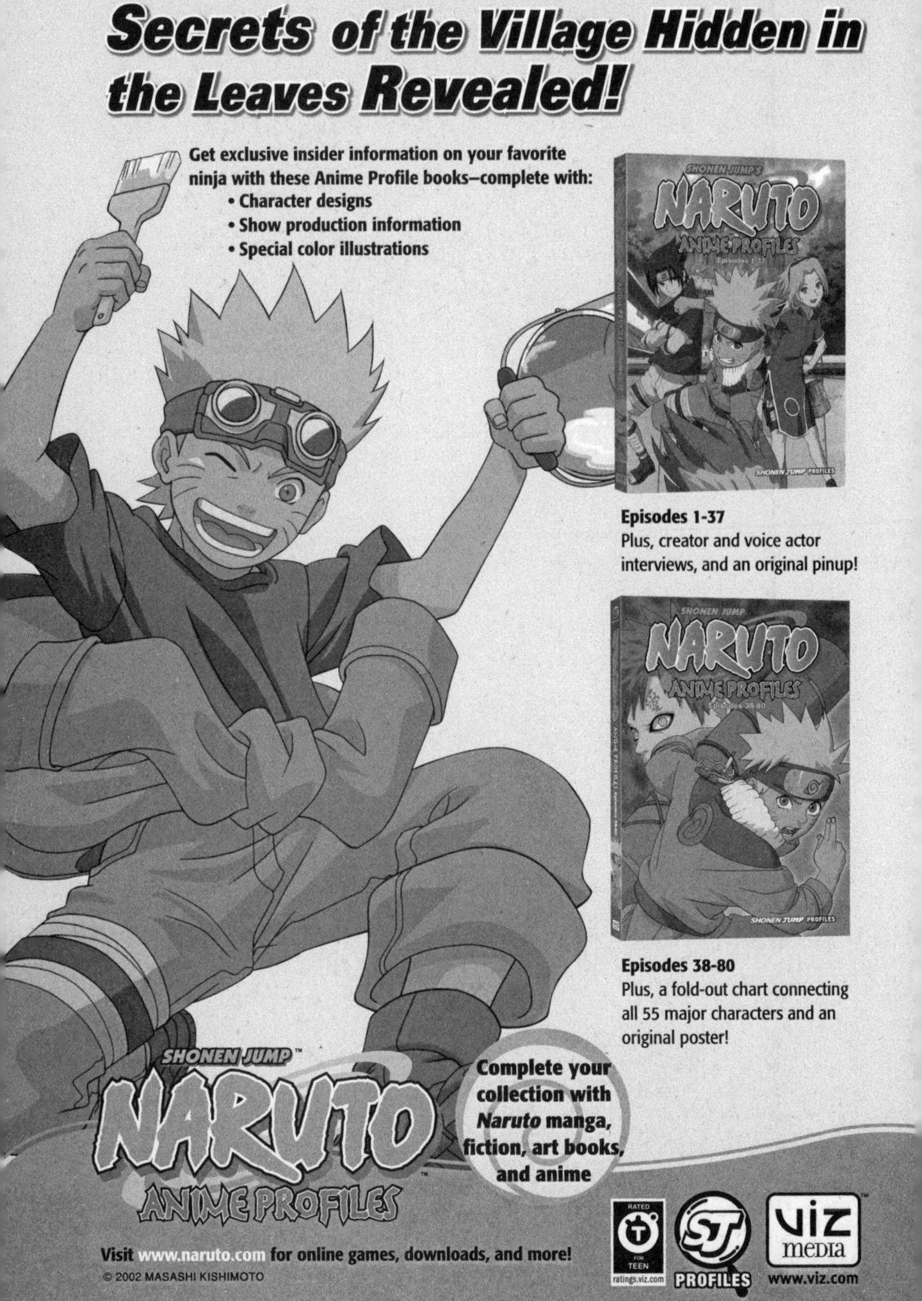
Secrets of the Village Hidden in the Leaves Revealed!
Get exclusive insider information on your favorite ninja with these Anime Profile books—complete with:
• Character designs
• Show production information
• Special color illustrations
SHONEN JUMP'S NARUTO ANIME PROFILES
SHONEN JUMP PROFILES
Episodes 1-37
Plus, creator and voice actor interviews, and an original pinup!
SHONEN JUMP NARUTO ANIME PROFILES
Episodes 38-80
SHONEN JUMP PROFILES
Episodes 38-80
Plus, a fold-out chart connecting all 55 major characters and an original poster!
SHONEN JUMP™
NARUTO™
ANIME PROFILES
Complete your collection with Naruto manga, fiction, art books, and anime
RATED T FOR TEEN ratings.viz.com
SJ PROFILES
VIZ MEDIA
www.viz.com
Visit www.naruto.com for online games, downloads, and more!
© 2002 MASASHI KISHIMOTO

Tell us what you think about SHONEN JUMP manga!

Our survey is now available online.
Go to: **www.SHONENJUMP.com/mangasurvey**

Help us make our product offering better!